POSITIVE EDUCATION

SERIES IN POSITIVE PSYCHOLOGY

Christopher Peterson and Ralf Schwarzer, Series Editors

A Life Worth Living: Contributions to positive psychology
Mihaly Csikszentmihalyi and Isabella Selega Csikszentmihalyi (eds)

International Differences in Well-Being
Ed Diener, Daniel Kahneman, and John Helliwell

Well-Being for Public Policy
Ed Diener, Richard Lucas, Ulrich Schimmack, and John Helliwell

Oxford Handbook of Methods in Positive Psychology
Anthony D. Ong and Manfred H.M. Van Dulmen (eds)

A Primer in Positive Psychology
Christopher Peterson

Designing Positive Psychology: Taking stock and moving forward
Kennon M. Sheldon, Todd B. Kashdan, and Michael F. Steger (eds)

POSITIVE EDUCATION

The Geelong Grammar School Journey

JACOLYN NORRISH, PhD.

foreword by
MARTIN SELIGMAN, PhD.

OXFORD
UNIVERSITY PRESS

Great Clarendon Street, Oxford, OX2 6DP,
United Kingdom

Oxford University Press is a department of the University of Oxford.
It furthers the University's objective of excellence in research, scholarship,
and education by publishing worldwide. Oxford is a registered trade mark of
Oxford University Press in the UK and in certain other countries

© Oxford University Press 2015

The moral rights of the author have been asserted

Impression: 1

Published in the United States of America by Oxford University Press
198 Madison Avenue, New York, NY 10016, United States of America

British Library Cataloguing in Publication Data
Data available

Library of Congress Control Number: 2014953105

ISBN 978-0-19-870258-0

Printed in Great Britain by Clays Ltd, St Ives plc

In Memory of Professor Christopher Peterson
18 February 1950—9 October 2012

With gratitude from the Geelong Grammar School community

Professor Chris Peterson did so much to enrich the lives of so many at this School as we journeyed together to unlock how best to utilize the tenets of Positive Psychology/character strengths among our students and staff. With Nansook always at his side, he challenged our pedagogy, supported our initiatives, and guided our direction in a kind and meaningful way. As everybody knows, he had a wonderful sense of humor. This strength was used as a means of helping to embed concepts aimed at improving the lives of individuals and helping to create flourishing and enabling institutions. Chris would observe and listen intently before offering advice and great wisdom. He made the teachers at Geelong Grammar School feel comfortable. He showed them respect, and no matter what was uttered in discussions he treated each thought or observation with grace and dignity.

Every member of the Geelong Grammar School staff involved in the 2008 and 2009 training with Marty Seligman and Karen Reivich was provided with a copy of Chris's *Primer in Positive Psychology*. He was amused when he was told teachers were instructed that they could do what they wanted with the book. There was no compulsion to read it if they did not want to ("Do not evangelize, but use the drip method" was his advice in 2006 when Geelong Grammar School staff attended the Medici Conference). He envisaged some using it as a doorstop or frisbee! Perhaps some did, but the vast majority went on to read it from cover to cover and still use it to support their learning. It was Marty who strongly recommended Chris's book as the best introduction to Positive Psychology one could find.

I know that whenever a member of the Geelong Grammar School community picks up a copy of *Primer in Positive Psychology* or reflects on their use of signature strengths in the future, their thoughts will turn to Chris. They will be saddened by his premature departure from this world, they will recall his brilliant mind, they will picture Chris and Nansook presenting—almost telepathically—their lectures, and recall the tall, kind, humorous, considerate, "I hate flying," passionate soul who will always be remembered with affection at Geelong Grammar School.

Charlie Scudamore, Vice Principal, Geelong Grammar School expression
of gratitude to Professor Peterson, October 2012

Perhaps the true testament to the character of a man is what people say about him when he is not there. Within hours of Chris's unexpected death on 9 October 2012, a waterfall of hundreds of remembrances filled the ether. Their main theme was how Chris had touched people's lives, and how he had made each and every one of us feel like we mattered. He left giant footprints not only in Positive Psychology, but also in the hearts of so many people whom he touched through his life. When Chris was asked to explain Positive Psychology, he said "Other people matter. Period." He always found joy in letting other people shine. He had a gift for seeing the best in each person. He also had a strong sense of fairness and duty, without being rigid. He always had fun, whatever he did, and also brought fun for others. While Chris lived such a frugal life, he always generously shared his time and resources. It is no accident that his nickname was "Mother Teresa."

Chris loved teaching. He loved being a teacher. He was a caring and inspirational teacher. When he met with students, he did not talk to who they were but to who they would become. Students often said that when they were in his class, he made them feel that he knew them, and that they mattered. He made everyone around him feel comfortable and respected. He inspired young people to develop a love of learning and a desire to be better people not by simply lecturing, but by living by example. Although his scholarly contributions are significant, his lasting legacy will be what he shared with other people.

Chris left a great challenge that we should willingly accept—to explore what makes life worth living and how we can achieve this for all of us. His work has begun but is not finished. Now it is our responsibility to carry on his legacy. There is no better place to start than Positive Education.

Professor Nansook Park, 2013

The iconic clocktower of Geelong Grammar School's Corio campus, built in 1914.

FOREWORD

What do you most want for your children?

If you are like the thousands of parents I've asked this question, your responses included "happiness," "confidence," "contentment," "fulfillment," "balance," "purpose," "good stuff," "kindness," "health," "satisfaction," "love," "being civilized," "meaning," and the like. In short, *wellbeing* is what you most want for your children.

What do schools teach?

If you are like most parents, your responses included "achievement," "thinking skills," "success," "conformity," "literacy," "mathematics," "work," "test taking," "discipline," and the like. In short, what schools teach is how to succeed in the modern workplace.

There is almost no overlap between these two lists.

I am all for success at work, but this book asks you to imagine that schools could, without compromising either side, teach both the skills of wellbeing and the skills of achievement.

Imagine Positive Education.

Here's how Positive Education began. I was on a speaking tour in Australia in January 2005 when I had a phone call from a voice I had never heard before. "G'day, mate," he said, "This is your student, Dr Trent Barry."

"My student?"

"Yeah, you know that live 6-month telephone course—I woke up at four in the morning every week to listen to your lectures from the outskirts of Melbourne, where I live. It was fantastic, and I was a fanatic, but I never spoke up. (I had given four iterations of 24 lectures on the telephone to about 1000 "listeners" a few years earlier.)

"We want to helicopter you to Geelong Grammar School. I am actively involved in the School and my children go there. We are in the middle of a fundraising campaign for a Wellbeing Centre. We want you to talk to the alumni and help us raise money for the campaign."

"What is the Geelong Grammar School?" I enquired.

"It is one of Australia's great schools, it has deep pockets, and it needs a new gym," he went on, "but the Council said we want wellbeing for the kids, not just a building. I told them about Seligman—they had never heard of you—and now they want you to come and convince the donors that wellbeing can actually be taught, and that a curriculum can be mounted to give the new building real meaning."

So my wife, Mandy, the kids, and I boarded a helicopter on a rickety platform in the middle of Melbourne's Yarra River, and 6 minutes later we were at Trent's home. Mandy whispered to me as we landed, "I have an uncanny feeling that we are going to spend our sabbatical here."

Mandy, as usual, was prescient. I spent the day meeting the council members, donors, and senior faculty. The financial goal, I'm told, was reached that day. We did spend our sabbatical at Geelong Grammar School in 2008, and Positive Education was founded then and there.

However, the tale would be incomplete without a few words about our family time at Geelong Grammar School. Nikki, the founder of Positive Psychology ("If I can stop whining, you can stop being such a grouch," uttered at the age of 5 years), was now 16. She boarded at The Hermitage, and flouted the parietal rules on the very first day. Moreover, she and her friends would appear for huge American breakfasts most mornings at the Chaplain's house where we lived. Darryl, now 14, chose to enter Year 10 at Corio rather than live at Timbertop doing Year 9, which would have been the chronological choice. He boarded at Manifold House and became a rugby fanatic. We followed him and his team around Victoria every weekend getting to know this wonderful sport as well as the surrounding schools. Darryl and Nikki thought the work was easy, and they tried to emulate the laid-back attitude of their classmates towards the present and the future—without any success. They speculated that the ingredient that East Coast American kids lacked for a laid-back attitude was the confidence of their place in their culture that their classmates had about Australia. Carly and Jenny, aged 4 and 7, lived with us at the Chaplain's house, where we continued to home school them, concentrating on Australia's history and culture. Lara stayed at home in Philadelphia to complete her Freshman year at Penn.

Most significantly the family was welcomed into a positive *community*—the Geelong Grammar School community. The concept of "community" was new to us. We have lived in Wynnewood, Pennsylvania, for 25 years, but it is not a community. It is a bedroom suburb of Philadelphia, and it does not even have sidewalks. I have worked at the University of Pennsylvania's Psychology Department for 50 years, but it is not a community. What unites the faculty of the University is little more than a common interest in finding good parking spaces, and as the Psychology faculty has grown more diverse, it has become half a dozen feudal kingdoms, each primarily concerned with enhancing its own territory. Consequently, living in a positive community for 6 months was a new adventure for our family.

You will read at length in the following chapters how Positive Psychology came to pervade the whole Geelong Grammar School community. The lesson I draw from my family's experience was that Positive Psychology will most easily take root within an already existing positive community.

Professor Martin Seligman

ACKNOWLEDGMENTS

I wish to thank the Geelong Grammar School Principal, Stephen Meek, for supporting this book from start to finish and for encouraging all of those who contributed to it.

I am also grateful to the Geelong Grammar School Council and the Geelong Grammar School Foundation for making this project possible.

The School is honored that so many leading scholars in the field so generously contributed their time and words to the introductions for the chapters in this book. I thank Professor Seligman for writing the Foreword, and for being an ongoing and valued friend of Geelong Grammar School. The School would also like to extend its deep appreciation to the many other researchers and practitioners in the fields of Positive Psychology and Positive Education who have visited the School over the past few years and shared their expertise and wisdom, enriching the program and curriculum.

I am grateful to Charlotte Green, Martin Baum, Angela Butterworth, Jo Hargreaves, and the team at Oxford University Press for their invaluable guidance and ongoing help in bringing this story to life.

This book started with a vision of sharing Geelong Grammar School's learning about Positive Education with other schools and educators, with the aim of inspiring them to also embrace the quest to incorporate the science of wellbeing and flourishing as part of daily life at their schools. It has been a privilege to work with so many people who are deeply committed to wellbeing, and especially to the wellbeing of children and young people. I wish to thank educators and families everywhere who share in the vision of a world where care, compassion, forgiveness, and health are at the heart of how schools educate children.

Within the pages of this book are case studies, stories, and examples from many staff members who generously took the time to contribute their thoughts and words. It is these stories and examples that perhaps best demonstrate how Positive Education is brought to life at Geelong Grammar School. Thank you to all who contributed, and to the more than 50 staff members, students, parents, and friends of the School from across all four campuses who took the time to be interviewed and share their experience of Positive Education.

I am most grateful to the wonderful team at the Institute of Positive Education (formerly the Positive Education Department), including Shannan O'Neill, who brought her strength of appreciation of beauty and excellence to selecting the photos and artwork, and Georgiana Cameron, who assisted with several chapters and contributed substantially to the Glossary and Recommended Resources. I give heartfelt thanks to Paige Williams for being an ongoing and invaluable support for the project since the beginning stages, and to both Elaine Pearson and Judy Hand for supporting the book in countless ways—nothing was ever too much. Thank you also to Janis Coffey and David Bott for being both respected colleagues and trusted friends.

I am grateful to Meredith O'Connor and Paige Williams for their invaluable contributions to Chapter 13 on research and evaluation, and to Fiona Fitzgerald for generously sharing her postgraduate research as well as her time.

This project has only been possible because of the hard work of the Community Relations Department, under the leadership of Tony Bretherton. In particular, sincere thanks are extended to Brendan McAloon, who was particularly instrumental in the early stages of creating the vision and synopsis for the book. I also thank Claire Robson for the numerous Positive Education images she has created over the years, and Frances Loughrey both for her enduring passion for wellbeing, and for her ongoing commitment to spreading the message of Positive Education to the wider community. In addition, I am grateful to Andrew Moore for his invaluable and ongoing support for this book and for Positive Education at Geelong Grammar School.

Special thanks are due to John Hendry, Steve Andrew, and Debbie Clingeleffer-Woodford for their willingness to spend hours discussing key ideas and events, for providing feedback and suggestions, and for their commitment to ensuring the authenticity of the story—as well as their generosity of spirit in contributing to education in and beyond Geelong Grammar School.

The School is grateful to Robyn Brook for her significant contribution to developing the Geelong Grammar School Model for Positive Education, and her experience and passion in assisting the growth of Positive Education at Geelong Grammar School during the early stages of the project.

I wish to thank Michelle Badior for giving such thoughtful, perceptive, and helpful feedback on all aspects of the writing, and for doing so with such kindness and grace.

Perhaps the biggest thank you should be extended to Justin Robinson and Charlie Scudamore, who read each version of every draft of all chapters, providing invaluable guidance and authentic examples and stories to elucidate key points. The field of Positive Education is the better for your passion, wisdom, and tireless commitment to wellbeing.

Finally, thank you to all members of the Geelong Grammar School community who have embraced Positive Education and who have helped to create a culture of wellbeing at the School. For every story that is told within this book, there are countless other moments of profound kindness, innovative teaching, and breathtaking grit that could not be included. It has been an honor to be part of the warm, caring, and inclusive community that is Geelong Grammar School. The memories of this experience will always be treasured.

Jacolyn Norrish

CONTENTS

LIST OF CONTRIBUTORS

Foreword

Professor Martin Seligman

Introduction

Stephen Meek

International expert contributors

Professor Roy Baumeister, Eppes Eminent Scholar, Professor of Psychology, Florida State University

Dr Tal Ben-Shahar, Maytiv, IDC Herzliya, Israel

Professor Barbara Fredrickson, Department of Psychology, University of North Carolina, Chapel Hill

Dr Craig Hassed, Senior Lecturer, Department of General Practice, Monash University

Professor Felicia Huppert, Emeritus Professor of Psychology and Director of the Well-being Institute, University of Cambridge, and Professor, Institute for Positive Psychology and Education, Australian Catholic University, Sydney

Dr Sue Jackson, Queensland University of Technology, University of Queensland, and Body and Mind Flow Psychological Consulting

Professor Nansook Park, Department of Psychology, and Director, Michigan Positive Psychology Center, University of Michigan

Dr Karen Reivich, Department of Psychology, University of Pennsylvania

Pninit Russo-Netzer, Department of Counseling and Human Development at the University of Haifa, Israel

Professor Martin Seligman, Zellerbach Family Professor of Psychology, and Director, Positive Psychology Center, University of Pennsylvania

Professor George Vaillant, Professor of Psychiatry, Harvard Medical School

Geelong Grammar School contributors

Steve Andrew
Michelle Badior
Pam Barton
Martin Beaver
Sarah Bell
Clare Bennetts
Margaret Bennetts
Rebecca Bettiol
David Bott
Wendy Breer
Tony Bretherton
Georgiana Cameron
Geoff Carlisle
Stacey Clancy
Debbie Clingeleffer-Woodford
Janis Coffey
Dean Dell'Oro
Janet Etty-Leal
Rob French
Andrew Groves
Simon Haigh
John Hendry
Roger Herbert

Glenn Hood
Kate Hood
Jo Kearney
Mary-Anne Lewis
Frances Loughrey
Brendan McAloon
Alice Macmillan
Christian Machar
Jane Marney
Julie Molloy
Andrew Monk
Daryl Moorfoot
Jacqui Moses
Meredith O'Connor
Eleanor O'Donnell
Stephen Pearce
Garry Pierson
Justin Robinson
Claire Robson
Charlie Scudamore
Justine Siedle
Paige Williams

ADVANCE PRAISE

In this welcome contribution to the literature on wellbeing in schools, a variety of academics and teachers provide theory, ideas and practical strategies to inspire and support other educators in putting wellbeing alongside academic attainment. Geelong Grammar School is a pioneer in the field of Positive Education and it has been my privilege and pleasure to work with some of its committed and wise teachers over the years.

Jenny Fox Eades, Author of *Celebrating Strengths*

We think a child is learning if they are acquiring new knowledge, thinking skills, and get high test scores. But is that it? In *Positive Education*, Norrish tells Geelong Grammar School's journey of making students' health, wellbeing, and flourishing just as important as academic learning. With introductions by world-renowned experts in Positive Psychology, the chapters discuss how classrooms were infused with positivity, and quotes from students, teachers, and administrators provide color. It is critical that we attend to our children's Wellbeing to make both their lives and the future brighter, and the Positive Education model used at Geelong will help accomplish these goals. I applaud Norrish for her commitment to bringing positive psychology to the classrooms, and I encourage everyone interested in helping youth flourish to read this book.

Jeffrey J. Froh, Psy.D., Associate Professor of Psychology at Hofstra University and Co-Author of *Making Grateful Kids: The Science of Building Character* and Co-Editor of *Activities for Teaching Positive Psychology: A Guide for Instructors*

Hopefully there is a moment in your life when you realize that you are the leader that you have been waiting for. At that moment of realization, you stand at the threshold of possibility for yourself and you begin to see a way to shape your positive contribution to the world. The ideas and values contained in this book provide a launching pad for these insights in young people and through this, have the capacity for changing the world.

Dr Andrew Fuller, Clinical Psychologist, Department of Psychiatry, University of Melbourne, Scientific Consultant for the ABC series "Whatever: the science of teens"

A deeply impressive book—an inspired and inspiring story of how a school decided that the health and wellbeing of students could, and should, be as important as their academic achievement and how they used the science of flourishing and Positive Psychology to implement that radical vision. Every school, teacher, parent, and policy-maker who truly cares about education and the welfare of young people should read this book.

Dr Maureen Gaffney, Author *Flourishing*

Congratulations Geelong Grammar School on creating the "Jewel in the Crown" of Positive Education texts. This book is filled with inspirational narratives and case studies that bring the science of Positive Psychology to life in the educational sector. Geelong Grammar School have been the leader in the emerging field of Positive Education and many schools, both independent and state, have been inspired to take action by the pioneering, work they've done. The character strengths of bravery, creativity, love of learning, and leadership shine brightly and it's my hope that this text becomes essential reading for all schools.

Dr Suzy Green, Clinical & Coaching Psychologist, Founder, The Positivity Institute

Positive Education should transform the focus of educational systems, and the outcomes they deliver for children, around the world. This outstanding book shows how and why, relating the stunning experiences and outcomes of Geelong Grammar School in Australia. Packed with insight, experience, and practical examples, it will inspire a new generation of educators and policy makers with a renewed belief in what is possible, raising the levels of what we should expect, and accept, for our children.

Dr Alex Linley, Chief Executive Officer, CAPP

Positive Education convinces you that schools should be the world's wellbeing centers where students strive to feel good and do good for a lifetime.

Dr Shane Lopez, Research Director, Clifton Strengths Institute

To simply call this book "groundbreaking" would be an under-statement. You will not find a more comprehensive and complete book on Positive Education. Period. Packed with case examples, in-depth content, a myriad of scientific findings, and practical applications it represents the best of what a Positive Psychology book can become.

As I read the book, I experienced something similar to my visit at Geelong—a feeling that I was amidst greatness . . . greatness coming from the compassion exemplified, from wisdom saturating, and from the sense that I was part of something deeply meaningful and impactful, much bigger than myself.

Ryan M. Niemiec, Psy.D., Education Director, VIA Institute on Character, Author of *Mindfulness and Character Strengths: A Practical Guide to Flourishing*

I've been aware of Geelong Grammar School's Positive Education program from the very early days and I've been lucky enough to get to know most of the key players along the way. As such, it's little surprise to me that these incredible people are achieving incredible results and leading the world in this all important area. The publication of this fantastic resource continues the Geelong Grammar team's great work by providing an amazingly valuable summary of all the core areas written by all the best people. I can highly recommend this book for anyone interested in Positive Education; in fact, it's a must read.

Dr Timothy Sharp, Chief Happiness Officer—The Happiness Institute

The Geelong Grammar School community understand that effective education nurtures kids to both "love to learn for life", and to "learn to love life" to the full. This book offers a fascinating window into the heart and soul of the School's transformational journey and into the lasting value of Positive Education for all.

Dr Helen Street, Applied Social Psychologist and Chair of the National Australian Positive Schools Initiative

Geelong Grammar School is a world leader in Positive Education. This book provides a detailed and thought-provoking insight into Geelong Grammar's journey from their pioneering years through to their latest cutting edge pedagogy and research. An interesting blend of insights are offered from prominent scholars in the field and, importantly, from Geelong Grammar staff themselves who have been at the "chalk face" of practice and development. The Geelong Grammar School Applied Model for Positive Education offers a robust framework for other schools to follow and has clearly been successful in the contexts of boarding and day school. Readers of this book will come away with a deeper understanding of the field of Positive Education and I am sure will be filled with energy and ideas to try out in their own schools.

Lea Waters, Professor, Gerry Higgins Chair in Positive Psychology, and Director of the Centre for Positive Psychology, Melbourne Graduate School, University of Melbourne, Australia

This book sets out the courageous and effective journey of Positive Education in one school, but does so in ways that make it accessible to all who are wanting to bring about enduring personal and institutional transformation. The elegant nexus of theory and practice offers an honest critical appraisal of many dimensions of Positive Education *in action*. One of the important themes is the centrality of positive relationships at all levels of education: a message that is needed now more than ever. I am sure this book will become a core text for all who are interested in researching and implementing positive education.

Dr Kerry Howells, Author of *Gratitude in Education: A Radical View.*

There are many books nowadays on how to do Positive Education. This is the first one on how to live it.

Dr Ilona Boniwell, iMAPP Course Director, Anglia Ruskin University and CEO, Positran

What makes a well-resourced, well-accomplished and well-groomed institution pursue wellbeing purposefully? Perhaps, Geelong Grammar School, like many educational institutions, recognize that challenges faced by the Millennial generation—from cyber bullying to escalating rates of depression—may not be handled only through scholastic accomplishments. Many institutions recognize but don't take the risk of taking a new and bold initiative, which Geelong Grammar School did through Positive Education. In this book, Norrish has artistically coalesced the collective wisdom of twelve eminent scholars, who have seen Positive Education unfolding in the corridors, courtyards, and classrooms of Geelong Grammar School, affecting in meaningful ways from the Principal to pupils, from parents and patrons. The book makes a compelling argument that Positive Education is not a collection of self-esteem boosting strategies; it has scientific arms and legs spanning into positive emotions, character strengths, positive relationships, health and resilience, engagement, accomplishment, mindfulness and meaning, to inspire and to translate this inspiration into applicable and replicable action, habit, and purpose.

Tayyab Rashid, Ph.D., C.Psych, University of Toronto Scarborough, Canada

LIST OF INTERVIEWS

Ildi Anderson

Steve Andrew

Pam Barton

David Bott

Debbie Clingeleffer-Woodford

Janis Coffey

Michael Collins Persse

Justin Corfield

Dr John Court

Janet Etty-Leal

Fiona Fitzgerald

Kylie Griffiths

Andrew Groves

Hayden Gyles

Simon Haigh

Paddy Handbury

John Hendry

Kate Hood

Ron Howell

Tony Inkster

Rita Jenkins

Xara Kaye

Stuart Kearney

Hugh Kempster

Jeremy Kirkwood

Malcolm Leigh-Smith

Mary-Anne Lewis

Frances Loughrey

Ian McIntosh

Christian Machar

Jane Marney

Annabel Meek

Stephen Meek

Andrew Moore

Daryl Moorfoot

Richard Munro

Michael Nelson

Keven O'Connor

Eleanor O'Donnell

Stephen Pearce

Garry Pierson

Marshall Radcliff

Steve Radojevic

Justin Robinson

Charlie Scudamore

Janet Stephens

Anthony Strazzera

George Vickers-Willis

Paige Williams

INTRODUCTION · Stephen Meek,

Principal, Geelong
Grammar School

Great schools get even better because they have vision and are prepared to take risks. They see society's problems and they take the lead by doing something about them. When that something has never been tried before, that is a risk. Such was the position when Geelong Grammar School committed to training its staff in Positive Psychology with Professor Martin Seligman and the team from the University of Pennsylvania in January 2008. No school before had committed to training its entire staff in Positive Psychology, so that they in turn could teach these ideas to all of the students in the School.

The risk of failure was high, and the risk of ridicule was even higher. Would the training be successful? Would the staff be receptive? Would the students be open to the ideas? Would parents accept that this was a good idea or would they feel that the School was trespassing in areas that belonged to families? Would the benefits justify the cost? Would all staff and students constantly have to have a smile on their faces to show that the training had worked? Was a "happiology" to be the School's new Mission Statement? What happened when the smiling stopped? The first questions were legitimate concerns. The last three questions were the types of points made by cynics who dismissed the whole notion of Positive Psychology. With so many questions, was it worth the risk? With student (and staff) wellbeing the prize, the answer was always yes.

The search for wellbeing

The search for wellbeing began in 2003 when the then Principal, Nick Sampson, and the School's Chief Medical Officer (from 1995 to 2010), Dr John Court, concluded that the School needed to do more to help students to cope with the issues that were confronting young people in the community. Everyone was clear that issues related to drugs, alcohol, stress, body image, depression, and anxiety were on the increase in society at large, but that schools were doing little to help students to learn how to manage these issues. Our students were not more prone to these difficulties, but nor were they immune to them. What could the School do to help?

When I started as Principal of Geelong Grammar School in 2004, one of the first questions the Council asked me was whether I supported the idea of constructing the

Wellbeing Centre. This would be a space combining five separate entities—the medical center, the sports facilities (including the swimming pool, fitness center, and sports hall), a social space, a dance studio, and the School shop—in one place. In essence, the aim was to combine the two key facilities of the medical center and the sporting facilities so that students would link exercise with health. We already knew that exercise was helpful in terms of alleviating stress and depression, and thus we hoped to encourage students to go to the Wellbeing Centre if they were feeling under pressure, so that they could exercise and meet with other people. However, we were also committed to encouraging students to get fitter so that they would feel better within themselves.

First steps into Positive Psychology

It was at this stage in 2005 that a parent, Dr Trent Barry, introduced us to the ideas of Professor Martin Seligman and the whole notion of Positive Psychology, as Trent could see that our ideas mirrored the essential beliefs of Positive Psychology. By chance, Marty came to Australia in 2006 and Trent arranged for him to come to Geelong, thereby introducing us to him. Marty gave an introductory talk to some staff at the School, and we decided to find out more.

I asked Charlie Scudamore, Vice Principal, Debbie Clingeleffer-Woodford, the Director of Learning, and John Hendry, the Director of Student Welfare, to conduct two trips to visit Marty at the University of Pennsylvania. Their task was to evaluate not only the benefits and costs that would come to the School from embracing Positive Psychology but also, more importantly, how well it would fit with our ideas for wellbeing and the culture of the School. Asking Charlie Scudamore to investigate whether there are ways to improve student wellbeing is like asking Don Bradman to find out whether there are any benefits to playing the game of cricket. A teacher more passionate about and dedicated to the cause of wellbeing would be hard to find. It was therefore not a huge surprise that his recommendation, along with those of Debbie and John, was that we should go ahead and undertake the training. After all of our investigation and due diligence, I felt confident that I could accept this recommendation and work it into a proposal to take to the School Council.

It was clear to me that the School's wish to do something for the wellbeing of the students in its care was a fundamentally important one, and I embraced it wholeheartedly. Thus when I brought the proposal for the introduction of Positive Psychology to the School Council, there was a willingness to consider the idea. We had a good debate, weighing up the advantages for our students and staff, and in the end the Council agreed to do this. Overall, the Council must be given great credit for being willing to back the School leadership over the desire to take positive steps to improve student wellbeing.

Much credit (and thanks) must also go to the Geelong Grammar Foundation for paying the significant cost of bringing Marty Seligman and his 20-strong team from the University of Pennsylvania to Corio for the 9-day training of 120 staff. Without the support of the Foundation, under its Chairman, Paddy Handbury, this training would never have gone ahead. However, with such high costs, inevitably a lot was hanging on the success of the training and the future implementation of Positive Psychology in the School program. It was a real risk.

What was it about the program that made it worth investing so much time and effort in it, especially given that the whole discipline of Positive Psychology was a relatively young one? First and foremost, Positive Psychology was based upon tested scientific experiments, with the results having been peer-reviewed by other academic staff. Secondly, it was a program that was for the benefit of everyone—all staff and all students—not just for a minority. Thirdly, it was an extremely good fit with our other programs. It built easily upon the Year 9 program at Timbertop which aims to strengthen resilience among students, and it followed naturally from the strong pastoral care that we provide in our Houses—both boarding and day. Fourthly, it was a natural fit with our ideas about wellbeing and our hopes for the construction of the Wellbeing Centre. I therefore felt that our staff would be receptive to the program.

Training the staff

The training of 100 School staff started in January 2008 with a mixture of senior staff from each campus, Heads of Houses, Heads of Faculty, some teaching staff who were keen to be involved, and some members of the non-teaching staff. The entire Principal's Advisory Committee, including all Heads of Campus, Directors, and staff in senior leadership positions and myself, attended all 9 days of the training, which was an indication of how highly the School valued the program. The inclusion of non-teaching staff was also important, as from the start we had always believed that this training was for all of our staff—teaching and non-teaching. It would have been very easy just to train the teachers, as they would be teaching the students, but I believed that there were benefits which would reach people personally as well as professionally, and thus it was incumbent upon us to make those opportunities available to all of our staff. I also felt that these benefits should be available to students and staff in other schools. From the very beginning we believed that we should share these ideas with other schools and not keep the benefits of Positive Psychology to ourselves.

The 9-day course was led by Dr Karen Reivich, from the University of Pennsylvania. She is the most remarkable and gifted trainer I have ever encountered, and she inspired us all with her vitality, knowledge, clarity, and charisma. She established a wonderful rapport with her audience, who soon became immersed in the world of Positive Psychology. Adding to the course was Marty, who gave key lectures and contributed periodically to the sessions with his own insights. The combination of Marty and Karen was inspiring and, aided by the other members of the team, we had a remarkable 9 days of training.

Some staff had approached the course with a degree of skepticism. They knew little about Positive Psychology, and this was not helped by the fact that they had been asked to give up 9 days of their summer holidays. However, by the end of the week it was clear that everyone felt that they had been given skills and insights which would enable them to transform their personal and professional lives. Apart from the sheer brilliance of the training by Marty and Karen, my lasting memory of the week was the incredible sense of unity and camaraderie that existed among all of the staff who were doing the course.

I remember talking to Karen at the start of the second day, when she asked me how I thought it was going. I replied that I was not sure it was going well, as everything we had been told on the first day was contained in the book we had all read in preparation for the course. My concern was that if the training was a rehash of the book, it would be one of the most expensive book reviews in history. In the event I need not have worried—the training was brilliant.

In his book, *Flourish*, Marty describes my transformation in the course of the 9 days from a "reserved … chilly … British headmaster" to someone who was "glowing and hugging my faculty." I suspect I would not have put it quite like that, but I certainly did feel that the course had reached inside me and made me look at myself and my approach differently. On a practical note, I was certainly happier at the end of the course than I was at the beginning, because I knew now that the training had been an outstanding success.

I think that it is fair to say that the brilliance of the course gave us a momentum and energy that carried us through the year, and years, ahead. Without that momentum it is possible that the training would have become smothered by the busyness of every-day school life. If that had been the case, the whole Positive Psychology journey would have floundered. We have more to thank Marty and Karen for than just the course, or just changing our personal lives. We thank them for giving us the launching pad that has allowed us to change the lives of so many others. How we built on that foundation, and created a School with flourishing at its very heart, is the story told in the following chapters.

Positive Education

During the 9-day training, a group of staff met with Marty to discuss the way ahead, and in the course of the meeting the term "Positive Education" was born. It seemed so much more applicable to what we were doing at the School. For us the definition of Positive Education is the bringing together of the science of Positive Psychology with best practice teaching, to encourage and support schools and individuals to flourish.

We had made a start with regard to bringing Positive Education into the culture of the School, but we needed to go further. We had trained 100 staff, but we employ over 400 staff in total—teaching and non-teaching—and ultimately I wanted everyone to be trained. Therefore, in 2009, Marty, Karen, and the team returned to the School and ran two 6-day courses for another 120 School staff members. Today, all of our staff have been trained in Positive Education. Karen Reivich returned to the School in 2011 to train 25 staff to an even higher level so that they could in turn become trainers.

It is now a condition of working at the School in any capacity that new staff must attend a 3-day course in Positive Education, which we run every year. It is so important that everyone understands what Positive Education is about. I spoke to a visitor to the School this term who had come to find out more about Positive Education. He told me that he had spoken to one of the gardeners and had been impressed by just how knowledgeable he was and how he used the same language as the visitor had heard in the formal presentations. You could not ask for more.

Has it worked?

Traditionally schools focus on achievement, with academic performance being a measure of success. One of the benefits of Positive Education is that it does not just focus on your academic achievements, but on who you are as a person. I think that has been a benefit for many students. I have no doubt at all that at the basic level we have raised the profile of wellbeing for all of our students. They now have a greater understanding of the significance of wellbeing, and how it can determine so much in terms of the quality of their lives. Moreover, they know how to boost their resilience when they encounter low points in their lives, and indeed they know that they can be proactive and act positively to increase their life satisfaction.

I know that the overwhelming majority of them have enjoyed the courses. These have provided them with a common language with which to converse with other students and staff, and also with which to express insights into their own wellbeing. That is power in itself.

For the staff I think there have been a number of similar results. They have felt personal benefits in their own lives, in terms of their own wellbeing. I believe that we have a happier staff than we did previously (and I thought they were content before!), and I feel that they have a pride in the initiative which the School has shown and the leadership which it has demonstrated. I think that it has helped to close the gap which can exist between teaching and non-teaching staff. It has certainly been very important for staff morale to have included all staff in our training, and to have clearly invested so heavily in professional development for staff.

Many parents also share that same sense of pride that the School has again shown international leadership in education, as had earlier been the case with the creation of Timbertop. The ideas that are central to Positive Education resonate with many of our parents who are encountering similar ideas at work. We are now running courses for parents not only so that they can benefit personally, but also so that they can support at home what we are doing at School.

A wider impact

There have been many benefits for us as a School. The amount of interest in the School's initiative has been remarkable, not only in the rest of Australia but also worldwide. We have a constant stream of enquiries and visitors coming to see what we are doing. I believe that the initiative has lifted the profile of the School higher on the world stage. I am equally sure that our willingness to help others with their investigation into wellbeing and Positive Education has also been appreciated. It has demonstrated far more powerfully than words could ever do that we take wellbeing seriously and are committed to the wellbeing of our staff and students. I think that the School is a fitter and healthier place than it was before.

I believe that there is a changed momentum in schools in Australia, and around the world, about the importance of wellbeing for students and staff, and that more schools are now embracing Positive Education. Student wellbeing was always a core objective for us as a School, and it is what led us into Positive Psychology in the first place. Our aim from the start was to encourage students to be more proactive in managing their health. We believed that there were techniques and approaches which they could use that would enable them to cope better with what life had to throw at them. Our hope was also that we would be able to share ideas with other schools. In many ways our initial aims were innovative, but modest. The actual outcome has been radical and on a scale that we could never have anticipated. The difference has been achieved through Positive Education. This book explains that journey and that outcome.

GUIDE TO THE READER

The Geelong Grammar School context

The School

Geelong Grammar School is one of the largest co-educational boarding and day school in Australia. It has four campuses—Corio and Bostock (both in Geelong), Toorak (in Melbourne), and Timbertop (outside Mansfield in the Victorian High Country). Its religious affiliation is Anglican.

- The Bostock campus, which is a day school, comprises the Early Learning Centre (ELC) (for students from 3 years old, kindergarten) to Year 4. It is located in the Geelong suburb of Newtown.
- The Corio campus, which is a boarding and day school, comprises the Middle School and Senior School. The Middle School encompasses Years 5 to 8, and the Senior School comprises Years 10 to 12. In the Senior School, students may study either the International Baccalaureate (IB) Diploma or the Victorian Certificate of Education (VCE).
- Timbertop, a boarding campus, is located in the Victorian Alps and caters exclusively for girls and boys in Year 9. At this campus there is a crucial balance between the academic and outdoor education programs.
- The Toorak campus, which is a day school, comprises the ELC to Year 6 and is located in suburban Melbourne. It offers the Primary Years Programme (PYP) of the International Baccalaureate from Prep to Year 6.

Corio campus

- The Corio campus comprises two Senior School co-educational day boarding houses (Allen and Fraser) and eight Senior School boarding houses (Clyde, Elisabeth Murdoch, Garnett, and the Hermitage are female boarding houses, and Cuthbertson, Francis Brown, Manifold, and Perry are male boarding houses), two Middle School day boarding houses (Highton and Otway), and three Middle School boarding houses (Barrabool and Barwon for boys, and Connewarre for girls).
- The Handbury Centre for Wellbeing is a space designated for sport, health, and overall wellbeing, and consists of a multi-purpose sports hall, a 25-metre pool, a fitness

center, a dance studio, the John Court Café, the Geelong Grammar School Shop and the School's Medical Centre, Kennedy, which also has rooms for counseling services and physiotherapy.

- The Co-Curricular Program is an after-school program that runs on weekdays and weekends, encompassing sport (which is compulsory) as well as activities that include art and the performing arts (dance, drama, and music), community service, debating, and a wide range of recreational and personal development interests.
- The Chapel of All Saints is at the spiritual center of the School. All students must attend a weekday service, and boarders must also attend on Sundays.

Community

- The Old Geelong Grammarians Association (OGGs) consists of Geelong Grammar School alumni and selected long-serving members of staff. The OGGs networks are complex, and offer important points of connection between past and present students, including support groups in sports and in the arts.
- The Geelong Grammar School Foundation encourages the strong tradition of generosity for the benefit of future generations of students. Its collaborative efforts enable the planning of important School projects and initiatives, including sponsoring staff professional development through the funding of study scholarships.
- *Light Blue* is the Geelong Grammar School triannual publication. It contains news of innovations in the curriculum, programs at the different campuses, reports from the Principal and Vice Principal, and reports from the various affiliated organizations.

GEELONG GRAMMAR SCHOOL: FOUR BRAVE STEPS

Schools have one of the most precious and instrumental roles in the community—educating the young. Parents trust schools with the vital mission of helping children and adolescents to develop the knowledge, skills, and values that enable them to grow up as contributors to society. Through teaching the basics and beyond of languages, mathematics, science, social sciences, and the arts, schools help to shape the minds of the future. Teachers and other school staff are some of the most important adult figures in students' lives, with their influence continuing for years, even decades, after students have left the classroom.

For over 150 years Geelong Grammar School has approached the role of educating students with courage and compassion. Over time it has grown to be an international leader in progressive and innovative teaching and learning—the provider of an exceptional education. The strong academic curriculum and the wide range of sporting and co-curricular activities combine to create nourishing opportunities for students to learn and grow. Rich social relationships and supportive pastoral care help to form a kind, respectful, and nurturing culture. Members of staff are renowned for their genuine love of young people and for their commitment to going above and beyond for their students (see Figure 1.1).

Positive Education is a new kind of exceptional education, where the science of wellbeing and flourishing meets best practice teaching and learning. Pos Ed, as it is known by the School community, provides pathways towards perhaps the most important learning of all—learning to know the self. Through committing to Positive Education, Geelong Grammar School has shown that schools can, and should, consider health, wellbeing, and flourishing to be as important as academic learning.

Figure 1.1 Stephen Meek, Principal, walking with 2013 School captains—Kate McGeoch and John Badgery.

The role that schools play in an increasingly complex and competitive society is changing. As rates of mental illness and psychological distress continue to increase, schools play an even more important role in supporting, protecting, and empowering young people. This book is the story of how Geelong Grammar School embraced that challenge through a whole-school commitment to Positive Education. It explores the initial thinking behind the move towards wellbeing, the creation of the powerful partnership with Professor Seligman and his team, and the decision to place "learning to flourish" at the center of the School's core purpose. The Geelong Grammar School Model of Positive Education—with its domains of Positive Relationships, Positive Emotions, Positive Health, Positive Engagement, Positive Accomplishment, and Positive Purpose—is explored as a framework for the cultivation of flourishing in a school setting. An exploration of the forward journey illustrates how Geelong Grammar School is continuing to help to lead a growing shift towards the value of wellbeing.

In many ways the dramatic growth of Positive Education within the School has only been possible because of the fertile soil provided by decades of education committed to cultivating well-rounded, resourceful, and resilient human beings. Therefore, before exploring the recent journey, it is important to look back and consider the rich history that has helped the School to pave the way for Positive Education. The School's history is described as comprising five significant steps, each of which was progressive in its day. These steps consist of its founding as a boys' school in 1855 in Geelong, the move from Geelong to the current site at Corio in 1914, the establishment of the Timbertop campus in 1953, becoming a co-educational school in 1976, and more recently the introduction of Positive Education in 2008. The common thread across these pivotal moments in the School's history is the belief that education happens both within and beyond the classroom.

The first step: founding of the School (1855)

In October 1855, Geelong Grammar School opened its doors to its first students, welcoming 14 boys (see Figures 1.2 and 1.3). At the time, the city of Geelong was in its early stages of development, having quickly grown over the preceding 20 years to become a thriving community of almost 20,000 inhabitants. The School was founded on a unique combination of the values of traditional English boarding schools and the free and egalitarian spirit of a young colony in what would later become Australia. These somewhat differing influences combined to create a founding philosophy that encompassed both respect for tradition, and courage with regard to change and innovation.

From the outset the School demonstrated resilience—surviving competition, economic depression, and financial challenges in the early 1860s, and even being

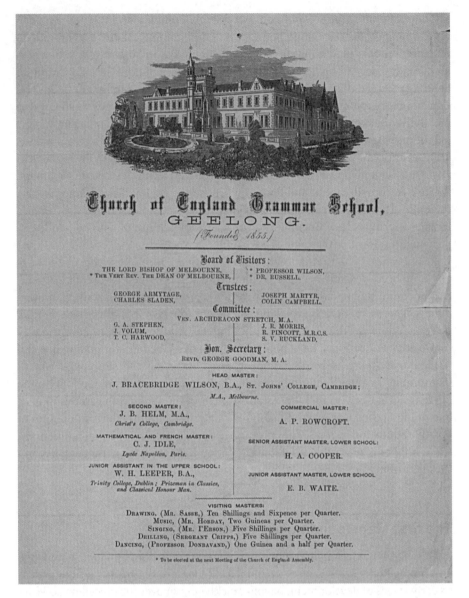

Figure 1.2 The School's 1857 prospectus displaying the foundation date of 1855.

forced briefly to close. John Bracebridge Wilson, headmaster from 1863 to 1895, was instrumental in reviving the School, and is credited with instilling many of the values and qualities that have shaped it ever since. Wilson believed that education should be about the whole child, not just about academic learning, and he placed a high priority on building character through service to others and the community. Through his leadership the School developed a well-rounded approach, including

Figure 1.3 The Geelong Grammar School building in 1860.

high standards for teaching and learning, a wide range of athletic and cultural opportunities, and a strong focus on pastoral care.

The second step: move to Corio (1914)

By the early twentieth century the School had outgrown its site in central Geelong. The School Council had dreams of a rural setting, a sense of space, and an array of separate buildings—boarding houses, classroom blocks, a hall, and a chapel—reminiscent of the great English public schools. The vision was to create a school community similar to a village, with staff and their families and students living alongside each other. A number of sites in Geelong were considered before the Council of the day bravely decided to move the School to the relatively remote, windswept, yet spacious grasslands on the shores of Corio Bay (see Figure 1.4).

The first foundation stone at Corio was laid in April 1913, and the School opened its doors on the new site the following February (see Figure 1.5). The 262 acres at Corio provided space for the boys to connect with nature, and enabled a range of activities, including sports such as cricket, rowing, and football, as well as swimming and sailing. Being exposed to the natural environment was considered paramount for the students' health, and the move to Corio provided room for them to exercise and explore with the support and security of staff living amongst them. The move also helped to solidify the School's strong foundation

Figure 1.4 School Council members (E. A. Austin, H. P. Douglass, W. F. Volum, Archbishop Lowther Clarke, H. A. Austin, and T. E. Bostock) surveying the new site at Corio in 1911.

of pastoral care, with the creation of a House structure that nurtured the development of close, supportive relationships between students and key members of the house staff.

The third step: Timbertop (1953)

Sir James Ralph Darling, headmaster for over 30 years (from 1930 to 1961), was instrumental in shaping the School in many ways. Darling's time as headmaster was characterized by expansion, both physical and curricular, and under his leadership the School grew to include Bostock House in Newtown and Glamorgan in Melbourne (later to be renamed Toorak Campus). One of Darling's greatest contributions was the creation of Timbertop in the Victorian Alps, where students are encouraged to live in harmony with the land, with the community, and with each other. An early stage in the creation of the Timbertop campus is shown in Figure 1.6.

Darling was interested in the work of Kurt Hahn, an international leader in experiential education who is best known for founding the Salem School in Germany and

Figure 1.5 The laying of the foundation stone at Corio in 1913.

Figure 1.6 The early stages of the building of the Chapel of St John the Baptist at Timbertop.

Gordonstoun in Scotland. Like Hahn, Darling believed that schools play an invaluable role in shaping character, and that students' schooling experiences should be authentic and challenging. Darling was known for his belief that learning to serve others is vital to healthy growth and development. Timbertop was founded on the philosophy that experience is the most powerful path to resilience, sensitivity, and courage.

Geelong Grammar School students now spend the entire Year 9 academic year at Timbertop, which provides a uniquely beautiful setting for them to reflect, think, and grow. While living in a small, supportive community, students develop skills and qualities beyond those possible at traditional schools. Supporting others through community and school service is a critical foundation. Students are

Figure 1.7 The view from Mount Timbertop in 1952.

responsible for looking after their environment, and do daily chores and "long jobs." During Term 2 they spend their weekends giving back to the broader community by working at farms, schools, and wineries in Mansfield and its hinterland.

Despite the scenic location (see Figure 1.7), time spent at Timbertop is not easy. The campus is purposefully designed to remove students from the comforts that most young people would consider necessities. Students do not have access to the Internet, television, or mobile phones, and are required to cut wood for the fires used to heat the boilers that provide hot water for their showers. A broad academic curriculum is combined with a rigorous exercise and outdoor education program, including regular long runs and multi-day hikes in the mountains. The aim is to help students to develop the belief and confidence that they can meet the challenges that life presents.

The fourth step: co-education (1971)

In the early 1970s the School made its move to co-education. The first steps, under headmaster Tommy Garnett, were tentative. In 1970 and 1971, senior girls studying at the Hermitage, or the Geelong Church of England Girls' Grammar School, attended the Corio campus to study subjects better provided for by Geelong

Grammar School. Over the ensuing years, girls were welcomed as members of the School, and in 1974, under the leadership of the new headmaster, Charles Fisher, the decision was made to integrate girls at all levels of the School. In 1976, with the amalgamation of Geelong Grammar School, the Hermitage, and Clyde School, the move to co-education was complete (see Figure 1.8).

This was an exciting time for the School. The following years saw the School embrace the challenge of not only becoming fully co-educational, but also educating a much larger student body. Although controversial at the time, the move to co-education was seen as instrumental in the development of the whole person and in preparing students for the adult world where men and women work, live, and learn alongside each other. The focus was on helping students to develop confidence in interacting with peers of both genders, and to cultivate the personal skills and qualities that result from being valued members of an inclusive school community.

The fifth step: Positive Education

Geelong Grammar School is now Australia's largest co-educational boarding and day school. At the time of writing it has a total of 1550 students and just over 400 members of staff. It is one School comprising four campuses, each of which has a

Figure 1.8 An early marketing shot of co-education at Geelong Grammar School in 1972.

unique, special atmosphere. Bostock House has the feel of a small country town school and welcomes students from the Early Learning Centre (ELC) to Year 4. The Toorak campus combines historic buildings with contemporary architecture and accommodates students from ELC to Year 6. Timbertop, in the Victorian Alps, is a beautiful and challenging residential campus, solely for Year 9s. The School's largest campus, Corio, comprises both day and boarding students, and houses students from Years 5 to 8 (Middle School) and Years 10 to 12 (Senior School). Corio is a vibrant community that includes over 900 students (of whom more than 600 are boarders), and more than 250 teaching and non-teaching staff, with over 100 staff members residing on campus in school accommodation.

The growth of the School since the first classes with 14 boys has been dramatic. However, much of the essence of the School remains the same—the dedication to ensuring a well-rounded education, the commitment to service to others, and the devotion to ensuring that students have meaningful and authentic experiences. It is with this fertile foundation and nurturing environment that Geelong Grammar School took its brave and pioneering fifth step—to Positive Education.

RECOMMENDED RESOURCES

Bate W (1990). *Light Blue Down Under: the history of Geelong Grammar School*. Melbourne, Australia: Oxford University Press.

Clarke M R (2003). *Timbertop: celebrating 50 years*. Victoria, Australia: Geelong Grammar School, Corio.

Collins Persse M (1995). *Well-Ordered Liberty: a portrait of Geelong Grammar School 1855–1995*. Melbourne, Australia: Cliffe Books.

Corfield J J and Collins Persse M (1996). *Geelong Grammarians: a biographical register*. Victoria, Australia: Geelong Grammar School.

THE FIFTH BRAVE STEP: POSITIVE EDUCATION

> The eyes of the educational world are upon us. Geelong Grammar School is the place where the seed crystal will happen. We will bring together the world's leading experts with the students and staff of this great School and ask the question: Can we change international education so that we not only teach mathematics and the like, but we also teach people how to lead lives that have more positive emotion, more achievement, and more meaning and purpose?
>
> Professor Martin Seligman at the Official Launch of Positive Education,
> Geelong Grammar School, February 2007

Around the turn of the new millennium, members of the School community were becoming increasingly concerned. There was an undeniably growing trend in stress, depression, anxiety, eating disorders, self-harm, and substance abuse across Australia and in other countries (Sawyer et al., 2000). Hearing stories of young people who were suffering, both within the School community and beyond, deeply worried many staff and parents. Staff were concerned that existing educational models and frameworks were no longer equipped to deal with the demands of adolescence. There was a need for new ideas and new ways of teaching to help young people not just survive, but thrive, in an increasingly complex society. The School wanted to help students who were experiencing physical or mental health problems. There was also a deep desire to help students to experience more purpose in their lives, to set and work towards fulfilling goals, to connect meaningfully with others, and to engage deeply in their learning. The vision was for Geelong Grammar School to become a beacon or lighthouse school in promoting child and adolescent health and teaching the skills for nourishing wellbeing.

The Handbury Centre for Wellbeing

Geelong Grammar has integrated the wellbeing and care of students from the day it was first built. It has always been an example of how you can't separate your work educating students from your work fostering wellbeing and healthy attitudes.

Dr John Court, Senior Medical Officer (1995–2010)

A catalyst for thinking strategically about health was the plan to build a new Wellbeing Centre, later to be named the Handbury Centre for Wellbeing. The School was in need of a new space for sports and recreation. Nick Sampson, School Principal at the time (2000–2004), and Dr John Court, Senior Medical Officer (1995–2010), had a vision for facilities that nurtured the whole student. The plan was to shift the focus on health from responding when students were unwell, to enriching wellbeing and promoting healthy behaviors such as good diet and exercise.

The aim was to create an integrated building where students could access medical and counselling services, healthcare information, exercise facilities, classrooms, open learning spaces, and a community social area. In contrast to a medical facility that was only used when a student needed help, the objective was to create a space where students and staff could swim, exercise, play basketball, socialize with friends, have a hot drink, or buy something from the uniform shop. While visiting, they would be exposed to a range of health information and have options for healthy practices such as meditation, yoga, and Pilates. When students walked over to the Wellbeing Centre, it would be unclear whether they intended to see a counselor, attend a meditation session, or play basketball. The aim was to reduce the stigma associated with accessing the counseling services and provide privacy for students seeking medical advice or psychological support. The integrated building also symbolized advancements in science in terms of the growing recognition of the complex interconnectedness between physical and psychological health.

Fundraising for wellbeing

The vision for the Wellbeing Centre was inspiring; however, there was a great deal to be done to bring the dream to fruition. The project fundraising team, led by Paddy Handbury, Chairman of the Geelong Grammar Foundation, worked tirelessly to raise resources for the project. Vice Principal Charlie Scudamore was integral to these efforts and spoke regularly to different audiences about the School's vision for proactive health. Charlie's reflections on this were that when he spoke about raising money for a gymnasium, the audience started to doze off. When he spoke about raising money for a Wellbeing Centre, a place that challenged the medical model with its focus on treatment and that placed student wellbeing at the forefront of education, the audience sat up—interested, intrigued, and curious. Clearly this issue was close to people's hearts.

An especially powerful and important moment in the School's journey was when Charlie visited the Handbury family in 2004. Geoff and Helen Handbury were well known for their commitment to philanthropic causes and for their support of medical and educational services. Helen Handbury, daughter of Dame Elisabeth Murdoch, was extremely ill with cancer when she met with Charlie. Her son, Paddy Handbury, tells the story:

> Charlie came up to meet with us a month before Mum died. It was fascinating, reflecting back on it. We laid out the plans for the building, and Mum wasn't feeling well, and you could see the look on her face—"Oh no, another building that they want us to give money to." She and Dad politely listened but with no real interest. I said "Let's put these plans away Charlie, why don't you just tell Mum what you want to do." So Charlie started talking about wellbeing and resilience, about changing the way that schools approach health, and about helping adolescents to feel better about themselves. Mum just lit up all over … she loved it. The way her eyes glowed and the happiness that came over her face when she understood what it was really all about is something I will always remember. Dad embraced it too. Children and adolescents have always been very special to them. It was so wonderful for Mum to have that moment, in the last few weeks of her life.

The generosity of Geoff and Helen Handbury, along with the Richard Hinds Bequest, with support from the parents and friends of Geelong Grammar School, made it possible for the Handbury Centre for Wellbeing to be built and the vision to begin to come to fruition.

Enter Positive Psychology

The School's Sesquicentenary in 2005 was a year of celebration and reflection. At the last celebration of the year, the School hosted 1,000 people in a big marquee on the oval with plenty of food and music. At the end of the festivities, Charlie Scudamore was left reflecting on the success of the day with one remaining guest, Dr Trent Barry. Dr Barry posed Charlie a thought-provoking question: what philosophy or framework was going to underpin the Wellbeing Centre? Dr Barry went on to explain his understanding of Positive Psychology, emphasize the importance of an evidence-based approach to wellbeing, and recommend that the School look at the work of Professor Martin Seligman, who was a personal friend.

When Professor Seligman visited Australia in 2006, the School leadership team took the opportunity to meet with him at Dr Barry's home in Geelong. The team learned that in 1998, during his term as President of the American Psychological Association, Professor Seligman had challenged the field of psychology to increase its focus on what makes life worth living (Seligman and Csikszentmihalyi, 2000). Whereas, historically, psychologists, psychiatrists, and healthcare professionals have focused predominantly on healing distress and dysfunction, Positive Psychology shifts the focus to considering in addition how people can be mentally, emotionally, and socially well (Gable and Haidt, 2005). The underpinning premise is that building strengths, cultivating wellbeing, and helping people to thrive are just as important and powerful as helping them to overcome hardships and weaknesses.

Positive Psychology resonated with the School staff because of its preventative and proactive approach. It challenges the disease model where the focus is on treating mental illness, and instead empowers each individual by exploring what they can do to live richer, fuller, and more purposeful lives. The intention to cultivate wellbeing was already there within the School—the nurturing of well-rounded, confident students was largely what the School had been about for the 150 years of its existence. The initial conversations with Professor Seligman offered a more concrete and formalized foundation for wellbeing. The ideas were consistent with the School's existing plans and intentions; however, Positive Psychology offered a cohesive language, a clearer structure, and, most importantly, a base of scientific research to support the approach.

A powerful partnership

It seemed to be a good marriage of where Positive Psychology was going and where Geelong Grammar School was going in terms of the focus on wellbeing, our work at Timbertop on resilience, and certainly the focus of service in the School. The School already had a deep commitment to wellbeing. We were on a journey and we were very interested in how Positive Psychology could make it a better one, a more effective one.

Debbie Clingeleffer-Woodford, Director of Learning

After initial conversations with Professor Seligman, the School was intrigued. However, there were still many unanswered questions. It was unclear how Positive Psychology concepts would work in education contexts, and whether the theories would stand up in Australian culture. There were also questions specific to Geelong Grammar School, including how the ideas would fit in with the existing practices of the School, such as the strong Anglican tradition and Christian values, and the Timbertop program. At this stage, under the direction of the new Principal, Stephen Meek, the School Council underwent a thorough research and decision-making process.

In 2006, two leading members of staff, Charlie Scudamore and Debbie Clingeleffer-Woodford, flew to Philadelphia to meet again with Professor Seligman and his colleagues and to find out more about Positive Psychology. Professor Seligman put together a team of experts, including Dr Angela Duckworth, Randy Ernst, Dr Jane Gillham, Professor Felicia Huppert, Mark Linkins, Professor Chris Peterson, and Peter Schulman, to discuss the opportunity to integrate Positive Psychology in schools, and specifically the potential for integrating it at Geelong Grammar School. This meeting was part of the Medici Conference, showcasing cutting-edge advancements in the scientific exploration of purpose, spirituality, psychological health, and wellbeing.

Charlie and Debbie returned to Australia ready to share information and ideas. They wrote a paper outlining the opportunity, and made a presentation to the School Council and the School Principal, Stephen Meek. Like Charlie and Debbie, the School Council was impressed by the science underpinning the approach, the depth of experience of the leading scholars, and the quality of the research that was emerging. Positive Psychology resonated with the School because of the innovative idea that wellbeing skills can be taught, and that people of all ages can learn skills which can help them to better manage their emotions, develop healthy thinking styles, and enrich their understanding of themselves and others. Furthermore, these skills can give individuals the confidence to take more productive risks, to embrace challenges, and to step outside their comfort zones and thrive.

After due consideration, the School Council made a decision to engage in Positive Psychology in a wholehearted way. Debbie and Charlie, along with John Hendry, the Director of Student Welfare, returned to the USA in 2007 to develop a concrete and strategic plan around the collaboration between Geelong Grammar School and Professor Seligman and the team from the University of Pennsylvania. Geelong Grammar School was taking the early steps down the path of becoming the first school in the world to adopt a whole-school approach to teaching and embedding the skills of wellbeing based on the science of Positive Psychology.

The official launch of Positive Psychology at Geelong Grammar School took place on 28 February 2007 (see Box 2.1 for an extract from the School periodical, *Light Blue*, from that time). The Principal, Stephen Meek, announced the plans to construct the Handbury Wellbeing Centre, the School's collaboration with Professor Seligman, and the plan to introduce Positive Psychology across the School. When the Handbury Centre for Wellbeing was opened the following year, on 20 April 2008, it represented a coming together of innovative thinking with the grit and courage necessary to make it happen (see Figures 2.1 and 2.2).

BOX 2.1: A commitment to wellbeing

We know that the current educational model and curriculum are no longer equipped to deal with the issues which our students will face in their time at school and beyond. Our intention is to help our students to develop strategies which will enable them to take a proactive approach in dealing with issues which may confront them in their lives—issues such as drugs and alcohol, obesity and eating disorders, bullying and peer pressure, depression and suicide. In doing so, we will give our students the opportunity to lead lives that have more positive emotion, more achievement, and more meaning and purpose. This in turn will enable them to have confidence in themselves, to look to the future with optimism, and to be successful.

Stephen Meek, Principal, Extract from *Light Blue*, 2007

Figure 2.1 Professor Seligman, along with Principal Stephen Meek and Vice-Principal Charlie Scudamore, announcing the introduction of Positive Education at Geelong Grammar School.

Figure 2.2 An early planning meeting with Professor Seligman in the Hawker Library at Corio.

From Positive Psychology to Positive Education

Positive Psychology fits so beautifully with the School's values and principles, in particular the whole concept of service and the wonderful warmth you get from contributing to something beyond yourself.

Malcolm Leigh-Smith, Human Resources Manager

The launch of Positive Psychology was undoubtedly a wonderful opportunity for Geelong Grammar School, but it was also a big step for Positive Psychology. By that point in time, Professor Seligman and his team had worked extensively on implementing specific programs within schools. Never before had they had the chance to contribute to the shaping of a whole educational institution according to the tenets of Positive Psychology (Seligman, 2008). Geelong Grammar School was to be a beacon of what could be achieved when the science of wellbeing was combined with an outstanding educational institution. It provided the fertile soil that would allow applied Positive Psychology to thrive.

Early on in the journey, the decision was made to no longer refer to the approach as Positive Psychology, but as Positive Education. The team felt that the term "psychology" was too closely associated with pathology and mental ill health. "Positive Education" was believed to reflect more clearly the School's broad vision of enriching wellbeing, and the unique opportunities and challenges of building on what is right with people within educational settings. The term "Positive Education" was thought to encapsulate the scientific and theoretical backbone of Positive Psychology while recognizing the unique features and complexities of school-based approaches to wellbeing.

Professor Seligman defines Positive Education as education for both traditional academic skills and the skills that foster wellbeing (Seligman, 2011). Dr Suzy Green and colleagues define Positive Education as "applied Positive Psychology in education" (Green et al., 2011, p. 16). Geelong Grammar School takes these definitions one step further by emphasizing the unique contribution that educators bring to the teaching of wellbeing via their expertise in children, adolescents, and learning. The official Geelong Grammar School definition is as follows: "Positive Education brings together the science of Positive Psychology with best practice teaching and learning to encourage and support schools and individuals within their communities to flourish." This definition aims to clearly articulate that Positive Education benefits greatly from best practice teaching and educators' wisdom regarding the knowledge transfer process. Positive Education complements and strengthens what many great teachers already do well in supporting students to flourish.

Training the staff

At the end of the first nine-day training course, there really was a fantastic buzz about the group. You could see how it resonated with people. I had presumed that this was going to be an intellectual exercise that people would engage with on a cognitive level. This was not like that. There was an intellectual element, but there were also emotional, psychological, and personal elements. That caught me by surprise: that people could see there was a way of changing their own lives through this. It was a very exciting thing to see.

Stephen Meek, Principal

The first major step in implementing Positive Psychology involved training the teaching staff. A 9-day Positive Education training course was held at Geelong Grammar School in January 2008. Professor Seligman and Dr Karen Reivich, along with their team of experts, led 100 staff from all four Geelong Grammar School campuses in comprehensive resilience and Positive Psychology training (see Figure 2.3). The School's highest priority was "getting it right in our own backyard," but there was also hope that one day all schools would embrace Positive Psychology. With this end in mind, Stephen Meek and Professor Seligman went to Canberra to visit Lisa Paul, the Australian Secretary of Education at the time, and offered the Department of Education, Employment, and Workplace Relations

Figure 2.3 Dr Karen Reivich conducting staff training in 2008 at Geelong Grammar School.

(DEEWR) 20 free places on the training course. An upcoming federal election posed a challenge to this plan, so instead the School offered the 20 free places to local teachers, counselors, and university staff (although one person from DEEWR did attend). The first 6 days of the training course focused on core resiliency concepts, and the remaining 3 days focused on character strengths and active constructive responding. "Transformational," "humbling," and "profoundly inspirational" were some of the terms that these outside guests used to describe their experience of the training.

Staff wellbeing is essential to a thriving School community, and genuine engagement with Positive Psychology is a prerequisite for teaching it to others. Therefore, whereas most school health programs focus on student wellbeing, the 9-day training course focused on staff wellbeing. It is important for staff to feel the impact of the training on their own lives in order to model and enact the principles in their everyday actions. Staff who attended the training explored their character strengths, identified unhelpful ways of thinking, and spoke about times when they were at their best. Throughout the course there was time and space for personal reflection and contemplation. Feedback on the program revealed that staff derived great meaning from sharing personal stories with colleagues, and that there was a general feeling of being at the frontier of something new and exciting.

Visiting experts

To help to build and sustain the program, Professor Seligman and his family resided at the School from January to June 2008. Randy Ernst and Mark Linkins, expert teachers and Positive Psychology facilitators, lived in residence for the first and second halves of the year, respectively, and worked with staff to implement Positive Education across the School. Randy and Mark collaborated with teachers to explore and plan the introduction of Positive Psychology into the classroom and across the School. These American visitors (and their families) quickly became more than expert teachers—they became treasured members of the School community.

This ongoing support from the University of Pennsylvania team was supplemented by a program of visiting scholars who came to the School to share their wisdom and expertise with staff and students. Throughout 2008, the School was privileged to host numerous leading experts in the field, including Professors Roy Baumeister, Ray Fowler, Barbara Fredrickson, Frank Mosca, Nansook Park, Chris Peterson, Stephen Post, Dianne Tice, and George Vaillant. Many staff, especially those with a love of learning or curiosity as signature strengths, have fond memories of deeply enriching discussions over lunch in the dining hall or at dinner at someone's home on campus. Marty, as he was fondly known among the School community, was often seen walking the beautiful School grounds, and was always happy to have company for a chat.

Positive Education in the curriculum

Many staff were eager to embark on teaching Positive Education from the moment the training stopped. However, the School was committed to ensuring that the implementation of the program with students was undertaken in a considered and sustainable manner. Therefore the whole of 2008 was devoted to training and planning, with the Heads of House trialing one semester of teaching Positive Education to Year 10 students, under the guidance of Randy Ernst. During Semester 2, a great deal of planning took place with the support of Mark Linkins.

The official roll-out of Positive Education into the curriculum occurred in 2009. At this stage, the School staff taught the Penn Resiliency Program (Gillham et al., 2008) to the Year 7 students, and followed the Strath Haven Positive Psychology Curriculum (Seligman et al., 2009) with Year 10 students. Staff also created materials for teaching resilience skills to Year 9 students at Timbertop, as core resiliency concepts complemented the existing program at the campus beautifully. Over the ensuing years, the integration of Positive Education into the curriculum has grown substantially (see Chapter 3 for more information on the teaching of Positive Education across year levels).

Debbie Clingeleffer-Woodford, Director of Learning, explained that when she and Charlie Scudamore first presented the idea of creating room in the academic day for Positive Education to the Heads of Faculty, she was concerned about how they would feel about losing valuable teaching and learning time. No more time could be found from any elective subject, as these subjects had already had the number of lessons reduced to accommodate other timetabling needs. The only possible available time for Positive Education came from the subjects of Mathematics and Science. Charlie and Debbie approached the meeting with the Heads of Faculty "with their boxing gloves on," ready with every argument they could think of as to why it was a good idea to take one lesson from every 10-day (2-week) cycle and allocate it to Positive Education. They were surprised and delighted when the Heads of Faculty, after completing the 9-day training course themselves, were supportive of the idea, so Mathematics and Science now have nine classes every 10-day cycle.

Data showing improved academic results for students in the Strath Haven research project added weight to this proposal (Seligman et al., 2009). The School's confidence was further supported by research which has found that student wellbeing has profound benefits for student engagement, commitment, concentration, motivation, and overall learning (for research evidence on the association between wellbeing, learning, and academic performance, see Durlak et al., 2011; Suldo et al., 2011). It is a measure of the support from the Heads of Faculty and their belief in Positive Education that compromises were made to create some space in the timetable. Since that time point, neither faculty has asked for the teaching time back; this is fundamental to the sustainability of Positive Education throughout the School.

Coming together for young people's wellbeing

It was the best professional development I have ever been involved in, because the political barriers came down. The State, Catholic, and Independent sectors were all working together towards the wellbeing of young people.

Charlie Scudamore, Vice Principal

In January 2009, the team from the University of Pennsylvania returned to Australia for more training. This time, in addition to further strengthening the School's knowledge base, the aim was to open the opportunity to other schools and communities so that teachers and students from a range of schools could benefit. Two 6-day training courses, each catering for 180 educators, were opened to people from all sectors of Australian education. This was followed by a 6-day course for 100 staff from DEEWR, also held at Geelong Grammar School. The Australian Government provided some support for this training in the quest to make it accessible to a wide range of schools. However, as with many world-class training opportunities, the cost was still substantial. Geelong Grammar School felt so strongly about helping other schools to commence their own journeys with Positive Education that Stephen Meek wrote to parents in the School community to ask them to contribute financial support to supplementing the costs for teachers from other schools. The parents were extremely generous and made the training highly accessible for all. Stephen Meek's reflections on this moment are included in Box 2.2. The School

---

BOX 2.2: Supporting other schools

It was not just our staff we wanted to train in Positive Education. We wanted other schools to be able to have the chance to have their staff trained and so we made the courses available to staff from other schools, Independent, Catholic, and State. Despite doing all that we could to keep the prices to a minimum, there was still quite a cost for doing the six-day course. As a result, the number of applicants from the State sector was very low, but I was particularly keen that the ideas of Positive Education should be in the State sector. I therefore sent an email out to the Geelong Grammar parent community explaining that I wanted to reduce the cost for the teachers coming from the State sector to as close to zero as I could, and would parents like to help to fund the shortfall. A number of parents responded very generously and, in total, we received $250,000. This enabled us to reduce the cost substantially for the State school teachers. Pleasingly, the number of State school teachers undertaking the training increased dramatically. It was a powerful moment, for it showed me the level of support we had from our parents for the initiative which we had undertaken.

Stephen Meek, Principal

community continued to feel honored that parents and friends gave so much to support children and schools from all parts of Australia.

HOPE and the Positive Education Department

During the initial stages of the Positive Education initiative, the School relied heavily on the team from the University of Pennsylvania. As the initiative evolved, Geelong Grammar School took increasing ownership of it, looking for opportunities to add to its existing knowledge, and to refine resources to suit the Australian context. The challenge was to ensure that the program remained sustainable once the intensive support from the University of Pennsylvania team was no longer present. The School entered a phase of consolidation where the focus was on embedding the approach and keeping the concepts fresh and dynamic.

The introduction of a Head of Positive Education (HOPE) was a large step in terms of creating a dedicated team with a focus on wellbeing. Dr Mathew White commenced the role in 2009, and was instrumental both in further embedding Positive Education and in sharing the School's journey with worldwide audiences. One of Dr White's key achievements was the organizing of a colloquium on Positive Psychology in Schools at the First World Congress on Positive Psychology in Philadelphia, 2009. Sharing the School's collaboration with Professor Seligman and the successes and challenges of implementing Positive Education across the curriculum stimulated conversations around the globe about the role of wellbeing in the future of education.

When Dr White left the School to pursue other opportunities, Justin Robinson became the Head of Positive Education. The Positive Education department was further strengthened by Paige Williams, who focused on strategic thinking with regard to how Geelong Grammar School could become a Positive Institution, with Positive Psychology embedded throughout the School community. A team of dedicated Positive Education teachers was brought together to teach the explicit Positive Education lessons. These teachers represented great diversity, being selected from eight academic departments across the School, but they all shared a passion for student wellbeing.

An internal training team

The training of the non-teaching staff was a monumental moment. It fulfilled in my mind what Geelong Grammar School is all about. Positive Education needs to be embedded throughout the whole community. It needs to be for everyone.

Garry Pierson, Head of Toorak Campus

After a strategic review of the School's progress in 2009, the Positive Education department made two key recommendations. The first recommendation was to create an internal training team so that the School could be sustainable in its professional development in Positive Education. The second recommendation was to train non-teaching staff alongside teaching staff to ensure a whole-school commitment to flourishing.

Dr Reivich and her colleagues returned again to the School in 2011 to run a 5-day "Train the Trainer" course that equipped key staff members with skills that could be used to teach Positive Education to others. Development of an internal training team provided the School with the independence and flexibility to train new staff members, offer ongoing staff refresher training, and share Positive Education with the wider School community and with other schools and organizations. The up-skilling of staff members who played key roles across the four campuses also ensured that there were people at each site who could contribute to the integration of Positive Education more locally.

Another pivotal moment in the journey was the first training session aimed specifically at non-teaching staff. Non-teaching staff include the hundreds of people who contribute to keeping the School community running smoothly, such as administrative staff, cleaning staff, gardeners, information technology support personnel, medical professionals, and House assistants. The training team for this course consisted entirely of Geelong Grammar School staff. Justin Robinson and Paige Williams took the roles of lead trainers and worked hard to ensure that everyone felt confident and comfortable within the training—even those individuals who were stepping inside the classroom for the first time in over 30 years. There was a strong focus within this training on visual images, storytelling, and experiential activities. Several members of the Positive Education team cite this initial training of the non-teaching staff, undertaken entirely by trainers from within the School, as one of their proudest moments in the School's journey.

Training parents and families

The vision for whole-community wellbeing did not stop at training the non-teaching staff; the next priority was the inclusion of families. Education is most powerful when it is discussed at the dinner table as well as in the classroom. Children derive the greatest benefits when there is consistency between the messages they learn at home and those they receive at school. In the early days, the involvement of parents and families in Positive Education grew organically. Parents were invited to attend lectures by visiting scholars as well as information sessions on topics such as mindfulness, resilience, and mindsets. The School communicated regularly with families through emails and newsletters, and the wider Geelong Grammar School community was kept informed of progress through articles published in *Light Blue*. The aim was for families, the School, and the community to function as a team in supporting both the wellbeing and the learning of students.

Although this was all a step in the right direction, increased inclusion of parents and families was identified as a top priority in the sustained implementation of Positive Education. In April 2013, the School ran its first multi-day Positive Education course for parents and family members. Most of the parents who attended the training did so out of a desire to support their children's wellbeing. Within a short time frame this focus shifted, as parents realized the potential for taking time out of the busyness of life to nurture their own wellbeing. Parents wrote gratitude letters, identified sources of flow in their lives, and shared stories about the things that gave them a sense of purpose and meaning. Over the course of the training there was much laughter as well as tears, with new connections made and friendships formed. The long-term objective is for this training to be available to all members of the extended School community, from parents, grandparents, and family members to Old Geelong Grammarians.

Moments for Positive Education

> The principles of Positive Education reaffirm Geelong Grammar School's long-tested educational foundation and the method of their implementation in our community complements the needs, circumstances, and challenges of the present.
>
> Anthony Strazzera, Senior English Teacher

In some ways, the development of Positive Education at Geelong Grammar School can be summarized as a series of important and significant advancements. However, the danger of doing so is that the School fails to capture the idea that Positive Education is a continually evolving and changing endeavor and process. When staff members are asked to recall their proudest moment in the School's journey, often they do not think of the significant "steps." Instead, they recall a moment that moved them—a speech made by a student at an assembly, seeing young children practicing mindfulness, students spotting character strengths in each other, or a courageous conversation with a colleague. Thus, as much as Positive Education is about brave and courageous steps, it is also equally about small but meaningful moments.

In his book, *Flourish*, Professor Seligman describes the Positive Education project at Geelong Grammar School as a world-leading initiative, but he also astutely calls it a "work in progress" (Seligman, 2011, p. 93). Like any ambitious, large-scale, worthwhile endeavor, there have been moments of resounding success and achievement, but also moments of setback, failure, and disappointment. Along the way, there have been lessons that students have not connected with, some training sessions that have been less successful than others, and moments when different concepts have failed to gain momentum. Concerns and criticisms have been raised from within and beyond the School community—some misguided and some warranted. Key staff have moved on, taking with them vast experience and knowledge. In many ways, Positive Education at Geelong Grammar School has had to embody many of the attributes that it aims to instill in students—resilience, grit, hope, and an openness to growth despite challenge. Through the ups and downs of the journey, described in detail in the following chapters, the School has never lost the vision of a society in which care, character, and wellbeing are at the heart of how schools educate children.

REFERENCES

Durlak J A et al. (2011). The impact of enhancing students' social and emotional learning: a meta-analysis of school-based universal interventions. *Child Development, 82*, 405–32.

Gable S L and Haidt J (2005). What (and why) is positive psychology? *Review of General Psychology, 9*, 103–10.

Gillham J E, Reivich K J, and Jaycox L H (2008). *The Penn Resiliency Program (also known as the Penn Depression Prevention Program and the Penn Optimism Program): leader's manual.* Philadelphia, PA: University of Pennsylvania.

Green L S, Oades L, and Robinson P (2011). Positive education: creating flourishing students, staff and schools. *InPsych, April issue*, 16–18.

Sawyer M G et al. (2000). The National Survey of Mental Health and Wellbeing: the child and adolescent component. *Australian and New Zealand Journal of Psychiatry, 34*, 214–20.

Seligman M E P (2008). Positive education and the new prosperity: Australia's edge. *Education Today, 12*, 20–21.

Seligman M E P (2011). *Flourish.* London: Nicholas Brealey Publishing.

Seligman M E P and Csikszentmihalyi M (2000). Positive psychology: an introduction. *American Psychologist, 55*, 5–14.

Seligman MEP et al. (2009). Positive education: positive psychology and classroom interventions. *Oxford Review of Education, 35*, 293–311.

Suldo S M, Thalji A, and Ferron J (2011). Longitudinal academic outcomes predicted by early adolescents' subjective well-being, psychopathology, and mental health status yielded from a dual factor model. *Journal of Positive Psychology, 6*, 17–30.

THE MODEL FOR
POSITIVE EDUCATION

Geelong Grammar School undertook what some believed to be an impossible task: the infusion of Positive Psychology-based principles across all levels within a large educational institution. This was not the sort of reform that simply involved bringing in new approaches and strategies to address a narrowly defined set of goals and objectives. This sort of reform required nothing short of a paradigm shift—a new way of framing, understanding, and applying our individual and collective capacities.

Mark Linkins, Positive Psychology Master Trainer at Geelong Grammar School, 2008 and currently Lead Consultant for Educational Practices at the VIA Institute and the Mayerson Academy, Cincinnati, Ohio

Positive Education at Geelong Grammar School has never been seen as an add-on component or as just a support for existing structures and processes. From the beginning of the School's journey, the objective has been to embrace Positive Education as a whole-school commitment to wellbeing and as a long-term vision for the School. The aim is to develop a sense of community across the campuses with the shared purpose of supporting staff and students to learn, grow, and thrive. However, shifting the culture of an organization as large as Geelong Grammar School is an ambitious endeavor, and requires substantial planning, continuous development, and constant revision.

Developing a conceptual and applied framework was viewed as a pivotal step in embedding Positive Education across all levels of the School community in a sustainable and science-informed way. With the objective of creating such a framework, Justin Robinson, Paige Williams, and Jacolyn Norrish joined with Robyn Brook, from nearby Avalon College, to create a Model for Positive Education. Robyn brought many strengths to the collaboration. She had a deep passion for

Positive Education, and in 2010 completed her Masters in Positive Psychology at the University of Pennsylvania. With ongoing support and assistance from other staff, this team created the Model for Positive Education which serves as a conceptual model and applied framework for guiding the planning, implementation, and evaluation of Positive Education at the School.

In June 2010, the School invited more than 20 experts in the fields of Positive Psychology and Education to review the Model for Positive Education. Throughout 2011 the team integrated feedback from these experts, and fine-tuned definitions and key topics based on their growing knowledge and evolving experience of applying Positive Education. In March 2012, after this thorough development and review process, the School shared the Model for Positive Education at the Third Australian Positive Psychology and Wellbeing Conference, which was hosted by the University of Wollongong. Another key accomplishment for the School was having an academic paper on the model published in the *International Journal of Wellbeing* (Norrish et al., 2013).

The Model for Positive Education

It might have been easier to implement if we saw it as a stand-alone unit or program—but we wanted more than that. We looked at how we could infuse it into everything we do: in the pastoral care structures, in the classrooms, in the way we interact with the kids, in the way we interact with each other.

Malcolm Leigh-Smith, Human Resources Manager

The Model for Positive Education is visually depicted as six "leaves" coming together in a circle that is supported by character strengths, with flourishing at the core (see Figure 3.1). The leaves represent the six "domains" of Positive Education—positive relationships, positive emotions, positive health, positive engagement, positive accomplishment, and positive purpose. The domains are an extension and adaptation of Professor Seligman's PERMA model (Seligman, 2011), with the most notable difference being the inclusion of positive health. Each of the domains includes a subset of evidence-informed concepts and skills that are described in detail throughout the following chapters of this book. Character strengths underpin the model and act as supporting pathways to the domains, and are especially valuable for introducing Positive Education to younger students. An alternative depiction of the model is presented in Figure 3.2.

Character strengths

The Model for Positive Education is underpinned by character strengths, which are morally valued traits that come naturally to a person and lead to a sense of fulfillment

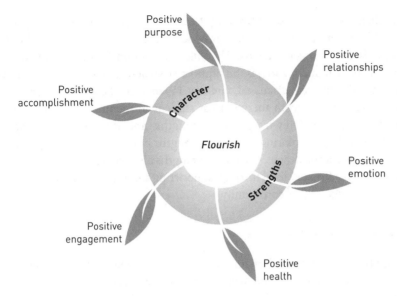

Figure 3.1 The Geelong Grammar School Model for Positive Education.

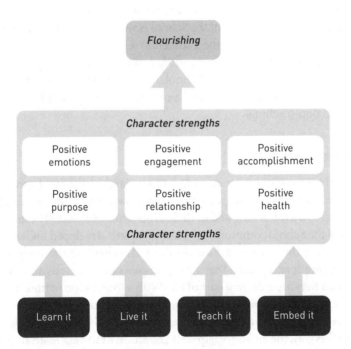

Figure 3.2 The Geelong Grammar School Applied Model for Positive Education, emphasizing the key levels of "learn it," "live it," "teach it," and "embed it."

and authenticity when used (Park and Peterson, 2009). Character strengths create links between the domains and provide access points to Positive Education, particularly for younger students. The Values in Action framework of strengths (Peterson and Seligman, 2004) is the supportive structure around which strengths are identified, explored, discussed, and developed at the School. Members of the School community—from the youngest student to members of staff—have an understanding of their own signature strengths, and experience in identifying strengths in others. Exploring character strengths builds self-knowledge and confidence in students of all ages. Character strengths also contribute to resilience and flourishing on a broader level through supporting a culture of connectedness and respect across the School community.

Positive relationships

The positive relationships domain recognizes the fundamental importance that feeling connected to others and having supportive relationships plays in a thriving life. The focus of the domain is on helping students to develop social and emotional skills that nourish their relationships with self and others. At Geelong Grammar School, this domain builds on the strong School community and its culture of compassion and respect. Kindness and forgiveness are the two leading values that are used to support the School's pastoral care structures and behavioral management policy. The caring culture of the School is supported by the teaching of skills that help to deepen and strengthen students' relationships. For example, active constructive responding (Gable et al., 2006) and mindful listening (Burgoon et al., 2000) have become gateways in the School to interpersonal communication that is authentic, attentive, and respectful, and also help to enrich staff relationships (both teaching and non-teaching).

Positive emotions

For a long time emotions were considered to be largely separate from education. The positive emotions domain recognizes that how students and staff feel is absolutely central to their learning and to their experience of school. The aim is to help members of the School community to cultivate a well-developed understanding of emotions—both their own and those of others. Another important aspect of emotional wellbeing is acceptance that strong, unpleasant emotions such as sadness, anger, and anxiety are a normal part of life. With a foundation in the broaden-and-build theory of Fredrickson (2001), there is also a focus on seeding frequent positive emotions, such as love, joy, contentment, gratitude, and hope, into daily life at the School. In this way, the aim is to help staff and students to anticipate, initiate, experience, prolong, and build positive emotions, as well as to reach out for help and support when necessary.

Positive health

The positive health domain focuses on supporting staff and students to develop sustainable habits for optimal physical and psychological health that are developed from a sound knowledge base. Central to this domain is an understanding of the mind–body connection and the inextricable link between physical and psychological health. In addition, the positive health domain encompasses the two core skill sets of mindfulness and resilience. Mindfulness, or attending to the current moment with open and curious awareness, is an evidence-based approach to supporting health and wellbeing that also has a benefical impact on student learning (Burke, 2010; Grossman et al., 2004). Positive health is also supported through fundamental skills for increasing resilience that help staff and students to embrace challenges and to bounce back from adversity, as well as to engage more fully in opportunities. Underpinning these skills and mindsets for flourishing are broader health behaviors such as exercise, good nutrition, and healthy sleep habits. These "basics" for health can be viewed as an essential foundation from which optimal wellbeing and flourishing can be nurtured.

Positive engagement

Building on the seminal work on flow by Csikszentmihalyi (1990), the positive engagement domain helps students and staff to experience complete immersion in activities through understanding the nature of engagement, the pathways to it, and its importance to individual wellbeing. Engagement is especially pertinent in the classroom, as it maximizes student motivation and learning. There is an equally strong focus on helping students to develop their interests and passions outside the classroom, with the understanding that immersion in a broad range of activities is central to a flourishing life. Another important objective is to support staff members to become engaged in their roles at the School and to cultivate a wide range of passions and interests in their broader lives.

Positive accomplishment

The positive accomplishment domain aims to develop individual potential through striving for and achieving meaningful outcomes. This domain encompasses the central business of schools in helping students to learn and achieve academically. However, the domain is broader than academic competence, as it also entails supporting students and staff to set and strive for goals that are deeply rewarding to the self as well as beneficial to others and the wider community. There is a strong focus on supporting members of the School community to embrace challenges with hope, grit, and openness to learning from their experiences. Embedded in a School culture that aims to help students to become independent, curious, lifelong learners, the positive accomplishment domain equips students with skills and mindsets that enable them to set and strive for worthwhile goals long after they have left the School grounds.

Positive purpose

Deeply engrained in the very fabric of Geelong Grammar School is a commitment to community and to service to others. The School is proud of its strong Anglican tradition and its dedication to helping students to explore the roles of faith and spirituality in their lives. Building on this rich foundation, the positive purpose domain involves understanding, believing in, and serving something greater than the self, and consciously engaging in activities for the benefit of others. The related concept of meaning concerns how people make sense of the world and their place in it. A particular focus of the positive purpose domain is altruism, and students are continually encouraged to reflect on ways in which they can use their character strengths for the benefit of others. This domain also recognizes that belonging to a close school community is a protective factor for mental and physical health, and a pillar of a purposeful and meaningful life.

Learn, live, teach, embed

The Model for Positive Education comes to life at the School on four levels, described as "learn it," "live it," "teach it," and "embed it." Staff and parents "learn" about Positive Psychology in regular training opportunities, and are supported and encouraged to "live" the principles of Positive Education and model the behaviors in their actions and interactions with each other and with students. "Teach it" refers to student learning in Positive Education that occurs through two key pathways. Dedicated or "explicit" Positive Education classes are devoted to cultivating wellbeing, and provide students with time to reflect meaningfully on the relevance of concepts to their lives. The "implicit" teaching of Positive Education refers to the infusion of wellbeing concepts into the wider curriculum so that academic objectives are approached in ways that also support flourishing. "Embed it" refers to the broader vision of creating a whole-school culture and community for wellbeing. Each level is approached as part of an ongoing, continually evolving process, as opposed to a mere objective to be achieved. The four levels can also be described as additive, synergistic, and dynamic in that they continually influence and inform each other.

"Learn it"

Throughout her extensive relationship with Geelong Grammar School staff, Dr Karen Reivich has regularly emphasized that the quantity and quality of staff training are critical to the effectiveness of Positive Education. Indeed, research suggests that the effectiveness of school-based wellbeing interventions decreases when staff training and support are minimal (Brunwasser et al., 2009; Weare and Nind, 2011). With this in mind, Geelong Grammar School has identified staff training in Positive Education as an ongoing priority, and is committed to ensuring that all staff (teaching and non-teaching) have a strong understanding of Positive Psychology and Positive Education.

As of 2014, over 450 Geelong Grammar School staff members have taken part in multi-day Positive Education training courses. Since 2012, attendance at these training courses has been a requirement for commencing employment at the School. The multi-day training courses comprise two primary learning formats. Plenary leaders present a summary of theory and research on topics covering the breadth of the model. At regular times, participants move into "break-out" groups of 12 to 16 people, in which they are led through deeper exploration and personal reflection by a group leader. These groups often bond closely as members share their stories, hopes, goals, and interests. Attendees who do not live close by stay at the Corio campus for the duration of the training course, and are offered opportunities to take part in health-supporting practices such as meditation, yoga, and Pilates classes.

The topics covered in the 3-day training course for new staff members, "Discovering Positive Psychology," in 2014 are listed in Box 3.1. In addition to the multi-day training courses, regular staff "refresher sessions" support the sustainable implementation of key ideas and behaviors, and enable staff to stay abreast of new developments in theory and research.

"Learn it" also emphasizes the importance of teaching parents and other family members the core theory, skills, and mindsets of Positive Psychology. There is no doubt that children derive the greatest benefits when there is consistency between the messages they are learning at home and those they receive at school. Since 2013,

---

BOX 3.1: "Discovering Positive Psychology" course outline

1. Introduction to positive psychology.
2. Positive accomplishments: mindsets.
3. Positive emotions: positivity.
4. Positive engagement: flow.
5. Positive relationships: active constructive responding.
6. Positive health: resilience.
7. Positive purpose: making a difference.
8. Character strengths.
9. From discovering to living.
10. Panning for gold.

Geelong Grammar School has provided residential courses for parents so that they can learn the skills and mindsets for wellbeing and keep abreast of what their children are learning in Positive Education. This commitment to Positive Education helps to create a shared language for wellbeing, resilience, and character strengths for students at home and at the School.

"Live it"

> When you are making such a commitment to Positive Education it needs to be authentic. It can't just be taught; it also has to be lived.
>
> Simon Haigh, Head of Barrabool House

Staff at Geelong Grammar School, who have been trained in Positive Education, are encouraged and supported to take regular action to nurture their own wellbeing. The aim is to help staff to live their lives with more positive emotion, engagement, accomplishment, and purpose. Adults who are committed to nurturing their own wellbeing become authentic role models for students—to best share Positive Education with others, a person should him- or herself meaningfully live by it. One teacher explained this by citing as an example the fact that conducting a classroom activity on kindness is a highly valuable activity—modeling kindness in their actions and interactions is arguably a much more powerful endeavor that helps to support a culture for respect and wellbeing across the School. These concepts are equally pertinent for parents and family members, and it is hoped that they too actively apply Positive Psychology concepts in their personal, professional, and family lives.

"Teach it": explicit learning

Explicit lessons refer to the teaching of wellbeing in classes specifically designated for Positive Education. The initial foundations of the explicit teaching curriculum were the *Penn Resiliency Program* (Gillham et al., 2008) and the *Strath Haven Positive Psychology Course* (Seligman et al., 2009) shared with the School by the team from the University of Pennsylvania. These explicit programs have been continually amended and expanded by Geelong Grammar School as the Positive Psychology research base has grown, and as staff have received helpful feedback from students and refined the content to suit the Australian context.

As of 2014, Positive Education is taught in dedicated classes in ELC through to Year 10 of the School. Students are allocated to weekly or fortnightly classes where they attend "Pos Ed"—as it is known by students—just as they attend classes in English, Geography, or Science. Over 30 staff members are actively involved in the teaching of Positive Education, including numerous staff in leadership positions (see Table 3.1 for a summary of how Positive Education is taught explicitly across year levels and campuses).

Table 3.1. Explicit teaching of Positive Education across year levels

Campus	Year level	Teaching staff	Time dedicated
Bostock House	ELC to 4	Classroom teachers, Head of Campus, Deputy Head of Campus	1 period* per fortnight
Toorak	ELC to 6	Classroom teachers, Head of Campus, Deputy Head of Campus	1 period per fortnight
Middle School, Corio	5 and 6	Classroom teachers	1 period per fortnight
Middle School, Corio	7 and 8	Head of Middle School, Deputy Head of Middle School, Heads of House	1 period per fortnight
Timbertop	9	Head of Campus, Deputy Head of Campus, Timbertop Positive Education Coordinator	1 period per fortnight
Senior School, Corio	10	Core team of 20 teachers, including Vice Principal, Director of Learning, Director of Student Welfare, Heads of House, Assistant Heads of House, Heads of Department, and Positive Education Institute staff	1 double period* per week

*A period is 45 minutes in duration; a double period is 90 minutes in duration.

In addition to this, Middle School and Senior School tutors are actively involved in delivering specific Positive Education topics as part of the House pastoral care system. An extract from a letter written by Justin Robinson to his Year 10 class, welcoming students to Positive Education and explaining some key ideas, is provided in Box 3.2. An explanation of "Pos Ed" written by a student

---

BOX 3.2: Welcome to Pos Ed

I just wanted to welcome you to our Pos Ed class. I hope we get to know each other well. I will also be on duty in Clyde House one night each week, and I look forward to supporting you with your academics as well as with your wellbeing. If you are wondering what "Pos Ed" is, in a nutshell, I say it is about learning, discussing, and exploring your wellbeing. I will be presenting to you a wide range of activities which are designed to nurture your wellbeing. I hope you will keep an open mind to each of the activities and I hope you will complete all assignments to the best of your ability. We will regularly share in small and large group discussions, and there will be time dedicated to allow you to reflect and jour-nal on the various topics. Throughout the year you will build up a comprehensive Pos Ed folio, which I hope you take great pride in and that you will keep well into the future. I will read and respond to various sections of your folio and look forward to supporting you on your individual wellbeing journey.

Justin Robinson, Director of the Institute of Positive Education

> **BOX 3.3: "Pos Ed"**
>
> Positive Education is very much a part of the Year 10 program, with two sessions a week embedded into our normal school schedule. We usually meet in our House groups, giving us a chance to get to know our fellow peers and how they think a little better. Occasionally, we get the privilege to hear from world-renowned specialists who have done extensive research on such topics as love, neuroscience, and flourishing. Recently we focused on the virtue of gratitude and how to make people know how much you appreciate them in a personal way. I found the activities associated with this topic very rewarding. This term we have also been focusing on the 24 character strengths that each of us has. To give us some insights into people who have strengths, we were introduced to a panel of strengths representatives from within the School community. This was a good chance to ask people how they use their strengths in daily life, which will hopefully in turn help us to use our strengths as much as possible in the future. We are all looking forward to seeing what impact Positive Education will have on our long-term wellbeing in the future.
>
> Rose, Year 10, Fraser House, Corio Campus

is shown in Box 3.3. Staff members who teach Positive Education classes have regular meetings at which they share their successes, discuss areas for improvement, and explore upcoming lessons and activities. This peer support is viewed as essential to the successful implementation of Positive Education, as giving teaching staff the time and space to talk about their lessons enhances the quality of their teaching.

The explicit Positive Education lessons are complemented by "Pos Ed focus days" that have a strong experiential focus and aim to deepen students' learning of core topics. A Positive Education focus day is held once a year for each year level from Years 7 to 12, and once a year for the Junior School campuses. Each focus day has a theme, such as teambuilding, community, and character strengths, and is devoted to immersing the students in a range of wellbeing-building activities. Where possible, a committee of student volunteers assists staff members in planning and facilitating the focus day, and on occasion senior students have helped to arrange focus days for younger age groups. Students do not attend normal classes on these days, but instead participate in activities that aim to enhance relationships and promote wellbeing, engagement, and health.

"Teach it": implicit learning

The implicit teaching of Positive Education involves the integration of the science of wellbeing into the wider curriculum. Across academic departments, teachers look for opportunities to create links between Positive Education concepts and core learning objectives. As all staff have been trained in the tenets of Positive Education, they share the responsibility for adapting the existing curriculum,

Figure 3.3 Junior School blessing journal. Expressing gratitude is an important element of the Model for Positive Education.

tailoring assignments, and weaving appropriate language and concepts into their academic classes to support and strengthen the message of wellbeing at the School. Examples include creating self-awareness through self-portraiture in Visual Arts, considering signature strengths in different characters in stories during English, and studying how different physical environments support or hinder wellbeing in Geography. Figure 3.3 shows an example of embedding gratitude into the teaching curriculum. Supporting the core messages of Positive Education on multiple levels adds depth to students' learning and facilitates consistency between the messages that students receive across classrooms. Case Study 3.1 provides an overview of a Year 2 Drama Production that helps students to develop many skills that complement Positive Education.

Positive Education influences pedagogy and the ways in which teachers approach teaching and learning. Common examples are starting a class with 5 minutes of mindfulness, providing feedback in ways that support growth mindsets, and increasing student engagement through a focus on character strengths. In a well-known example within the School, John Hendry, Director of Student Welfare, writes "Thank you" on every piece of work he assesses. John does this to commend the effort the student has put in, independent of their final grade, and believes that

CASE STUDY 3.1

Positive Education in action—*Wombat Divine*! Year 2 production

Rebecca Bettiol, Drama teacher, Toorak Campus

The idea for *Wombat Divine* emerged from the wonderful children's picture book by Mem Fox (Fox, 1996). This book not only examines the wonderful Australian out-back and animals, but also encapsulates a beautifully rich story. When we choose a stimulus for the children's writing, we need to select something that has a strong message which is easily transferable through dialogue and, of course, the stage!

We introduce the stimulus (in this case the storybook) to the entire lower primary school as one. No one knows prior to this gathering what the production will be about. As you can imagine, there is quite a buzz of excitement and trepidation among the children; it is a definite highlight of their year. The Drama and Music Specialists read the book to the children, with the aid of a projector, so that all of the children are able to understand the narrative. What follows is a brainstorming session, which is broken into class groups, led by the classroom teacher.

The discussions are steered towards understanding the story, looking more closely at the characters (in particular the protagonist) and the central message of the story. What we learn from this story, and how we can make connections with our own lives, is a major focus for the children. We also begin to discuss how the book can be adapted for the stage. What colors can we use? What props? What sets? The ideas that the children have are quite amazing. All of the responses are recorded and used for development of the script.

The story of *Wombat Divine* follows a Wombat's quest to be involved in the annual nativity play. However, due to his physical attributes, he cannot find the appropri-ate character. The children at our campus loved this story—they admired Wombat's resilience in finding a role, but also the absolute support and encouragement of Wombat by his friends (the other characters).

> *Possum:* There are heaps of different characters in the play. Surely there would be one just right for you, Wombat. Emu, have you cast the Three Kings yet? Maybe you could be one of the Three Kings. Wombat, do you feel like a King?

The Year 2 children were the script writers. As a class, we broke down each section of the narrative and brainstormed dialogue for the characters. This really utilized the chil-dren's imagination and creativity. It also ignited a sense of pride and joy as each drama lesson was devoted to writing "spoken words" for these unique characters. Through the children's imaginations the characters became three-dimensional, and what emerged was a script full of stage directions and quirky dialogue. In order for the script to include every child (as every child in Year 2 takes on the responsibility of playing a principal character), the Drama teacher shapes the final draft of the script, ensuring its flow and inclusivity. Through this process the children also acquire the skill of mindfulness in a dramatic context—sustaining a role for the duration of a performance.

The Year 2 children later told me that they really felt like a team, and that they felt safe on stage because they were with their friends. As the process had been so highly collaborative, the relationships between the students became more defined as they took risks and learned how to move in a confident and free manner with each other. There were no complaints about how many lines they had, as they were the script writers; they understood how valuable each character was to the overall story. The lower year levels, who took on the role of ensemble, also understood their contribution to the performance—how they moved the story forward through dance and song, and not only enhanced the quality of the play, but also further defined its message.

The set and lighting design were created through the children examining photos of outback Australia and choosing colors and iconic Australian images (e.g. windmill, gum trees) and interpreting these through the medium of art on A3 sheets of paper. Then, to ensure that the set design was a culmination of all the children's ideas, every image was taken to an artist who had the task of coming up with a stage and lighting design that reflected and embodied the children's pictures. This process allowed the children the opportunity to understand how stage lighting can be manipulated to reflect the mood of a scene, a fundamental component of stagecraft.

The costumes were designed by the children (see Figure 3.4), who were also responsible for their creation. As every child designed their own costume on A3 paper and then, with the aid of a parent, translated that design onto a T-shirt and leggings,

Figure 3.4 Year 2 Toorak students performing *Wombat Divine*.

this process was highly creative. We achieved this through the use of a glue gun and chosen fabric and craft pieces. This could range from sequins to felt or even just colored paper. The School was very clear that the costumes needed to be the children's designs. We were not interested in "perfect" costumes, but rather a reflection of the child's imagination. This resulted in individual costumes, each beautifully unique and quirky, and a magnificent stage full of continuous color.

The children designed the programs and tickets for the final performances. They also designed the posters that were displayed throughout the School leading up to the event. There is always so much pride and commitment among children when you allow them to be creative through a process such as this one. I cannot begin to articulate the tremendous benefit of drama and dance for children within education. The connections that children draw through drama and, in this case, the production are integral to the development of their confidence and sense of self. Through drama, they role play the principles of Positive Psychology and see how they are applied. The focus that children achieve and the resilient nature they adopt throughout the construction of the script, learning of the choreography, design of the stage, learning of the lyrics and dialogue, design and creation of the costumes, the rehearsal and, of course, the final performance is one that instills creativity and positivity in a most meaningful, empowering, and accessible way.

this step helps students to become open to constructive feedback and engage positively with ideas on how they can improve their work.

"Embed it"

Positive Education has pervaded how we deal with staff welfare and counseling processes. Ideally Positive Education will enhance resiliency and therefore reduce the need for support services by providing people with the knowledge and skills to reflect on and resolve issues independently. However, whenever staff members are having difficulties we try to incorporate the principles of Positive Psychology: the focus on strengths, the proactive problem solving, the way you provide feedback, the language around resilience. It is a brilliant and practical framework for staff welfare, communication, and teamwork.

Malcolm Leigh-Smith, Human Resources Manager

A common saying around the School is that "Positive Education is in the water here." This phrase recognizes that Positive Education comprises more than staff training and student lessons, and is a way of life within the School. At Timbertop, staff meetings commence with "what went well," with staff sharing stories of teaching successes, achievements they are proud of, and special moments with their families. Across all of the campuses, assemblies and Chapel services are often devoted to character strengths and other Positive Education concepts. Students and staff at Corio are regularly invited to come to the Hawker Library and watch and discuss TED talks on a wide range of concepts relevant to wellbeing. The weaving of positive practices into daily life at the School aims to create a culture of resilience and flourishing.

A substantial component of embedding Positive Education at Geelong Grammar School has been undertaken as part of the Positive Institution Project initiated and led by Paige Williams, Positive Psychology Project Manager (2009–2013). Launched in 2010, the Positive Institution Project aimed to create positive cultural and work environments for school staff. A range of projects were implemented that created pathways for positive cultural change. One health-focused initiative, launched in 2011, in which more than 80 staff across different campuses took part, was the Global Corporate Challenge. This is an evidence-based workplace health and wellbeing program in which staff compete in teams in a virtual walking journey around the world, with the goal of achieving at least 10,000 steps a day. All of the staff who were involved reported feeling health, motivation and relationship benefits, and for some it was the beginning of a personal transformation through the positive changes that they embedded in their lifestyle. Another integral aspect of the Positive Institution Project was the Positive Leadership Development Program, which initially involved the School's senior leadership team (the Principal's Advisory Committee), and was subsequently implemented at the School's Toorak campus (see Box 3.4 for further details).

"Embedding" Positive Education also involves the infiltration of the skills and mindsets for wellbeing into organizational practices, processes, and cultural norms. Malcolm Leigh-Smith, Human Relations Manager, explains that understanding concepts such as resilience and character strengths is valuable when staff members experience conflict with colleagues or difficulties in their roles. Similarly, the School's Behavioral Management Policy is built around the values of forgiveness and kindness, and supports growth and respect across the School community. A powerful testament to the pervasiveness of Positive Education is the integration of wellbeing and flourishing within the School's Purpose Document, the process of which is described in Case Study 3.2.

A framework for flourishing

Positive Education is, in my view, one of the most inspiring developments of recent years. I believe it has enormous potential to transform the lives of young people. It is an outstanding example of the way in which the School can use its exceptional resources to build on the established strengths and values of the School, benefit the School and the wider community, and drive evidence-based innovation in education.

Bill Ranken, Chairman of the Geelong Grammar Foundation

BOX 3.4: The Positive Leadership Development Program

I firmly believe that organizational leaders play an important role in guiding and shaping cultural norms and behaviors. Understanding ways in which Positive Psychology can inform our approach to leadership at the School and developing leadership capacities and skills that are grounded in Positive Psychology will have a meaningful and positive impact at both an individual and organizational level.

Stephen Meek, Principal, *Light Blue*, August 2011

The Positive Leadership Development Program (PLDP) was designed to develop understanding and application of Positive Psychology principles to leadership knowledge and skills throughout Geelong Grammar School. The PLDP provided an opportunity for participants to explore and develop their understanding of Positive Psychology specifically in relation to their role as a leader and to leadership in general. The Program included research-led teaching through its evidence-based approach, collaborative learning through peer coaching, and reflective learning through participants using their own experience to build knowledge.

Over the course of three full-day workshops approximately 6 weeks apart, participants were introduced to the key ideas and science of Positive Organizational Scholarship, Positive Organizational Behavior, and Positive Organizational Psychology. From that basis they explored the role of leadership in creating a virtuous school environment, they engaged with the concepts and practice of authentic leadership (Walumbwa et al., 2008) as operationalized through self-awareness, balanced processing, relational transparency, and internal moral perspective, and they explored techniques that they could use to promote the wellbeing, strengths, learning, and resilience of themselves, their colleagues and team members, and their students.

The material for the original program was developed by Professor Lea Waters (PhD), from the University of Melbourne, in collaboration with Paige Williams. The redevelopment of the program for implementation with staff at the Toorak campus also included contributions from Dr Peter Kaldor, co-creator of the *Lead with Your Strengths* framework. The School is grateful for the contribution of both Lea and Peter to the School's learning journey.

The PLDP had a meaningful impact for both groups of participants, as is evident from the following feedback from a staff member who took part at the Toorak campus:

This week I have been thinking about how to do things differently. I have observed my colleagues and noticed the many clever ways they achieve during the day. I have been asking questions about the methods and applications they use when performing tasks very efficiently. Because of my questioning, heightened awareness, and interest in their successful methods I have learnt a lot this week. I have become more aware of the unique styles of leadership my colleagues use and the benefits they have on their work and those around them. My appreciation for their great attributes has made me more motivated to improve my own.

Paige Williams, Positive Psychology Project Manager

CASE STUDY 3.2

School Purpose Document

**Tony Bretherton, Director of Community Relations,
Geelong Grammar School**

Key issues for any educational institution are clarity of strategy and the coherence of strategy and brand. Geelong Grammar School proclaims "Exceptional Education", but what do these words stand for? It is important to unpack the philosophy that is embodied by these words. To help the School to clarify its own understanding and the assumptions behind these two key words, Professor Mike Pratt was invited to come and undertake a 2-day "purposing" exercise. Professor Pratt and colleagues from the Waikato University (New Zealand) Management School had developed a process of management strategic planning, based on the success of key international sports teams. The process resulted in the clarification of the School's Spirit, Character, Focus, Purpose, and Greatest Imaginable Challenge, all of which were to fit on one A4 page. This has become the philosophical foundation for an Exceptional Education (see Figure 3.5).

So with their Purpose theory already used by major corporations such as Saatchi & Saatchi, Proctor & Gamble, and Toyota, as well as select universities and schools, Professor Pratt prepared for the Geelong Grammar School adventure. Gathered together were members of the School Council, Foundation, leadership team, academic staff, general staff, alumni, and students. People listened, debated, broke into small groups and worked with words as they sought to express their deep understanding of the essence of their School and community.

The result after 2 days was a group of words that made sense to the participants—but how well had our representatives captured the essence of Geelong Grammar School? The test was to share the work done with the full School staff community and to see how well the work resonated with them. A committee that included the Director of Community Relations, the Vice Principal, and the Head of Positive Education reviewed the responses, and the first draft became a second draft. This was shared again, and additional changes were made to create the final draft, which was then signed off by the Principal and School Council. Interestingly, when it has been shared more widely, for more than 2 years now, people say "Yes, that's us." It reflects well who we are and where we are going. It has given us a common set of words to describe what we mean by "Exceptional Education."

The **philosophy** that underpins the School's understanding of Exceptional Education is manifest in our purpose, spirit, focus, character and beliefs

OUR CHALLENGE

is to demonstrate that Positive Education enhances student wellbeing and to lead in establishing wellbeing as an essential component of a thriving educational system

WE BELIEVE

- our rigorous academic programmes create wonder, curiosity and a desire to learn
- boarding and co-education provide valuable life skills
- Positive Education enhances wellbeing and enables individuals to flourish
- our exceptional staff bring character and richness to the life of the School
- partnerships between our parents, staff and students provide the best learning outcomes
- in nurturing strong relationships
- in fostering spirituality and celebrating our Anglican tradition
- in serving others and building social responsibility
- in growing our heritage through innovation

OUR PURPOSE

is to inspire our students and community to flourish and make a positive difference through our unique and transformational education adventures

OUR CHARACTER

is to be authentic, courageous, dedicated, forgiving, inquiring, loving, optimistic, passionate, resilient and trusting

OUR FOCUS

is learning to flourish

OUR SPIRIT

is making a positive difference

Figure 3.5 Geelong Grammar School's Purpose Document.

The Model for Positive Education facilitates the planning, implementation, and evaluation of Positive Psychology within school settings. The six domains are viewed as pillars of flourishing, and character strengths provide an underpinning base through which development in each domain can be enhanced. The model serves as an overarching framework that encapsulates the breadth of research in the field while providing practical pathways to support wellbeing across the school community. It is hoped that this model supports other schools in their own journeys with Positive Education and serves as a useful road map to integrating science-informed wellbeing strategies across a range of settings and organizations.

The Model for Positive Education helps students to reflect on what it means to live a flourishing life. There is sometimes a temptation for young people to think about a "good life" in quite a narrow way—for example, as a life filled with material possessions, physical beauty, and external success. Through exploring the breadth of the domains of the Model, students can see that a flourishing life is much deeper than solely external successes or material possessions. A life well lived includes a range of factors that support wellbeing. Furthermore, many of these factors are as focused on others as they are on the self—for example, nurturing strong relationships and making a difference to the community.

To emphasize the versatility of the model, students are often encouraged to consider the six domains as they approach an upcoming holiday or plan for a possible "gap year." Many people plan for holidays and adventures with "positive emotions" in mind. Students are prompted to broaden this understanding consciously by considering how their adventures can support and benefit others through the domains of positive purpose and positive relationships. They also reflect on their strengths and their passions as they consider how their adventure can build positive engagement and positive accomplishment. Underpinning all of this is consideration of how different activities and endeavors can nurture resilience and support positive health. Using this method, many students create plans for holidays and adventures that are creative, deeply enriching, and meaningful.

In many ways the model is a very functional framework. It serves as a crucial tool in the planning, implementation, and evaluation of Positive Education across the School community and throughout the curriculum. The Positive Education team can often be seen using the model to plan a training course or map out a sequence of curriculum. As it is such a useful tool, it is often easy to forget that it is so much more than a document for planning, implementing, and evaluating Positive Education. In its essence, the model can be thought of as a good road map or summary of what people want for themselves, their students, and their children, namely good health, frequent positive emotions, rewarding and supportive relationships, a sense of purpose and meaning, the accomplishment of worthwhile goals, and moments of complete immersion and absorption—a life where a person uses their character strengths in ways that support the self and others and which has flourishing at the heart.

RECOMMENDED RESOURCES

Achor S (2011). *The Happy Secret to Better Work. TEDx Talk.* <www.ted.com/talks/shawn_achor_the_happy_secret_to_better_work>

Bonniwell I and Ryan L (2010). *Personal Well-Being Lessons for Secondary Schools: positive psychology in action for 11 to 14 year olds.* Maidenhead: Open University Press.

Bott D, McCormick A, and Shaw J (2011). *Teach Positive: applying the science of positive psychology to the classroom.* London: Contemporary Brilliance Publications.

Collaborative Association for Social and Emotional Learning. <www.casel.org>

Collins M and Tamarkin C (1990). *Marva Collins' Way: returning to excellence in education.* New York: Jeremy P. Tarcher/Putnam.

Gilman R, Huebner E S, and Furlong M J (eds) (2009). *Handbook of Positive Psychology in Schools.* New York: Routledge.

Hattie J (2008). *Visible Learning: a synthesis of over 800 meta-analyses relating to achievement.* New York: Taylor & Francis.

Johnstone M and Kerr J (2009). *The Alphabet of the Human Heart: the A to Zen of life.* Sydney, Australia: Pan Macmillan.

MacConville R and Rae T (2012). *Building Happiness, Resilience and Motivation in Adolescents: a positive psychology curriculum for well-being.* London: Jessica Kingsley Publishers.

Morris I (2009). *Teaching Happiness and Wellbeing in Schools: learning to ride elephants.* London: Network Continuum.

Noddings N (2003). *Happiness and Education.* Cambridge: Cambridge University Press.

O'Grady P (2013). *Positive Psychology in the Elementary School Classroom.* New York: W. W. Norton & Company.

Pierson R (2013). *Every Child Needs a Champion. TED Talks Education.* <www.ted.com/talks/rita_pierson_every_kid_needs_a_champion>

Positive Education Schools Association (PESA) (Australia). <www.pesa.edu.au>

The Positive Times. <http://positivetimes.com.au>

REFERENCES

Brunwasser S M, Gillham J E, and Kim E S (2009). A meta-analytic review of the Penn Resiliency Program's effects on depressive symptoms. *Journal of Counsulting and Clinical Psychology, 77,* 1042–54.

Burgoon J K, Berger C R, and Waldron V R (2000). Mindfulness and interpersonal communication. *Journal of Social Issues, 56*, 105–27.

Burke C A (2010). Mindfulness-based approaches with children and adolescents: a preliminary review of current research in an emergent field. *Journal of Child and Family Studies, 19*, 133–44.

Csikszentmihalyi M (1990). *Flow: the psychology of optimal experience.* New York: Harper & Row.

Fox M (1996). *Wombat Divine.* San Diego, CA: Harcourt, Brace & Co.

Fredrickson B L (2001). The role of positive emotions in positive psychology: the broaden-and-build theory of positive emotions. *American Psychologist, 56*, 218–26.

Gable S L, Gonzaga G C, and Strachman A (2006). Will you be there for me when things go right? Supportive responses to positive event disclosures. *Journal of Personality and Social Psychology, 91*, 904–17.

Gillham J E, Reivich K J, and Jaycox L H (2008). *The Penn Resiliency Program (also known as the Penn Depression Prevention Program and the Penn Optimism Program): leader's manual.* Philadelphia, PA: University of Pennsylvania.

Grossman P, Niemann L, Schmidt S, and Walach H (2004). Mindfulness-based stress reduction and health benefits: a meta-analysis. *Journal of Psychosomatic Research, 57*, 35–43.

Norrish J M, Williams P, O'Connor M, and Robinson J (2013). An applied framework for Positive Education. *International Journal of Wellbeing, 3*, 147–62.

Park N and Peterson C (2009). Character strengths: research and practice. *Journal of College and Character, 10*, 4–13.

Peterson C and Seligman M E P (2004). *Character Strengths and Virtues: a handbook and classification.* Oxford: Oxford University Press; Washington, DC: American Psychological Association.

Seligman M E P (2011). *Flourish.* London: Nicholas Brealey Publishing.

Seligman M E P et al. (2009). Positive education: positive psychology and classroom interventions. *Oxford Review of Education, 35*, 293–311.

Walumbwa F O et al. (2008). Authentic leadership: development and validation of a theory-based measure. *Journal of Management, 34*, 89–126.

Weare K and Nind M (2011). Mental health promotion and problem prevention in schools: what does the evidence say? *Health Promotion International, 26*, 29–69.

FLOURISHING AND
POSITIVE EDUCATION

Introduction by
Professor Felicia Huppert

If you ask a parent what they want for their child, a common response is "I just want my child to be happy." But what do they mean by that? Presumably they don't want their child to be unhappy, but what if the child is happy yet unengaged, doing poorly at school, self-absorbed, or socially isolated? I think it is safe to conclude that parents want more for their child than just positive emotions. They want their child to thrive or flourish.

So what does it mean to flourish? Flourishing is a combination of feeling good and functioning well. Functioning well begins with attention—bringing an attitude of interest and curiosity to the world around us, which in turn leads to engagement, embracing opportunities, and developing our full potential. Functioning well also includes self-regulation—the ability to manage our thoughts, feelings, and behaviors, and to reflect on our experiences. This allows us to make better choices and to be resilient in the face of difficulties or challenges. Finally, functioning well extends beyond the self, by contributing to the wellbeing of others. Reviews of the state of knowledge about the science of wellbeing, and the causes and benefits of flourishing, can be found in Huppert (2009, 2014).

Although flourishing incorporates positive emotions, we would not be flourishing if we felt good all the time. There are periods in our life when it is appropriate to experience negative or painful emotions, such as sadness about the suffering of others, disappointment if a longed-for goal is not attained, or grief at the loss of a loved one. Flourishing is about managing such emotions effectively, not denying or burying them.

Flourishing in the context of school

For far too long there has been a disconnect between what parents want for their child and what schools have offered. Schools have traditionally focused on academic success, and preparing children for the world of work, rather than developing the whole child. They have tended to emphasize the acquisition of knowledge rather than cultivating the love of learning and the skills of mind that foster learning, accomplishment, and positive social interactions. Schools have too often failed to recognize that psychological wellbeing underpins successful learning, accomplishment, and relationships, and needs to be at the core of the educational curriculum. This view has been beautifully expressed by Siegel (2007, p. 260):

> So much of school experience focuses on acquisition of important skills and knowledge regarding the outer world. We learn to read, to write, to calculate numbers. Perhaps this approach stems from our educational system's emphasis on a curriculum of content rather than one that focuses on the process of cultivating the mind itself. Wouldn't it make sense to teach children about the mind itself and make reflection become a fundamental part of basic education? If teachers became aware that attuning to the self, being mindful, can alter the brain's ability to create flexibility and self-observation, empathy and morality, wouldn't it be worth the time to teach such reflective skills, first to teachers and then in age-appropriate ways to the students themselves?

The need to optimize psychological wellbeing and cultivate the mind itself has been increasingly recognized in recent years, and scores of programs have been developed to teach social and emotional skills, awareness, and self-regulation in the school context. Although the quality of these programs has varied widely, there is no doubt that they have overall benefits in terms of a variety of outcome measures, including cognitive skills, social relationships, academic performance, reduced symptoms of psychological distress, and increased wellbeing. Major reviews of this area include those by Durlak et al. (2011), Jennings and Greenberg (2009), Meiklejohn et al. (2012), and Weare and Nind (2011, 2014).

Defining and measuring flourishing

As in any area of science, our understanding of the determinants and consequences of flourishing requires that the concept be clearly defined and accurately measured. Definitions and appropriate measurements are usually obtained through a lengthy process of reaching a consensus by international experts. This applies whether one is looking at physical measures such as the amount of carbon dioxide in the atmosphere, economic measures such as the gross domestic product, or psychological measures such as depression or wellbeing. However, as wellbeing science is a relatively new discipline, there is not yet a consensus among experts on the definition of the terms "wellbeing" and "flourishing," or how to measure them.

That having been said, there are many convergent ideas that have been developed by scholars in the field. For example, Ryan and Deci (2001) propose that a person's level of wellbeing is determined by the extent to which their "basic psychological needs" for autonomy, competence, and relatedness are satisfied. For Ryff and Keyes (1995), psychological wellbeing comprises six dimensions, namely autonomy, environmental mastery, personal growth, positive relationships, purpose in life, and self-acceptance. In the recent book by Seligman (2011) on flourishing, he identifies five components or pillars of flourishing, which form the acronym PERMA—positive emotions, engagement, relationships, meaning, and accomplishment. It is clear from these few examples that although there is considerable overlap in the conceptual definition of wellbeing or flourishing, there is not yet a consensus.

Decades ago, the field of mental health was at a similar developmental stage in relation to defining mental disorders. Over time, an international consensus was reached, resulting in the *Diagnostic and Statistical Manual of Mental Disorders* (American Psychiatric Association, 2013) and the *International Classification of Diseases* (World Health Organization, 1993). Both are updated from time to time as our understanding of causal mechanisms and their underlying pathology develops.

One way to make progress in defining psychological wellbeing is to build on the extensive work undertaken in the field of mental health. We can conceptualize wellbeing not as the absence of mental disorder or ill-being, but as its *opposite*. Such a view has been explicitly proposed by Huppert and So (2013), although it is implicit in most models of psychological wellbeing. Huppert and So use the model of a mental health spectrum or bell curve, with the common mental disorders at one end of the spectrum, and flourishing at the other end. It is important to note that this conceptualization only applies to the common mental disorders, namely anxiety and depression, which anyone can experience. During the time when a person has a clinically significant anxiety or depressive disorder, they cannot be said to be flourishing. On the other hand, in the case of certain less common chronic disorders, such as schizophrenia or personality disorder, there may be periods when a person can flourish despite their chronic condition.

If flourishing is the opposite of the common mental disorders, then it can be defined in terms of the opposite of the internationally agreed symptoms of anxiety and depression. Taking this approach, Huppert and So (2013) identified 10 features of flourishing, namely positive emotions, engagement, relationships, meaning, accomplishment/competence, resilience, emotional stability, vitality, optimism, and self-esteem. It can be seen that the first five features correspond perfectly to Seligman's notion of PERMA—the five key components of flourishing (Seligman, 2011). The remaining five can be regarded as the characteristics displayed by flourishing people.

Once wellbeing and/or flourishing have been defined, measurement can follow. It is clear that we need to measure the elements of PERMA, and at this early stage in the science of wellbeing it would be wise to measure related constructs, such as the five characteristics of flourishing people identified above, and perhaps other characteristics such as autonomy and grit. Following an extensive search of existing measures of subjective and psychological wellbeing, Butler and Kern (2014) have administered a long list of survey questions to thousands of participants and, using psychometric analysis, have created a measure called the PERMA Profiler. This measure comprises the best three items for each PERMA construct, so there are 15 items in total. Further work is under way to establish the best items for capturing additional constructs, including the five characteristics of flourishing people (resilience, emotional stability, vitality, optimism, and self-esteem).

Until such time as these new instruments become available, ongoing studies are using a variety of measures of wellbeing or flourishing. The best validated of these, which has been used widely on representative population samples, including samples of adolescents, is the Warwick-Edinburgh Mental Well-being Scale (WEMWBS) (Stewart-Brown et al., 2009; Tennant et al., 2007), which exists in both a 14-item and a 7-item version. Other scales that are fairly widely used include Ryff's Psychological Well-being Scale (Ryff and Keyes, 1995), Keyes' Psychological and Social Well-being Scales (Keyes, 2003), and the Flourishing Scale of Diener et al. (2010). Selected questions from the European Social Survey, which cover the 10 features of flourishing, have been administered to 43,000 people (Huppert et al., 2009; Huppert and So, 2013). They have also been used as indicators of flourishing in a recent study of adolescents (Kuyken et al., 2013), and in a number of ongoing studies of the benefits of positive psychology or mindfulness training in students, including the Positive Education program at Geelong Grammar School.

Measuring what matters is really crucial. Many studies that purport to be about improving wellbeing have only used negative outcome measures such as symptom reduction. In the light of our imperfect understanding of what constitutes wellbeing, it is advisable to cast the net wide when we try to measure it, lest we omit a feature or characteristic that turns out to be very important.

Promoting flourishing in schools

In many schools, teachers are so preoccupied with preparing and teaching the formal curriculum that it feels as if there is no space in the timetable in which to teach the skills that children need to optimize their wellbeing. Yet the experience of schools which do combine the two approaches is that this creates a win–win situation. Students and teachers benefit from a more positive and less stressful school environment, and academic attainment does not suffer—indeed there is evidence that higher levels of wellbeing are associated with higher academic performance.

So how should a school decide which program to choose? Many programs have been developed that aim to improve wellbeing or increase social and emotional skills. Schools, like other organizations, may adopt such programs on the basis of their face validity, especially if the materials offered are engaging and attractive, and teachers are offered short and affordable training in how to deliver the program. However, no matter how good a program appears to be, it is essential that its benefits are properly evaluated. Unless wellbeing is measured before the program is initiated, following its delivery, and at some time afterwards, there is no way of knowing how effective the program really is. For example, does it work well for some groups of students or staff and not others? Does it work well for some outcomes but not others? Are there some elements of the program that work better than others? Are the benefits short-lived or long-lasting? Unless programs are properly evaluated, we shall never know if improvements are needed, and how to streamline them so that they are as effective as possible within resource limitations (see Chapter 13 for information on how Positive Education at Geelong Grammar School is currently being evaluated).

Furthermore, we need to think not only about what constitutes a good program in its own right, but also about how the program is delivered in the broader context of a school. A program might be extremely well conceived and well designed, but may fail to achieve its goals if it is poorly implemented (Durlak and DuPre, 2008). Research has identified the features that characterize the most successful programs, although none of the published studies to date have implemented all of these features. As summarized by Weare and Nind (2011), these features are as follows:

- a whole-school approach
- a focus on the whole child
- a focus on positives, not just problems
- high-quality implementation
- a universal approach, not just targeting those with the greatest need
- interactive learning
- involvement of parents and communities
- starting early and carrying on.

All of these elements form part of the Positive Education program which has been developed and refined by Geelong Grammar School. This School has led the world both as an early adopter of the principles of Positive Education and in the comprehensiveness of its approach. It is also committed to creating an evidence base, ensuring that this major investment in people really works in helping them to lead engaged, fulfilled, and socially beneficial lives.

Flourishing at Geelong Grammar School

As educators, we cannot go past the questions that lead to real lifelong learning. What are we doing to unlock a positive mindset in our students? How are we helping them to uncover their strengths and feel the power of positive emotions? What role are we playing in children's abilities to access a place within their world and their minds where they can flourish?

Janis Coffey, Associate Director of the Institute of Positive Education

Sometimes simple stories have a profound impact on a school community. One of these stories at Geelong Grammar School is a children's book called *The Golden Rule*, written by Irene Cooper and illustrated by Gabi Swiatkowska (Cooper, 2007). The book tells the story of a boy and his grandfather who contemplate the words "Do unto others as you would have them do unto you." The story describes the ways in which this profoundly simple but timeless phrase is represented in various religious faiths, and explores the Golden Rule as a powerful reminder of the importance of treating all people and beings with respect. This book is used frequently throughout the School community, and is read to young students, integrated into Chapel services, and explored within Positive Education staff professional development sessions.

The Golden Rule has an important message about treating other people with respect, kindness, and forgiveness. It also has a deeper message, which can be considered just as perennial. Through their conversations, the boy and his grandfather ponder what it means to live a good life—what it means to live life well. This enduring question is relevant to all children as they grow to make sense of the world, and to all adults as they make choices about their life and decide on the values they would like to instill in their family. The question about what it means to live well was certainly relevant to staff at Geelong Grammar School when they made the decision to embark on their journey with Positive Education.

In committing to Positive Education, Geelong Grammar School has helped to shift the discourse on what is important in education, and has adopted a strong stance that schools have a larger role to play in helping students, staff, and their families to live well. Over numerous decades the academic model of education—in which success is measured by academic indicators—has become so deeply ingrained in educational systems that it can be largely unquestioned. Through Positive Education, Geelong Grammar School has adopted a firm position that a high level of academic performance is only one aspect of education and, in doing so, has helped to shape the conversation about the true role that schools play in thriving societies.

Redefining the goals of education

Central to the successful implementation of Positive Education is a strong understanding of desired outcomes. Clearly articulating the goals of Positive Education supports the sustainability of the approach and allows for aims and objectives to be communicated across campuses and throughout the wider community. One of the first goals of the Positive Education team was to establish a strong definition of optimal wellbeing so that goals could be set, outcomes measured, and progress evaluated.

However, determining what it meant to have high or optimal wellbeing proved to be a challenging task. Although the scientific community had well-defined methods of measuring mental ill health, there was little consensus about how to measure positive human functioning. Mental health disorders such as depression, anxiety, and bipolar disorder are recognized by very specific sets of criteria and the presence of clearly articulated symptoms and characteristics (American Psychiatric Association, 2013). However, beyond the presence or absence of a disorder there was not a consensual definition of what it means to be mentally healthy. With the support of experts in the field, such as Professor Martin Seligman and Professor Felicia Huppert, the School explored different definitions of optimal wellbeing, and ultimately selected flourishing as the overall goal of Positive Education within the School community.

Hedonic and eudaimonic wellbeing

Scientific inquiry into wellbeing is often described as being aligned with one of two philosophical traditions—the hedonic approach and the eudaimonic approach (Deci and Ryan, 2008; Keyes and Annas, 2009). Hedonic wellbeing focuses on feelings and evaluations of quality of life (Keyes and Annas, 2009). The most established concept in this area is subjective wellbeing, which is defined as satisfaction with life and the relative predominance of positive compared with negative emotions (Diener, 2000). According to this approach, a student or staff member who experiences more frequent positive emotions than negative ones, and who rates their overall life as quite satisfying, could be considered to have high hedonic/subjective wellbeing.

In contrast, eudaimonic definitions of wellbeing propose that wellbeing is achieved by contributing to others and by fulfilling one's *daimon* or true nature (Deci and Ryan, 2008). From a eudaimonic perspective, being psychologically well involves more than feeling positive emotions; it entails personal growth, service to others, and living in accordance with values (Ryff and Singer, 2008). Whereas hedonic approaches focus on how people feel, eudaimonic approaches focus on what people do and the choices that they make (Keyes and Annas, 2009). While not denying the importance of good feelings, eudaimonic wellbeing recognizes that the ways in which people interact with others and their environments are integral components of optimal wellbeing. One way in which this difference is explained to students is that hedonic wellbeing focuses on the "I" world (individual wellbeing) whereas eudaimonic wellbeing focuses on the "we" world (wellbeing of the self and others).

Despite constructive debate within the scientific community about the advantages and disadvantages of the two approaches (Kashdan et al., 2008; Waterman, 2008), experts have increasingly proposed that hedonic and eudaimonic wellbeing are both central to optimal wellbeing (Henderson and Knight, 2012; Keyes et al., 2002; Seligman, 2002, 2011). This has led to an increased focus on both "feeling good" (hedonic) and "functioning well" (eudaimonic) as interconnected and dynamic aspects of optimal functioning (Keyes and Annas, 2009). The importance of feeling good and functioning well certainly resonated with School staff, who desired a definition of wellbeing that aligned with the School's long history of nurturing the whole child.

Happiness?

Positive Education is not a happiology—that is a poor description; it doesn't mean anything. Positive Education is about establishing a strong foundation for life for both students and adults. They will face challenges in life and they will experience ups and downs in their personal and professional lives. Positive Education is about being able to deal with what comes, both good and bad.

Andrew Moore, Commercial Director

At times it has been suggested that "happiness" should be the primary aim of Positive Education. Happiness as an outcome clearly emphasizes the presence of wellbeing as opposed to only the presence or absence of disorder. However, like many members of the scientific community, staff at Geelong Grammar School did not think the term "happiness" truly conveyed the depth of their vision for Positive Education. The term "happiness" often brings to mind people who are cheerful and buoyant, whereas the focus of Positive Education is much richer than the quest for constant positive mood states. Happiness as an outcome was considered to be too vague, too misunderstood, and subject to many misconceptions by the wider community.

Staff recognized that the term "happiness" did not truly reflect the sort of research that was being conducted under the banner of Positive Psychology, such as how people could grow from traumatic experiences (Peterson et al., 2008) or persist in moving towards their goals despite difficulties and setbacks (Duckworth et al., 2007). A conversation about Positive Education in Garnett House exemplified these issues. When asked what they thought Pos Ed was about, students volunteered the following responses: "Pos Ed teaches us how to deal with adversity," "It promotes a sense of self-worth," "It encourages realistic goal setting," "It focuses on the importance of helping others," "It emphasizes the need to slow down and reflect on life," "It helps us to understand how the mind works," and "It is not about being happy all the time." The consensus within the School and the wider community was that Positive Psychology was about much more than happiness, so the

School continued its search for a term that truly conveyed the depth and rigor of the Positive Education approach.

Flourishing

> One of the core aims of Positive Education is that individuals flourish—that they have greater wellbeing, a greater sense of purpose, and more life satisfaction. We want people to live the life that they have been given for the short portion of time they have been given it—and to enjoy it more.
>
> Stephen Meek, Principal

Professor Felicia Huppert visited Geelong Grammar School in 2010 and again in 2014, and during both visits shared generously with staff and students her extensive knowledge of the science of flourishing (see Figure 4.1). During her time at the School, Professor Huppert explained that as the field of Positive Psychology evolved, several leading experts were moving towards the term "flourishing" to describe optimal wellbeing (Diener et al., 2010; Huppert and So, 2013; Seligman, 2011). This term seemed to be an excellent fit with the vision for Positive Education at Geelong Grammar School.

The *Oxford Dictionary of English* defines flourishing as "to grow vigorously; to thrive, to prosper; to be in one's prime; to be in good health" (Oxford University Press, 2010). Professor Maureen Gaffney provides the example of a small flowering

Figure 4.1 Professor Felicia Huppert visiting the school in 2010.

plant that is vibrant with color, bursting with life, and straining towards the light (Gaffney, 2011). Professor Gaffney makes the link between this powerful symbol and a flourishing person who embraces life, connects deeply with others, grows from difficulties, and contributes meaningfully to society. These definitions emphasize that flourishing is more than the absence of disorder, and is a multi-dimensional and holistic concept that integrates a range of valued outcomes.

Professor Huppert and her colleagues have contributed extensively to the scientific understanding of flourishing, as she describes in her introduction to this chapter (see also Huppert, 2014; Huppert and So, 2013). Her work on conceptualizing flourishing—including the ten features of vitality, self-esteem, resilience, positive relationships, positive emotions, optimism, meaning, engagement, emotional stability, and competence—has informed the Positive Education evaluation strategy at the School (see Chapter 13 for a comprehensive discussion of the measurement of flourishing in both students and staff members).

Professor Corey Keyes' substantial contributions to the literature (Keyes, 2002, 2006) are also relevant to the conceptualization of flourishing. Keyes defines flourishing as comprising three components: first, emotional (hedonic) wellbeing or the presence of positive feelings about oneself and life; secondly, social wellbeing, which includes feeling valued by others and connected to the community; and thirdly, psychological wellbeing, which focuses on functioning well (Keyes, 2007). Keyes proposes that mental health exists on a continuum, from languishing, to moderately mentally healthy, to flourishing. People who are languishing have low subjective wellbeing, challenged relationships, and poor functioning, whereas those who are flourishing feel good, have thriving relationships, and function well.

Feeling good and doing good

It is my hope that if you ask a primary school student what Positive Education is all about, they would say it is about "feeling good and doing good." We want students to learn things that help them to experience more joy, hope, gratitude, and resilience, but just as importantly to think beyond themselves to the wellbeing of others.

Justin Robinson, Director of the Institute of Positive Education

The move within the scientific community towards the term "flourishing" seemed to be an excellent fit with how the community at Geelong Grammar School had come to understand the aims of Positive Education. While academic definitions of flourishing provided the approach with increased rigor, the School needed a simpler definition. The need was for a phrase that could be understood and embraced by everyone—from students in the Early Learning Centre to members of staff. With this aim in mind, the School arrived at the definition of flourishing as *feeling good* and *doing good*. It is also important that this understanding is supported by real-life experiences for staff and students. Case Study 4.1, written by Justine Siedle, an Art teacher at the Toorak campus, describes how Year 1 students explore wellbeing and flourishing through the process of creating mandalas.

Feeling good includes a wide range of emotions and experiences, such as feeling content about the past, happy in the present, and hopeful about the future. Feeling good also represents healthy acceptance of the range of human emotions and experiences,

CASE STUDY 4.1

Year 1 Art

Justine Siedle, Art teacher, Toorak Campus

A unit of inquiry titled *Peace Begins With Me*, completed during Art classes at the Toorak campus, gave Year 1 students an opportunity to demonstrate some of the key elements of wellbeing. The unique aspect of Art is that it enables children to explore the visual world and to work with a variety of media—crayons, watercolors, clay, and collages—to express their insights and emotions (Figure 4.2 shows Year 1 students engaged in creating their artworks). Art is a natural way of expressing the spirit of Positive Education.

As part of this inquiry, students analysed a number of Buddhist mandalas and collaborated to create their own artworks using mixed media. To capture the spirituality of Buddhism, students explored the symbols used to express the characteristics of fire, earth, water, and air, drawing shapes such as a circle for the sun in the fire element, and clouds in the air element. The students had two lessons in which to play with wooden blocks, rocks, shells, and pieces of fabric to further their imagination.

Figure 4.2 Year 1 students working on their mandalas.

They invented ideas for making waterfalls and raindrops, and discussed in teams how the elements could be combined, such as plants on top of the water or steam coming out of a volcano. The character strengths that the children developed during the two lessons were curiosity, teamwork, and a love of learning.

To illustrate the practice of Buddhism, students watched a video of Buddhist monks using sand to create a mandala. Learning about the ritualistic aspect of the Buddhist practice, and reflecting on the fact that, in order to create such intricate patterns in a mandala, the monks had to work together as a team, the students found meaning in creating symbols and learning about the mandalas. Positive emotion became a key part of their experience as they explored ideas through shared conversations and drawing patterns.

Working collaboratively to create symbols and patterns for the mandala enhanced in the children the character strength of perspective. They needed to listen to one another's ideas and consider each other's viewpoints. The teamwork aspect of the project also encouraged resilience, as they required problem-solving skills to incorporate everyone's ideas into one design.

As the children's work evolved, they began to savor the pleasure of creating. As this was the first unit of inquiry of the school year, many children had fresh memories of the waves on the beach, or memories from nature still resonating from their Christmas holidays. Drawing from these experiences and recognizing them as pleasures created pathways to happiness for these children.

As the students completed their painted construction of a mandala, they felt the joy of accomplishment. Creating a unique work of art, they had collaborated as a team. They felt proud of their achievements. Their Art project had enabled them to flourish.

with a focus on responding to negative or unpleasant emotions with acceptance and a willingness to grow and learn. Feeling good also embodies the power of flow and engagement, and the feelings that result from being absorbed in authentically meaningful challenges. It encompasses the importance of helping members of the School community to develop resilience, and the mindsets and behaviors that support them to embrace challenging goals and to grow from difficult experiences.

Feeling good focuses on an individual's wellbeing and functioning. However, it is hoped at the School that students and staff will think beyond themselves and consider how their actions influence others. According to Professor Nansook Park and Professor Chris Peterson a traditional priority for schools is to equip students with the skills and abilities to do well—a similar priority should be given to helping students to develop the will and passion to do good (Park and Peterson, 2008). Doing good embodies a desire and motivation to do the right thing, to cultivate kindness, compassion, and forgiveness in relationships, and to contribute meaningfully to society. Identifying doing good as a central component of flourishing is aligned with the School's strong history of service and the deeply embedded principle of helping students to become respectful of others, passionate about civic responsibility, and active contributors to the community (see Figures 4.3 and 4.4).

Figure 4.3 Individual and community wellbeing will be vitally important to this ELC student and all future ELC students.

Figure 4.4 A Bostock student warmly welcoming people to the campus.

Support and mental health

My favorite moment in Pos Ed was when someone came to talk about his bat-
tle with depression. This was an eye-opener because many of us didn't realize
the severity of the issue. Within Year 10 there is now far more awareness of the
importance of mental health.

Charlotte, Year 10, Senior School, Corio Campus

At a Positive Education information day, a member of the audience asked
whether visits to the school counselors had decreased since the implementation
of Positive Education, as surely this would be a clear indication that a higher percentage of students were flourishing. Justin Robinson, Director of the Institute
of Positive Education, responded that his understanding—and his hope—was
that trips to the school counselors had actually increased over recent years.
Research has shown that many young people with emotional and mental health
challenges do not seek professional help, and rates of help-seeking in young
men are especially low (Rickwood et al., 2005; Wilson, 2007). Through Positive
Education there is a strong focus on reducing the stigma associated with seeking
help, and supporting students (and staff) to feel more comfortable accessing care
and support.

Within any school community there will always be students and staff members who are experiencing a range of personal difficulties and hardships. In the
Handbury Centre for Wellbeing, students can visit a range of healthcare professionals. Psychologists are available to support students who have different concerns, including those students who are experiencing mental illnesses such as
depression or anxiety. Throughout the Positive Education explicit curriculum
there has also been a strong focus on building awareness of mental illness. For
example, Matthew Johnstone, author of *I Had a Black Dog* (Johnstone, 2005),
speaks to students about depression as part of the Year 10 Positive Education
curriculum.

Alongside building awareness of mental health there has been a focus on communicating the idea that counseling is more than a service to be accessed in times
of distress; it can also be a useful pathway to enhancing wellbeing and flourishing. In a concrete example of how this message is communicated, all Year 10 students receive a bookmark outlining the School's counseling services. Prior to
Positive Education, these bookmarks listed a range of common issues for which
students could access help, including sleep problems, bullying, anxiety, depression, stress, grief, friendship issues, and homesickness. Since the increased focus
on wellbeing, the bookmarks have been redesigned and a range of positive issues,
such as resilience, learning to thrive, and how to flourish, have been integrated
(see Figure 4.5). The bookmarks represent a wider message that students can
seek counseling when they are feeling overwhelmed or isolated *or* they can seek

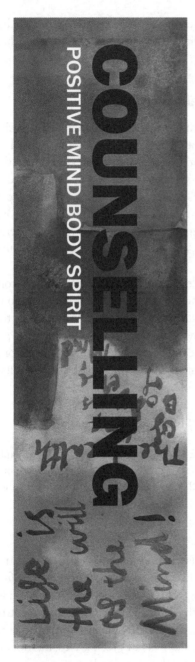

FREE confidential service for all students

Counsellors:
Ian McIntosh
Janet Stephens

Counsellors are available at the **Kennedy Medical Centre (Handbury Centre for Wellbeing)**

Appointments:
by email to the counsellor or in person at Kennedy

Services:
Individual counselling and advice

Types Of Issues:
- Sleep
- Stress
- Relationships/Friendships
- Learning to thrive
- Grief, Loss/Trauma
- Anxiety/Depression
- Strengths
- How to flourish
- Study skills
- Homesickness
- Psychological assessment
- Resilience
- Positive Focus Group Sessions

Services provided by counsellors are free and confidential

All appointments are voluntary and negotiated individually with each student

Kennedy Medical Centre

Figure 4.5a and 4.5b New counseling bookmarks created in 2010 listing additional issues to complement Positive Education.

counseling if they want to empower themselves to be emotionally, socially, and psychologically able to perform at their best in their studies and their broader lives.

A powerful reminder of mental health

In a salient example of the increased openness to discussing mental illness that has developed in the School, a Year 12 student made a speech at a Senior School assembly about his experience with depression (see Box 4.1 for an extract from the first half of this speech). This student was a very accomplished all-round student—a good sportsman, a strong student, and a lead in the senior School musical production. From the outside it might have been assumed that he was the epitome of flourishing. His courage in openly discussing his experiences was a moving reminder that no one is immune to mental illness, and that often external success can mask deep internal conflicts and hardships.

As is evident from his speech, this student made a firm call to the School community to look out for students who are lonely, anxious, and depressed. Responses to this speech where characterized by a mixture of emotions—admiration for the student's courage, empathy and compassion for his experience, pride that students feel safe enough within the community to speak openly about such issues, and ongoing determination to honor the student's wish for all members of the community to be more mindful of mental illness.

Flourishing at Geelong Grammar School

> People have often asked me what Pos Ed is all about. My favorite way to explain it is to "know thyself in order to help others." It reflects the great philosophers in this field, and also emphasizes one of the key foundations of Geelong Grammar School—service to others.
>
> Charlie Scudamore, Vice Principal

To explain flourishing during Positive Education information days and training courses, the School provides pictures of five oak trees (see Figure 4.6). The first tree is colorless, barren, and clearly struggling. This corresponds with a person who is languishing, who has poor mental health, challenged relationships, and struggles to find a sense of meaning and purpose. The next tree is in slightly better health, but looks bare and thirsty. The third tree shows a few green leaves; it is not unwell, but it certainly is not thriving either. This oak corresponds with a person who is moderately mentally well, but not necessarily content or fulfilled. The fourth tree is vital, and its leaves are a vibrant green. The final tree is bursting with life and color, providing food and shelter for birds and animals, its branches reaching for the sun. A connection is made between this powerful final image and a flourishing

BOX 4.1: The Blue Speech

Today I'm here to talk about something different. Something that has affected a lot of us deeply whether we know it or not. Colloquially it's referred to as "the blues." Medically it is known as "clinical depression." Now I know already that everyone here has probably had adverts, pamphlets and information thrown at them about the topic, and even as I speak here in front of you a small part of me wonders why I'm up here at all. But I am not here for personal gain. I am not here for your pity or consolation. I am here because I have had enough of the youth of today thinking that this problem is something that happens to other people, grown-ups outside the bounds of this School, out there in the real world—something that only happens to the homeless, drug addicted, and outcast. No, I'm here to make it personal and to bring this issue into the light. Whilst this is a confronting issue I believe that it is an issue which must be confronted; knowledge is power, and thus regardless of how stark or confronting the reality may be, it is reality nevertheless, and only by looking it in the eye can we learn anything of value from it.

In this School's mad rush for "wellbeing" unfortunately I feel as if certain aspects of our health have been neglected. Yes, we've built a multimillion dollar Wellbeing Centre so we can go to the gym and swim in the pool and, yes, we've embraced the forefront of Positive Psychology but, in the race for all this self-improvement, I feel as if we have forgotten about the little guy, the kid who can't go to the Wellbeing Centre because he gets intimidated at the gym, who feels alone and unsupported in this unimaginably huge and overwhelming world which he has found himself thrown into. Who has to juggle the pressures of home, work, social life, the Boarding House, sport, and countless other tasks alone whilst operating between the guidelines set by the School.

I had my first real encounter with a situation like this almost three years ago, here, in Year 10. Fresh out of Timbertop I descended into something very scary; I panicked as I saw the color slip from my little world. Today I know that I wasn't alone. I didn't know that back then. Three years on and things have changed, problems came, people hurt me. The school counselors, for all of their great work, weren't enough anymore; the treatment made me angry and sick. No one seemed to understand. I didn't understand.

However, I'm not here to scare you with my cynicism or tell you all about how horrible life is or to even ask you for your help, because I'm a lot further, and more capable now of dealing with my life than I was all those years ago. That said, I still freaked out all week about getting up here and speaking. The only thing that stops me from chickening out and running away right now is that I wish that I could have seen someone get up when I was going through all this, swallow their ego, face their fear, and just say: you are not alone—because you are not.

To me it comes back to basics. Simple actions and small steps help the great work of *beyondblue* and other organizations like it that help people like us. There is no silver bullet or magic pull to effortlessly rid us of such a far-reaching and influential problem. Mental illness does not differentiate between race, age, gender, or wealth; ironically we are all made equal in our vulnerability.

Year 12 Student, Senior School, Corio Campus

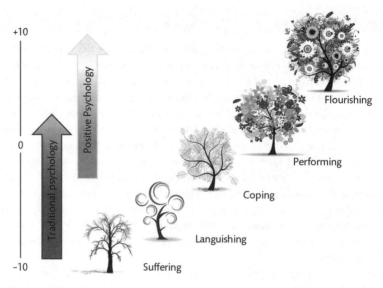

Figure 4.6 The different images of trees help to depict the wellbeing continuum.

person—someone who embraces life, connects deeply with others, and grows from difficulties.

In her introduction to this chapter, Professor Huppert discussed the spectrum of mental health, with mental ill health at one end and flourishing at the other. The greatest objective of the field of Positive Psychology is to shift this spectrum so that a greater percentage of individuals are at the flourishing end of the continuum (see Figure 4.7). In some cases the move towards greater flourishing involves providing care for someone who is experiencing distress; in other cases it means supporting someone to achieve a higher level of wellbeing. As key institutions in the community, schools are uniquely placed to nurture wellbeing in young people, and in doing so to contribute to a greater percentage of people who live optimally well. Case Study 4.2 describes how as simple a tool as a "What Went Well" board supports a flourishing community at the Timbertop campus.

Moving the spectrum of health towards flourishing requires attention to individual wellbeing. One goal of Positive Education is for students and staff to "know thyself," to practice behaviors that nurture wellbeing—such as exercise and mindfulness—on a daily basis, and to have the courage to ask for support when it is needed. Figure 4.8 shows students at a Year 11 Positive Education Focus Day, learning about the five ways to wellbeing, namely "Connect," "Be active," "Take notice," "Keep learning," and "Give" (New Economics Foundation, 2011). However, a

Figure 4.7 A Geelong Grammar School card that visually depicts the objective of supporting and encouraging members of the community to move to the right on the wellbeing curve (i.e. towards flourishing).

Figure 4.8 The 5 Ways to Wellbeing cards which are the building blocks of the Year 11 Positive Education Focus Day.

CASE STUDY 4.2

Timbertop's "What Went Well" Board

Andrew Monk, Timbertop Teacher and Positive Education Campus Coordinator (2008–2011)

For 14- and 15-year-olds, Timbertop is definitely a unique educational environment. It is important for students at a boarding school to build positive relationships and to focus upon what is working well. After attending Geelong Grammar School's Positive Psychology Conference, it dawned on me that the activity of recognizing three good things each day is not only an important ritual for adults to include in their daily life, but also presents an opportunity for students to practice thinking about "what went well" (WWW) while living away from home.

The idea of the WWW Board (see Figure 4.9) came about after it was shown that the three blessings activity promoted positive emotion and built optimism. Initially the students were encouraged to write in their journals each night what they believed were three good things that had occurred during their day. We found that although students were willing to consider the WWWs, not all of them were so enthusiastic about completing this reflection each night. There needed to be another avenue for us to accentuate positive emotion and optimism, while also building relationships.

Figure 4.9 Timbertop's "What Went Well" board in action.

The WWW Board represented not only students' recognition of what they perceived as highlights in their day, but also the opportunity for them to display gratitude toward others in the community. A whiteboard was placed in front of the Timbertop library, as this was a central point of the campus and also a place where visitors would regularly pass. Students, staff, visitors, and family members were all told about the WWW Board and its purpose. At first we had some reservations about the Board presenting an opportunity for students to write messages that compromised our positive theme, but we discovered in the first year, and in the years which followed, that the students had taken to this activity with great enthusiasm. The Board had to be wiped clean each week as it was so full of messages of WWWs and of gratitude that there was no room for others to write.

In contrast, we did find that writing on the Board ebbed and flowed over the course of the year. During the cold winter months, members of staff needed to make explicit efforts either to contribute to the Board themselves or to encourage students to write on the Board after they had chatted to them about what was going on in their life at the time.

What was notable with the WWW Board is that everyone made an effort to stop and read about the positive personal events that people wanted to share. For many staff members and students this built and enhanced positive relationships. We were able to talk to students already knowing that they had been thanked by somebody or having learned something new about their life at Timbertop. It was fascinating to see students rush to write on the Board after something had occurred in their life or that of others. What was most significant is that students learned not only to be grateful and to see the value of expressing gratitude, but also that sharing with others what went well in their day connected them powerfully to others.

flourishing school community occurs when people think beyond themselves to how they can enrich the lives of others. This message is perhaps the one viewed as most important by Positive Education staff at Geelong Grammar School—treating other people with kindness, compassion, and forgiveness is integral to the wellbeing of others, but it is absolutely essential to the wellbeing of the self. A person cannot flourish in isolation; it is in their connections and relationships that true wellbeing is found.

RECOMMENDED RESOURCES

Belic R (2011). *Happy* (documentary). <www.thehappymovie.com>

Ben-Shahar T (2010). *Even Happier: a gratitude journal for daily joy and lasting fulfilment.* New York: McGraw-Hill Professional.

Bonniwell I (2006). *Positive Psychology in a Nutshell.* London: Personal Well-Being Centre.

David S, Bonniwell I, and Conley Ayers A (eds) (2013). *The Oxford Handbook of Happiness.* Oxford: Oxford University Press.

Gaffney M (2011). *Flourishing.* London: Penguin Books Ltd.

International Positive Psychology Association (IPPA). <www.ippanetwork.org>

Jarden A (ed.) (2012). Positive psychologists on positive psychology. *International Journal of Wellbeing, 2,* 70–149.

Lyubomirsky S (2007). *The How of Happiness.* London: Sphere.

McKay H (2013). *The Good Life: what makes life worth living?* Sydney, Australia: Macmillan.

New Economics Foundation. *Five Ways to Wellbeing,* <www.fivewaystowellbeing.org>

Peterson C (2013). *Pursuing the Good Life: 100 reflections on positive psychology.* Oxford: Oxford University Press.

Positive Psychology News Daily. <http://positivepsychologynews.com>

Seligman M E P (2011). *Flourish.* London: Nicholas Brealey Publishing.

Think and Be Happy. <www.thinkandbehappy.com.au>

University of Pennsylvania. Authentic Happiness website. <www.authentichappiness.sas.upenn.edu>

REFERENCES

American Psychiatric Association (2013). *Diagnostic and Statistical Manual of Mental Disorders,* 5th edn. Washington, DC: American Psychiatric Association.

Butler J and Kern M L (2014). *The PERMA-Profiler: a brief multidimensional measure of flourishing.* Philadelphia, PA: International Association of Positive Psychology.

Cooper I (2007). *The Golden Rule.* New York: Abrams Books for Young Readers.

Deci E L and Ryan R M (2008). Hedonia, eudaimonia, and well-being: an introduction. *Journal of Happiness Studies, 9,* 1–11.

Diener E (2000). Subjective well-being. The science of happiness and a proposal for a national index. *American Psychologist, 55,* 34–43.

Diener E et al. (2010). New well-being measures: short scales to assess flourishing and positive and negative feelings. *Social Indicators Research, 97,* 143–56.

Duckworth A L, Peterson C, Matthews M D, and Kelly D R (2007). Grit: perseverance and passion for long-term goals. *Journal of Personality and Social Psychology, 92,* 1087–101.

Durlak J A and DuPre E P (2008). Implementation matters: a review of research on the influence of implementation on program outcomes and the factors affecting implementation. *American Journal of Community Psychology, 41*, 327–50.

Durlak J A et al. (2011). The impact of enhancing students' social and emotional learning: a meta-analysis of school-based universal interventions. *Child Development, 82*, 405–32.

Gaffney M (2011). *Flourishing*. London: Penguin Books Ltd.

Henderson L W and Knight T (2012). Integrating the hedonic and eudaimonic perspectives to more comprehensively understand wellbeing and pathways to wellbeing. *International Journal of Wellbeing, 2*, 196–221.

Huppert F A (2009). Psychological well-being: evidence regarding its causes and consequences. *Applied Psychology: Health and Well-being, 1*, 137–64.

Huppert F A (2014). The state of well-being science. In: F A Huppert and C Cooper (eds) *Interventions and Policies to Enhance Wellbeing*. Oxford: Wiley-Blackwell.

Huppert F A and So T T (2013). Flourishing across Europe: application of a new conceptual framework for defining well-being. *Social Indicators Research, 110*, 837–61.

Huppert F A et al. (2009). Measuring well-being across Europe: description of the ESS well-being module and preliminary findings. *Social Indicators Research, 91*, 301–15.

Jennings P A and Greenberg M T (2009). The prosocial classroom: teacher social and emotional competence in relation to student and classroom outcomes. *Review of Educational Research, 79*, 491–525.

Johnstone M (2005). *I Had a Black Dog*. Melbourne, Australia: Pan Macmillan.

Kashdan T B, Biswas-Diener R, and King L A (2008). Reconsidering happiness: the costs of distinguishing between hedonics and eudaimonia. *Journal of Positive Psychology, 3*, 219–33.

Keyes C L M (2002). The mental health continuum: from languishing to flourishing in life. *Journal of Health and Social Behavior, 43*, 207–22.

Keyes C L M (2003). Promoting a life worth living: human development from the vantage points of mental illness and mental health. In: R M Lerner, J Jacobs, and D Wertlieb (eds) *Promoting Positive Child, Adolescent, and Family Development: a handbook of program and policy innovations*. Volume 4. Thousand Oaks, CA: Sage Publications, Inc. pp. 257–74.

Keyes C L M (2006). Mental health in adolescence: is America's youth flourishing? *American Journal of Orthopsychiatry, 76*, 395–402.

Keyes C L M (2007). Promoting and protecting mental health as flourishing: a complementary strategy for improving national mental health. *American Psychologist, 62*, 95–108.

Keyes C L M and Annas J (2009). Feeling good and functioning well: distinctive concepts in ancient philosophy and contemporary science. *Journal of Positive Psychology, 4*, 197–201.

Keyes C L M, Shmotkin D, and Ryff C D (2002). Optimizing well-being: the empirical encounter of two traditions. *Journal of Personality and Social Psychology, 82*, 1007–22.

Kuyken W et al. (2013). Effectiveness of the mindfulness in schools programme: non-randomised controlled feasibility study. *The British Journal of Psychiatry, 203*, 126–31.

Meiklejohn J et al. (2012). Integrating mindfulness training into K-12 education: fostering the resilience of teachers and students. *Mindfulness, 3*, 291–307.

New Economics Foundation (2011). *Five Ways to Well-being: new applications, new ways of thinking.* London: New Economics Foundation.

Oxford University Press (2010). *Oxford Dictionary of English.* New York: Oxford University Press.

Park N and Peterson C (2008). Positive psychology and character strengths: application to strengths-based school counseling. *Professional School Counseling, 12*, 85–92.

Peterson C et al. (2008). Strengths of character and posttraumatic growth. *Journal of Traumatic Stress, 21*, 214–17.

Rickwood D, Deane F P, Wilson C J, and Ciarrochi J (2005). Young people's help-seeking for mental health problems. *Australian e-Journal for the Advancement of Mental Health, 4 (Suppl. 3)*, 1–34.

Ryan R M and Deci E L (2001). On happiness and human potentials: a review of research on hedonic and eudaimonic well-being. *Annual Review of Psychology, 52*, 141–66.

Ryff C D and Keyes C L M (1995). The structure of psychological well-being revisited. *Journal of Personality and Social Psychology, 69*, 719–27.

Ryff C D and Singer B H (2008). Know thyself and become what you are: a eudaimonic approach to psychological well-being. *Journal of Happiness Studies, 9*, 13–39.

Seligman M E P (2002). *Authentic Happiness: using the new positive psychology to realize your potential for lasting fulfillment.* New York: Free Press.

Seligman M E P (2011). *Flourish.* London: Nicholas Brealey Publishing.

Siegel D J (2007). *The Mindful Brain: reflection and attunement in the cultivation of well-being.* New York: W W Norton & Company.

Stewart-Brown S et al. (2009). Internal construct validity of the Warwick-Edinburgh Mental Well-being Scale (WEMWBS): a Rasch analysis using data from the Scottish Health Education Population Survey. *Health and Quality of Life Outcomes, 7.* <www.hqlo.com/content/7/1/15>

Tennant R et al. (2007). The Warwick-Edinburgh Mental Well-being Scale (WEMWBS): development and UK validation. *Health and Quality of Life Outcomes, 5.* <www.hqlo.com/content/5/1/63>

Waterman A S (2008). Reconsidering happiness: a eudaimonist's perspective. *Journal of Positive Psychology, 3,* 234–52.

Weare K and Nind M (2011). Mental health promotion and problem prevention in schools: what does the evidence say? *Health Promotion International, 26,* 29–69.

Weare K and Nind M (2014). Promoting mental health and wellbeing in schools. In: F A Huppert and C L Cooper (eds) *Interventions and Policies to Enhance Wellbeing.* Oxford: Wiley-Blackwell. pp. 1–48.

Wilson C J (2007). When and how do young people seek professional help for mental health problems? *Medical Journal of Australia, 187 (7 Suppl.),* S35–9.

World Health Organization (1993). *The ICD-10 Classification of Mental and Behavioural Disorders: diagnostic criteria for research.* Geneva: World Health Organization.

CHARACTER STRENGTHS

**Introduction by
Professor Nansook Park**

How can we build good character in young people? For centuries, building and strengthening good character among young people have been universal goals for education and parenting. Character is important not only for personal wellbeing, but also for societal wellbeing. A young person's character strengths play an important role in their positive development. Character strengths not only act as broad protective factors, preventing or mitigating psychopathology and problems, but also enable conditions that promote thriving and flourishing.

Despite the importance of good character, scholars largely neglected this topic throughout much of the twentieth century. Positive Psychology has refocused scientific attention on character, identifying character strengths as one of the pillars of this new field, and central to understanding the good life. Positive Psychology specifically emphasizes building the good and fulfilling life by identifying individual strengths of character and fostering them.

For over a decade, our research team, led by Professor Chris Peterson, has been focusing efforts on the study of character strengths and virtues, and specifically on what character strengths are, how we measure them, why they are important (i.e. their consequences), how they are developed, and how we cultivate them effectively. In our project, character strengths are not simply the absence of deficits and problems, but rather a well-developed family of positive traits reflected in feelings, thoughts, and actions. Each character strength is expressed in terms of degree, with some people having more or less of any given strength. Character is not singular, but plural, and must be measured in ways that do justice to its breadth.

Accumulating research evidence is showing that character strengths have important consequences, which vary depending on the character strengths involved. Children and young people with certain sets of character strengths are happier, do better at school, and have fewer psychological and behavioral problems. For example, hope, kindness, social intelligence, self-control, and perspective can potentially buffer against the negative effects of stress and trauma, preventing or mitigating serious emotional and behavioral problems in their wake. In addition, character strengths help young people to thrive. Although all character strengths contribute to wellbeing, in general the strengths of character that are consistently related to life satisfaction are gratitude, hope, zest, curiosity, and—perhaps most importantly—love, defined as the ability to sustain reciprocated close relationships with other people. Thus, in order to have a thriving life, individuals need to cultivate these five strengths in particular. Furthermore, our research showed that students' academic achievement was significantly influenced by a set of character strengths above and beyond intelligence. Among middle-school students, the character strengths of perseverance, fairness, love, gratitude, honesty, hope, and perspective predicted end-of-year grade point average.

These findings imply that the encouragement of certain character strengths would not only make students happier and healthier, but also help them to attain better grades. Working on students' character is not a luxury but a necessity, and does not entail a trade-off with traditional "academic" concerns.

Character has a developmental trajectory. Although there is a degree of convergence when comparing the relative prevalence of strengths among young people and adults, there are also interesting developmental differences. Specifically, hope, teamwork, and zest are relatively more common among young people than in adults, whereas appreciation of beauty, honesty, forgiveness, and open-mindedness are relatively more common among adults than in young people. These latter strengths require maturation in order to be displayed. One implication of this is that educators and parents often try to teach young people the character strengths that adults value. However, it is also important to know that children and young people naturally possess many of the components of good character. If attention is not paid to strengthening these, children may lose them as they mature.

Good character can be cultivated and strengthened by appropriate parenting, schooling, various youth development programs, and healthy communities. Although this work is still in its infancy, it seems that a variety of factors contribute to the development of good character, including genetics, family, schools, peers, and communities. According to Aristotle, virtues—a reflection of the individual's character—can be taught and acquired only by practicing them. Other scholars have also emphasized that character must be developed by action, and not merely by thinking or talking about it. These various notions about virtues all suggest that character can be cultivated by good parenting, schooling, and socialization, and that it becomes instantiated through habitual action.

Character development programs should teach specific activities relating to strengths, and encourage young people to keep using them in their daily lives. Children and young people should be instructed to choose a target character strength that they want to focus on, then set a specific and measurable goal, and devise a concrete action plan for achieving that goal.

Positive institutions play an important role in character development among young people by providing positive role models, creating more opportunities to practice character strengths, and setting cultural norms that value character strengths.

Our character strength project is founded on strengths-based approaches. By measuring character strengths in plural terms, it allows the comparison of character strengths not only across individuals but also within individuals. We believe that everyone has strengths regardless of where those stand compared with others. This strength-based approach is particularly useful when working with students with a history of disability, low achievement, or troubles. When we compare these students with the norm or with other students, as we often do, it is hard to find anything they are good at. However, if we compare the character strengths *within* an individual, we can identify those strengths that are stronger than others, and educators, parents, and professionals can then help these children and young people to use those strengths in their lives. These strengths-based approaches can be used with children and young people at any level. Once they have started to build their confidence by using their signature strengths, they can be taught how to use the latter to work on less well-developed strengths. Problem-focused approaches can be useful for reducing and treating the specific targeted problem, but they do not necessarily prepare young people to have fulfilling lives. Attention to both strengths and weaknesses is critical, and no useful purpose is served by regarding these as mutually exclusive goals.

Franklin D. Roosevelt stated that "We cannot always build the future for our young people, but we can build our young people for the future." Perhaps helping young people to identify their character strengths and use them in their everyday lives may provide a route toward a psychologically fulfilling life.

The strengths of character and virtues project is arguably the most ambitious and ground-breaking work undertaken in the field of Positive Psychology. It is often considered to be the core of Positive Education. What made this project rigorous and significant was the man behind this project from the beginning—Professor Chris Peterson. It was his life's work.

This project was not only the result of Chris's scholarly brilliance and hard work but also, more importantly, it was a reflection of the way that he lived his life. Chris not only studied and taught character strengths and virtues but also lived them—he was the embodiment of good character and virtues. He had that rare combination of a great mind and a giant heart. His brilliance was accompanied by warmth, generosity, humility, fairness, integrity, genuineness, and a gentle sense of humor. To put it simply, he was a "gentle giant."

Chris and I treasured our time at Geelong Grammar School during a month-long visit, and we then followed this up with a short second visit 2 years later. We realized that Geelong Grammar School was a natural home for Positive Education initiatives. Although the School had great resources, its real assets were people. We were very impressed by the dedicated teachers, the innovative administrators, and the kind staff who truly care about education—not just educating minds, but also educating the hearts of young people. Their passion for education was observed not only in the classroom, but also throughout campus life. We felt privileged to be part of such an innovative effort at such a great institution with wonderful people. We came away from both visits with more learning and inspiration from the people at Geelong Grammar School than we ourselves had shared with them. I believe that the success of the Positive Education initiative at the School was in large part due to the unique, natural assets of the School community. I think that it would be highly desirable for other schools looking to embark on Positive Education to identify and utilize the unique assets and capabilities that exist in their own institutions and communities, in order to maximize the likelihood of success and sustainability.

Character strengths at Geelong Grammar School

Many people take for granted the things they can do well, and focus instead on the things they cannot do well. To be reminded that one has strengths is therefore wonderful, and being encouraged to use those signature strengths actively, on a daily basis, makes enormous sense for increasing one's satisfaction with life.

Stephen Meek, Principal

Professor Chris Peterson and Professor Nansook Park had an extended stay at Geelong Grammar School in 2008, and returned for a second visit in February 2010. During these visits they gave a number of inspiring presentations on character strengths, made thoughtful contributions to the School community, and celebrated Chris Peterson's sixtieth birthday.

Chris Peterson and Nansook Park made an invaluable contribution in helping to develop and embed the character strengths language and framework in the School community. Sadly, Chris Peterson died suddenly in 2012. With his passing, the School took the opportunity not only to reflect on his character strengths, including kindness, humor, and modesty, but also to be grateful for his legacy in helping the School to engage in Positive Education in an authentic and meaningful manner.

As Nansook Park explained in her introduction to this chapter, character strengths were at the core of Chris Peterson's work. Character strengths are also at the heart of Positive Education at Geelong Grammar School. They serve as the underpinning framework of the Model for Positive Education, and work as access points to flourishing across the domains, particularly for younger students. Introducing character strengths to young students is especially powerful, as this is a pivotal time in their understanding of themselves, others, and the world. Through the lens of character strengths, the School celebrates the unique ways in which each student and staff member contributes to the community.

Values in Action Classification of Character Strengths (VIA)

The Values in Action Classification of Character Strengths (VIA) is the language in which character strengths are identified, talked about, and developed at the School (Peterson and Seligman, 2004). The VIA is based on a historical study of character strengths that have been valued in a diverse range of cultures and traditions (Dahlsgaard et al., 2005). The strengths included in the VIA are a set of universally recognized character traits that are relatively stable and have a wide impact on thoughts, feelings, and actions. Character strengths are valued in their own right, as well as being important pathways to wellbeing and flourishing. They are powerful routes to treating others, the community, and the environment with integrity and respect.

The VIA comprises six virtues that are further broken down into 24 character strengths (Peterson and Seligman, 2004). The virtue of Wisdom recognizes the character strengths of the "head", such as creativity, curiosity, open-mindedness, perspective, and love of learning. The character strengths of honesty, bravery, persistence, and zest make up the virtue of Courage. The virtue of Justice focuses on strengths that contribute to healthy communities, such as fairness, leadership, and teamwork. The Transcendence strengths of gratitude, hope, humor, spirituality, and the appreciation of beauty and excellence provide meaning and help people to connect to others and the larger universe. The virtue of Temperance recognizes the importance of controlling against excess, and includes the character strengths of humility, prudence, self-control, and forgiveness. Character strengths of the "heart" that nurture and enrich positive relationships, such as kindness, social intelligence, and love, come under the virtue of Humanity.

The focus on character strengths

When students move into the Boarding Houses at Geelong Grammar School, parents are asked to provide comprehensive information about their child, including any learning difficulties, concerns about particular subjects, or behavioral problems. Parents go into careful detail about health problems and special dietary needs. They devote substantial time to ensuring that the Boarding House staff, who will be helping to care for their child over the ensuing months and years, have a thorough understanding of the challenges, difficulties, or worries they have about their son or daughter. Throughout the students' time at the Boarding House, staff and families maintain regular communication about any issues or concerns that arise.

Since the implementation of Positive Education, parents are also often asked to describe their son or daughter at their best (see Box 5.1 for an email sent to parents by Simon Haigh, Head of Barrabool House). Parents are invited to share times when

---

BOX 5.1: Dear Barraboolian Parents

It was wonderful to have all the Barrabool lads together again this evening—they settled excitedly into their new dorms, and seemed very happy to be back together after a 2-week break. I would love it if you could please find the time to write a story about your son "at his best." We plan to devote time this term towards the investigation of our personal character strengths. If you could please spend some time thinking about a specific instance of your son "at his best"—it might be on the sporting field, working at home, helping his brother/sister, interacting with his friends ... whatever the context, I would love to be able to read about your son acting in ways that made you proud. I plan to use your story to help us identify the character strengths that your son uses when he is at his best. This is a great opportunity to celebrate what is wonderful about your son.

Many thanks,

Simon Haigh, Head of Barrabool House

their child has thrived in the classroom, at a family event, at play, or during sports. They are encouraged to provide information on their child's character strengths and the attributes of which they are most proud. This information provides the Boarding House staff with a valuable head start in getting to know each child. It also creates a point of connection between staff and parents, who often take great pride in sharing their children's strengths and great comfort in knowing that the staff want to see the best in their children. This simple activity represents the essence of the character strengths approach. So often in life there is a tendency to prioritize worries, concerns, and difficulties. Focusing on character strengths is an intentional shift towards also celebrating the good in each person. Discussions about character strengths lead to a richness of conversation and a quality of connection that do not result when conversations focus on problems or challenges.

Creating a shared language for character strengths

> Strengths are one of our main focuses here at Bostock because we have such little ones. They love reading a story and reeling off the signature strengths they identify in different characters. The justifications they can come up with and the conversations they can have are wonderful. For young children, they really have a good understanding of what the strengths are and what they mean in their lives.
>
> Jane Marney, Bostock House Teacher and Positive Education Coordinator

Schools are notoriously good at recognizing talent or aptitude in subjects, sports, and co-curricular activities through prizes, recognitions, awards, and colors. Through the focus on character strengths, the emphasis moves beyond external markers of success to the morally valued attributes of each child and adult. For example, a student who is a natural athlete may receive a prize for winning an event. Through a focus on character strengths, there is equal importance placed on teamwork in supporting other athletes or gratitude in acknowledging the coaches. The result of several years of Positive Education at Geelong Grammar School is a deeply embedded vocabulary of character strengths across the School culture. Throughout the campuses, there is a common language that allows character strengths to be noticed, discussed, and explored by members of the School community (Figures 5.1 and 5.2 provide examples of how students explore character strengths).

Substantial time is devoted to helping students to cultivate a deep understanding of all of the character strengths, and during their time at the School even young children develop a rich understanding of the various strengths. Bostock House staff allocate the 24 character strengths across the five year levels taught at the campus, so each year the students develop an understanding of a few strengths. For example, they learn about kindness in Prep, honesty in Year 1, fairness in Year 2, humor in Year 3, and leadership in Year 4. Each teacher spends time exploring the assigned character strengths so that students' knowledge and understanding of strengths build

Figure 5.1 A Year 6 student with his personal shield of character strengths.

Figure 5.2 Year 3 drawing of the character strength of bravery in action.

over their time at Bostock House. Helping young children to understand character strengths is invaluable in supporting the development of their social and emotional learning skills. Children can talk about their own strengths in the context of how they interact with others, and also have the vocabulary to identify strengths in their peers.

Building character strengths through celebrations and stories

School assemblies often have a theme of celebrating a particular strength, which is based on Jenny Fox Eades' approach to cultivating strengths through celebrations and rituals (Fox Eades, 2008). Similarly, Chapel services are focused on character strengths, through an identification of Bible readings and stories that exemplify values such as wisdom, kindness, gratitude, and appreciation of beauty and excellence. Students identify individuals within the School community and beyond who epitomize particular character strengths, commonly referred to as character strengths "paragons." Case Study 5.1 describes an activity in which students interview panels of character strengths paragons from across the School community.

At Bostock House and Toorak campus, the 24 character strengths are displayed and used as a visual prompt for students to think about how various strengths may be useful in the playground. Literature is also valuable in creating strengths

CASE STUDY 5.1

Character strengths paragon panel

Justin Robinson, Director, Institute of Positive Education

Spotting character strengths in action in others is a great habit to develop. This habit, or skill, is available to all students, staff members, and parents, and is actively practiced and nurtured at the School. Although for some the spotting of strengths comes easily and naturally, others may need to override their tendency to spot weaknesses. We often ask staff and students in our Positive Education sessions to "Think of a person whom you have had difficulties with, and suggest one or more of their signature strengths." Individuals commonly recognize strengths authentically in the person whom they were having difficulties with, and this simple reflective awareness can assist in moving the relationship forward. The VIA Classification of Character Strength has provided the School with a common language that is used on a regular basis—whether informally in conversations, formally in classroom activities, or embedded in documentation such as student reports or meeting agenda items.

Although it is great to spot character strengths in action, a school community can reap tremendous benefits when, on occasion, students and staff go one step further and truly celebrate individuals who embody particular character strengths. One way in which we have done this at Geelong Grammar School is to hold character strengths paragon panels. Prior to holding such a panel, students (and/or staff members) are asked to work in small groups and nominate members of the Geelong Grammar School community who embody or exemplify a particular character strength. The group (a House, year level, or class) provides a shortlist of Geelong Grammar School members whom they recognize as exemplars or role models of a particular strength. Students then formally invite these chosen individuals to attend a character strength paragon panel where the students can celebrate their actions (virtuous behavior), and gain valuable insights by asking a range of relevant questions. Generally a panel of between three and five participants representing a range of different areas of the School community is gathered for the session. Students have selected peers from their year level, older and younger students, teachers, coaches, support staff (such as cleaners, catering staff, or grounds and maintenance staff), and School leaders. The mix of "paragons" often adds another dimension to the discussion.

Students prepare questions for the panel members and, depending on the age group, they will lead the paragon panel activity, thanking the participants for coming and guiding the discussion. A typical opening question might be as follows: "We are looking forward to getting to know you further. Could you share a little bit of your story, your past, and what is important to you?"

Other questions asked by the students have included the following: "Would you call the strength we are discussing today one of your signature strengths?," "How important is this strength to you?," "When do you use this strength the most, and could you give us an example?," "Have you used this strength to overcome adversity?," "Where do you think this character strength came from?," "Did your use of this strength ever get you into trouble?," "Do you think there might be a shadow side to this character strength for you?," and "What advice would you give to someone who wanted to nurture this character strength?"

The success of this activity becomes apparent in the attentive attitude of the students actively listening to and learning from the dialogue between the students and the panel members. Another positive side effect is the validation experienced by each and every panel member. On many occasions, panel members have taken the time to write to the group of students thanking them for the experience. Recognizing and celebrating paragons of character strengths, whether formally or informally, has had a positive impact on the culture of our School.

connections for students. Young students are regularly read stories and encouraged to explore the character strengths of the main characters. When exploring Anzac Day (a national day of remembrance in Australia and New Zealand), students read the book *Simpson and his Donkey*, which tells the story of John Simpson, a stretcher bearer during the First World War (Greenwood, 2011). According to the story, shortly after landing at Anzac Cove, Simpson located a donkey and used it to carry injured soldiers away from the front line. He transported the wounded over the hills, often under fire, and ultimately lost his life in this service. The children identify Simpson's unique mix of character strengths, including persistence, love, courage, and even his creativity and resourcefulness in acquiring the donkey.

Older students identify character strengths in stories and texts, television shows, and movies. Although it may be easy for students to identify strengths in the hero of the story, students are challenged to consider the character strengths of the main villains or rivals—making the point that everyone has character strengths, although these may be misused or overused at times. A rich example of this is the way that students identify character strengths in famous "heroes and villains" during their Year 9 History curriculum (see Case Study 5.2).

Signature strengths

Character strength building has been the most valuable thing we have done in Positive Education. I have learnt more about myself just by knowing what my top signature strengths are. I can put them into action more and also work on the ones towards the bottom of the list.

Phoebe, Year 10, Senior School, Corio

CASE STUDY 5.2

Year 9 History "Heroes and Villains" assignment

Christian Machar, Coordinator of History, Timbertop

The idea of the "Heroes and Villains" assignment was born during my induction to Geelong Grammar School, at which staff complete an Introduction to Positive Education training course. In the process of learning about myself, I was curious as to how I could make key components of Positive Education become more relevant in the History curriculum.

It is obvious that the individuals who have left imprints on history have displayed character strengths in their words and actions. For example, Nelson Mandela demonstrated forgiveness and mercy to his jailers of 27 years, as well as leadership in reconciling South Africa, while Mother Teresa showed kindness and love in her humanitarian work with the poor, sick, orphaned, and dying.

The brief to my Year 9 students was, on the surface, relatively simple, namely to present a portrait of a person of historical significance and identify three character strengths that they displayed. Students would then write an essay and reflect on these findings collectively as a class.

To provide an accurate representation of the individuals chosen, it was important to obtain as much information as possible when researching, and not just examine a tiny snapshot of the person's life. It was also important for me to encourage strong student engagement. I allowed the students to choose individuals from a diverse range of fields. They chose an eclectic mix of historical and contemporary figures, such as Alexander the Great, Leonardo da Vinci, Marie Antoinette, Edward "Weary" Dunlop, Anne Frank, Martin Luther King, Madonna, and Jessica Watson.

At a deeper level it was important for the students to go beyond simply writing an essay. I wanted them to make a link to their own personal experiences, to perhaps observe highly desirable character strengths and set goals to develop them. The students were asked to present to the class a brief overview of their person of interest, to outline the three character strengths, and to explain how they were demonstrated.

Prior to the students' presentations, we predicted which character strengths might be highly ranked among the heroes and villains, and why this was so. Our top five strengths were bravery, creativity, hope, leadership, and persistence. Students made such comments as "Often people persist through something difficult" and "Many famous people do something courageous." Not surprisingly, the evidence of our research project mirrored the top five character strengths we had chosen.

Further questions explored such ideas as the following: Are we born with character strengths or can we acquire and develop them? What factors influence character strengths? Can character strengths be viewed as a weakness? What character strengths would you like to develop, and why?

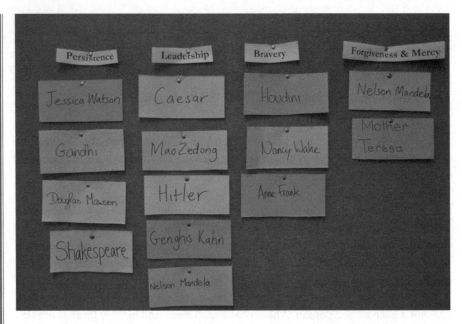

Figure 5.3 Character strengths: Year 9 History "Heroes and Villains" assignment.

The students enjoyed this assignment as they learned about individuals who might have been of interest to them before, but more importantly they now had a deeper awareness of, and insight into, character strengths. I was impressed by the range of character strengths that were identified (for some examples, see Figure 5.3). For example, the students reflected on mountaineer Tenzing Norgay's modesty and humility in relation to his historic Mount Everest climb, and Jessica Watson's open-mindedness in relation to her solo sailing voyage around the world. Although learning outcomes in History courses may be constrained by time limitations, I do believe that even topics of study such as the First World War or the Industrial Revolution could allow for the discussion of one or more key individuals and their character strengths.

Each member of the Geelong Grammar School community has a unique blend of character strengths that serve as an excellent foundation for flourishing. Signature strengths are ways of thinking, feeling, and behaving that enable high levels of functioning and performance (Linley and Harrington, 2006). Each person has a subset of character strengths that come most naturally to them and help to define them as a person (Park and Peterson, 2009). Peterson and Seligman (2004) have outlined several criteria for signature strengths, including that the use of the strength leads to feelings of excitement, invigoration, and authenticity. Signature strengths are also easily noticed by others and used across different settings and situations. A person continually identifies new opportunities to apply their signature strengths and feels intrinsically motivated to use them.

The School works on the principle that each student in the community will develop a rich understanding of their signature strengths, creating important pathways towards self-knowledge and acceptance. As Professor Park outlined in her introduction to this chapter, substantial research evidence supports the power of strengths in building wellbeing and contributing to a full and flourishing life (Govindji and Linley, 2007; Linley et al., 2010). Signature strengths have been found to be positively associated with academic performance, motivation, and effort (Lounsbury et al., 2009).

Identifying signature strengths requires comprehensive exploration and reflection. A person's "gut feeling" is considered to be important information when identifying signature strengths. Students are encouraged to write in their journals about times when they feel most authentic and energized. They also reflect on their strengths through the evidence-based "best possible self" activity (Sheldon and Lyubomirsky, 2006; see Box 5.2 for further details). Students describe feeling a sense of fulfillment and meaningfulness when helping a friend, taking photographs, writing, or raising awareness for an important social justice issue. This understanding is built upon by asking for other people's perspectives, and students are encouraged to ask several people who know them well to nominate their signature strengths. Hearing examples of their character strengths from friends, teachers, coaches, and family members is often very meaningful for students.

BOX 5.2: Me at my best

I feel at my best when I am talking to my friends. I show respect for other people. It helps me to feel included.

Georgia, Year 4, Toorak Campus

I feel at my best when I am playing footy. I show confidence and it helps me to get hyped up before a game.

Max, Year 4, Toorak Campus

In a "me at my best activity," students write a story about a time when they were at their very best—a time when they felt at their most authentic, alive, content, or energized. Students then read their story to a partner, and together the two students identify signature strengths used in the story. Through this activity, students identify times when they are at their best—for example, this might be when helping others, working in teams, creating things, or performing on stage. Variations of this activity are used with students of all ages. In a version used at Toorak Campus, students explore times when they feel at their best and write a description on colorful flowers. They then display their flowers together to create a flower bed of students' strengths.

Having explored their strengths from these diverse viewpoints, students complete the VIA Youth Survey (Park and Peterson, 2005), an online tool that explores the 24 character strengths included in the VIA classification. Similar to the longer, adult VIA Inventory of Strengths (Park et al., 2004; Peterson and Park, 2011), the VIA Youth Survey is aimed at children and adolescents (aged 10–17 years), and uses language, contexts, and examples that are appropriate for young people. Once the survey has been completed, students are provided with a detailed report on their strengths, including their top five signature strengths (for further information on this process and report, see <www.viacharacter.org>).

The results of the VIA report are combined with self-reflections and information obtained from friends, family, and teachers, so that each student has thorough information on his or her strengths from different sources. Through this comprehensive exploration, students select a set of four to six signature strengths with regard to which they feel a sense of ownership and connection. Awareness of one's signature strengths is just as relevant for staff, and all staff have completed the adult version of the VIA Inventory of Strengths. For example, Justin Robinson, Director of the Institute of Positive Education, has the top strengths of perseverance, fairness, zest and enthusiasm, honesty, and love of learning. Often staff members encourage their partners and family members to complete the VIA Inventory of Strengths themselves, so the language of character strengths spreads through the wider School community. All senior students and staff have their signature strengths displayed in their online portal and are reminded of their strengths whenever they log in to check their email or timetable.

Developing character strengths

> All of our staff and students are aware of the field of character strengths; they are aware of their own strengths, aware of strengths spotting in others, and have a language around strengths.
>
> Charlie Scudamore, Vice Principal

Often character strengths develop naturally through life events, lifestyle changes, or exposure to new role models. For example, during the transition to Timbertop, students are stretched in new ways and may discover strengths of which they were previously unaware. The development of character strengths can also be planned and deliberate; staff and students may devote time to learning more about a strength, read a biography of someone who exemplifies a strength, or spend time with a strengths paragon. At the School, the term "actioning strengths" is used to describe the process of intentionally using character strengths or brainstorming ways of applying them to new situations. An activity in which students make a plan to nurture a character strength is described in Box 5.3.

Many staff members have found that focusing on character strengths is especially powerful when working with students who have behavioral, learning, or emotional

> **BOX 5.3:** Nurturing a character strength
>
> Students are encouraged to consider all 24 character strengths and pick one they would like to grow and develop. The students are placed in small groups, where they describe their reasons for selecting a particular strength. In their groups they discuss the potential benefits and costs of using the selected strength more often. Together the students brainstorm new and varied ways in which they could action the strengths over the coming month, including how they could use the character strength.
>
> Next, working as individuals, the students develop a concrete action plan for developing their chosen character strength. This often takes the form of a "new day, new use" challenge, where students create a plan for using one of their strengths in a new and creative way each day. They are asked to keep a log book or diary for a month about the ways in which they have actioned the strength each day. At the end of the month, the students write a report or give a presentation on their experience, identifying not only the ways in which they were successful in growing the strength, but also anything that hindered their progress, and concluding with their plans for continued use of the strength after the end of the project.

difficulties. Such students may spend hours every week hearing about their challenges and focusing on areas for improvement. For such students, a conversation about their character strengths—what is right with them—can be valuable in building self-worth and confidence. A commonly used phrase at the School is "What you focus on grows." In other words, if you acknowledge character strengths such as self-control, love of learning, or persistence, students are more likely to repeat these behaviors in the future.

A community that celebrates strengths

> Character strengths help people to appreciate difference and value people for who they are. This is the heart of Positive Education—recognizing difference, seeing the difference as strength, and understanding that people contribute to the School community in unique but complementary ways.
>
> Anthony Strazzera, Senior English Teacher

At the beginning of Year 5, Pam Barton gives each of her students a piece of a giant floor puzzle. Students write their strengths on their piece of puzzle and then have the challenge of putting the puzzle together. The result is a completed puzzle in which individual students' character strengths fit together to create the overall picture. Whether a student is a section of the sky or a piece of a flower, they know that they are all part of the picture and help to make up the diversity of the group—the puzzle would not be complete without them.

Although there is power in knowing individual signature strengths, there is just as much value in knowing the combined strengths of a class, House, team, or group. At Corio campus, the character strengths of the students who live at the Boarding

Houses are presented in creative ways such as radar graphs and pie charts. Many staff find knowing the character strengths of each person in their team valuable in creating supportive and respectful relationships. One year, each staff member at Bostock House was asked to nominate signature strengths for their colleagues. The strengths for each staff member were tallied and the five most common strengths identified. Year 2 students then painted portraits of each staff member to correspond with their strengths. These portraits were showcased in the staff room, with the character strengths displayed underneath.

Identifying signature strengths in others is invaluable for nurturing relationships. One way to enrich connections is to learn about a friend's football team or their favorite food. In a similar way, learning about a friend's signature strengths, and spotting those strengths in action, also nurtures a deep connection and fosters meaningful relationships. One senior student explained that thinking about signature strengths helps her to know how best to support a friend who is going through a difficult time. If the friend's signature strength is appreciation of beauty, she may pick her flowers or give her a scented candle, whereas if her character strength is humor, she may write her a funny card or note.

Spotting character strengths

Strengths spotting involves identifying and communicating strengths noticed in others (Fox Eades, 2008; Linley, 2008). Some character strengths, such as kindness or leadership, may be easy to spot, but the challenge for students and staff is to spot strengths that can be more subtle, such as social intelligence, humility, or prudence. This skill in noticing character strengths develops over time, and many children across the campuses are now excellent strengths spotters. Strengths spotting can be used to add depth to active constructive responding (for further information, see Chapter 6) as students and staff members take time to listen carefully to people's good news and spot their character strengths in action. Activities aimed at cultivating strengths spotting across the School community are described in Boxes 5.4 and 5.5.

BOX 5.4: Strengths spots

One Middle School activity that takes strengths spotting one step further involves providing students in the class with blank, colorful stickers in the shape of spots. If a student sees another student actioning a character strength, the student picks out a spot, writes the character strength and a brief summary on it, and gives it to the student. A young girl received a poor score on her Science test. She sat down and went through all her corrections until she had them all right. The student sitting next to her noticed her diligence, picked a strengths spot, and wrote the character strength of "persistence" on it. Instead of feeling bad about getting a poor result, the student felt proud of herself for turning the situation around.

> **BOX 5.5: Barrabool House strengths board**
>
> Barrabool House is a Middle School Boarding House for boys. Barrabool House staff encourage students to identify times when other members of the House display character strengths. Although some of the stories are about big accomplishments, most of the stories are about little moments of humor, gratitude, kindness, or bravery. The stories are displayed on a noticeboard and the result is a vibrant board that displays a rich array of the students' use of character strengths. Simon Haigh, the Head of House, reflects that while it is good to see the examples of students using their character strengths, he is most proud of seeing students develop their ability to notice the strengths of others. One student in particular identified character strengths of his peers every day throughout a term, himself demonstrating the strengths of curiosity, kindness, persistence, and zest. Simon took this activity one step further by integrating character strengths stories in his regular email communication with families. This had the wonderful benefit of engaging parents in their children's daily lives at the School.

Strengths spotting is especially powerful for nurturing relationships between staff and students. One year, at the beginning of their time at Timbertop, students interviewed staff members about their life story, with the aim of identifying staff signature strengths. Many students were surprised by their teachers' stories of family, adventure, travel, or overcoming adversities. This activity was an invaluable way of helping students to see the human side of the adults who taught them.

Strengths spotting also helps staff members to get to know their students. Teachers are given a class roll with a blank space next to each student's name. They are encouraged to identify a character strength for each student—whether that student displays love of learning, kindness, leadership, or a combination of strengths. Teachers sometimes have trouble identifying a character strength for one or two students. This difficulty serves as a reminder to spend more time with these students, asking them questions and getting to know their strengths. A friend of Geelong Grammar School, Dr Denise Quinlan, often refers to the 24 character strengths as "24 ways to like a difficult child," and prompts teachers to use the framework for building stronger relationships with students from whom they may feel disconnected.

The shadow side of character strengths

> When the girls make mistakes or poor decisions, I start with their strengths. Often it is the shadow side of the strength that may have caused their poor decisions. For example, the strength of zest can lead to energy, fun, and loudness, but the shadow side of it can be acting in ways that are intimidating to others, or not settling at night. We talk about how to balance this with other strengths such as kindness or self-control. The students really get it.
>
> Mary-Anne Lewis, Head of Connewarre House

Across the School community, students and staff explore their own character strengths and acknowledge the strengths of others. It is important that students understand that although character strengths are valued across times and cultures, any of the strengths can be overused, misused, or underused. Similarly, strengths can be forgotten, or expressed in harmful or unbalanced ways. In order to expand their understanding, students are encouraged to brainstorm what the exaggeration, absence, or opposite of particular strengths may be (for example, the exaggeration of persistence could be stubbornness, and the opposite of humility might be vanity). One student talked about how she often sees the shadow side of her strength of prudence—she is very cautious when meeting new people, and as a result does not make new friends as easily as she would like to.

Different situations also require the use of different strengths (Biswas-Diener et al., 2010). A student might call on his or her social intelligence and kindness when with friends, draw on curiosity or persistence when studying, and use teamwork and leadership when engaging in a community service project. A focus is on helping students to consider when, how, and why certain strengths are important and useful in different situations. In Box 5.6, Justin Robinson, Director of the Institute of

---

BOX 5.6: An orchestra of strengths

According to the orchestra of strengths metaphor, each person is the conductor of their own 24 instruments. The beauty of orchestral music comes from the different combinations of instruments playing together, often in harmony, and often with changing and contrasting dynamics. On occasions the piece of music is quiet and led by the strings—this could be likened to occasions in life that call for supporting a friend, drawing on the character strengths of love, kindness, social intelligence, and hope. At other times, orchestral music is loud, as trumpets and trombones contrast with flutes and clarinets. This could be likened to a balance of the use of leadership, courage, curiosity, and zest. Although some instruments, such as the triangle, may not be required on many occasions, listeners will always notice the contribution of this rarely used—yet still important—instrument, which may be likened to an individual's lesser strengths, perhaps modesty or prudence.

The aim for all of us is to become a "master" conductor of our 24 character strengths—knowing when to call upon different strengths, when to temper particular strengths, and when to ask more of certain strengths. The Geelong Grammar School Symphonic Orchestra (see Figure 5.4) is used as a metaphor for the importance of becoming a "master conductor" of character strengths. Some students may initially think, incorrectly, that the metaphor implies that they are one instrument or strength and the goal is to become a master of that particular strength. However, it is made clear to students that they are not one instrument, but rather they are the conductor, and they have at their disposal 24 different strengths that they can use throughout their lives.

Justin Robinson, Director of the Institute of Positive Education

Figure 5.4 The Geelong Grammar School Symphonic Orchestra in action.

Positive Education, explains how the metaphor of an orchestra of strengths is used to help students to engage with their unique profile of character strengths. Other valuable metaphors that students have suggested for the 24 character strengths include a box of 24 Derwent pencils, a quiver of 24 arrows, and a golf bag containing 24 different clubs.

Character strengths and overcoming difficulties

It is important for staff and students to understand that the character strengths approach is not about avoiding weaknesses, but rather that focusing on strengths can actually be a useful strategy for working on areas of improvement. Students may use their strengths of teamwork and perseverance when trying to master a challenging visual design technique, or their strengths of forgiveness when resolving a conflict with a friend. Over time, building on what works improves confidence, commitment, and determination, and has a run-on effect to other areas.

One activity in the explicit Positive Education program starts with an exploration of realistic and relevant difficulties that students may encounter during the year. Together, students brainstorm different scenarios, such as struggling with a subject, having a difficult time getting along with someone in the Boarding House, adjusting to life in a new country, overcoming procrastination, or feeling pressured into doing something they do not want to do. The whole class then considers each scenario and identifies different ways in which character strengths may be useful in each situation.

After this foundation, students identify a challenge or difficulty that they are facing personally, and explore ways in which they can use their strengths to help them in this challenge. One student from Garnett House identified her challenge as being to "stop being too much of a perfectionist," and decided to apply her strengths of perspective, fairness, teamwork, open-mindedness, and modesty to overcome this.

Many students who complete this activity have an "aha" moment when they understand more fully what it means to action their strengths. Often this process is valuable for students, and once they have grasped the skill they can use it on a regular basis throughout their lives.

Summary and conclusions

The character strengths approach has added great depth and value to the implementation of Positive Education at Geelong Grammar School. Strengths are woven into daily life at the School as staff and students use their own character strengths and celebrate the strengths of others. The VIA framework has provided all members of the School community with a shared language for communicating respect for each other. Exploring the language of strengths creates an appreciation of difference among staff and students, and provides points of connection for parents and other members of the School community. Although character strengths are powerful for all students, they have particular relevance for young children. Character strengths are seen so often in the playground, for example, as children use the strength of kindness to include others in their games, or demonstrate courage by asking to join in themselves.

Encouraging students, staff, and members of the School community to identify, explore, use, and develop their character strengths is a powerful strategy for supporting them to thrive and flourish. The underlying premise is that everyone has unique abilities and capacities that help them to perform at their best. Although, at first glance, character strengths may seem like a way of celebrating individuals, the real heart of the approach is celebrating others and building a sense of meaning and community. The character strengths of each individual are interwoven as each person contributes to the community in diverse and complementary ways.

RECOMMENDED RESOURCES

Fox Eades J M (2008). *Celebrating Strengths: building strength-based schools.* Coventry, UK: CAPP Press.

From Strength to Strength. Lesson plans, posters, and activities. <www.fromstrengthtostrength.com>

Gallup. *Strengths Finder.* <http://strengths.gallup.com>

Geelong Grammar School. *Character Strength Wheel.* <www.ggs.vic.edu.au>

Krouse Rosenthal A (2007). *The OK Book.* New York: Harper Collins. (Illustrated juvenile fiction.)

Let it Ripple. *The Science of Character* (8-minute film). <www.letitripple.org/character>

Linley A (2008). *Average to A+: realising strengths in yourself and others.* Coventry, UK: CAPP Press.

Linley A, Willars J, Biswas-Diener R, and Garcea N (2010). *The Strengths Book.* Coventry, UK: CAPP Press.

Niemiec R M (2014). *Mindfulness and Character Strengths: a practical guide to flourishing.* Ashland, OH: Hogrefe Publishing.

Niemiec R M and Wedding D (2014). *Positive Psychology at the Movies: using films to build character strengths and well-being,* 2nd edn. Ashland, OH: Hogrefe Publishing.

Peterson C and Seligman M E P (2004). *Character Strengths and Virtues: a handbook and classification.* Oxford: Oxford University Press; Washington, DC: American Psychological Association.

Rashid T. <www.tayyabrashid.com> (Character strengths website.)

St Luke's Innovative Resources. <www.innovativeresources.org> (Wide selection of practical resources.)

Values in Action Institute on Character. <www.viacharacter.org> (Resources and assessments.)

Yeager J, Fisher S, and Shearon D (2011). *Smart Strengths: building character, resilience and relationships in youth.* New York: Kravis Publishing.

REFERENCES

Biswas-Diener R, Kashdan T B, and Minhas G (2010). A dynamic approach to psychological strength development and intervention. *Journal of Positive Psychology, 6,* 106–18.

Dahlsgaard K, Peterson C, and Seligman M E P (2005). Shared virtue: the convergence of valued human strengths across culture and history. *Review of General Psychology, 9,* 203–13.

Fox Eades J (2008). *Celebrating Strengths: building strength-based schools.* Coventry, UK: CAPP Press.

Govindji R and Linley P A (2007). Strengths use, self-concordance and well-being: implications for strengths coaching and coaching psychologists. *International Coaching Psychology Review, 2,* 143–53.

Greenwood M (2011). *Simpson and his Donkey.* Sydney, Australia: Walker Books.

Linley A (2008). *Average to A+: realising strengths in yourself and others.* Coventry, UK: CAPP Press.

Linley P A and Harrington S (2006). Playing to your strengths. *Psychologist, 19,* 86–9.

Linley P A et al. (2010). Using signature strengths in pursuit of goals: effects on goal progress, need satisfaction, and well-being, and implications for coaching psychologists. *International Coaching Psychology Review, 5,* 8–17.

Lounsbury J W, Fisher L A, Levy J J, and Welsh D P (2009). An investigation of character strengths in relation to the academic success of college students. *Individual Differences Research, 7,* 52–69.

Park N and Peterson C (2005). The Values in Action Inventory of Character Strengths for Youth. In: K A Moore and L H Lippman (eds) *What Do Children Need To Flourish? Conceptualizing and measuring indicators of positive development.* New York: Springer. pp. 13–23.

Park N and Peterson C (2009). Character strengths: research and practice. *Journal of College and Character, 10,* 4–13.

Park N, Peterson C, and Seligman M E P (2004). Strengths of character and well-being. *Journal of Social and Clinical Psychology, 23,* 603–19.

Peterson C and Seligman M E P (2004). *Character Strengths and Virtues: a handbook and classification.* Oxford: Oxford University Press; Washington, DC: American Psychological Association.

Peterson C and Park N (2011). Classifying and measuring strengths of character. In: S J Lopez and C R Snyder (eds) *Oxford Handbook of Positive Psychology,* 2nd edn. New York: Oxford University Press. pp. 25–33.

Sheldon K M and Lyubomirsky S (2006). How to increase and sustain positive emotion: the effects of expressing gratitude and visualizing best possible selves. *Journal of Positive Psychology, 1,* 73–82.

POSITIVE RELATIONSHIPS

**Introduction by
Professor Roy Baumeister**

For centuries, thinkers have sought to understand the human mind by analyzing how it operates, understands, responds, initiates, thinks, and more. In recent years, however, some critics have pointed out that analyzing the individual human mind may miss a key dimension. The human mind is social, which is to say it is designed to work together with others.

Almost all of human progress reflects this pattern. If you grew up on a deserted island and never spoke to other people, how much could you figure out on your own? In fact, a single mind working alone cannot get very far. All the great achievements of human culture and progress—computers, automobiles, electric lighting, television, recorded music, and myriad others—were the result of many different people building on the achievements of others. Even something as basic as mathematics had to be built up over many generations. If you started on a deserted island, you would have to be a genius even to invent simple counting. The complexities of mathematics (subtraction, multiplication, algebra, trigonometry, and calculus) could only be achieved by people who started where others had left off. It took many centuries before human beings even got the idea of the number zero.

Human beings are animals, and are like many other animals. However, unlike other animals, we have achieved great cultural progress. This difference arises because humans can work together and accumulate knowledge across generations. For every other animal species, each new generation of babies essentially has to start over to discover the world anew. That is why they do not get very far. For example, wolves are highly social animals, just like humans. They seek each other out, form bonds, cooperate, compete, and pursue common goals, just as humans do. However, unlike human beings, each new generation of wolves starts out having to figure everything out for itself. In contrast, each human generation starts by building on what they learned from previous generations. The result is an astonishing difference. Wolves born today live pretty much the same lives as their ancestors did thousands of years ago. In contrast, human life has changed almost beyond recognition over thousands of years, indeed even over hundreds of years. Even just one century ago there was no Internet, no television, hardly any indoor plumbing, cars were rare, and telephones and electricity scarcely existed. Social life and work were radically different to what they are today.

The cultural animal

The key point here is that there is something extraordinary about how human beings relate to each other. To be sure, humans are animals, and we have much in common with other animals. We grow up and grow old, get sick and get better, feel pain, desire contact and pleasure, compete, fight, mate, cooperate, and so forth. Wolves do these things, too. However, there is something else. Humans form a kind of relationship that is different from what other animals do, and that has profound effects.

Some years ago I decided to write a book about human nature. I wanted to read all the research about how human beings think, feel, and act, and pull it together to furnish a portrait of what kind of creature the human being is. After several years of work, I called this book *The Cultural Animal* (Baumeister, 2005). To me, that was the best way to understand what makes human beings human.

By way of context, we need to start with the scientific theory of evolution. Plants and animals were created by evolution, as were human beings. Evolution proceeds by natural selection, which is a ruthless process that forces creatures to compete against each other. The basic principle is that life seeks to sustain life—but nature has never found it possible to create something that will live forever. If immortality (living forever) is impossible, the only way to sustain life is for living things to reproduce—that is, create new life. Crucially, the traits that produce the most offspring are the ones that increase in future generations. If two baby animals were born, and one wanted to eat healthy food while the other wanted to eat stones or did not want to eat at all, only the first one would live long enough to reproduce, and the next generation would consist of its offspring having its appetites. Survival and reproduction are the ways in which nature measures success. Traits that promote survival and reproduction spread and become more common, whereas traits that undermine survival and reproduction tend to die out and disappear. These can even be cultural traits. For example, there have been several religions (such as the Shakers) that strongly disapproved of sexual intercourse. They may have attracted some converts, but they soon died out because the followers of these religions did not produce any children. In contrast, most of the world's great religions have encouraged marriage and the family as ways of producing offspring and providing further generations of believers.

Survival and reproduction are thus the basic challenges for all living things, and species that survive across many centuries find ways to accomplish these. Human beings manage to survive and reproduce by forming relationships with others, sharing information, and developing complex systems with cooperative roles (such as business corporations, governments, musical and theatre groups, and schools), in which different people perform different roles. This is essentially what culture is—a system for cooperating, performing different roles, sharing knowledge, and working together.

The human being is thus naturally designed to form attachments to other people and work with them. It is easy but misleading to think of the human brain as something designed to figure things out and solve problems. It certainly does some of that, but most of what the brain does involves connecting with other people. Of all the things an adult human being knows, only a small part involves what that person has figured out for him- or herself. Most of one's knowledge is learned from others.

The role of schools

Schools are a good example of this. You probably think of school in matter-of-fact terms as something that young people take part in every day. But consider this. Of all the thousands of other creatures that exist on our planet, none of them—not a single one—has schools. Only humankind has schools. The lack of schools is a serious handicap to all other creatures—apes, kangaroos, dogs, bugs, and the like. Without schools, the young animals cannot learn from the older ones, except occasionally by watching and imitating them. If you were a non-human animal, your success would not depend on how much you learned in school. However, there is overwhelming evidence that, for human beings, success in life is strongly linked to how one performs at school. People who do well at school and university make much more money than people who drop out of school early, which is one (imperfect) measure of how much the culture values them. This is partly because schools impart the knowledge that has been built up over many generations. Without schools, humans would be like wolves, with each generation having to start from zero and figure everything out for itself. The human inventions of fire, the wheel, language, and the like were huge steps forward, and although they are taken for granted, if humans did not pass their knowledge on, every new generation of young people would have to invent these things all over again—or try to cope without them.

The purpose of the human brain is thus to connect with other people. It cannot do much on its own, but it can connect with the body of knowledge that has been built up over many generations and use it. The chances that you could invent a mobile telephone by yourself, if you knew nothing and never went to school or learned from other people, would be extremely small. However, if you are born today you will learn how to use these devices very effectively from the culture that has developed around them.

That is why people have a need to belong. Alone, a human being is weak, vulnerable, and ineffective. Imagine a human child abandoned in the jungle alone—it would not live for very long. Even a strong, healthy adult would find it difficult to survive alone in such an environment. People need to work with others to create knowledge, cities, money, technology, and more. People have an innate drive to connect with others, because that is what enabled our ancestors to survive and reproduce.

There are different kinds of relationships. Close, intimate relationships are powerful, important, and satisfying. Casual relationships also matter. Most people have a few intimate relationships and many casual acquaintances. Research suggests that in order to be happy, you need roughly four to six other people who care about you, whom you can talk to, whom you like and who like you. Forming these close bonds is important. Yet the broader networks of shallow relationships are also important, because culture arises from these. For example, there have been remarkable advances in scientific knowledge of physics and chemistry, mainly based on the work of many people who barely knew each other but who shared the results of their own work, allowing knowledge to build up across many generations.

Positive relationships at Geelong Grammar School

I spend a significant amount of my time developing relationships with students. This is what every teacher does at our School. We do this by our involvement in pastoral care, our work in music, drama, sport, and so many other co-curricular activities. The hours spent on pastoral care, and the way in which so many of our House staff carefully manage complex situations, is in the end the difference between good and great outcomes in terms of academic results but, more importantly, life outcomes for students.

Dean Dell'Oro, Head of Corio

In the beautiful Chapel at Timbertop, towards the end of a school year, a student got up to sing. The first few moments were uncertain and the look on his face was one of fear. While performing in front of others may come easily to some people, that was not the case for this young man. However, after a few moments he hit his stride and the song came out clear and smooth. When he had finished singing there was resounding applause. By mid-morning there were notes of encouragement on the Timbertop "What Went Well" board. This student showed many character strengths in this moment—courage, appreciation of beauty and excellence, and humility. More than his individual strengths, however, it was the trust and faith he showed in the other students and the staff that made this moment possible.

This story is not an isolated one. Each year at Timbertop students perform by singing or playing musical instruments in front of their peers. Across all of the campuses, young people take risks and challenge themselves in varied and courageous ways. This is perhaps most evident in the Senior School assemblies, where several students have spoken openly about topics that require great courage, and faith in the School community (for further information, see Box 6.1). A priority at Geelong Grammar School is creating a safe environment where students feel loved and cared for irrespective of their age, gender, sexuality, race, ethnic background, or physical appearance or capabilities. Students who retreat into their comfort zones when around people who are critical and judgmental of them truly thrive when surrounded by people who value them and believe in them. This is the heart of the Positive Relationship domain—the quest to nurture kind, caring, and forgiving relationships across the School community so that students and staff can flourish.

Other people matter

The things that define us as human beings are the relationships we form.

John Hendry, Director of Student Welfare

The role of positive relationships in flourishing cannot be overstated. Feeling connected to other people is a deeply embedded human need (Baumeister and Leary,

> **BOX 6.1: Flourishing relationships at School assemblies**
>
> So often, in schools, events such as assemblies can be seen as "unnecessary" and time-consuming endeavors that take important time away from the core business of teaching and learning. This view could not be further removed from the attitude of staff at Geelong Grammar School, who view School assemblies, celebrations, and Chapel services as the settings where some of the most important lessons are learned. Staff spend time preparing assemblies and planning for students to be involved. Over the years, students have shown incredible courage at the Senior School assemblies in particular. One student made a speech about sexuality and shared his experience of being gay during a celebration of diversity. This student received a standing ovation. Another student spoke about his depression and emotional and mental health difficulties. Another student, who was terrified of public speaking, spoke to the audience about facing her fear, and prompted other students to explore how they too could take small but brave actions to make the School and the world a better place. Assemblies have become known as safe, supportive, and accepting environments, and this has emboldened students, who know that their voices will be heard.

1995). There is a large body of research indicating that social relationships are essential for physical health (Uchino et al., 1996), wellbeing (Diener and Seligman, 2002; Myers, 2000), meaning in life (Hicks and King, 2009; Lambert et al., 2010), and resilience (Cohen and Wills, 1985). In his introduction to this chapter, Professor Baumeister shared the important role that social cooperation has had in the evolution and progress of the human species. Social connectedness is so important for wellbeing that, when asked to summarize Positive Psychology, Professor Chris Peterson responded with the phrase "Other people matter" (Peterson, 2013, p. 127).

Perhaps nowhere is the statement "Other people matter" more relevant than in schools. Feeling connected to their friends and families is essential for students' emotional and social wellbeing in the present, and for their healthy development as they approach adulthood (O'Connor et al., 2011). Research has consistently found that safe and supportive school environments are essential to young people's wellbeing (McGraw et al., 2008). In contrast, critical and turbulent school environments, bullying, and poor social relationships are major risk factors for poor health and for engagement with at-risk behaviors (Resnick et al., 1997). Interestingly, there is also evidence that staff wellbeing is related to how connected staff members feel to their students (Spilt et al., 2011) (see Figure 6.1).

Relationships and learning

> If little kids are happy being at school—if they feel valued and secure and feel a sense of belonging—learning falls into place 99 out of 100 times.
>
> Daryl Moorfoot, Head of Bostock House

Figure 6.1 The importance of positive staff and student relationships.

Most teachers can share a story of a student whose academic work suffered when the student experienced discord in their relationships at school, with their peers, at home, or online. Equally, many teachers can share a story of a student who was struggling academically and who turned their grades around when a teacher found a way to connect meaningfully with them. In fact, many staff working with students who require academic support or assistance focus first on their relationship with the student, trying to understand the student's unique personality, interests, and strengths, and in particular reinforcing what the student does do well.

The quality of students' relationships with their families, teachers, and peers is integrally linked to their school engagement and academic performance (Furrer and Skinner, 2003; Wentzel, 1998; Wentzel and Caldwell, 1997). In one of the most extensive research endeavors in the field to date, Professor John Hattie reviewed more than 800 meta-analyses (or the combined results of over 50,000 research studies) of the role of various influences on student achievement. He found that the greatest predictors of achievement were factors related to the individual students—their prior knowledge, their health and wellbeing, and their expectations of themselves as learners. The second strongest predictor of student learning and academic achievement was the student's relationship with his or her teacher. Across the thousands of research studies included in the meta-analysis, teachers were as powerful in predicting student performance as home, school, and peer factors put together.

It appears that although all relationships are essential for student flourishing, the teacher–student relationship is especially important for student learning.

Connectedness at Geelong Grammar School

The feeling of togetherness generated in a hike group that arrives at Fry's Flat late at night after walking all day battling the heat and the mountains is a memory never to be forgotten.

Roger Herbert, Head of Timbertop

Students involved in the School Productions demonstrate an incredible amount of belonging over the development and rehearsal processes and the performance week. It is such a bonding experience as they feel part of something worthwhile. There is great value in students working with a range of people from different peer and social groups.

Nicholas Mawson, Drama Teacher

It could be said that Geelong Grammar School is built upon a foundation of positive relationships. Toorak campus and Bostock House are both close communities where staff, students, and families care for and support each other. At the Corio and Timbertop campuses, staff and their families and students live alongside each other. The closeness of the School community means that students really get to know their teachers and their families, and vice versa. Students often experience and display a strong sense of loyalty and connectedness to their Houses and Units. Reflections on time spent at Timbertop convey a sense of appreciation of lifelong bonds forged in a context of sharing different and challenging experiences. Across all campuses, the relationship reparation approach and the devotion to high-quality pastoral care have paved the way for caring and respectful relationships. Figures 6.1, 6.2, 6.3, 6.4, and 6.5 show a range of positive relationships across the Geelong Grammar School community. Case Study 6.1 includes a discussion of kindness, forgiveness, and relationships written by John Hendry, Director of Student Welfare, in 2012 and included in student diaries ever since. Case Study 6.2, written by Roger Herbert, Head of Timbertop, describes how supportive relationships are nurtured in Timbertop staff meetings through sharing "What Went Well" (WWW).

There is a growing recognition at Geelong Grammar School and across the educational sector more widely that schools provide an unparalleled opportunity for young people to cultivate strong communication and social skills. The aim of the positive relationships domain is to help students to develop social and emotional skills in order to create and promote strong and nourishing relationships between self and others. For the youngest members of the School community, these skills may involve joining in at the playground or sharing their toys with their friends. For older students such skills may include listening mindfully to others, responding

Figure 6.2 Hikes at Timbertop provide a rich opportunity for great conversations.

Figure 6.3 Junior School students at Bostock House.

Figure 6.4 Student buddies at Toorak.

Figure 6.5 Garry Pierson, Head of Toorak Campus, interacting with students.

CASE STUDY 6.1

Kindness, forgiveness, and reparation

John Hendry, Director of Student Welfare

> The quality of a community (individual relationships, family, community, nation) is not to be judged on its successes, but rather on the humane and constructive approach it employs to the management of mistakes.
>
> John Hendry

People *live* in relationships. However, when people live and work together, disputes are inevitable and errors are made. Relationships are tested. The intimacy of a school community is such that effective dispute resolution is essential if people are to live in relationships where individuals and the community flourish. Disputes can be resolved if the disputing parties accept the need for the reparation process to be transparent and believe that it should be transparent and fair, providing an opportunity to develop a shared understanding of the issues. If both parties feel that they will be well treated, the process can proceed; there will be no residual resentment, and a mechanism for restoring trust, honesty, integrity, compassion, and hope will be created. For this to occur, forgiveness must be exercised by all parties. The aim is to restore dignity to relationships.

The Geelong Grammar School community is one based on trust. When harmful behavior or conflict occurs, we emphasize the need to repair the damage caused to relationships and find mutually acceptable ways forward. This practical philosophy can transform the way in which community members think, feel, and act towards each other.

Forgiveness underpins the School approach to dealing with mistakes. Many mistakes are made by young people through lack of careful attention to others or to rules. Often there is no intention to harm, and when harm is intended, the young people involved may have little real understanding of the effects of their harmful actions. However, actions affect others, and this must be understood for the safety of all.

Geelong Grammar School's approach to relationships is based on moral precepts that value both the individual and the community. Our pastoral principles and behavior management practice promote wholesome, transformative relationships. Intimidation, fear, or the overt exercise of authority are antithetical to our way of thinking and responding. The relationship reparation practices that we use to resolve disputes encourage people to rethink, to learn, to appreciate, and to understand, value, and respect others. Our approach recognizes and attends to difference, and is fundamentally educative. Parties grow through this approach—recognizing mistakes, understanding that mistakes have to be addressed, and thus better understanding life. Parties acknowledge that relationships have been disturbed and need to be repaired, and this requires a co-created positive approach.

The quality of a relationship has many determinants, but fundamentally there are five significant ones, namely trust, forgiveness, integrity, optimism (hope), and compassion. The notion of a relational living world underpins *how* we live together. Errors are, of course, the way in which we learn, and they must be managed positively in a relational sense. Resilience is about recognizing an error and being able to repair in every sense the impact of that error on relationships. This is complex. The error has to be recognized, accepted, and fully understood in terms of its impact. The "error maker" must accept a pivotal role in starting to repair the relationships that have been disturbed. This process begins with acceptance—forgiveness of the self for committing the error, dislocating relationships, and perhaps causing hurt and a sense of loss. Those relational "partners" who have felt that the relationship has been harmed must also accept and acknowledge the error, understand the "error circumstance," forgive the "error maker," and then work *with* the "error maker" to repair the relationship that has been damaged. Collaboration during the repair process is essential, for although the "heavy lifting" is substantially done by the "error maker," the damaged party shares a responsibility to repair the relationship as far as possible. The obligations exist. The process requires all five determinants of a relationship to be addressed both individually and in concert. The objective is to repair and to restore peace.

CASE STUDY 6.2

What Went Well (WWW): one way to create a positive staffroom culture

Roger Herbert, Head of Timbertop

Timbertop students do not have access to mobile phones, social networking, online computers, or television. All members of staff live on campus alongside the students, who are required to make their own decisions in this very supportive environment without relying on Mum and Dad to help them. In this intense "around-the-clock" boarding environment, the staff have daily meetings so that everyone is aware of student wellbeing issues and any operational changes. These daily staff briefings are conducted in a positive atmosphere, adding to—and building on—an already positive culture.

While working in other schools my experience of staffroom meetings was, at times, not positive. Sometimes inappropriate and unthoughtful negative comments were made. It is important to us at Timbertop that the daily staffroom briefings encourage positive emotions for all involved.

Professor Martin Seligman visited Geelong Grammar School in 2007. Soon afterwards, members of staff were trained by Dr Karen Reivich in the major concepts of Positive Psychology. One of the concepts introduced by Dr Reivich and her team was "Blessings" or "Hunt the Good Stuff." Enhancing our gratitude and positivity by "thinking about why events go well, what the positive events mean to us, and how we can create circumstances that enable more good things to occur encourages a consciousness of blessings and molds a style of thinking that promotes optimism about the future" (Reivich, 2010). This counters the natural negativity bias that we have as humans. Negativity is our default setting, and is something that needs to be consciously countered. It is a legacy from our "caveman" days, when we had legitimate reasons for concern—the sabre-tooth tiger prowling around the mouth of our cave, waiting for us to emerge as its next meal, warranted concern.

The commitment to a positive staffroom culture and the arrival of Positive Psychology at Geelong Grammar School seemed a natural fit. The suggestion was that we should share our "Blessings" (or "Hunt the Good Stuff") as a way to start our daily staffroom briefing. The concept was discussed at a management meeting, but the term "Blessings" was considered a little too religious to be used in the context of our staffroom. At one of the first Positive Psychology conferences, Steve Andrew, a teacher from our Corio campus, suggested the title "What Went Well" ("WWW") as an alternative to "Blessings." Initially, What Went Well (WWW) was a challenge to the rapidly developing phenomenon of the "World Wide Web." However, we liked the sound of it, so the concept of WWW was adopted.

Implementation was our next challenge, and we decided that, at the beginning of every daily staff briefing, whoever was running the meeting would call for WWWs. Staff would then respond with little things that had gone well in their personal or professional lives recently. The first time, a few staff members were primed, and ready with positive comments, in case no one had anything to offer. Negative thoughts were discouraged. Staff needed to be ready to contribute, and prepared to think of positive ideas to share prior to the briefing.

The decision was made that three WWWs would be shared daily. A WWW provided me, and others, with a fantastic opportunity to thank staff for all the amazing things they were doing daily—a brilliant morning singing practice, a member of staff volunteering to cover a colleague's duty at lunchtime, or outstanding sensitivity and empathy shown when dealing with a difficult student emotional issue. The list is endless. Starting staff briefings with a number of positive comments countered our "negativity bias" and really set a positive tone for the remainder of the meeting (see Figure 6.6).

In the Timbertop staffroom, WWWs have now been used for a number of years to begin meetings, transforming the sometimes difficult daily briefing into a positive

Figure 6.6 Staff at Timbertop start their daily meetings with a "What Went Well" session.

and welcoming experience. Staff genuinely enjoy coming to briefings because they feel valued and appreciated, and enjoy having a good belly laugh that puts them in a good mood for the remainder of the day. Visitors to Timbertop, either from Corio or from other schools, frequently comment on the warm, humorous, and welcoming staffroom culture that now exists.

assertively to conflict, or giving and receiving help during difficult times. Students are provided with opportunities to practice good relationship skills via collaborative learning and team-based activities. The aim is to support these skills more widely by creating a School culture based on the values of kindness and forgiveness.

Kindness

Kindness is contagious—if you are kind to someone then they will be kind to others and it keeps growing.

Annabelle, Year 5, Middle School, Corio

Kindness provides fertile soil for the cultivation of positive relationships. It is one of the 24 Values in Action (VIA) character strengths, and is motivated by feelings of compassion and care towards others (Peterson and Seligman, 2004). Kindness is closely related to altruism, which is integral to the positive purpose domain (see Chapter 12). Although there is much overlap between the two concepts, the distinction used within the School is that kindness involves care and thoughtfulness among individuals, whereas altruism involves larger acts of service to charity or community groups. Helping a friend with his homework may be considered an act of kindness, whereas running a fundraising campaign for the Karen refugee community may be considered an act of altruism.

For many people across the Geelong Grammar School community and beyond, kindness needs no justification. Teaching young children values such as being compassionate and caring towards others is an important part of shaping their characters and helping them to grow into considerate members of society. Similarly, reminding adults of the power of kindness helps to create workplaces where people treat each other with respect and thoughtfulness. It can be considered an additional benefit, therefore, that research has found kindness to be a pathway towards wellbeing (Buchanan and Bardi, 2010; Dunn et al., 2008; Otake et al., 2006). Several research studies have found that simply being aware of kindness or deliberately practicing acts of kindness leads to improved mood and enhanced wellbeing.

As part of a Positive Education training session, staff members were shown an image of the ripple effect around a single drop of water. Staff were asked to consider this image in terms of how it relates to kindness—when someone receives an act of kindness, they are more likely to act kindly towards others, and the effect spreads. This image was used as the foundation of a Random Acts of Kindness (RAOK) campaign where, for one term, staff members were encouraged to perform and celebrate regular thoughtful acts towards each other. Examples of kind acts performed by staff included covering another teacher's yard duty, leaving flowers on a friend's desk, stopping by someone's office to wish them well before an important assembly or sporting match, and picking up a cup of coffee for a colleague on the way to work. On completing a RAOK, the benefactor would leave a card with a picture of the ripple on it. After receiving a RAOK, the staff member was encouraged to add their story to a staff blog, which became a celebration of kindness across the School. Although this project took place some time ago, staff members on different campuses still enjoy the occasional RAOK card turning up at unexpected times in unexpected but appreciated ways. Activities based on kindness and the student population are described in Boxes 6.2 and 6.3.

Forgiveness

We try to work on creating a culture of forgiveness. If you work from the basis that not everything has to be perfect, you can build a more accepting culture in the room.

Richard Munro, Teacher, Toorak Campus

> **BOX 6.2: Catching a kindness**
>
> A well-known Positive Education activity at Geelong Grammar School is "catching a kindness." Year 5 students are provided with bright fluorescent paper cut into the shape of butterflies. When students notice another student doing a kind deed, they write it on a butterfly and place it in a butterfly net positioned at the front of the classroom. Examples of kind acts that have been "caught" include "sharing snacks at recess when I left mine at home," "helping me pick up all my stuff when I dropped my pencil case," "comforting me and helping me feel better after my dog died," and "To Peter, the bus driver: For being so friendly and driving me safely to school each day." A photo of the students and their butterflies is shown in Figure 6.7. At the end of the week, the butterflies are tipped out of the net and read out loud to the class. They are then stuck on a glass window and the children watch the "swarm" get bigger and bigger as the weeks go by.

Figure 6.7 Students with their 'Catching a Kindness' butterflies.

During Pos Ed we spoke about forgiveness in depth. We learnt that you cannot really move on without forgiving somebody. If you hold a grudge against someone, it is like a burden. If you want to move forward in both of your lives, you actually have to forgive them and acknowledge the wrong-doing and move forward.

Thomas, Year 10, Senior School, Corio

Students in the Early Learning Centre at Toorak Campus were asked what it means to be forgiving. Hamish thought forgiveness meant to "say OK when someone

---

BOX 6.3: Genuine Good Bloke (G²B) Awards

Senior School Captains took the concept of kindness one step further by devising the "Genuine Good Bloke (G²B) Award," with the term "bloke" being used in a gender-inclusive way. Several times throughout the year the School Captains created a staged opportunity where someone needed help, and they filmed the other students' responses. One day, a student deliberately dropped a tray of food in the Dining Hall. Two or three students immediately went to help and comfort her, picking up the food from the floor, while another student went to get a mop. These students were unaware that they were being filmed. The film was played at the following School assembly, and the students who helped were asked to come up on the stage to receive a "G²B Award" for their actions. The films were generally highly entertaining and, more importantly, represented the School Captains demonstrating creativity in their leadership, sending a message to the student body that they wanted to have a School community in which people help each other out.

---

says sorry." Ben's perspective was "saying you are friends again." According to Serene, forgiveness is "giving a big cuddle." While more simple than academic definitions, these children's ideas certainly get to the heart of what it means to forgive. In the research literature, forgiveness is defined as a decrease in angry and revenge-seeking motivations and an increase in empathetic and compassionate motivations (Bono and McCullough, 2006).

Forgiveness is one of the VIA character strengths, indicating its central place in human relationships across time and cultures (Peterson and Seligman, 2004). Andrew Groves, a teacher at Bostock House, explored this concept with his Year 4 class in a Chapel service devoted to the theme of forgiveness. Andrew worked with his students to create a short video on "wise words on forgiveness from Bostock House and from religions around the world." Students interviewed members of the School community about their thoughts on saying sorry and forgiving others. The comments of staff and students were then interwoven with messages of forgiveness from across different religions and in stories, music, and prayers. In particular, students explored the Bible story of Joseph, son of Jacob, who forgave his brothers decades after they had sold him into slavery. The video ended with students sharing their key learning on forgiveness, including "Forgiveness does not fix your past, but it does improve your future" and "Forgiveness starts with me."

Forgiveness has deep roots in empirical literature, and forgiving others is consistently found to be good for both physical and psychological health (Bono et al., 2008; McCullough, 2000). Forgiveness also has social benefits, and is related to empathy, compassionate and satisfying relationships, and pro-social behaviors (Breen et al., 2010; Karremans et al., 2005; Tsang et al., 2006). In contrast, alternatives to forgiveness, such as anger, resentment, and hostility, do little to nurture people physically or emotionally, and can be the cause of enduring distress and dysfunction.

When working with younger children, a key to forgiveness is considering the importance of apologizing sincerely and accepting apologies graciously. Children explore what it means to have empathy and to reflect on different events or scenarios from different people's perspectives. The exploration with older students focuses on helping them to develop a rich understanding of forgiveness, and to practice cultivating it in their lives. Teachers often share stories or examples from the media to stimulate group discussion about the consequences of forgiving or not forgiving others. Some students can mistake forgiveness for being "soft" or "weak." However, through meaningful discussion and reflection they can begin to see that it actually takes great strength to be forgiving.

Often the most meaningful connections are made when students explore the role of forgiveness in their own lives. Dr Michael McCullough, an expert in the field, suggests that people are most likely to forgive when they remember how they have been forgiven in the past, and think about how being forgiven made them feel (McCullough, 2008). With this in mind, students are asked to recall stories of times when forgiveness has played an important role in their own lives. They are also encouraged to explore what it means to hold a grudge and how they can go about letting go of past grudges.

Relationship reparation

> We do not want to shame the child who has made the mistake, or "rub their faces into the ground." We tell students they are still respected citizens of the School community, to hold their heads up, to understand the mistakes they may have made, and to learn from them.
>
> Charlie Scudamore, Vice Principal

When people of all ages work together as closely as they do in schools, mistakes and conflicts are inevitable. At Geelong Grammar School, the aim is to create a culture where forgiveness and empathy are valued over punishment and retribution. Complementing the ethos of Positive Education, the relationship reparation approach involves a shift from how a child should be punished for poor behavior to how all parties can learn from an experience and how hurtful behaviors can be minimized in the future. Students learn that there will be consequences to their actions, but ultimately the goal is to repair the relationship that has been damaged and to help all involved to move forward with dignity.

John Hendry, Director of Student Welfare, and Charlie Scudamore, Vice Principal, have managed student discipline since the implementation of Positive Education. Their aim is to ensure that the way mistakes and transgressions are managed within the School community is consistent with the ethos of Positive Education. This is why the two core values that underpin behavioral management are kindness and forgiveness. As a result of this approach, recidivism has decreased substantially. In order to share key learning with other schools, John Hendry runs training courses for teachers and staff who are looking at how their pastoral care and behavioral management practices can support Positive Education.

Cooperation and communication

I am really good at sharing. I can share toys and books and I can even share friends, too. I always share with my friends at school, and at home with my brother and sisters.

Zara, Early Learning Centre, Toorak Campus

A few years ago, Janis Coffey and Amy Walker, who were Toorak staff members at the time, spread out 100 cardboard boxes on the School oval as part of the unit of inquiry, *Peace Begins with Me*. They gave Year 1 students the challenge of building a city with the boxes, but with certain rules and parameters. There had to be at least three "buildings" that were three boxes high, there had to be a bridge, there had to be something to step over, and there had to be something to crawl through. Janis and Amy set the children to work, videotaping them as they worked. The students launched themselves into this task with zest and determination. However, what they lacked was teamwork and a clear plan. Buildings were built and unbuilt at the same time as different children moved boxes for different tasks. One child would finish making a part of the city and move on, only to have another child take the newly constructed boxes down to use for something else.

After the task had been completed, the students were shown the video and had the opportunity to watch themselves, full of enthusiasm, but often working against each other. After discussing the activity with their teachers, the students could see that the reason why the box city did not work was because they were not talking to each other—they were not collaborating or cooperating. Over the course of the term, the class considered different skills related to communication and conflict resolution. After a couple of months, the students were given the opportunity to repeat the box city activity. This time the first thing they did was to divide themselves into teams and make a plan for the city. Conflicts and competing goals were resolved calmly. The second time around the students constructed a beautiful box city built on a foundation of teamwork and collaboration.

On all Geelong Grammar School campuses there is a strong focus on creating a culture based on respect and cooperation. Schools are often places of competition, especially in the more senior years, when students can be vying for limited university places, positions on selective sports teams, or coveted opportunities such as being a School Captain or the lead in a School performance. Although some degree of competition can be healthy, if the focus on competitiveness is too strong,

> **BOX 6.4: Collaborative handshakes**
>
> In this activity, students gave each other competitive and collaborative handshakes. When instructed to give competitive handshakes, students tried to outdo each other, their grip was tight, and their body language was hostile. When instructed to give collaborative handshakes, the students' grip was firm, their body language was warm and positive, and they looked each other in the eye and smiled. When asked what cooperative relationships look like, students came up with words and phrases such as "friendly," "safe," "tolerant," "full of laughter," and "respectful." Based on this understanding, students were asked to brainstorm principles to guide the development of a School culture based on cooperation. They came up with a range of ideas, such as respect for different people's beliefs, mutual acceptance, safety, empathy, trust, honesty, and harmony.

students can end up assessing their accomplishments in terms of how well they perform relative to their peers, rather than reflecting on their own learning and growth. This can lead to the unhelpful social comparisons that are known to undermine wellbeing (Buunk et al., 1997). To balance this perspective, there is a strong focus on teaching students both the skills and the values required for collaboration. Box 6.4 includes an example of a simple Middle School and Senior School student activity that demonstrates the difference between competitiveness and collaboration.

Positive communication

One of Pam Barton's favorite activities with her Middle School students is called "Compliment Crown." Each morning, Pam pulls the name of a student out of a hat. The students have until just before recess to think of a genuine compliment to pay that person. When the time is right, the student sits in a special chair and wears a special crown. Members of the class take turns to share genuine compliments about the child. In addition to cultivating gratitude for others, Pam uses this activity to teach students about good communication, the importance of eye contact and open body language, and giving and receiving compliments graciously.

Several years ago, Pam had a student in her class who lacked confidence and struggled to make friends. When it was the young boy's turn to wear the "Compliment Crown," he appeared to be embarrassed and uncomfortable. He was slumped in his chair and looked at the ground. His body language seemed to say "Who is going to have anything nice to say about me?" As the class members started talking about the student's strengths and sharing genuine things they liked about him, the boy started to open up more and more. By the end of the activity he was beaming, and threw his head back with laughter. This was a special moment for the young boy, who learned that there was much about him that his peers liked and respected. It was also a special moment for the other students in the class, who learned the power of a few moments spent going out of their way to pay someone a genuine compliment.

Schools are valuable places in which to teach social and communication skills. Although it may be assumed that good communication skills develop naturally, there is growing recognition that such skills can be taught explicitly (Collaborative for Academic, Social, and Emotional Learning, 2003). Needs differ according to age. For example, the youngest students may learn how to take turns in conversations, while the focus with older students may be on how to interact with others safely and respectfully online. With students of all ages, mindfulness plays an important role in good communication. A simple mindfulness exercise that encourages students to spend 2 minutes truly listening to a partner without responding verbally demonstrates the power of being present and attentive during conversations (for a discussion of mindful communication, see Burgoon et al., 2000). Another important social skill, assertive communication, is described in Box 6.5.

Active constructive responding

Active constructive responding is very powerful to use in the Boarding House where you actually have time to sit down with the kids. In giving someone else joy

---

BOX 6.5: Assertiveness role plays

This year, I not only discovered what assertiveness means, but how to use it in my daily life without being rude.

Eliza, Year 7, Middle School, Corio

Many students find it useful to learn the difference between aggressive, passive, and assertive communication. Aggressive communication occurs when a person's own needs are put first. This form of communication is often confrontational, and can lead to conflict. Passive communication occurs when a person's own needs are put last, and the person avoids expressing how they feel and what they want. Assertive communication involves having a balanced view so that the needs of all parties are considered and different perspectives are explored calmly and respectfully. Assertiveness is a key skill for resilience, and is taught at the School in Year 7 as part of the Penn Resiliency Program (Gillham et al., 2008).

At the School, communication skills are often taught through role play. A teacher enlists the help of a colleague to enact aggressive, passive, and finally assertive communication. Following this introduction, students are divided into small groups and given time to create role plays on the various communication styles themselves. This exploration can be insightful, as some students find it extremely difficult to voice their own needs, while others are unaware of a tendency to be overly aggressive. An additional outcome is often that students can be more attuned to times when others may be communicating passively. They can then take steps to support their friends or peers in feeling comfortable expressing their point of view.

in telling their story, it is almost as if you are able to be a little part of it. Often, as teachers, we are the ones standing up at the front of the class. It is really important for students to know that we will actually sit down with them and that we are genuinely interested in what they have to say.

Michael Nelson, Head of Physical Education,
Health and Wellbeing and Assistant Head of Perry House

Active constructive responding (ACR) is a relatively simple skill that involves responding to good news in ways that allow the experience to be shared, deepened, and savored. ACR was developed by Professor Shelly Gable and her colleagues, and has been found to be associated with wellbeing and relationship satisfaction (Gable et al., 2004, 2006).

How people respond to good news generally differs in terms of whether it is active or passive and constructive or destructive. Active destructive responding is critical and dismissive. For example, if a child excitedly brings home to her parents a school result of which she is proud, an active destructive response would be to tell the child that the score was not high enough and that she should have worked harder. This form of responding deflates the child and reduces positive emotions. However, a passive destructive response is also negative, but in a less vocal and communicative way. In this case the parents may either ignore the good result or else warn the student not to be too confident or not to become complacent. If the parents were to divert attention from the child's score and talk about their own performance at school, this would be yet another form of passive destructive response.

Passive constructive responding is a common pitfall in many busy schools and homes. While still supportive, this form of communication is unenthusiastic and uncommunicative. For example, in the above scenario, a passive constructive response might be "Well done. Now please help set the table" or "That's great, we will talk about it later." In contrast, ACR is both positive and communicative. In this form of responding, the parents may compliment their child on her hard work, ask her how she felt when she received the good grade, ask questions to find out more, and spot character strengths that have been used.

At the School, these four types of responses are commonly referred to as "deflate" (active destructive), "steal" (passive destructive), "stall" (passive constructive), and "amplify" (active constructive). Of the four communication types, responding to good news using ACR is the most beneficial for wellbeing and for relationships (Gable et al., 2004). As people tell their stories, they relive and savor the experience, enhancing the positive emotions drawn from it. Within the School, ACR has become an access point to communication that is deep, authentic, and engaged. Staff often comment on its usefulness in the classroom and Boarding Houses as they use the skill to connect meaningfully with students who share good news with them. Box 6.6 presents a discussion of the "bucket-and-dipper" theory, which is another helpful way of exploring relationships with students (Rath and Clifton, 2004).

> **BOX 6.6: Bucket-and-dipper theory**
>
> Based on the work of Tom Rath and Dr Donald Clifton, the simple bucket-and-dipper theory (Rath and Clifton, 2004) has become a metaphor for positive relationships around the School. The underlying idea is that everyone has an invisible bucket. When buckets are full or overflowing, people feel happy, connected, and energized. When buckets are depleted, people feel miserable and exhausted. Everyone also has an invisible dipper. This dipper can be used either to fill other people's buckets or to dip from them. Examples of behaviors that fill a bucket include listening attentively, spotting strengths, and performing kind or thoughtful acts. Examples of behaviors that dip from a bucket include bullying, excluding others, or criticizing. This simple language provides a useful starting point for even the youngest students to explore what positive and negative behaviors look like. With their teachers, students may consider the case of a new student arriving at the School. They may brainstorm bucket-filler behaviors such as saying hello, learning the person's name, and asking him questions about himself. They may also brainstorm bucket-dipper behaviors such as ignoring the new person, leaving him out of games, or making comments about him to others.

Self-compassion and forgiveness

The positive relationships domain of the Model for Positive Education prioritizes strong and nourishing relationships with the *self* and others. The inclusion of nourishing relationships with the self in the domain was a very deliberate decision by the Positive Education team. The team felt strongly that the relationship with the self is often overlooked within efforts to promote healthy relationships. Furthermore, in many instances, people are a lot less kind to themselves than they are to their friends or even their acquaintances. It is easy for young people (and adults) to be extremely critical of their own actions, appearance, and social interactions.

Exploring self-compassion is one avenue towards developing a warm and caring stance towards the self. According to Associate Professor Kristin Neff, self-compassion involves being kind to the self, recognizing that making mistakes is a part of life, and having a balanced and mindful view of both positive and negative emotions (Neff, 2011). The similar concept of self-forgiveness involves forgiving the self in much the same way that one would forgive *someone else* (Hall and Fincham, 2005). These concepts also dovetail with Dr Tal Ben-Shahar's concept of "the permission to be human," discussed in Chapter 7 (Ben-Shahar, 2007). Through cultivating self-compassion, students are encouraged to treat themselves in the same way that they would treat a close friend (for an activity based on this concept, see Box 6.7). This exploration can also be supported by loving-kindness meditations that focus on generating warm and nurturing feelings towards the self and others.

> **BOX 6.7:** Nurturing self-compassion
>
> As part of their "Pos Ed" classes, Year 10 students are asked to pick one critical statement that they say to themselves on a regular basis. This could be something about their physical appearance, their academic performance, or their personality (e.g. "I am too tall," "I am always so disorganized," or "I always say the wrong thing and look stupid"). Students are asked to consider what they would say to a friend who was criticizing him- or herself in such a way. This can lead to meaningful insights as students realize how much kinder they are to their friends than they are to themselves. The students are encouraged to write in their journals about this process, and to explore any thoughts or feelings that arise.

Self-compassion has been a recent addition to the multi-day Positive Education training courses for staff and parents. During the training, staff and parents learn that one important aspect of self-compassion is seeking and accepting help and support. Together, the group explores the idea that sometimes people have a tendency to avoid asking for help, as they would like to appear strong, as if they have everything under control. Accepting support from others is discussed as a form of kindness to the self, which leads into a discussion of the benefits of seeking help in personal, health, and work contexts.

Summary and conclusions

> I do think love is the right word for a lot of things I see happening or I experience at this School ... I am talking about love in the form of compassion, kindness, respect, and a genuine enjoyment of another person's company. I see love as something we have within the majority of our friendships. I see love as something present within the dynamic of most Houses.
>
> Dani Davidovits, School Prefect, 2013, Senior School Assembly

When adults are asked to think back to their schooling experiences, it is often their relationships that they remember most clearly. They describe teachers who inspired them or made them feel important, and close friends with whom they shared the ups and downs of the journey. Rather than stories describing how they achieved something on their own, adults often reminisce about moments of togetherness, such as being part of a close sports team, an engaging camp, or a meaningful community project. Although many memories of school may fade, relationships often stand the test of time, and students maintain friendships and connections years or even decades after they have left the school grounds.

Geelong Grammar School has a rich history of nurturing strong relationships. Within the close and supportive community, the School has long upheld the notion that "other people matter." The positive relationships domain is a pertinent example of how existing practices and structures within the School have been strengthened and deepened by Positive Education concepts and language. The character strengths of kindness and forgiveness are cornerstones of the School community, and help to create a culture in which mistakes are responded to with compassion and dignity. ACR has become a reference term for taking the time to listen to and communicate with others in mindful and authentic ways. Another valuable endeavor involves helping students to cultivate feelings of warmth and compassion towards themselves, with the recognition that young people can be their own worst critics.

The positive relationships domain is a case in point of the power of a preventative and proactive approach. Schools commonly use reactive models that focus on responding quickly and effectively to poor behavior, conflict between students, and bullying. The aim at Geelong Grammar School is to create a culture in which such behaviors are minimized in the first place. A conviction held by staff is that people have the power to harm each other and to heal each other, and they should always aim to heal. When students have strong social and emotional skills and when they are aware of how their behaviors impact on others, conflict will be minimized. The result is a School community in which staff and students feel safe, valued, and respected, and where there are meaningful and authentic connections between staff, students, and other members of the community.

RECOMMENDED RESOURCES

Brene B (2010). *The Power of Vulnerability. TED Talk.* <www.ted.com/talks/brene_brown_on_vulnerability>

Cooper I (2007). *The Golden Rule.* New York: Abrams Books for Young Readers. (Children's picture storybook.)

Cozolino L (2013). *The Social Neuroscience of Education: optimising attachment and learning in the classroom.* New York: W. W. Norton & Company.

Fetzer Institute. <www.fetzer.org>

Forgiveness Project. <http://theforgivenessproject.com>

Goleman D (2006). *Emotional Intelligence: why it can matter more than IQ,* 10th anniversary edn. New York: Bantam Books.

Gottman Institute. <www.gottman.com>

Hicks D (2011). *Dignity: the essential role it plays in resolving conflict.* York, PA: Yale University Press.

Krznaric R (2012). *The Power of Outrospection: RSA Animate.* <www.thersa.org/events/rsaanimate/animate/power-of-outrospection>

Life Vest Inside. <www.lifevestinside.com> (Videos and projects.)

Neff K. Self-Compassion. <www.self-compassion.org> (Exercises, videos, and information.)

Random Acts of Kindness Foundation. <www.randomactsofkindness.org> (Lesson plans and activities.)

Rath T and Clifton D (2004). *How Full is your Bucket?* New York: Gallup Press.

Rath T and Reckmeyer M (2009). *How Full is your Bucket? For kids.* New York: Gallup Press. (Children's picture storybook.)

The Art of Conversation. <www.taoc.com.au> (Cards and games.)

REFERENCES

Baumeister R F (2005). *The Cultural Animal: human nature, meaning, and social life.* Oxford: Oxford University Press.

Baumeister R F and Leary M R (1995). The need to belong: desire for interpersonal attachments as a fundamental human motivation. *Psychological Bulletin, 117,* 497–529.

Ben-Shahar T (2007). *Happier.* New York: McGraw Hill.

Bono G and McCullough M E (2006). Positive responses to benefit and harm: bringing forgiveness and gratitude into cognitive psychotherapy. *Journal of Cognitive Psychotherapy, 20,* 147–58.

Bono G, McCullough M E, and Root L M (2008). Forgiveness, feeling connected to others, and well-being: two longitudinal studies. *Personality and Social Psychology Bulletin, 34,* 182–95.

Breen W E, Kashdan T B, Lenser M L, and Fincham F D (2010). Gratitude and forgiveness: convergence and divergence on self-report and informant ratings. *Personality and Individual Differences, 49,* 932–7.

Buchanan K E and Bardi A (2010). Acts of kindness and acts of novelty affect life satisfaction. *Journal of Social Psychology, 150,* 235–7.

Burgoon J K, Berger C R, and Waldron V R (2000). Mindfulness and interpersonal communication. *Journal of Social Issues, 56,* 105–27.

Buunk B P, Gibbons F X, and Buunk A (1997). *Health, Coping, and Well-Being: perspectives from social comparison theory.* Mahwah, NJ: Lawrence Erlbaum.

Cohen S and Wills T A (1985). Stress, social support, and the buffering hypothesis. *Psychological Bulletin, 98*, 310–57.

Collaborative for Academic, Social, and Emotional Learning (CASEL) (2003). *Safe and Sound: an educational leader's guide to evidence-based social and emotional learning (SEL) programs.* Chicago, IL: CASEL.

Diener E and Seligman M E P (2002). Very happy people. *Psychological Science, 13*, 81–4.

Dunn E W, Aknin L B, and Norton M I (2008). Spending money on others promotes happiness. *Science, 319*, 1687–8.

Furrer C and Skinner E (2003). Sense of relatedness as a factor in children's academic engagement and performance. *Journal of Educational Psychology, 95*, 148–62.

Gable S L, Reis H T, Impett E A, and Asher E R (2004). What do you do when things go right? The intrapersonal and interpersonal benefits of sharing positive events. *Journal of Personality and Social Psychology, 87*, 228–45.

Gable S L, Gonzaga G C, and Strachman A (2006). Will you be there for me when things go right? Supportive responses to positive event disclosures. *Journal of Personality and Social Psychology, 91*, 904–17.

Gillham J E, Reivich K J, and Jaycox L H (2008). *The Penn Resiliency Program (also known as the Penn Depression Prevention Program and the Penn Optimism Program): leader's manual.* Philadelphia, PA: University of Pennsylvania.

Hall J H and Fincham F D (2005). Self-forgiveness: the stepchild of forgiveness research. *Journal of Social and Clinical Psychology, 24*, 621–37.

Hicks J A and King L A (2009). Positive mood and social relatedness as information about meaning in life. *Journal of Positive Psychology, 4*, 471–82.

Karremans J C, Van Lange P A M, and Holland R W (2005). Forgiveness and its associations with prosocial thinking, feeling, and doing beyond the relationship with the offender. *Personality and Social Psychology Bulletin, 31*, 1315–26.

Lambert N M et al. (2010). Family as a salient source of meaning in young adulthood. *Journal of Positive Psychology, 5*, 367–76.

McCullough M E (2000). Forgiveness as human strength: theory, measurement, and links to well-being. *Journal of Social and Clinical Psychology, 19*, 43–55.

McCullough M E (2008). *Beyond Revenge: the evolution of the forgiveness instinct.* San Francisco, CA: Jossey-Bass.

McGraw K, Moore S, Fuller A, and Bates G (2008). Family, peer and school connectedness in final year secondary school students. *Australian Psychologist, 43*, 27–37.

Myers D G (2000). The funds, friends, and faith of happy people. *American Psychologist, 55,* 56–67.

Neff K (2011). *Self-Compassion: stop beating yourself up and leave insecurity behind.* New York: William Morrow.

O'Connor M et al. (2011). Predictors of positive development in emerging adulthood. *Journal of Youth and Adolescence, 40,* 860–74.

Otake K et al. (2006). Happy people become happier through kindness: a counting kindnesses intervention. *Journal of Happiness Studies, 7,* 361–75.

Peterson C (2013). *Pursuing the Good Life: 100 reflections on positive psychology.* Oxford: Oxford University Press.

Peterson C and Seligman M E P (2004). *Character Strengths and Virtues: a handbook and classification.* Oxford: Oxford University Press; Washington, DC: American Psychological Association.

Rath T and Clifton D O (2004). *How Full is your Bucket?* New York: Gallup Press.

Reivich K (2010). *Master Resilience Training Trainer Manual.* Philadelphia, PA: University of Pennsylvania.

Resnick M D et al. (1997). Protecting adolescents from harm. *Journal of the American Medical Association, 278,* 823–32.

Spilt J L, Koomen H M, and Thijs J T (2011). Teacher wellbeing: the importance of teacher–student relationships. *Educational Psychology Review, 23,* 457–77.

Tsang J, McCullough M E, and Fincham F D (2006). The longitudinal association between forgiveness and relationship closeness and commitment. *Journal of Social and Clinical Psychology, 25,* 448–72.

Uchino B N, Cacioppo J T, and Kiecolt-Glaser J K (1996). The relationship between social support and physiological processes: a review with emphasis on underlying mechanisms and implications for health. *Psychological Bulletin, 119,* 488–531.

Wentzel K R (1998). Social relationships and motivation in middle school: the role of parents, teachers, and peers. *Journal of Educational Psychology, 90,* 202–9.

Wentzel K R and Caldwell K (1997). Friendships, peer acceptance, and group membership: relations to academic achievement in middle school. *Child Development, 68,* 1198–209.

POSITIVE EMOTIONS

**Introduction by
Professor Barbara Fredrickson**

In early 2008, I spent several weeks on the Geelong Grammar School campus, teach-ing about the science of positive emotions and learning first-hand about Geelong Grammar School's noble aspirations. Never before have I seen an entire school so committed to taking a holistic, ambitious, and proactive approach to protecting and elevating the emotional wellbeing and health of all of its students. When speaking with teachers, staff, and administrators, I was struck by the compassion, sincerity, and in-vestment that each member of the Geelong Grammar School community was already devoting to their shared vision of transforming their School to become a beacon of Positive Education.

Now, 5 years later, I am even more impressed with how thoroughly and judiciously all in the Geelong Grammar School community have worked to bring their visions to life, transforming their culture and practices from the inside out for the benefit of their stu-dents, and also, not incidentally, for the benefit of the entire Geelong Grammar School—community, teachers, staff, and parents as well. Their Model for Positive Education may now serve as the model for any school in the world that is open to, and interested in, helping students to learn the essential life skills—beyond the standard curricula in

Science, Mathematics, and Literature—that will help them to flourish in life, to find both happiness and meaning, and to make important and lasting contributions to their communities and the world.

I am honored to have played even a small part in Geelong Grammar School's admirable goal of transforming educational practices, not just at their own school, but also—through sharing their insights—worldwide. I was delighted, therefore, to accept the invitation that was extended to me to write an introduction to this chapter on positive emotions. The chapter offers an impressive application of the scientific evidence on how all emotions— negative and positive—together with a toolkit of emotional skills can set students on a pathway towards lifelong flourishing. My goal in this brief introduction is to provide a state-of-the-science overview of theory and research on positive emotions, in order to ground the reader's appreciation of Geelong Grammar School's efforts to apply this science.

Are emotions in fact malleable? This is a reasonable question to raise. As is the case for all people, students' daily lives can brim with emotional upsets. Unforeseen obstacles, incivilities, rebuffs, insults, and arguments abound. These and other upsets often ignite the pain of anger, anxiety, or sadness, with their attendant downward spirals and destructive behaviors.

Although the link between negative events and negative emotions can seem automatic and altogether inescapable, kids and teenagers—like all people—actually have enormous choice in how they respond to the slings and arrows of daily life. What does it take for a student to experience these and other upsets *without* inner turmoil or outer destructiveness? Is it possible?

Indeed it is possible. What it takes is the ability to regulate one's own attention and cognition in the service of recognizing and appreciating negative emotional states. This provides a strong foundation for cultivating inner states that are more open and optimistic—states that till the soil for positive emotions to take root, ranging from serenity and inspiration to joy, gratitude, and more. This overview, anchored in empirical evidence, outlines why these skills are important, and how they can be learned.

The beneficial correlates of positive emotions

People who experience positive emotions more frequently than others seem to have it made. Scientific evidence documents that they are more resilient to life's adversities, more socially connected, and more successful in their personal and work lives. They are also healthier, with lower rates of hypertension and cardiovascular disease. They even fall prey to fewer viruses, such as the common cold. Added to this, they live up to 10 years longer than those who experience the least positive emotions (for an accessible review, see Fredrickson, 2009).

To the extent that people assume that trait-positive affect is an immutable, biological given, encountering research findings like these can be disheartening. Still, there is reason for hope. Although heritable, evidence suggests that only about 50% of individual differences in trait affect are genetically determined, with the remaining 50% reflecting a combination of life circumstances and daily habits (Lyubomirsky et al., 2005), which can and do change, especially with age. Indeed, age-related changes in emotions are striking, with younger adults favoring negative information and older adults favoring the positive (Mather and Carstensen, 2005). Key to this wisdom of old age appears to be the ability to accept negative emotions (Shallcross et al., 2013) and flexibly self-generate positive emotions.

More than a decade of empirical work on the broaden-and-build theory of positive emotions (Fredrickson, 1998, 2001, 2009) casts these emotions as key drivers of personal growth and resilience, not simply the products of them. Below, I describe how positive emotions can widen one's perspective on life and build personal resources such as mindfulness and the ability to connect with others. Through incremental broaden-and-build processes, micro-moments of positive emotions grow into stable affective dispositions that foster people's physical health and render their lives more satisfying. In short, positive emotions are a key engine of flourishing.

Positive emotions as means, not ends

The first tenet of the broaden-and-build theory is that positive emotions expand people's awareness, temporarily allowing them to take in more of their surrounding contextual information than they do during neutral or negative states (Fredrickson, 1998, 2001). This momentary cognitive effect of positive emotions has been demonstrated in a wide range of tightly controlled experiments carried out in multiple laboratories. For instance, experimentally induced positive emotions have been shown to broaden the scope of people's visual attention in behavior tests (Fredrickson and Branigan, 2005), including tests that measure fine-grained behavioral responses using reaction times of milliseconds (Rowe et al., 2007) and eye-tracking technology (Wadlinger and Isaacowitz, 2006). Moreover, experiments with brain imaging (e.g. functional MRI) reveal that positive emotions expand people's field of view at very early perceptual encoding stages (Schmitz et al., 2009; see also Soto et al., 2009). Positive emotions, then, quite literally widen people's outlook on the world around them (for a contrasting view for approach-motivated positive affect, see Gable and Harmon-Jones, 2008).

Although the expansion of awareness that comes with positive emotions is as subtle and as short-lived as the emotion itself, it accounts for positivity-related increases in creativity (Rowe Hirsh and Anderson, 2007), and may well account for the documented benefits of positive emotions for autobiographical memory, integrative decision making, test and work performance, coping and resilience, interpersonal trust, social connection, teamwork, and negotiation ability (for a review, see Fredrickson, 2009, 2013). In short, open and flexible awareness and thinking are core attributes of positive emotional states.

Positive emotions transform lives

The second tenet of the broaden-and-build theory is that, over time, the momentary states of expanded awareness sparked by positive emotions accumulate and compound to build durable personal and social resources that ultimately reshape people's lives for the better (Fredrickson, 1998, 2001, 2009, 2013). This means that people who learn skills to self-generate positive emotions (which in turn allow them to increase their daily diets of positive emotions) build resources and resilience that help to minimize future suffering and cultivate future health and wellbeing. Recent randomized controlled trials have tested the effects of learning loving-kindness meditation as a means of self-generating positive emotions more frequently (for further information on this ancient Buddhist mind-training practice, see Salzberg, 1997). The results indicate that, relative to a control group, loving-kindness meditation practice reliably elevates positive emotions (Fredrickson et al., 2008). Most importantly, however, the upward shift in positive emotions evident in people practicing loving-kindness meditation also increases their personal resources, including their mindfulness, their environmental mastery, their positive relationships with others, and their self-reported health. In turn, these increased resources account for reduced depressive symptoms and improved life satisfaction (Fredrickson et al., 2008). As loving-kindness meditation increases daily positive emotions, it has also been shown to increase cardiac vagal tone (Kok et al., 2013), which is a marker of both physical health and behavioral flexibility (Thayer and Sternberg, 2006). This growing research on the long-range health and psychological benefits of cultivating positive emotional states provides a compelling rationale for considering the value of learning to self-generate positive emotions in daily life.

Upward spirals counter downward spirals

Because both positive and negative emotions alter people's attention, thinking, motivation, and behavior, they also trigger self-perpetuating dynamics—or spirals—that can either drag people down or buoy them up. For example, the negative emotions of anger, stress, or sadness each narrow people's attention and reinforce emotion-consistent appraisal patterns (e.g. blame, threat, or loss, respectively) that initiate further bouts of anger, stress, or sadness, with attendant social friction or isolation. These cycles perpetuate themselves to produce the downward spirals that are all too familiar to teachers and school counselors.

The broaden-and-build theory holds that positive emotions create opposing upward spiral dynamics, in which the broadened awareness that accompanies positive emotions allows people to step back or "decentre" from stressful circumstances and appraise them in a more positive light, which in turn can trigger further experiences of positive emotions. As this upward spiral unfolds, it creates resilience, wellbeing, and greater opportunities for social connection. A number of prospective studies have now documented this upward spiral dynamic, and there is also emerging evidence that upward spirals might drive neuroplasticity in ways that can be productively applied within psychotherapy (Garland et al., 2010).

Using the broaden-and-build theory to help students to flourish

The broaden-and-build theory originated to explain how positive emotions were shaped by the forces of natural selection. The key is that, over time and through repeated experiences, these fleeting pleasant states augmented our human ancestors' resources for survival. Although the theory has been tested primarily in healthy adult populations with typical life stressors, experienced teachers at Geelong Grammar School have created education-based applications of the theory, suitable for a wide age range of students. These applications are the focus of the following evidence-based chapter.

When students and educators alike come to understand how positive emotions work—how they open minds, transform futures, and create uplifting spiral dynamics—they are more likely to see the wisdom of cultivating these heartfelt momentary experiences more frequently. Seen from the perspective of the broaden-and-build theory, unlocking more momentary experiences of positive emotions is not simply the end goal of a desire to feel good, but rather it is an important vehicle for reshaping students' abiding levels of resilience, health, and wellbeing as well as a host of other resources and personality traits that make life more satisfying and meaningful. In short, trait affect can change—children, adolescents, and teachers can learn to self-generate more frequent positive emotions, which can have sweeping repercussions throughout their lives as a whole.

Positive emotions at Geelong Grammar School

It is not eliminating or ignoring emotions. It is good to be angry, it is good to be scared, it is good to have the full gambit of emotions. Positive Psychology is really about engaging with your full emotional range and understanding it—but also identifying when you are in a downward spiral and learning how to recover, how to move on.

Charlie Scudamore, Vice Principal

Year 7 students were asked to share what they had learned from Positive Education. One young student explained that he no longer gets so upset when he is started on the bench during a football game. Another student described how she is better at controlling her anger and as a result is receiving fewer technical fouls on the basketball court. One student shared that she is better able to keep calm during tests. Another said that he does not yell so much when things do not go his way.

The aim of the positive emotions domain is to cultivate emotional health and wellbeing in students, staff, and members of the Geelong Grammar School community. Students of all ages experience a range of emotions on a daily basis. Interactions with their friends can be a source of joy and happiness, but also of conflict and frustration. Students can feel stress and anxiety about upcoming deadlines or exams, as well as pride and excitement about their goals and accomplishments. One of the gifts that schools can give students is an enhanced understanding of their emotions and of the emotions of others. These skills are also relevant for staff and members of the wider School community, as adults benefit equally from emotional health. At a wider level, emotional wellbeing is supported by a school culture that fosters inclusion and belonging, where everyone feels safe and respected.

Although all emotions are central to the Model for Positive Education, positive emotions have a special place. Professor Fredrickson's broaden-and-build theory (Fredrickson, 2004), as she eloquently describes in her introduction to this chapter, and the substantial research evidence that supports the power of positive emotions in creating upward spirals towards wellbeing, provide a rich rationale for building positive emotions in schools. Therefore a core aim of Positive Education is to help people to anticipate, initiate, experience, prolong, and build positive emotional experiences. Figures 7.1, 7.2, 7.3, and 7.4 show students from different campuses having fun and experiencing positive emotions.

Emotional wellbeing

A building block of emotional wellbeing is identifying and understanding the emotions of the self and others. It is hoped that students and staff learn to recognize and acknowledge their feelings without being consumed by them. Research has consistently found that young people who can communicate how they are feeling and regulate their emotions experience good mental health (Eisenberg

Figure 7.1 Nothing like good old-fashioned fun.

Figure 7.2 Toorak students displaying zest and enthusiasm.

Figure 7.3 Senior students sharing and celebrating birthdays within their tutorial group.

Figure 7.4 Timbertop students embracing the adventure of their hike.

et al., 2003; Rydell et al., 2003). Students who have strong emotional awareness cope well with distressing situations, whereas students who struggle to understand their emotions can be overwhelmed when faced with everyday hassles and challenges. Understanding feelings is a pathway to good communication, and students with high levels of empathy often flourish socially. Researchers have even found a connection between emotional health and academic performance, suggesting that students who have well-developed emotional regulation skills thrive in their studies (Gumora and Arsenio, 2002).

An objective of Positive Education is to help students to develop emotional literacy, or the language to express and communicate their feelings. In the early primary years, prompts such as pictures, toys, and books are used to teach students about different emotions. Students are read stories and encouraged to explore how various characters may have been feeling, and how their feelings could have influenced their actions. Another useful activity is to ask children to brainstorm how they would explain various emotions to an alien who is totally unfamiliar with the concept. Students come up with creative physical sensations and clever metaphors in response to this (e.g. joy is like having bubbles in your heart, and sadness feels dark, heavy, and grey). Such activities help young children to become competent and confident in talking about their feelings.

Just as importantly, older students are taught explicit classes on identifying the range of human emotions. One activity uses emotion cue cards as a basis for role plays that help students to create meaningful connections between feelings and actions. These explicit lessons are supported by implicit learning, such as investigating how the body responds to different emotions in Science, or exploring the impact of songs on feelings in Music. Further details about a lesson that uses colorful lollies or sweets to help students to develop confidence in talking about their feelings are provided in Box 7.1.

BOX 7.1: Emotional Skittles

An engaging way of increasing students' understanding of emotions is through using colorful pieces of confectionary. Each student is given a small bag of Skittles. The teacher encourages the class to select one color. The students then brainstorm emotions that this color may represent—for example, blue may be associated with serenity or alternatively with sadness, yellow with happiness, red with anger, or brown with frustration. There are no right or wrong answers—the class decides together as a group. Next, the students are invited to reflect on a recent time when they have felt this emotion, and to discuss it with a partner. Together the students explore the experience in some depth, including their thoughts, feelings, and actions at the time. Once the students have practiced talking about the particular feeling, they are welcome to eat any Skittles of this nominated color. The students are generally eager to move on to sharing stories about the next color.

Emotional responsibility

Within the School, "emotional responsibility" refers to being aware of emotions and mindful of the impact of behaviors on others. One pertinent example is anger. Everyone feels angry sometimes, but it is important to be aware of the danger of becoming overwhelmed by anger and acting in ways that hurt others. Staff and students of all ages are taught skills that help them to regulate strong emotions. Many of these skills are covered in Chapters 8 and 9, and focus on an awareness of how thoughts, feelings, and behaviors are connected. In addition, students are taught calming techniques such as slow breathing, walking away, and counting to 20. These emotional regulation skills were initially taught to students by staff. However, students are increasingly encouraging each other to slow down when they are at a point of crisis. A technique that started in Garnett House and caught on is called "fluttering hands," and involves fanning oneself with both hands, with the fingers pointing inwards. This action often leads to tension dissolving into fits of laughter. Such simple skills and strategies give students time and space to find perspective before addressing the underlying issue.

Positive emotions and flourishing

While at Geelong Grammar School, Professor Seligman spoke several times to the wider School community. At these presentations he asked parents in the audience to share their deepest wishes for their children. Several parents said they hoped that their children would experience love. Others said they wished for them to have contentment, hope, or peace. Many cited happiness. Not one parent said a perfect report card, plenty of money, or abundant success. The message of this activity was clear—a flourishing life entails experiencing frequent positive emotions such as joy, contentment, and excitement. Positive emotions are powerful signals that life is going well, whereas a sustained absence of positive emotions is often a symptom of mental ill health and depression.

The broaden-and-build theory of Fredrickson (2004), as she outlines in her introduction to this chapter, provides an explanation as to why positive emotions are so valuable in schools. Negative emotions lead to a narrowing and restricting of attention. When a child misbehaves, a teacher may experience frustration or disappointment. The teacher's attention may narrow to focus on the student until the challenging behavior has been responded to appropriately. In contrast, positive emotions widen focus and support broad, creative, and flexible thinking and behaviors. A teacher who experiences interest or curiosity may explore and investigate, creating new ideas for use in the classroom. Shared amusement may help staff members to reach out and connect with each other. Over time, positive emotions build enduring resources and lead to an enhanced ability to capitalize on opportunities, cope with challenges, and deal with adversity.

Fredrickson (2009) proposes 10 positive emotions that are especially important for flourishing—joy, gratitude, serenity, interest, hope, pride, amusement, inspiration, awe, and love. Fredrickson selected these 10 emotions because they have been the focus of substantial scientific research, and because she believes that they are the positive emotions people most commonly experience. She makes a special mention of love as the most powerful and encompassing emotion, with feelings of love including a range of other key positive emotions, such as joy, gratitude, and hope.

The explicit Positive Education program in the later years at the School involves an overview of the broaden-and-build theory and a replication of some of Fredrickson's experiments. This empowers young people with enriched knowledge of how their emotions influence their thoughts, actions, and relationships. In addition, the broaden-and-build theory has infiltrated classrooms and influenced pedagogy. Teachers may start a class with a short activity or media clip that creates positive emotions, generating a platform for creative and open thinking. Similarly, the evoking of joy or amusement can be used to defuse tension or conflict that might disrupt cooperation or distract from learning. Prior to examinations, Year 10 students are given the opportunity to choose one activity from a range of experiences aimed at boosting positive emotions, including taking part in a drumming workshop, doing yoga and meditation, or watching an inspiring movie. Box 7.2 provides an example of an explicit activity based on the broaden-and-build theory, which is used with senior students.

Cultivating positive emotions

Evidence suggests that many young people do not experience a healthy ratio of positive to negative emotions. In an Australian study of more than 10,000 children and adolescents, a substantial proportion of students were found to experience frequent negative states, such as stress, depression, and anger, and few positive feelings, such as happiness and a sense of belonging (Bernard et al., 2007). For example, 41% of the students in the study reported that they worried a lot, and 21% reported that they often felt hopeless and depressed. Such statistics underscore why it is essential that schools help students to develop emotional health and wellbeing and, just as importantly, provide access to supportive services for students who are struggling.

Fredrickson's positivity toolkit includes 12 evidence-based strategies for cultivating positive emotions (Fredrickson, 2009). These strategies are integrated across the Model for Positive Education. For example, students and staff are exposed to mindfulness activities, including mindfulness meditation and loving-kindness meditation. They are also encouraged to be open and curious about their surroundings and experiences. Resilience lessons have a strong focus on disputing unhelpful negative thought patterns and developing healthy distractions for times of excessive negativity. Across the Model, students are encouraged to nurture high-quality

---

BOX 7.2: Exploring positivity

The broaden-and-build theory provides a useful point for discussion and exploration within the explicit curriculum. In one lesson, the class is asked to brainstorm as many positive emotions as they can. The students are then introduced to Fredrickson's 10 key positive emotions and provided with an overview of research on the broaden-and-build theory (interested students are also provided with relevant research articles to extend their knowledge and understanding).

Following this introduction, the students take part in a mini-replication of a broaden-and-build experiment. The class is divided into three groups—neutral, negative emotions, and positive emotions. First, the neutral group is given 2 minutes to write a list of all the things they would like to do in their next hour of leisure time. Secondly, students in the negative emotions group are shown an appropriate clip designed to evoke mild sadness or frustration. These students are then given 2 minutes to create a leisure activity list. Thirdly, a clip designed to cultivate humor or happiness is played, followed by a chance for the positive emotions group to generate their lists.

After all of the groups have had their turn, the students count the number of leisure activities they generated and group totals are calculated. Often—but not always—the results within the classroom replicate the research findings, and the positive emotions group have compiled the longest and most creative list of potential leisure activities. Students who have been "primed" with positive emotions often brainstorm a broad range of activities that use a diverse array of strengths, such as composing music, performing a random act of kindness, or planning for a community service project. This mini-experiment invariably leads to inter-esting discussion and debate, with students often sharing creative and thought-provoking insights into how both positive and negative feelings impact on behaviors in different contexts.

---

relationships, engage in acts of service and altruism, visualize future possibilities, spend time in nature, and explore and apply character strengths. Two positivity toolkit strategies that are especially relevant for the building of positive emotions across the School are gratitude and savoring. Case Study 7.1 (Awesome) and Case Study 7.2 (the Book of Blessings) showcase projects within the School community that build positive emotions with staff and young students, respectively.

CASE STUDY 7.1

Awesome

Paige Williams, Positive Psychology Project Manager

Understanding the important and unique role that each individual has within the School community, equal emphasis and importance is placed on the development of Positive Psychology skills and knowledge with both non-teaching and teaching staff. Therefore a 90-minute Positive Psychology workshop for non-teaching staff is held during core working hours each term.

A particularly successful workshop entitled "Awesome" was held, based on the work of Neil Pasricha (Pasricha, 2010). Pasricha's work reminds us of the simple pleasures in the things that we love but rarely stop to appreciate—the things that are "awesome." The focus is on building positive emotions, gratitude, and mindfulness through noticing and celebrating the small good things that happen to us every day. It connects to Fredrickson's work on the broaden-and-build theory of positive emotions (Fredrickson, 2001), which suggests that we need to actively search for opportunities to feel positive emotion in order to overcome our natural tendency to focus on the negative (also known as the negativity bias).

As a group we watched Neil Pasricha's TED talk in which he explains how he began his journey with "Awesome" to help him to cope with a time of personal tragedy. This gave us a powerful insight into the way in which we can choose to focus our attention on the frequent small good things that happen every day, and the significant impact that doing this can have on our wellbeing. Following a group discussion about the TED talk, members of staff were asked to think about what they find "awesome" about Geelong Grammar School, and to share and then write down examples for the development of a book of "Awesome@GGS."

By sharing the awesome things, we engaged social contagion, creating a ripple effect of positive emotion and gratitude about the opportunities and experiences encountered at Geelong Grammar School, and shifting people's perspective about their workplace. The workshop ended with an afternoon tea which gave participants a further opportunity to talk about what they find "awesome" outside of work, and to develop and deepen relationships with colleagues outside of their departments.

The "Awesome@GGS" book is filled with examples of small, special moments in which staff find value, such as people phoning just to say hello, being able to go for a run at lunchtime around the beautiful campus, the library staff going the extra mile to help out, receiving thank you cards from students, and mornings—when the campus is quiet and ready for a new day of possibilities.

CASE STUDY 7.2

The Book of Blessings

Geoff Carlisle, Year 2 Teacher, Bostock House

The Book of Blessings is a valuable and enriching addition to the Year 2 classroom. At this age, many students have a positive outlook on life and are naturally optimistic and full of hope for the future. Given minimal prompting, they are able to express thanks and consider the positive aspects of their lives. However, it is often more difficult for them to consider how others are blessed and to attend to the finer details of their lives that give them joy and promote happiness.

The Book of Blessings provides students with a way to share, with their peers, the parts of their lives for which they are grateful. It encourages children and families to talk about their blessings and to multiply their sense of joy through the process of sharing. Each week a student is selected to take home the Book of Blessings. They are encouraged to return it when they have completed a reflection on an important part of their life. Parents are encouraged to help students to edit their writing and select photographs or decorations to enhance the presentation. Due to the open-ended and personal nature of the task, even the most reticent of writers completes a page of which they can be proud. Once they have completed their entry, the student makes a presentation to the class, with students delighting in displaying their work and sharing the details of their lives (some student examples are showcased in Figures 7.5 and 7.6).

This task has created many positive outcomes in Year 2. First, it enables the teacher–student relationship to develop as the student is able to tell stories about his or her life. Secondly, the discussion that ensues from the student's presentation encourages the class to consider someone other than themselves. Thirdly, the audience learns to ask questions that allow the presenter to relive the positive emotion

Figure 7.5 A sample Book of Blessings page.

My hunt the good stuff is when I got my puppy. It was so good. because I have always wanted one. She's is so cute.

Holly
Year 3

Figure 7.6 Another sample Book of Blessings page.

of that memory. The ritual of sharing a blessing each week is one of the highlights of my teaching at this level. The process has helped many students to notice the small things that they are blessed to experience, and has supported relationships within and beyond the classroom.

Gratitude

Dr Robert Emmons, leading researcher in gratitude, explains that gratitude has been the topic of religious and philosophical discussions and practices for centuries, but that scientists have started to investigate gratitude only recently (Emmons, 2007). Gratitude is defined as thankfulness or feelings of appreciation that result from perceived fortune or the kindness of others (McCullough et al., 2002). People with dispositional gratitude have a tendency to notice and appreciate good outcomes in the world. Interestingly, these ideas dovetail with definitions provided by Year 2 students from Bostock House. These young minds propose that gratitude is:

Not taking something or someone for granted.

To appreciate what others do for you.

To be happy with what you have.

Expressing gratitude appropriately acknowledges others and cultivates an attitude of open appreciation of blessings in life and within oneself. Unsurprisingly, gratitude has a powerful impact on friendships, and helps people to feel valued and respected within the context of their relationships. Gratitude has been found to be positively related to relationship satisfaction (Algoe et al., 2010), friendship formation and development (Algoe et al., 2008), and trust and pro-social behavior (Bartlett and DeSteno, 2006).

What is perhaps more surprising is the impact that gratitude has on the benefactor's health and wellbeing. Dr Alex Wood and his colleagues contrast gratitude, with its focus on attending to the good in life, with depression, with its orientation towards the negative in life, the self, and the future (Wood et al., 2010). Empirically, gratitude has been associated with reduced depression and enhanced subjective wellbeing (Wood et al., 2010). Associate Professor Jeffery Froh runs a research laboratory on gratitude in children and adolescents, and has led several studies on the impact of gratitude on young people. In one study, Froh et al. (2010) found that gratitude led to upward spirals of wellbeing over 6 months. In another study, cultivating gratitude was found to be an especially powerful strategy for enriching wellbeing in students with low baseline levels of positive emotions (Froh et al., 2009). Gratitude connects people to things outside of themselves—to other people, to the community, and to nature.

Research on gratitude has often focused on the "three good things" or "daily blessings" activity. This activity encourages a person to pay deliberate and regular attention to things that he or she is thankful for. Compared with control activities, this simple practice has been found to lead to enhanced wellbeing (Emmons and McCullough, 2003; Seligman et al., 2005). Attending to daily blessings has been found to have an especially powerful impact on young people's satisfaction with their school experiences (Froh et al., 2008).

Hunting the good stuff

When I pick my young children up from school I now ask them "What good things happened today? What did you do well? What made you laugh?"

Fiona Fitzgerald, Member of the School community

At Geelong Grammar School, deliberately looking for things that make life meaningful and enjoyable is referred to by many terms, including "What Went Well," "panning for gold," and "hunting the good stuff." The term "hunting" appropriately reflects that it often requires a conscious effort to turn attention away from hassles and pressures and towards things that are going well. Across the School community, regular rituals and practices are focused on cultivating gratitude. Staff meetings often commence with people sharing "What Went Well" or things that have gone well for them, both at school and in their family and personal lives. Young students start many school days by reflecting on things that make them happy. Students and staff are encouraged to complete a gratitude diary, or even take part in a "365 project" where they take a photo each day of something they are thankful for (see Box 7.3 for an explanation of this activity written for the School community by Janis Coffey). A lesson that is part of the explicit program in the later years, encouraging students to conduct personal expressions of gratitude, is described in Box 7.4.

Communicating gratitude

I went down to the playground looking for someone to play with; straight away Kasey said that I could join in, even when they were already playing.

I think Sophie was a great leader because she encouraged me and helped when I was a bit scared on the first night in our bunk.

Tristan was a big help because he made me laugh and smile at canoeing.

Year 3 and 4 students at the end of camp, Bostock House

BOX 7.3: Beating the winter blues

With chilly mornings and even colder nights, we can certainly say that we are in the throes of winter. While you might love the chance to enjoy all the things that winter brings, including skiing and warm, fuzzy jumpers, you might also be looking forward to spring coming sooner rather than later. But don't wish the days away! There are daily events and beautiful things that happen every day, and if we take the time to acknowledge them, they can warm our hearts.

Research has shown that taking the time to write down three things that you are grateful for every day can improve your overall outlook on life. We know that negative events and stressors in life stick to us easily. They keep us up at night and they may even seem to outweigh the positives that may have happened that day. So get yourself a notebook, put it on your bedside table, and every day go out and "hunt the good stuff." Write down three things that you are grateful for and what this means to you. You can even take this one step further with a "365 project," which involves taking a photo every day of something that makes you happy. Taking a photo of little moments in the day, over the course of a year, builds up a portfolio of photos and memories of the things that make your life special and unique.

Janis Coffey, Associate Director of the Institute of Positive Education

BOX 7.4: A personal expression of gratitude

Students benefit from an activity that helps them to cultivate and express gratitude by writing and delivering a heartfelt letter of gratitude. First, the students are asked to think of someone who is important to them. The person they select could be a family member, friend, coach, mentor, or teacher. In pairs, the students then reflect on their relationship with this person, thinking about how he or she has influenced them and how they have grown as a result of knowing this person.

The students are provided with time and a comfortable space in which to write a letter of gratitude to the person of their choice. There is a lot of flexibility in style and approach. Students are encouraged to personalize their letters by including specific memories and details, and elements of creativity such as drawings or poems. Often a good letter will take some time to write, and may even require several sittings. If possible, the student should aim to personally hand-deliver the letter and read it out loud to their important person. Students are encouraged to write a summary of their experience of this activity, from the initial stages of writing the letter to the feelings and emotions that are experienced on delivery of it.

A special way of cultivating gratitude involves peer nominations in which students identify reasons why they appreciate each other. It is one thing for a student to receive a compliment from a staff member, but to be acknowledged by a peer is often infinitely more powerful. Peer nominations can be made on a daily or weekly basis, or they can take place at the end of an event such as a camp, class project, or sports game. The key is to challenge students to remember that peer nominations are not just about patting their friends on the back, but also about recognizing admirable qualities in a diverse range of people. Frequently students go to great lengths to find things out about each other. A Middle School activity that took this one step further, by making and distributing "compliment cookies," is described in Box 7.5.

BOX 7.5: Compliment cookies

Students engaged in an activity that celebrates gratitude by giving compliment cookies. As a first step, the students thought of someone in the School community or beyond who had done something special for them. They then made biscuits in the spirit of fortune cookies; however, instead of having fortunes inside, they included messages of thankfulness and appreciation. The students gave these cookies to their friends, to their teachers, to the bus driver for driving them to School safely, and to the gardener for always saying hello. This activity helped to create meaningful connections across the School community, and also encouraged the students to consider important—and often unacknowledged—people in their lives.

Savoring

Modern life is busy and complicated. Often taking the time to enjoy big and small moments is trumped by daily life and hassles. Many important things get taken for granted. Savoring helps students and staff to slow down and appreciate the present moment. Professor Fred Bryant and Professor Joseph Veroff explain that savoring is acting or thinking in ways that prolong or maximize the impact of positive emotions and experiences (Bryant and Veroff, 2007). Savoring can be about the past, the present, or the future. Savoring the past involves reminiscing, sharing experiences with others, and thinking back to past successes. Savoring the present involves deliberately focusing on enjoyable experiences. Savoring the future involves anticipating future events and enjoying the process of making plans.

One teacher shared a story about the impact that savoring had had on parenting his young children. Coming home tired at the end of a long day, he often found it easy to get caught up in the pressures of evening family life, such as cooking dinner, helping his kids with their homework, and preparing for the next day. Now, when he arrives home, he dedicates a few minutes to savoring some quality time with his children, asking them about their day, and reflecting on how lucky he is to have a strong and healthy family. A time that can be chaotic and stressful now seems precious and wonderful.

Adding to the intuitive benefits, several research studies have found that savoring increases positive emotions and enhances wellbeing. For example, Bryant (2003) found that people who practice savoring experience high levels of wellbeing and frequent positive emotions as well as infrequent negative feelings such as hopelessness, depression, and guilt. An experimental study found that savoring strategies that focused on being present in the moment, vividly remembering or anticipating positive events, and sharing memories with others were associated with increased wellbeing, whereas suppression techniques such as fault finding and rumination were associated with decreased wellbeing (Quoidbach et al., 2010).

Many children could teach adults a lot about savoring. Bostock House and Toorak campuses are filled with young children who are looking forward to something with excitement and exhilaration, or bursting to tell their stories and share their memories with their families. As children grow older it is valuable for them to consciously reconnect with savoring. Students and staff across campuses are encouraged to savor the moment by attending to their senses. Students are also encouraged to practice sensory savoring by using food, songs, or everyday objects. Once they have practiced these skills, they are encouraged to transfer their learning to other situations in their lives. Recently, a staff member was walking across Corio campus when two senior male students stopped him and pointed out a beautiful sunset. The staff member described his admiration that the young men had taken the time to enjoy the sight, and his appreciation that they had included him in the moment.

Savoring has an especially important place at Timbertop, and students are regularly given time and space to reflect on their year. For a long time, Timbertop students have been encouraged to write regular journal entries, as well as to exchange letters with their families. Regularly writing about their experiences encourages students to stop and reflect on their lives and to process the ups and downs of the week. For many students, these journals and letters provide vivid recollections of their time at Timbertop and are savored and treasured for years (or decades) to come. Parents also often cherish the letters written to them by their children during their time at Timbertop.

Permission to be human

When Dr Tal Ben-Shahar visited Geelong Grammar School he spoke to a theatre full of students about his area of expertise—happiness. He started by sharing the importance of accepting emotions, explaining that at times every person feels sad, jealous, angry, or frustrated. He spoke about the danger of suppressing or denying emotions, and explained that it often takes a lot of courage to accept painful feelings and reach out to others for support. He recommended that everyone should give themselves the "permission to be human" or the freedom to experience the whole range of human emotions without trying to ignore, suppress, or deny them.

This message plays a central role in Geelong Grammar School's journey with Positive Education. Positive Psychology is not about feeling happy or joyful all the time. The approach holds that people can actively look for ways of building positive emotions, while simultaneously accepting that they will at times experience emotions that are not positive, pleasant, or comfortable. It is valuable for students to develop curiosity, self-awareness, and insight into their range of emotional experiences. For example, one activity encourages students to write in their journals about three highlights of their day. In another activity, considered just as valuable, students are encouraged to write about three lowlights or down points, or three feelings or experiences they are curious about—whether these are pleasant or unpleasant. Reflecting on times when they have experienced different emotions increases self-knowledge, wisdom, and understanding, and serves as an important foundation for resilience.

Emotional flourishing

Seeding positive emotions into daily life across the four campuses has been one of the most powerful strategies in the School's journey with Positive Education. Life at a large and complex school will always involve challenges and complexities. Despite the potential temptation to focus on stressors or conflicts, directing attention to the positive aspects shines light on the many exciting, wonderful, and inspiring things that happen at a school on a daily basis. The impact on the Geelong Grammar School community has been tangible. Across year levels, students have benefited from enriched skills in understanding and communicating their emotions. Staff members recall how "What Went Well" activities have helped them to get to know their colleagues on a more personal level, creating moments of humor and heartfelt connection. Relationships between students, staff, and families have grown through the focus on savoring and gratitude. As Professor Fredrickson explained in her introduction to this chapter, over time these simple strategies for positive emotions foster social, psychological, and cognitive resources and lead to upward spirals of wellbeing and flourishing. The objective is a kind and supportive school culture in which students and staff experience frequent positive emotions in the present, and develop emotional skills and capacities that will hold them in good stead for their future.

RECOMMENDED RESOURCES

365 Grateful Project. <http://365grateful.com/original-365-project> (App and website.)

Bryant F and Veroff J (2007). *Savoring: a new model of positive experience.* Mahwah, NJ: Lawrence Erlbaum Associates.

Emmons R. Emmons Lab website. <http://psychology.ucdavis.edu/labs/emmons>

Emmons R A (2007). *Thanks! How the new science of gratitude can make you happier.* Boston, MA: Houghton-Mifflin.

Emmons R A (2013). *Gratitude Works! A 21-day program for creating emotional prosperity.* San Francisco, CA: Jossey-Bass.

Fredrickson B. Love 2.0 website. <www.positivityresonance.com>

Fredrickson B L (2009). *Positivity.* New York: Three Rivers Press.

Fredrickson B L (2013). *Love 2.0: how our supreme emotion affects everything we feel, think, do, and become.* New York: Hudson Street Press.

Howells K (2012). *Gratitude in Education: a radical view.* Rotterdam, The Netherlands: Sense Publishers.

Kimochis. <www.kimochis.com.au> (Classroom resource for emotional literacy.)

Pasricha N (2010). *The 3 A's of Awesome. TED Talk.* <www.ted.com/talks/neil_pasricha_the_3_a_s_of_awesome.html>

Random Gratitude. <www.apple.com> (App available through this website.)

Silverstein S (1964). *The Giving Tree.* New York: HarperCollins Publishers. (Children's picture storybook.)

Soulpancake. <http://soulpancake.com> (Inspiring and mood lifting videos.)

Steindel-Rast D (2013). *Want To Be Happy? Be grateful. TED talk.* <www.ted.com/talks/david_steindl_rast_want_to_be_happy_be_grateful>

REFERENCES

Algoe S B, Haidt J, and Gable S L (2008). Beyond reciprocity: gratitude and relationships in everyday life. *Emotion, 8,* 425–9.

Algoe S B, Gable S L, and Maisel N C (2010). It's the little things: everyday gratitude as a booster shot for romantic relationships. *Personal Relationships, 17,* 217–33.

Bartlett M Y and DeSteno D (2006). Helping when it costs you. *Psychological Science, 17,* 319–25.

Bernard M E, Stephanou A, and Urbach D (2007). *ASG Student Social and Emotional Health Report.* Melbourne, Australia: Australian Council for Educational Research and Australian Scholarships Group.

Bryant F B (2003). Savoring Beliefs Inventory (SBI): a scale for measuring beliefs about savouring. *Journal of Mental Health, 12,* 175–96.

Bryant F B and Veroff J (2007). *Savoring: a new model of positive experience.* Mahwah, NJ: Lawrence Erlbaum Associates.

Eisenberg N et al. (2003). Longitudinal relations among parental emotional expressivity, children's regulation, and quality of socioemotional functioning. *Developmental Psychology, 39,* 3–19.

Emmons R A (2007). *Thanks! How the new science of gratitude can make you happier.* New York: Houghton Mifflin Harcourt.

Emmons R A and McCullough M E (2003). Counting blessings versus burdens: an experimental investigation of gratitude and subjective well-being in daily life. *Journal of Personality and Social Psychology, 84,* 377–89.

Fredrickson B L (1998). What good are positive emotions? *Review of General Psychology, 2,* 300–19.

Fredrickson B L (2001). The role of positive emotions in positive psychology: the broaden-and-build theory of positive emotions. *American Psychologist, 56,* 218–26.

Fredrickson B L (2004). The broaden-and-build theory of positive emotions. *Philosophical Transactions of the Royal Society B: Biological Sciences, 359,* 1367–77.

Fredrickson B L (2009). *Positivity.* New York: Three Rivers Press.

Fredrickson B L (2013). Positive emotions broaden and build. In: Devine P and Plant A (eds) *Advances in Experimental Social Psychology.* Volume 47. Burlington, MA: Academic Press. pp. 1–53.

Fredrickson B L and Branigan C (2005). Positive emotions broaden the scope of attention and thought-action repertoires. *Cognition and Emotion, 19*, 313–32.

Fredrickson B L et al. (2008). Open hearts build lives: positive emotions, induced through loving-kindness meditation, build consequential personal resources. *Journal of Personality and Social Psychology, 95*, 1045–62.

Froh J J, Sefick W J, and Emmons R A (2008). Counting blessings in early adolescents: an experimental study of gratitude and subjective well-being. *Journal of School Psychology, 46*, 213–33.

Froh J J, Kashdan T B, Ozimkowski K M, and Miller N (2009). Who benefits the most from a gratitude intervention in children and adolescents? Examining positive affect as a moderator. *Journal of Positive Psychology, 4*, 408–22.

Froh J J, Bono G, and Emmons R (2010). Being grateful is beyond good manners: gratitude and motivation to contribute to society among early adolescents. *Motivation and Emotion, 34*, 144–57.

Gable P A and Harmon-Jones E (2008). Approach-motivated positive affect reduces breadth of attention. *Psychological Science, 19*, 476–82.

Garland E L et al. (2010). Upward spirals of positive emotions counter downward spirals of negativity: insights from the broaden-and-build theory and affective neuroscience on the treatment of emotion dysfunctions and deficits in psychopathology. *Clinical Psychology Review, 30*, 849–64.

Gumora G and Arsenio W F (2002). Emotionality, emotion regulation, and school performance in middle school children. *Journal of School Psychology, 40*, 395–413.

Kok B E et al. (2013). How positive emotions build physical health: perceived positive social connections account for the upward spiral between positive emotions and vagal tone. *Psychological Science, 24*, 1123–32.

Lyubomirsky S, Sheldon K M, and Schkade D (2005). Pursuing happiness: the architecture of sustainable change. *Review of General Psychology, 9*, 111–31.

McCullough M E, Emmons R A and Tsang J A (2002). The grateful disposition: a conceptual and empirical topography. *Journal of Personality and Social Psychology, 82*, 112–27.

Mather M and Carstensen L L (2005). Aging and motivated cognition: the positivity effect in attention and memory. *Trends in Cognitive Sciences, 9*, 496–502.

Pasricha N (2010). *The Book of Awesome*. New York: Penguin Books Ltd.

Quoidbach J, Berry E V, Hansenne M, and Mikolajczak M (2010). Positive emotion regulation and well-being: comparing the impact of eight savoring and dampening strategies. *Personality and Individual Differences, 49*, 368–73.

Rowe G, Hirsh J B, and Anderson A K (2007). Positive affect increases the breadth of attentional selection. *Proceedings of the National Academy of Sciences, 104*, 383–8.

Rydell A M, Berlin L, and Bohlin G (2003). Emotionality, emotion regulation, and adaptation among 5- to 8-year-old children. *Emotion, 3*, 30–47.

Salzberg S (1997). *Lovingkindness: the revolutionary art of happiness*. Boston, MA: Shambhala Publications.

Schmitz T W, De Rosa E, and Anderson A K (2009). Opposing influences of affective state valence on visual cortical encoding. *Journal of Neuroscience, 29*, 7199–207.

Seligman M E P, Steen T A, Park N, and Peterson C (2005). Positive psychology progress: empirical validation of interventions. *American Psychologist, 60*, 410–21.

Shallcross A J, Ford B Q, Floerke V A, and Mauss I B (2013). Getting better with age: the relationship between age, acceptance, and negative affect. *Journal of Personality and Social Psychology, 104*, 734–49.

Soto D et al. (2009). Pleasant music overcomes the loss of awareness in patients with visual neglect. *Proceedings of the National Academy of Sciences of the United States of America, 106*, 6011–16.

Thayer J F and Sternberg E (2006). Beyond heart rate variability. *Annals of the New York Academy of Sciences, 1088*, 361–72.

Wadlinger H A and Isaacowitz D M (2006). Positive mood broadens visual attention to positive stimuli. *Motivation and Emotion, 30*, 87–99.

Wood A M, Froh J J, and Geraghty A W A (2010). Gratitude and well-being: a review and theoretical integration. *Clinical Psychology Review, 30*, 890–905.

POSITIVE HEALTH
AND RESILIENCE

**Introduction by
Dr Karen Reivich**

Geelong Grammar School is leading the way in Positive Education. Central to Positive Education is the development of student resilience. Resilience has been defined as a "dynamic process of positive adaptation or development in the context of significant adversity" (Luthar et al., 2000, p. 543), and research shows that young people who display resilience have "good outcomes in spite of serious threats to adaptation or development" (Masten, 2001, p. 228). More broadly, resilience can be thought of as the ability to persist in the face of challenges, and to bounce back and grow from adversity. There are a number of evidence-based protective factors that contribute to resilience, including optimism, effective problem solving, sense of meaning, self-efficacy, flexibility, impulse control, empathy, close relationships, faith and spirituality, among others (Masten and Reed, 2002; Reivich and Shatté, 2002). Many of these qualities can be developed through learning and practicing skills. Thus resilience is not a process limited to a lucky few, but rather it can be learned and developed in all children.

Family, school, and community environments are critical to youth development of capacities that enable resilience. Students with strong connections to school and family are less likely than their peers to develop depression or engage in substance use, violence, and other risky behaviors (Benard, 2004; Resnick et al., 1997; Rutter et al., 1982; Wang, 2009). These connections may be especially important for children who grow up in communities plagued by poverty and violence (Rutter et al., 1982). However, regardless of one's background, resilience skills are essential in that they prepare young people for lives rich in positive emotion, meaning, strong relationships, and success.

Schools can, as Geelong Grammar School has done, enhance resilience by creating educational environments that cultivate students' personal skills, strengths, and strong relationships. Because of the daily complex social interactions and academic challenges that attending school entails, schools are the ideal place to teach children skills that enable them to react to challenges and adversity with effective problem solving, a positive attitude, and the ability to manage their emotions effectively. Education that focuses on resilience has the potential to promote students' growth and wellbeing both in school and outside it, as well as to equip young people with tools that will benefit them long after their formal education has ended.

The research on resilience shows that this process can be effectively taught in schools. The Penn Resiliency Program (PRP) (Gillham et al., 2007) is a school-based, group program for students from late elementary to middle school age (approximately age 10–14 years). PRP grew out of cognitive–behavioral theories and interventions used to treat psychological disorders, especially depression (Beck, 1976; Beck et al., 1979; Ellis, 1962; Seligman, 1991). The major goal of the PRP curriculum is to increase students' ability to handle day-to-day stressors and problems that are common for most students during adolescence. PRP promotes optimism by teaching students to think more realistically and flexibly about the problems they encounter. PRP also teaches assertiveness, decision making, relaxation, and several other coping and problem-solving skills.

PRP is one of the most widely researched programs designed to prevent depression in young people. During the past 20 years, 17 studies have evaluated PRP in comparison with a control group. Most of these studies used randomized controlled designs, and together the studies include over 2,000 children and adolescents between the ages of 8 and 15 years. The findings on PRP show that students who are taught resilience skills are less likely to experience depression and anxiety, and they report less hopelessness, have fewer negative behaviors, and show greater optimism (Brunwasser et al., 2009; Cutuli et al., 2006; Gillham et al., 1995, 2006). In addition, a meta-analysis of PRP showed no evidence that the effects of PRP vary by race or ethnicity (Brunwasser et al., 2009).

The data are compelling—when resilience skills are taught in schools, important changes are reflected in the students. However, reviews of PRP research indicate that the program's effectiveness varies considerably across studies (Gillham et al., 2008). On average, the effects are small; PRP has moderate to large effects in some studies and no effect in others. This variability in effectiveness appears to be related at least in part to the level of training and supervision that group leaders receive. Program effects are strongest when group leaders are either members of the PRP team or are trained and closely supervised by the PRP team. Program effects are smaller and less consistent when group leaders receive minimal training and supervision. The quality of curriculum delivery also appears to be critical. For example, a study of PRP in a primary care setting revealed significant reductions in depression symptoms for adolescents in groups with high rates of adherence to the program. In contrast, PRP did not reduce depressive symptoms relative to controls in groups with lower rates of program adherence (Gillham et al..

2006). Thus we believe that current best practice for PRP includes intensive training and supervision of group leaders.

The variability in the magnitude of the results of resilience training in the school might relate to the degree to which the school makes resilience more than a "stand-alone" curriculum. Schools that integrate resilience into their school culture might see greater and more sustained changes in their students. This is where I believe Geelong Grammar School leads the way.

I have been fortunate to be part of a team, led by Professor Martin Seligman, who worked with the leadership, faculty, and staff at Geelong Grammar School during their initial development and execution of Positive Education. The goal of the collaboration was to shift the focus from training a subset of classroom teachers how to teach resilience to imbuing an entire school with the principles, interventions, and skills of Positive Psychology—of which resilience plays a key part. Across the years of this collaboration I was inspired (and continue to be) by Geelong Grammar School's deep and thorough commitment to living, teaching, and embedding resilience skills throughout the culture and community of the School. All of the faculty and staff at Geelong Grammar School participate in workshops designed to enhance their own resilience and wellbeing. These workshops contribute to creating a community in which resilience is seen not as a "program," but as an essential part of a culture that enables young people to thrive. In addition, the Geelong Grammar School community engages in ongoing conversations, development work, and research to explore how best to create a lasting culture that promotes the wellbeing of staff and students—not just in the classroom, but on the sports field, in the dining hall, and in communications with parents and families. The work conducted at Geelong Grammar School will further our understanding of how to inculcate resilience and, more generally, how to create a system of education that enables our young people to flourish.

Resilience at Geelong Grammar School

Resilience is not about minimizing difficulty—it is not trying to achieve happiness by shutting off everything that makes you human. Being human is being able to thrive at the crossroads, opening oneself up to as many different emotions, experiences, and challenges as possible. Geelong Grammar School provides the opportunity and support for this self-defining journey.

Anthony Strazzera, Senior English Teacher

It is the responsibility of adults to create communities and environments in which children and young people are safe from harm. However, it can be a natural instinct of adults to want to protect children from *all* difficulties, to spare them from pain, sadness, stress, and anger. The danger of sheltering young people from all disappointments is that they can be confronted and overwhelmed when they experience life's inevitable challenges and hardships. At Geelong Grammar School it is understood that there is great value in a moment when a child does not get picked for the school musical, or has conflict with a friend, or receives a disappointing score on a test. Such moments help students to practice the skills and mindsets for resilience, and to develop resources that can help them throughout their lives. The aim is not to protect children and adolescents from all difficulties, but to support them in thriving through the natural ups and downs of life.

The definition of resilience adopted by the School, courtesy of Dr Karen Reivich, is as follows: "Resilience is the ability to grow and thrive in the face of challenges and bounce back from adversity. Resilience enables you to take calculated risks and capitalize on opportunities" (Reivich, 2010). This definition underscores the belief that resilience is the ability to maintain a healthy and flourishing life, despite sometimes experiencing hardships and difficulties. Importantly, resilience entails much more than an ability to bounce back from setbacks. Having skills of resilience helps people to step outside their comfort zones, take risks, and engage more fully in life. Students who are resilient may feel confident enough to try out for the school play, despite feeling apprehensive, or bravely introduce themselves to someone whom they have not met before, even though they feel nervous.

Resilience is also shown when a person is able to confront a difficult issue without resorting to anger or poor communication. Many people avoid conflict even though expressing the truth or speaking their mind would greatly benefit them and the relationship. Resilience helps people to deal proactively with stressful situations or challenging interpersonal interactions before the experience causes excessive distress or conflict. In this way, resilience and assertive communication are mutually beneficial skills that foster positive relationships as well as good psychological health.

Traditionally, it may have been assumed that resilience is a stable trait that some people have and others do not. As Dr Karen Reivich explained in her introduction to this chapter, there is increasing understanding that resilience can be taught and that the associated skills and mindsets can be practiced and cultivated intentionally. Dr Reivich and her colleague Dr Andrew Shatté propose that resilience comprises seven factors that can be developed and enhanced, namely optimism, managing and regulating emotions, controlling impulses, flexible thinking, empathy, self-efficacy, and reaching out to and connecting with others (Reivich and Shatté, 2002). At Geelong Grammar School, these skills are integrated throughout the Model for Positive Education. The aim is to create a School community and culture where the language of resilience is interwoven into daily life at the School, and is used throughout the classrooms, staff rooms, Boarding Houses and Units, sports fields, and co-curricular and activities programs.

Teaching resilience

If something goes wrong, the next day you can do better.

You can bounce back to a good life.

You can get back to your goals.

You can grow from the experience and not just bounce back but actually bounce forward.

Year 3 students define resilience, Bostock House

The development of resilience at Geelong Grammar School occurs through several key pathways. In professional development activities, staff explore core resiliency skills and reflect on the relevance of different ideas to their personal and professional lives. In explicit classes, students explore and practice resilience skills and mindsets. The pinnacles of this explicit learning are in Year 7, when students are taught a modified version of the PRP, and in Year 9, when they also undertake comprehensive resilience training during their time at Timbertop.

In these explicit programs, students learn core resiliency skills covered by the PRP training (Gillham et al., 2007; Reivich, 2010). These skills include understanding the relationship between activating events, thoughts, and consequences (ATCs), detecting thinking traps and icebergs, energy management, problem solving, putting it in perspective, and real-time resilience. Several of these skills are covered in this chapter. More information on the other skills, which are considered just as valuable for resilience, is available from the PRP Manual and related materials (Gillham et al., 2008; Reivich, 2010; Reivich and Shatté, 2002). At Geelong Grammar School, resiliency skills are also interwoven throughout the early schooling years and revisited in the senior curriculum. By offering multi-day Positive Education training courses for family members, the School has taken substantial steps towards sharing the language of resilience with parents. This helps to create consistency in the messages that children and young people are receiving about resilient thinking and behaving at home and at school.

What is resilience?

Some students place so much focus on being "macho" and "toughing it out." When you take the time to talk to them and challenge them to think about how much strength it actually takes to be vulnerable, the results are very powerful—you can literally see students grow.

Steve Andrew, Head of Fraser House

As a foundational base, students and staff of all ages are encouraged to consider what it means to be resilient (see Case Study 8.1 for a description of a project on resilience for Year 3 students by Jane Marney, a teacher from Bostock House). Students are asked to explore what resiliency means to them personally and think of times when they have seen resilience in action, both in themselves and in others. A "paragon" of resilience in the School community, often mentioned in these discussions,

CASE STUDY 8.1

Year 3 Resilience Project

Jane Marney, Classroom teacher, Bostock House

The Resilience Projects developed because I wanted to introduce my young students to the concept of resilience—but did not want to simply *tell them* what it was. My hope was that if my Year 3 students could find and study examples of resilience in plants and animals, they would understand the concept in a holistic sense and see the importance of resilience for themselves.

The "Habitats" Unit was planned with a focus on how plants and animals adapt to survive in different habitats. Through both shared and individual research, the students would learn about how changes occur in nature to ensure survival and prospering. The first research project was conducted in pairs, with each pair given a different habitat. Researching different types of plants found in their habitat, the students examined the adaptations that particular plants develop in order to survive. Each pair presented their information on posters, sharing examples of plant "survival skills." Although the word "resilience" had still not been used by the students, they were beginning to understand that living organisms face battles and make changes on a daily basis in order to survive and flourish.

The second research project was completed individually and involved students selecting an animal that they wanted to study. Normally such research would be focused on facts about their animal, but this time their attention was directed to how the animal survived the threats and challenges that it faced daily. Students began by listing the challenges they thought their animal faced, and then researched how it managed to survive these. Some of the areas they discovered included body shape and features, being part of a group, movement, sheltering, food, and using the features of its habitat. Through this process the students were developing their understanding of what animals and plants need to survive and live a good life.

The final part of the Unit was where we made the link to the students' own lives. Together we discussed some of the challenges they might face from day to day. Next, they explored how they could adapt to overcome these challenges. Having worked on the projects, the students were easily able to come up with suggestions. It was at this stage that I introduced the word "resilience." Now, for my Year 3 students, being resilient meant being able to adapt and overcome challenges positively—and as a normal part of the experiences of life.

Finally, the students were given a Super Ball to look after for 24 hours. They then had to protect an egg for the next 24 hours. They were excited to examine the differences between looking after the ball and looking after the egg. They decided that the ball was resilient because it could bounce back and survive even if the students dropped it, whereas the egg was not (as evidenced by the sad fate of some of our eggs). The students decided that the ball was a lot easier to take care of and "be with" for the day, and they made the connection that perhaps resilient people would go through their day without fear and therefore might flourish more easily.

The Habitats Unit proved to be a valuable "real-life" introduction to resilience. My students became aware of what challenges are, and that every living thing faces them. They also became aware of the many different ways in which adaptations can be made to combat challenges. Through the study of plants and animals, the students developed a clearer understanding that living organisms rely on each other to survive; this was reflected in our discussion about overcoming challenges. The idea of seeking help from others and not always trying to survive alone became a theme of our conversations, as did the fact that challenges are a normal part of life and that change can be made. I was excited to see their growing understanding of the importance of resilience—that being more resilient might make life a little easier, and that the capacity to adapt would make them stronger.

is Old Geelong Grammarian Cameron Rahles-Rahbula, who was diagnosed with a rare form of bone cancer when he was in Year 7 at the School. To stop the progression of the cancer, Cam's left leg was amputated above his knee. Despite his disability, Cam completed the entire year at Timbertop in Year 9, taking part in intense and extensive physical exercise. He also went on to represent Australia in alpine skiing at the Paralympic Games. More than Cam's notable achievements, however, it is the hope, courage, and grit he constantly displayed that continue to inspire staff and students at Geelong Grammar School. A story of resilience in action, written by a senior student, is included in Box 8.1.

Although it is valuable to share inspirational stories of resilience, it is also important for students to understand that resilience is about more than being tough or

> **BOX 8.1:** A story of resilience
>
> A good friend of mine found out last year that her Mum had cancer. I can clearly remember admiring and respecting my friend for the way she dealt with the news. She always stayed strong, not in an unfeeling kind of way, but in that she kept everything in perspective; her mum was still here and still the same person. Yes, they had recently and suddenly found out about the illness, but they had in fact been living with it unknowingly for some time. She didn't treat it like some taboo issue that she didn't want anyone to know about, but at the same time didn't attempt to gain any attention from it. Even though it would have been understandable for her grades to drop, she didn't ever slack off, and she remained a conscientious student and a contributing member of Geelong Grammar School. I often wondered if I had been in her place whether I could have shown the same level of integrity and resilience and, even though I guess I'll never know, I like to think that observing my friend's behavior will help me in the future when I am confronted with issues that concern me more directly.
>
> Senior School Student, Corio

achieving notable and admirable feats. One image of a resilient person is someone who is composed and stoical, who takes everything in their stride, and who never shows emotions. At the School, great care is taken to challenge this view and to communicate that resilient people do not always "have it together" on the outside. The most resilient people feel sad, angry, and frustrated sometimes and, importantly, they have the courage to ask for help. When asked to define resilience, a Year 10 student described it as "not how hard you can punch, but how many punches you can take and get back up again."

Staff, students, and parents are introduced to "real resilience" through an activity that asks them to identify different statements as resilience "myths" or "facts." Some resilience "myths" include "Never show emotions," "Always in control," and "Never needs help." Some resilience "facts" include "Accept support," "Know when to have a break," and "Feel sad sometimes." Students are encouraged to think of resilience not as a goal to be achieved, but as a process that is constantly developing and changing.

Foundations of resilience

> Nobody is going to be successful 24 hours a day, 7 days a week, so teaching confidence, resilience, and optimism is fundamental for young children. Positive Education improves student wellbeing while equipping them with the skills to manage failure, as well as to build from those life experiences found to be challenging.
>
> Garry Pierson, Head of Toorak Campus

During his time at Geelong Grammar School, Professor Martin Seligman shared the story of his journey in teaching resilience to young people. He explained that, for a long time, cognitive–behavioral therapy (CBT) has been a gold standard in the treatment of a range of mental illnesses, including depression and anxiety (Beck, 2005; Butler et al., 2006). Core goals of CBT are to develop awareness of how thoughts influence feelings and behaviors, to identify unhelpful patterns of thinking, and to create a balanced and flexible view of life experiences.

Professor Seligman and his colleagues researched why—when faced with similar traumatic life events—some people developed a sense of helplessness and others maintained effort and hope (Maier and Seligman, 1976). His explanatory style theory proposed that the way in which people interpret their experiences has a profound influence on how they feel and act in response to them. Seligman and his colleagues found that individuals could learn more flexible and healthy ways of interpreting negative experiences, which in turn decreased their symptoms of depression and increased their sense of hope and confidence (Seligman, 2006).

Aware of the mounting research on the importance of CBT skills in *treating* mental health disorders, Seligman became intrigued by the potential of such skills to *prevent* the disorders in the first place (Seligman et al., 1999). He had a vision of working with children and young people to teach them skills and mindsets that would be beneficial throughout their lives (Seligman, 1995). He recruited a team of hardworking and passionate professionals, and started a journey of developing, refining, and evaluating the Penn Resiliency Program, as outlined by Dr Reivich in her introduction to this chapter.

Foundations of resilience: the ATC model

One thing that is helpful is the ATC model. An example of an activating event is an exam. You might think you are going to fail. The consequences are that you feel anxious and procrastinate about studying because it all seems worthless. But if you challenge the thought and think you can do your best, the consequences could be very different. How you think about a situation can change the entire outcome.

David, Year 10, Senior School, Corio Campus

Understanding how experiences, thoughts, feelings, and actions are interconnected is a cornerstone skill for resilience. Staff and students are introduced to this through the ATC model. The "A" in the model represents an *activating event* or situation. Activating events can be daily occurrences, such as running late for a class or having a disagreement with a sibling, or more significant life experiences, such as family illness, relationship breakdown, or a career setback. The "T" in the ATC model represents *thoughts*. Staff and students are taught to tune into their "internal radio station" and pay attention to unhelpful or inflexible thoughts that may be amplifying their distress. Often people are largely unaware of this stage in the process, and attribute their feelings and behaviors to the situation itself, rather than to how they have perceived it. The "C" in the model represents "consequences," which are further divided into emotional and behavioral reactions.

The ATC model provides a tangible framework for understanding and analyzing the interrelationships between thoughts, feelings, and behavior. Although the ATC model is quite complex, even young children can be supported in considering how their perception of events influences their feelings. Staff carefully ask questions that help young students to reflect on their experiences, such as "Is your thinking helping or harming the situation at the moment?" or "You look upset—what are you thinking that may be causing you to feel this way?" Young children can also be helped further to understand the link between thoughts, feelings, and actions through visual cues, such as drawings of people with empty thought bubbles that require them to fill in what those people may be thinking in different situations.

Figures 8.1, 8.2, and 8.3 show diagrams of the ATC model, where students have drawn an activating event that they have experienced. Other students are provided with these drawings and asked to fill in the "thoughts" and "consequences" boxes, with the intention of developing their awareness of how different interpretations of situations influence how they feel and react to those situations. After this introduction, all of the students are encouraged to brainstorm and draw an activating event they have personally experienced, as well as the thoughts and consequences that may arise from it.

Self-talk and catastrophizing

Connewarre is a Middle School girls' Boarding House with around 45 girls from Years 6 to 8. The girls have about 50 minutes of leisure time each evening, when they are free to make phone calls, and this is precious time. One evening as I was

Figure 8.1 Student ATC drawings: 1.

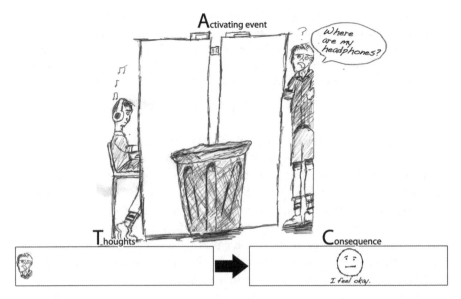

Figure 8.2 Student ATC drawings: 2.

Figure 8.3 Student ATC drawings: 3.

walking past a group of girls, I overheard one say "Nobody loves me because they never answer the phone when I ring them." Another girl said "Don't you think you are catastrophizing a little? They've missed one call." The concept of catastrophizing is something we teach in Year 7 Positive Education. The resilience language makes difficult situations within the Boarding House easier to manage.

Mary-Anne Lewis, Head of Connewarre House

To complement their understanding of the ATC model, students are introduced to the concept of self-talk or their internal "radio station." A Year 7 student explained negative self-talk as "thinking badly about yourself inside your head." Catastrophizing is a default way of thinking that can cause distress. Catastrophizing occurs when a person blows the severity of an event out of proportion, and thinks of the very worst-case scenario. If a teacher asks to see a student after class, that student may spend the rest of the lesson worrying about getting into trouble, and visualizing a range of possible punishments. The student may therefore have difficulty focusing for the rest of the lesson. In reality, the teacher may want to suggest a minor area for improvement, or even compliment the student on their good work.

One PRP activity for countering catastrophizing is "putting it in perspective" (Gillham et al., 2007). Students are taught three simple steps in which they think of the worst-case scenario, followed by the best-case scenario, and finally the most likely scenario. The following are examples of the three steps provided by a Year 10 student who was distressed after having a disagreement with a close friend:

- **Worst-case scenario thinking:** The conflict will never be healed. We will never be friends again. No one else will forgive me either and no one in the school will like me any more. I will end up with no friends at all.
- **Best-case scenario:** My friend will apologize today and say it was all her fault. She will respect me even more in the future. Everyone else will also develop more respect for me, and from now on everyone will listen to what I have to say.
- **Most likely scenario:** We will both feel mad for a few days but finally talk and make up once things have calmed down. Our friendship will heal in time and we can work on listening more respectfully to each other in the future.

By considering the absurdity of the worst-case scenario, and the improbability of the best-case scenario, students arrive at a more balanced and useful perspective and consider how to move forward with respect and dignity. After completing the three steps, students are encouraged to come up with an action plan to move the situation forward in a positive way. In this situation, the student made a plan to seek a different friend to talk to for support and understanding (while being careful not to spread the feud), and to apologize to her friend in a few days' time. Although this was difficult given her distress at the time, the student described how going

BOX 8.2: Resilience in action

Hi Scuddas,

   I just wanted to send you an email to let you know how grateful I am to have learnt Pos Ed. Today it was my first day in a German school and I was feeling pretty down, I thought everyone was laughing at me, then I realized it was a thinking trap and I did the worst case, best case, and most likely scenarios. It helped incredibly, and got my head back into the right place. I just thought I'd let you know, because from students you probably hear quite a bit of negative feedback and rarely the positive feedback!

   Hope you're well,

   Don

Dear Don,

   Good to hear from you and great to know that a skill taught in Pos Ed was put to good use. I have never been on an exchange to a foreign country where I have been the "odd one out." I did, however, live in Greece with my Greek family (there are lots of them) when I was about 18 or 19. Not one of them could speak English and I spoke a little Greek. A different scenario to you, in that I was surrounded by kin, but there were times when I got very frustrated with my inability to communicate properly or not quite come to terms with the cultural differences. You will have a great time. Once you get the first few days/weeks behind you, you will find a rhythm. I hope this is the case.

   Best wishes,

   Scuddas

through this process helped her to remain calm and avoid unhelpful or impulsive behavior that might have escalated the conflict.

   Box 8.2 includes email correspondence between Charlie Scudamore, Vice Principal, and Don, a Geelong Grammar School student, describing how resiliency skills helped Don while he was on exchange in Germany. This email started a chain of correspondence between Charlie, Don, and Don's parents, and with Don's permission was also shared throughout the School community. At the time of the last correspondence, Don was enjoying his time in Germany, picking up the German language quickly, and forming close connections with his host family and members of the wider community. The story was meaningful to many Geelong Grammar School staff as a rich example of how students use their knowledge of Positive Education in real-life situations.

Looking for evidence

Are you a Sherlock Holmes or a Merlock Worms? Do you look for evidence or believe the first thing that comes into your head? If you are a Sherlock Holmes you collect evidence. If you are a Merlock Worms you think about it for only a second or two and then just choose the first thought that pops into your head and stick with it. You don't research anything.

Winnie, Year 7, Middle School, Corio Campus

"Merlock Worms" is one of the most memorable activities from the PRP (Gillham et al., 2007). The activity is based on the story of a missing bike and the ensuing search for the bike thief. First, Merlock Worms helps to look for the bike thief. Merlock accepts the first explanation that he comes across and sticks with it, despite increasing evidence that the explanation is incorrect. In contrast, Sherlock Holmes searches for evidence, weighs up the different options, and in the end identifies the true bike thief. Through regular reminders, students become quite skilled at considering different perspectives, looking for evidence, and challenging their automatic negative thoughts.

In a pertinent story of the power of having this language for resilience across the School community, Mary-Anne Lewis, Head of Connewarre House, came home one night to find the Boarding House in disarray. She reprimanded the students and instructed them to go straight to bed. The next day, a few students came and politely asked to speak with her. They said that she had been a "Merlock Worms" and had not considered their side of the story. After the students had explained their version of events, Mary-Anne could see their point of view more clearly. She thanked the girls and acknowledged their use of the character strengths of honesty and bravery in coming to speak with her, and told them that the whole experience was a good reminder that "sometimes adults can be like Merlock Worms, too."

Confirmation and negativity bias

To create depth of understanding, students are taught about biases in human thinking that can undermine resilience. The metaphor that "Some thoughts stick like Velcro and other thoughts slide off like Teflon" is useful in helping students to understand that the way in which each individual sees the world is influenced by certain patterns in their thinking. The confirmation bias occurs when people pay attention to information that is consistent with their beliefs, and ignore or discount information that contradicts their beliefs (Nickerson, 1998). A student with a confirmation bias about being completely incompetent at a particular subject may focus heavily on their difficulties while completely ignoring their successes.

The Positive Education curriculum also covers the negativity bias—that is, the tendency for humans to be highly attuned to negative experiences compared with positive experiences (Vaish et al., 2008). This bias is often summarized by the phrase "Bad is stronger than good," as substantial research has found that people's emotional, behavioral, and physiological reactions to negative events and stimuli are much stronger than their reactions to positive events and stimuli (Baumeister et al., 2001). An activity that helps students to understand the negativity bias is described

> **BOX 8.3: Exploring the negativity bias**
>
> Students in Year 10 are shown a series of 20 powerful images in a random order. Ten of these images are chosen because they evoke positive emotions, such as a baby laughing, a beautiful beach scene, or elderly people holding hands. Ten of the images are chosen because they evoke negative emotions, such as a baby crying, the bush after a fire, or a person looking alone and defeated. After all of the images have been shown, the students are asked to estimate how many negative and positive images there were altogether. Most students overestimate the number of negative images in the set and underestimate the number of positive images, which supports the negativity bias theory. They are then asked to share which image had the most powerful impact on them. Again, this often favors the negative. Students are encouraged to gain personal meaning from these ideas by journaling about times when they have focused heavily on the negatives in a particular situation.

in Box 8.3. Through such exercises, students become skilled at going beyond taking their thoughts at face value, and become more aware of the unique factors that influence how they interpret the world. Students and staff make use of activities aimed at cultivating positive emotions, such as blessings journals and "What Went Well" exercises, which are deliberate techniques to combat the negativity bias and redirect attention towards the positive aspects of life.

Real-time resilience

> You are born neither with nor without resilience. Resilience develops as people grow, as they move through life experiences, as they develop more accurate thinking and self-awareness skills, more knowledge. Resilience is comprised a set of characteristics, abilities, and core competencies—many of which are teachable.
>
> Tony Inkster, Head of Middle School

Students in the 3rd VIII rowing crew used their learning in Positive Education during the Head of the Schoolgirls Regatta on the Barwon River (see Figure 8.4). The 3rd VIII had been working hard to prepare for their important race for several months. Just after the race had started, a team from another school, who were favorites to win the race, ran into difficulties and stopped rowing. The other three teams rowed for 500 metres before they were told to stop as the race was to be restarted. Puffed, disgruntled, and angry, the teams turned around and rowed the 500 metres back to the start of the race, where the fresh and determined favorite team was waiting for them. Rather than be overcome by their anger, the Geelong Grammar School team regrouped and made a conscious decision to remain positive. One crew member made a comment that they had an advantage over the other crews—they had learnt the skill of real-time resilience. The students smiled at this. The race was restarted, and the Geelong Grammar School team rowed the race of their lives, winning by 0.14 of a second.

Figure 8.4 Girls' rowing crew in action.

As this story exemplifies, resilience skills are often needed in the heat of the moment, at the time when a person has a strong emotional reaction to an experience, before they react in ways that may make the situation worse. The aim of real-time resilience is to challenge counterproductive thoughts as they occur, thereby allowing the individual to focus positively and productively on the task or challenge at hand (Gillham et al., 2007). Real-time resilience does not mean minimizing or ignoring the difficulty, but instead developing the skills necessary to react calmly to stress and pressures. Mindfulness also plays a key role in helping students and staff to regulate their emotions in the present moment, and greatly supports resilience (for further information, see Chapter 9).

Post-traumatic growth

Recently, the Positive Education curriculum has been expanded to include post-traumatic growth. Trauma occurs when a person is involved in or witnesses a life-threatening event that causes extreme levels of fear and helplessness. The majority of people will experience at least one traumatic event in their lifetime (Creamer et al., 2001). Normal reactions that people have after a trauma include feeling numb, feeling flat, having trouble sleeping, and withdrawing socially. In the majority of cases, these reactions will subside after a number of weeks. However, when these reactions are intense and prolonged it is best to seek help. Although the majority of people cope well with trauma and display resilience, a small number of individuals go on to develop post-traumatic stress disorder.

The emerging field of post-traumatic growth offers new insights into trauma and the effects that traumatic experiences have on people's lives. Post-traumatic growth challenges traditional ways of looking at negative life events, and emphasizes that stories of suffering do not always lead to negative life pathways (Tedeschi and Calhoun, 2004). Post-traumatic growth involves positive transformation after trauma, and can include greater appreciation of life and changed priorities, warmer, more intimate relationships with others, a greater sense of personal strength, spiritual development, and a sense of new possibilities. A useful metaphor used at the School is that of a caterpillar and a butterfly—perceptions of our world may change completely, but such change can lead to new possibilities and ways of looking at the world.

Post-traumatic growth is explicitly covered in Year 10 Positive Education lessons. These lessons aim to explore the meaning of trauma and its impact in terms of stress and growth. In considering the sensitivity of the topic, teachers emphasize that there are no hard and fast rules about how to respond to trauma and stress. Lessons look to inform students about typical psychological and physiological responses to trauma, such as flight, fight and freeze, as well as the normal reactions people have after stressful events, such as problems with sleeping. It is hoped that such lessons foster students' world readiness as time is spent considering how to seek help and develop healthy coping strategies if they ever find themselves struggling after a stressful event.

A training ground for resilience

The greatest gift a parent can give to their son or daughter is the ability to cope with the future world—the ability to have the resilience to deal with the unknown and the ability to cope with adversity. The only way this can happen is practice. Timbertop is a resilience training ground … a place to practice.

Roger Herbert, Head of Timbertop

Year 9 students complete their academic year at Timbertop, which is a fully residential boarding campus in the Victorian Highlands. Life at Timbertop requires resilience on a daily basis. Students are challenged in many ways—socially, academically, emotionally, and physically. It is difficult for many students to be away from their parents and families, and they are required to be largely responsible for themselves. Cultivating resilience has been at the heart of Timbertop since the foundation of the campus in 1953. The recent implementation of Positive Education has further supported this vision by creating a common language around resilience, complementing the lived experiences with explicit resilience lessons in the curriculum. More information on resilience and life at Timbertop is provided by Stephen Pearce, Deputy Head of Timbertop, in Case Study 8.2.

CASE STUDY 8.2

Resilience at Timbertop

Stephen Pearce, Deputy Head of Timbertop

Face the days that lie ahead with a spirit of adventure, compassion, honesty and confidence. Brave the stormy seas that are bound to confront you, determined to sail your ship on to the quiet waters that lie ahead. Help those whom you may find in trouble, and steer clear of the whirlpools of destruction which you will meet on your voyage through life.

Dr Kurt Hahn

Dr Karen Reivich describes resilience as a "dynamic process of positive adaptation or development in the context of significant adversity" (Reivich, 2010). Welcome to a year at Timbertop!

Timbertop began as a brave educational experiment, conceived by the then Headmaster of Geelong Grammar School, Sir James Darling, in the belief that students needed to be removed from the "usual school machine" to live in a "different and less clement environment." Influenced by the philosophies of Dr Kurt Hahn, Darling hoped that the Timbertop life would be "essentially one of self-reliance and the challenge to live up to this responsibility."

The Timbertop program has naturally evolved since 1953, but Darling's philosophy still resonates through the daily life of the campus. Past students return to sit on "their bed" in a Unit set-up that remains virtually unchanged. Metaphorically, at least, their initials are still scratched into the timber. They are connected and will always belong. The stories recounted by past and present students sound familiar, too, and are the result of shared adversities—the same steep mountains, long hikes, cross-country runs, blisters, fatigue, cold, and wet.

Inherent challenges have been experienced by every generation of boys and girls at Timbertop, while other challenges have been very personal and unique. Of course, what is a significant adversity for some may well be a moment of flourishing for others. Physically the program is demanding for all students and staff who must engage in its challenges. As the year progresses, so do the distances of the hikes and cross-country runs. There is always a new mountain! Students need to learn real-time resiliency skills in order to cope with the demands of living in the wilderness. Core human needs for shelter, food, and water require consideration—they must stay warm and dry, they must drink fluids, and they must cook, regardless of the weather conditions or their state of fatigue or social friction within the hiking group. Figure 8.5 shows a group of students on a hike during the colder months.

The Timbertop life asks students to surrender technology, so there are no televisions, mobile phones, emails, Facebook, or personal computers. For some, this

Figure 8.5 Opportunities to foster resilience and nurture relationships abound on all Timbertop hikes.

"digital detox" is the greatest adversity they face, certainly in the first school term, as their cyberspace existence is offline, at least until the school holidays. Students write letters home, and these letters are kept and re-read. They live in timber huts called Units and sleep in dormitories, so they must learn how to share space. They need to develop a culture of service. For the Unit and campus to function, students rely on one another to complete chores. They sweep, vacuum, mop, clean toilets, serve meals, sort recycling, collect rubbish, and tend the vegetables in the garden. They can only have a hot shower when wood has been collected and chopped, and the boiler has been lit. The boiler takes time to heat the water, so someone needs to get out of bed early to do this chore.

The social complexities of living with others for long periods of time in spartan accommodation can sometimes present the greatest adversities. There are no parents present to help to defuse an argument, to allocate jobs, or to change the linen and sort the laundry. Instead the students are supported by their Head of Unit—a teacher who is assigned to guide them through the year. The relationship between the students and their Head of Unit is very special, and the connections are strong. As Darling had hoped, Timbertop is indeed a challenging life.

Explicit teaching of Positive Psychology in the classroom plays a critical role in supporting the students so that they can manage adversity at Timbertop in a positive and dynamic way. As a timetabled subject, Positive Education aims to equip students with the resiliency skills necessary to help them to "bounce back," and to understand that adversity can provide opportunities for self-discovery and personal growth. We discuss inherently shared Timbertop challenges to help to build resiliency skills. Sometimes students raise personal issues, such as navigating the physical challenges and the socially complex life alongside the School's rigorous academic program. Either way, the adversities encountered in the Timbertop program are authentic and unique.

Dr Karen Reivich writes that when schools integrate resilience into their culture, this enhances greater and more sustained changes in their students. It is not uncommon for Timbertop students to truly acknowledge their achievements only once the year is over. Sometimes only then do they recognize that navigating Timbertop has been a journey of self-discovery and growth through adversity. They can draw on their experiences to help to manage adversity in later life. A Year 10 student recently wrote the following in a letter to me:

> Trust me, I don't miss the hiking part of it; for me that was the hardest part of the whole year. But then again, that is where I learnt the most about myself and my capabilities. When I reflect on my year, so many of my memories are ones where I had that stupid big pack on my back! I hope they realize what an amazing place Timbertop is, because I didn't fully understand it until I left. It was such a hard year, but one of the best experiences ever.

At Timbertop, you cannot opt out of a cross-country run because it is raining; you cannot determine the personality of the other students in your Unit. In the words of Dr Karen Reivich, "Schools can, as Geelong Grammar School has, enhance resilience by creating educational environments that cultivate students' personal skills, strengths, and strong relationships." Our work in Positive Education enhances our students' strengths in learning how to live a meaningful life.

This commitment to creating a culture that both supports and encourages resilience is not limited to Timbertop, but is an integral part of life at all four Geelong Grammar School campuses. In Box 8.4, Rob French, Deputy Head of the Middle School, describes how the "Year 8 journey" of paddling and hiking in the Victorian bush helps students to develop many new skills. The other option for the Year 8 journey, which involves taking part in the 9-day Great Victorian Bike Ride, is equally valuable in supporting students to develop resilience, persistence, and teamwork.

BOX 8.4: Resiliency on the Year 8 journey

The paddling and hiking camp is one of the best ways of fostering and promoting resilience in a group. Teams of approximately 12 students are chosen by staff, with the students having no input into who else is in their team. The members of each group are highly dependent on each other for the week of the camp. Leadership is shared, and the students themselves organize the paddling combinations, with the aim of keeping the combinations balanced. Students are given navigation tasks and must work together to organize breaks and lunch spots, with only the map as their guide. Once camp has been set up, the entire team is responsible for food preparation, and once again they rely heavily on working together as members of a team. For the hiking component, communal gear is sorted and distributed by the students to spread a fair load. The students are provided with maps, and need to navigate and arrange suitable locations for breaks. For many students this is their first significant outdoor experience, and their resilience is tested in a number of ways. The week is physically demanding, and they are pushed to play their part in maintaining group harmony and productivity. The groups are largely responsible for their own decision making, and must sort out conflicts between themselves. Many students finish this week having formed new connections with others, having used many of their character strengths to maintain harmony, and having undertaken many new and difficult tasks and responsibilities.

Rob French, Deputy Head of Middle School

Summary and conclusions

I've made up my mind that our lives are not determined by what happens to us, but by how we react to what happens; not by what life brings to us, but by the attitude we bring to life.

Steve Radojevic, Finance and Administration Manager

Dean Dell'Oro, Head of Corio Campus, shared the story of a Year 12 student who had trained for a specific athletics event for more than 6 months. In the final lead-up meet before the athletics final, the student ran badly and it looked highly unlikely that he would make the team for the final the following week. Although he was obviously deeply disappointed, the student did not complain, or blame the weather or an injury. The next day he asked a friend to come out to the track and record him running the same race again. He reran the race while his friend recorded his performance, and he managed to run a much better time. He then spoke to his coach, and showed him the footage, which ultimately meant that he was included in the team again. This student demonstrated the skills and mindsets necessary for resilience. Hopefully, when faced with challenges in their lives, many students will respond with the same dignity and courage.

Resilience is the capacity to maintain a healthy and thriving life despite the natural and inevitable ups and downs that go with it. As the world becomes increasingly complex and competitive, resilience skills will become more important than ever. Alongside developing healthy ways of seeing the world, it is important for students and staff to be reminded that a foundation of resilience is a willingness to seek and accept help and support. A wonderful bonus of having students with a well-developed understanding of resilience is that they are also better equipped to support their friends and family members at times of hardship. Thus students become more able to help the people they care about to cope with adversities and challenges, as well as living more fulfilling and flourishing lives themselves.

RECOMMENDED RESOURCES

Beyondblue. Australian National Mental Health Initiative, childhood and education program.<www.beyondblue.org.au/about-us/programs/childhood-and-education-program>

Beyondblue. Australian National Mental Health Initiative, SenseAbility communications portal (secondary school). <www.beyondblue.org.au/resources/schools-and-universities/secondary-schools-and-tertiary/senseability>

BounceBack! <www.bounceback.com.au>

Dr Seuss (1990). *Oh, the Places You'll Go!* New York: Harper Collins. (Children's picture storybook).

Edelman S (2006). *Change Your Thinking.* Sydney, Australia: ABC Books.

Fuller A (2011). *Life: a guide.* Sydney, Australia: Finch Publishing.

Ginsburg K (2011). *Building Resilience in Children and Teens: giving kids roots and wings.* Elk Grove Village, IL: American Academy of Pediatrics.

Johnstone M (2007). *I Had a Black Dog.* London: Robinson Publishing. (Picture book.)

Joseph S (2011). *What Doesn't Kill Us: the new psychology of posttraumatic growth.* New York: Basic Books.

KidsMatter. Australian National Mental Health Initiative for early years and primary schools. <www.kidsmatter.edu.au>

MindMatters. Australian National Mental Health Initiative for secondary schools. <www.mindmatters.edu.au>

Positive Psychology Center, University of Pennsylvania. *Resilience Research in Children: the Penn Resiliency Project.* <www.ppc.sas.upenn.edu/prpsum.htm>

Reivich K and Shatté A (2012). *The Resilience Factor: 7 keys to finding your inner strength.* New York: Three Rivers Press.

Seligman M E P (2006). *Learned Optimism: how to change your mind and your life*. New York: Vintage Press.

Southwick S M and Charney D S (2012). *Resilience: the science of mastering life's greatest challenges*. New York: Cambridge University Press.

REFERENCES

Baumeister R F, Bratslavsky E, Finkenauer C, and Vohs K D (2001). Bad is stronger than good. *Review of General Psychology, 5*, 323–70.

Beck A T (1976). *Cognitive Therapy and the Emotional Disorders*. New York: International Universities Press.

Beck A T (2005). The current state of cognitive therapy: a 40-year retrospective. *Archives of General Psychiatry, 62*, 953–9.

Beck A T, Rush A J, Shaw B F, and Emery G (1979). *Cognitive Therapy of Depression*. New York: Guilford Press.

Benard B (2004). *Resiliency: what we have learned*. San Francisco, CA: WestEd.

Brunwasser S M, Gillham J E, and Kim E S (2009). A meta-analytic review of the Penn Resiliency Program's effects on depressive symptoms. *Journal of Counsulting and Clinical Psychology, 77*, 1042–54.

Butler A C, Chapman J E, Forman E M, and Beck A T (2006). The empirical status of cognitive-behavioral therapy: a review of meta-analyses. *Clinical Psychology Review, 26*, 17–31.

Creamer M C, Burgess P, and McFarlane A C (2001). Post-traumatic stress disorder: findings from the Australian National Survey of Mental Health and Well-being. *Psychological Medicine, 31*, 1237–47.

Cutuli J et al. (2006). Preventing co-occurring depression symptoms in adolescents with conduct problems. *Annals of the New York Academy of Sciences, 1094*, 282–6.

Ellis A (1962). *Reason and Emotion in Psychotherapy*. New York: Lyle Stuart.

Gillham J E, Reivich K J, Jaycox L H, and Seligman M E P (1995). Prevention of depressive symptoms in schoolchildren: two-year follow-up. *Psychological Science, 6*, 343–51.

Gillham J E et al. (2006). Preventing depression among early adolescents in the primary care setting: a randomized controlled study of the Penn Resiliency Program. *Journal of Abnormal Child Psychology, 34*, 195–211.

Gillham J E, Reivich K J, and Jaycox L H (2007). *The Penn Resiliency Program (also known as the Penn Depression Prevention Program and the Penn Optimism Program): leader's manual*. Philadelphia, PA: University of Pennsylvania.

Gillham J E, Brunwasser S M, and Freres D R (2008). Preventing depression in early adolescence: the Penn Resiliency Program. In: JRZ Abela and BL Hankin (eds) *Handbook of Depression in Children and Adolescents*. New York: Guilford Press. pp. 309–32.

Luthar S S, Cicchetti D, and Becker B (2000). The construct of resilience: a critical evaluation and guidelines for future work. *Child Development, 71*, 543–62.

Maier S F and Seligman M E (1976). Learned helplessness: theory and evidence. *Journal of Experimental Psychology, 105*, 3–46.

Masten A S (2001). Ordinary magic: resilience processes in development. *American Psychologist, 56*, 227–38.

Masten A S and Reed M J (2002). Resilience in development. In: S J Lopez and C R Snyder (eds) *Oxford Handbook of Positive Psychology*, 2nd edn. Oxford: Oxford University Press. pp. 74–88.

Nickerson R S (1998). Confirmation bias: a ubiquitous phenomenon in many guises. *Review of General Psychology, 2*, 175–220.

Reivich K (2010). *Master Resilience Training Manual*. Philadelphia, PA: University of Pennsylvania.

Reivich K and Shatté A (2002). *The Resilience Factor: 7 essential skills for overcoming life's inevitable obstacles*. New York: Broadway Books.

Resnick M D et al. (1997). Protecting adolescents from harm. *Journal of the American Medical Association, 278*, 823–32.

Rutter M, Maughan B, Mortimore P, and Ouston J (1982). *Fifteen Thousand Hours: secondary schools and their effects on children*. Cambridge, MA: Harvard University Press.

Seligman M E P (1991). *Learned Optimism*. New York: Knopf.

Seligman M E P (1995). *The Optimistic Child*. Sydney, Australia: Random House.

Seligman M E P (2006). *Learned Optimism: how to change your mind and your life*. New York: Vintage Books.

Seligman M E P, Schulman P, DeRubeis R J, and Hollon S D (1999). The prevention of depression and anxiety. *Prevention and Treatment, 2*, 1–24.

Tedeschi R G and Calhoun L G (2004). Posttraumatic growth: conceptual foundations and empirical evidence. *Psychological Inquiry, 15*, 1–18.

Vaish A, Grossmann T, and Woodward A (2008). Not all emotions are created equal: the negativity bias in social-emotional development. *Psychological Bulletin, 134*, 383–403.

Wang M (2009). School climate support for behavioral and psychological adjustment: testing the mediating effect of social competence. *School Psychology Quarterly, 24*, 240–51.

9

POSITIVE HEALTH
AND MINDFULNESS

**Introduction by
Dr Craig Hassed**

Mindfulness seems to be the "flavor of the month." One only has to pick up a magazine or turn on the radio and it is not long before the topic of mindfulness comes up. The term is becoming part of modern parlance, but can something that has been around for thousands of years really be called a fashion or fad? Or is it just a matter of what was old becoming new again as more people search for meaning or clarity in a world that looks to be a little short on those two qualities?

Mindfulness is both a form of meditation and a way of living. As a form of meditation it might initially be thought of as a way of providing welcome respite from this increasingly frenetic and fast-paced modern world, but to see it as only that greatly limits the usefulness and scope of mindfulness. One of the main reasons why we practice mindfulness meditation is so that we have a greater capacity to live more mindfully or more consciously when we re-engage with the world—whether that means communicating with more attention, savoring life more, or being less anxious and preoccupied.

Mindfulness is both old and new—old in the sense that for millennia the world's great wisdom and spiritual traditions have used various meditative or contemplative practices, and new in the sense that the world appears to have suddenly discovered mindfulness. Over the last 20 years, but particularly over the last 10 years, there has been a veritable explosion of research and clinical interest in mindfulness-based approaches for enhancing or managing just about anything. Mindfulness has been applied in a vast range of situations, from improving mental and physical health to its use in education, sport, and leadership training.

William James' classic textbook, *The Principles of Psychology*, laid the foundations for all that followed in twentieth-century psychology. In it he wrote: "The faculty of voluntarily bringing back a wandering attention over and over again, is the very root of judgment, character, and will. No one is compos sui (a master of themselves) if he have it not. An education which should improve this faculty would be the education par excellence" (James, 1890).

It would seem as though William James recognized the importance of being able to train or focus attention, and that this was, in a manner of speaking, the ultimate education underpinning the development of "judgement, character, and will." Unfortunately, the West had all but lost touch with its ancient contemplative roots, so the skills of meditation were not widely known about or used. Consequently, the importance of attention in Western psychology remained largely a footnote for the next century. However, the situation has now changed rather dramatically.

Is mindfulness therefore a panacea? The answer is both yes and no. Yes, in that awareness or attention is the prerequisite for understanding or doing anything, or at least for doing it well. We cannot live or respond consciously without it. Living without awareness is like living without light—we cannot see or understand much, and we tend to be afraid of the dark. No, mindfulness is not a panacea in that it is not always a replacement for other things that might be necessary. For example, the fact that it helps in the management of pain—whether this is emotional or physical—does not mean that there may not also be a need for other kinds of support and treatment.

How do we know that mindfulness helps? Well, we can study it, but studying things like mindfulness that can be a little intangible can be somewhat challenging. As Mark Twain said, "Studying humor is like dissecting a frog. You may know a lot, but you wind up with a dead frog." In some ways it is the same when we are trying to study and define mindfulness. As useful as it might be to define it or put it in a pigeonhole, as soon as we do that we potentially limit something that has an infinite number of aspects and applications. We potentially take the life out of the very thing we are trying to study. Nevertheless, it is on the back of research—especially in the fields of clinical medicine, neuroscience, and psychology—that mindfulness has become of interest to a much wider audience.

Mindfulness practitioners in ancient times did not have modern laboratories, physiological measures, or techniques for measuring brain activity such as magnetic resonance imaging (MRI). Their laboratory was their own mind and body. They studied it from the inside out, as it were, not from the outside in as is the way with science. This helped the ancients to understand it in a deeper, more intuitive, nuanced way than would be the case if one only had an intellectual understanding of it. Mindfulness can only really be learned and understood through practice and experience. A mere intellectual understanding devoid of experience is about as useful as giving a lecture on hydration to a thirsty man. Theory alone will not satisfy that deep longing. We have to understand ourselves more deeply and to experience life more fully.

Having said all of this, let us nevertheless try—without killing the frog—to define mindfulness and to explore why it is such an important foundation for Positive Education. A simple way of defining mindfulness could be as a mental discipline aimed at training attention. There are a few other implied aspects of mindfulness training. For example, mindfulness-based practices generally utilize the senses as a point upon which to train the attention, engage the mind in the present moment, foster self-control through non-attachment to transitory experiences such as thoughts, feelings, and sensations, encourage an attitude of openness, acceptance, or non-judgment towards those experiences, and cultivate calmness and a sense of stillness through being unmoved by or less reactive to moment-by-moment experience.

In what way are such capacities valuable to education? In what way is mindfulness a life skill that every child needs in order to learn and flourish? Here are a few considerations. First, without attention there is no memory. We cannot remember things—from the most mundane to the most profound—if we did not see them happen because we were not paying attention. For example, we may not recall where the car keys are because our mind had already begun worrying about what we were going to do next at the precise moment when the keys were being put down.

Secondly, we cannot understand something or learn how it works unless we observe impartially and objectively. Often we find it difficult to engage our attention with what we are trying to learn. For example, a student might find it difficult to learn Mathematics because their attention is eclipsed by the thought "I'm no good at Mathematics," and is therefore unable to engage with the teacher or the Mathematics in front of them. Such a distracted and unengaged state of mind not only makes learning onerous, but also causes procrastination and wastes a huge amount of time.

Thirdly, there is little wonder or enjoyment in learning when we are not paying attention. As Gilbert Chesterton said, "There are no uninteresting things, there are only uninterested people." When we are not paying attention we do not see what is of interest, and when we are uninterested we become uninteresting and live in an uninteresting world. The younger the child, the more wide open their eyes are and the more they live in a fascinating and miraculous world. Einstein was a classic deep learner with an almost child-like fascination. This is what he said: "The most beautiful thing we can experience is the mysterious. It is the source of all true art and all science. He to whom this emotion is a stranger, who can no longer pause to wonder and stand rapt in awe, is as good as dead: his eyes are closed."

Fourthly, one of the greatest roadblocks to learning is mental rigidity—that is, a fixation or attachment to an opinion, belief, or assumption even in the face of evidence to the contrary. It could also be a fixation on a way of doing things even when the method that we are using is not working, or at least is not working well. The non-attachment that is developed through mindfulness helps us to cultivate the mental flexibility required to adapt, innovate, and create. This is closely related to the concept of fixed and growth mindsets as described by Professor Carol Dweck (see Dweck, 2006) and discussed in Chapter 11 of this book.

Fifthly, mindfulness is an essential skill that helps not only to cultivate wellbeing but also to build resilience and assist in the management of the stress, anxiety, and depression that are so much a part of life for many of our young people today. One particular form of anxiety that students, especially more senior ones, find troublesome is exam anxiety. The distracted focus on oneself results in a lack of engagement with the exam question in front of one. Stress will only drive performance so far. It is the art of being alert and not alarmed that is learned by the most capable people.

Lastly, one of the key aims of education is to do with a focus not on the individual, but on the individual as a connected member of family, community, society, humanity, and the environment. In order to understand others, to develop social skills, or to experience empathy and compassion for others, we have to unhook our attention from our preoccupation with ourselves for long enough to allow us to engage with the person who is in front of us. Cruelty and insensitivity are easy to inflict when we are not really looking at what we are doing and the impact that it is having on those around us. Compassion, on the other hand, is one of the most natural and important "side effects" of mindfulness—perhaps the most important.

I have had the great pleasure and honor of being invited over recent years to provide mindfulness courses for staff members and presentations for senior students at Geelong Grammar School. These have focused on how to apply mindfulness in academic and personal life. Other mindfulness teachers, such as Janet Etty-Leal and Dr Jacolyn Norrish, have provided further input throughout the School community. Geelong Grammar School, is, I believe, taking the right approach to implementing mindfulness and Positive Education in that these are not being added as an afterthought to a packed curriculum, but as a practical and philosophical underpinning to the whole education process. It is in integrating mindfulness, revisiting it, and reinforcing it over a number of years and in a variety of contexts that students and staff can really understand it from the inside.

In my experience at Geelong Grammar School I have been struck by the sincerity and openness with which the students and staff have engaged with mindfulness. This makes me believe that the principles of Positive Education are not just finding a home there, but are taking root deep within the very fabric of the School. This brave pioneering work not only augurs well for education in Australia, but will also resonate around the world. There is a natural synergy between mindfulness and the aims of Positive Education. Perhaps mindfulness could be seen as the yeast in the bread mix. It is up to the current generation of brave and innovative educators to measure, mix, and bake the ingredients well. Heaven only knows, the world is hungry for what a Positive Education can provide.

Mindfulness at Geelong Grammar School

The most valuable skill I have learnt in Pos Ed is to press the pause button. Taking a step back is important. Meditation helps you clear your mind of worries and focus on the present moment.

Alice, Year 7, Middle School, Corio

Simon Haigh, Head of Barrabool House, shared a story of a time on a recent family holiday when he was walking along the beach with his wife, Lucy, and their two young children, Bella and Charlie. The sea was rough and waves were crashing, leaving water running up and down the sand. Bella and Charlie, both students at Bostock House where mindfulness is regularly practiced, were talking to each other, unaware that Simon and Lucy were listening to them. As she walked along the sand, Bella said "I think this is like a meditation." Later on in the day, the whole family was in the water. The kids were jumping as the waves were breaking, feeling the bubbles against their faces. As he focused on the sensations of the water on his face, Charlie said to his sister "This is like a meditation, too." To watch young children be fully alive in the moment is a wonderful experience. For children as young as 4 years old to be able to communicate their understanding of mindfulness and share their experiences with each other is something quite special.

Reflection and contemplation have always been an important part of Geelong Grammar School. Students are often provided with clear points at which to pause, celebrate their journey so far, and look to the future with fresh eyes. In particular, the regular Chapel services allow students the time and space for deep contemplation and introspection. Similarly, reflective learning is a core skill that is embedded throughout the four campuses, and helps to create space for personal exploration and growth. Through journaling and letter writing, students reflect on their experiences and make sense of their feelings. These important skills for self-awareness and insight are supported and enhanced by Positive Education and the dedicated focus on mindfulness and meditation.

Mindfulness and meditation

I feel floaty and very quiet inside.

I feel calm when I close my eyes. I see rainbow colors and feel light.

It is calm for my body. I feel calm and relaxed and the whole world is peaceful.

I feel like I am floating on a cloud.

Prep students from Bostock House explain what meditation feels like

A student hiking on Mount Timbertop may be fully present in the moment, focusing on the sights before them, the smells in the air, and the sounds that their steps make on the bush floor. In comparison, another student may be largely oblivious to their surroundings, caught up in thinking about a recent conversation with a friend, or worrying about an upcoming assignment. The difference between these two students in this moment can be summarized as one student being mindful and the other being mindless (or even mind*full*). In the academic literature, mindfulness is defined as attending to the current moment in a curious, open, and non-judgmental way (Kabat-Zinn, 2003). A useful explanation for students is that mindfulness is like "tuning in" and paying attention, whereas mindlessness is like "tuning out" and being unfocused.

Meditation practices involve the deliberate direction of attention and awareness. There are many forms of meditation, such as breathing meditations, guided visualizations, and active/movement meditations, many of which are integrated in different ways throughout Geelong Grammar School (for an example of a walking meditation used with students, see Box 9.1). Mindfulness is a meditative practice that includes bringing open and accepting awareness to the activities of daily living. Individuals can mindfully take part in a range of activities, such as having a conversation, listening to music, exercising, or studying. The aim of mindfulness is to be "in the moment," as opposed to being preoccupied with thoughts about the past or future.

BOX 9.1: A walking meditation

This short mindful meditation is used with a range of age groups and is often completed at the start of the day or as a break during a lesson. The practice starts with a standing meditation where the focus is on feeling balance. Students are asked to stand with their knees slightly bent. Once they are comfortable, the students rock slightly forward to the point where their heels are just about to leave the ground, rock slightly back until their toes are just about to leave the ground, and then find the point of balance in between. Next, they are asked to move their body slightly to the right, and then to the left, again finding their balance between the two points. This introduction helps students to become centered prior to the commencement of the walking meditation. Students are invited to walk in a circle around the classroom or around a suitable area outside, breathing as they transfer their weight from one foot to the other. As they calmly place one foot in front of the other, they intentionally observe the transfer of balance.

At Corio campus, this walking meditation is extended by leading students through a mindful walk around the Chapel of All Saints. Students visit different points of interest in the Chapel surrounds mindfully, such as the Gallipoli oaks on the Chapel lawn, the diverse and flowering garden beds, the House of Commons bird bath, and the bronze effigy of the dog, Chippie Mark IV. By mindfully attending to the details in their surroundings, the students learn the value of pausing to take in and appreciate those aspects of their environment that can be easily missed.

Through mindfulness, students and staff members develop increased awareness of just how much time is spent analyzing past disappointments or worrying about things that may or may not happen in the future. The aim of mindfulness is for people to notice their thoughts coming and going without trying to judge or control them. As a result, when someone is mindful, they are more able to notice, appreciate, and savor the present moment. The capacity for mindfulness builds over time, and regular practice strengthens a person's ability to remain present despite distractions.

Mindfulness and flourishing

Contemporary life can be full and hectic. Often even young children have structured timetables filled with extra-curricular activities. Students of all ages juggle academic, co-curricular, sporting, performing arts, and community service endeavors. Many adults work long hours and balance substantial family, professional, and personal commitments. Sources of technology compete for people's attention and can lead to the danger of almost constant stimulation. There is such little time for children, young people, or adults to just "be." Mindfulness offers points of stillness, calm, and balance in the day. It enhances the experience of the current moment and helps individuals to be present, even in the midst of busy or hectic surroundings. Mindfulness recognizes that there is great value in allowing students and staff to take a step back, press "pause," and devote a few moments to relaxation and rejuvenation.

However, as Dr Craig Hassed explained in his introduction, mindfulness offers much more than a respite from busyness—it is a foundation for flourishing. Mindfulness is located within the positive health domain due to its robust influence on physical and mental health. Enduring stress is a major contributing factor for a range of physical health conditions, and acts to cause prolonged wear and tear on the body. Mindfulness calms the stress response and helps the body to regulate and heal (Kabat-Zinn, 1990). Reviews of mindfulness programs have consistently found positive results in terms of the prevention and treatment of illness, improved immune functioning, and decreased pain (Greeson, 2009; Grossman et al., 2004).

Cultivating awareness through mindfulness and meditation is also linked to enhanced psychological health. Research studies indicate a beneficial connection between mindfulness and a reduction in depression, anxiety, and psychological distress (Baer, 2003; Fjorback et al., 2011; Hofmann et al., 2010). Mindfulness has been associated with increased psychological wellbeing and more frequent positive feelings such as joy, inspiration, hope, gratitude, and vitality (Greeson, 2009). Especially relevant to schools, mindfulness reduces misbehavior and aggression, and has valuable consequences for young people with attention deficit hyperactivity disorder (Meiklejohn et al., 2012). Taken together, the research in the field provides promising evidence for the value of meditation and mindfulness in contributing to flourishing living and learning.

Staff mindfulness

A school culture of mindfulness and meditation starts with the staff. Having a personal mindfulness practice equips staff to teach such skills to their students with authenticity. Being mindful throughout the day enables adults in the School community to lead by example and to role model behaviors that they would like to instill in their students. Mindfulness has particular value within constantly changing classrooms, where teachers are required to balance and respond to many competing demands for their attention. By training their awareness, teachers become more able to sustain focus and carefully shift their attention from task to task or from student to student.

Dr Hassed, a respected expert in the field, ran experiential courses for Geelong Grammar School staff which aimed to help them to develop or expand their own mindfulness and meditation practices (for further information on the concepts covered by this program, see Hassed, 2008). The first 8-week course was run with all Heads of House; the second course was open to any interested Corio staff members. Dr Hassed gently led staff through mindfulness exercises and facilitated deep exploration of mindfulness as a path to self-knowledge and understanding. A concept that resonated with many staff related to Dr Hassed's ideas of mindfulness "full stops" and "commas." A "full stop" is a time within the day that is dedicated to a longer meditation practice. A "comma" is a short pause or break, and may be as simple as directing attention to the breath while waiting for the kettle to boil, or performing some mindful stretches before going for a run. Commas and full stops provide the individual with time and space to center the self before proceeding with the tasks of daily living with increased focus and renewed vitality.

Dr Hassed's comprehensive course enabled informative discussion and rich growth. The experiential mindfulness practice was supported by personal reflection and non-judgmental discussion of each person's experience of mindfulness—and often mindlessness—throughout the week. This course supported many staff in practicing mindfulness with increased confidence and regularity. Several staff described feeling more focused, content, and at peace after regularly practicing mindfulness. Conversations about mindfulness are continuing. For example, the team at the Institute of Positive Education takes 10 minutes for meditation every morning, which provides a foundation for mindfulness throughout the day (for a reflection on this, written by Dr Georgiana Cameron, see Box 9.2).

Mindfulness and younger students

We want children to understand the concept of quiet time before they get entirely caught up in the schedules of their own increasingly demanding lives and the

BOX 9.2: Mindfulness and the Institute for Positive Education

In February 2014, Professor Felicia Huppert visited Geelong Grammar School (her second visit), and the Institute team were privileged to spend time with her. As a team we were inspired by the emphasis and value that Professor Huppert placed on mindfulness. Although we have always considered mindfulness to be an essential aspect of wellbeing, Professor Huppert's visit reminded us of the need to continue to devote time and energy to creating opportunities for mindfulness practices across the whole School. In considering how to encourage others to practice mindfulness, we felt it was important to look first at our own practice of mindfulness. We value authenticity strongly, and endeavor always "to walk our talk," so we began a daily practice of mindfulness. This practice involves all Institute staff stopping at 9.00 a.m. and sitting together and listening to a guided mindfulness meditation for 10 minutes. This seemingly simple activity continues to give us insight not only into ourselves, but also into the benefits and difficulties associated with sustaining a daily mindfulness practice. At times we have found ourselves "too busy" and have let the practice slip for a few days, only to realize the following week that we need to remind each other again of its importance and re-establish the habit. In many ways our continued commitment to this 10-minute mindfulness practice has not only been helpful to us as individuals, but has also been powerful in increasing our awareness and strength as a team.

Georgiana Cameron, Content Developer and Trainer, Institute of Positive Education

busyness of their worlds in the future. We want them to learn the pleasure and value in, once in a while, having a break from their routine and commitments to take some quiet time just for themselves.

Daryl Moorfoot, Head of Bostock House

Mindful meditation offers huge potential in positively developing the minds of children. As children progress through sequential mindful experiences, they can learn to manage stress, calm down, self-monitor, and reap the benefits of developing self-mastery in every facet of their lives.

Janet Etty-Leal, Mindful Meditation Consultant

Introducing young students to mindfulness at the very beginning of their formal education provides them with years of practice in this important life skill, and equips them with lifelong skills for health and wellbeing. Young children are often naturally mindful, and can be completely absorbed in simple activities such as looking at leaves and pebbles, reading a story, or playing with their friends. The aim is to build on this rich foundation so that as children grow up they have a well-developed capacity for self-awareness and focus. Reflections on mindfulness activities run with students in the ELC and Prep at Bostock House are described in Box 9.3.

BOX 9.3: Mindfulness in ELC and Prep

Janet explained that we have a "pause" button, like that on a DVD player. We can pause and create a space in which to see and feel things differently. She read *The Rainbow Fish* and we explored the importance of noticing and paying attention and what we can give and share. Lucan suggested we can share love. Taj suggested we can share toys. We talked about how we can share these things with cuddles, smiles, saying kind things, and doing nice things. We finished with a beautiful mindful movement experience where we swayed and moved different parts of our bodies gently.

Julie Molloy, Early Learning Centre, Acting Director, Bostock House

Each day we do 5 minutes of meditation and gratitude circle time where we all get to express gratitude for things/people in our lives. I change the time of day we do it so the children become aware of the things that happen throughout their whole day. We focus on the fact that the very small things in life deserve thanks as much as the more elaborate things and moments. When we start a meditation, some children take significantly longer than others to settle but, in general, all children allow themselves to quieten inwardly and benefit from the sessions. I find the classroom meditation sessions provide the children with a wonderful "space" to just be themselves and let their busy little minds and bodies relax and sift out the busyness of their day.

Jo Kearney, Prep Teacher, Bostock House

Mindfulness is integrated in many ways throughout Toorak campus and Bostock House. Starting the school day with a few moments for mindfulness helps students to become open, curious, and ready to learn. Similarly, students can return to the classroom from playing during recess or lunch full of energy and enthusiasm. Teachers may devote a few moments to mindful storytelling, listening to music, or drawing, to help the students to refocus for the upcoming lesson. Several teachers have commented that mindfulness is a foundational skill for concentration, cooperation, and creativity, and that a few moments of mindfulness benefit students' focus for the remainder of the day.

Mindfulness goes beyond preparing students for learning, and helps them to develop strong emotional and social skills. Richard Munro, a teacher at the Toorak campus, uses visualization techniques to encourage his Year 5 students to imagine the place where they feel most calm, at peace, and grateful. This mindful place may be a room in a house, a place in nature, or somewhere near the water. Richard gives each student a piece of paper with an empty oval on it, which he refers to as a "mindful spot" (Richard attributes this activity to past Toorak teacher, John Reddan, who referred to these ovals as "magic spots"). When the students have spent time imagining their calm and serene place, they are invited to draw a picture of it in their "mindful spot." The students can then use this drawing, or recall their mindful place, if they are feeling anxious or distressed. This skill of pausing helps students to regulate their emotions and behaviors, and provides a valuable foundation for resilience.

Meditation capsules

Self-knowledge is the key benefit of the practice of meditation. Over time, children can begin to understand the "shifting sands" of emotions, impulses, and habits. Moment-by-moment choices are gradually illuminated by self-awareness. As confidence grows with practice, increasingly children feel like they are in good hands—their own!

Janet Etty-Leal, Mindful Meditation Consultant

The School's journey with mindfulness has been greatly enriched by a long-term relationship with Janet Etty-Leal (for further information on Janet's programs, see Etty-Leal, 2010). Janet is an experienced mindful meditation consultant who guides Junior and Middle School students in the practice of mindfulness and meditation (see Figure 9.1). She spends up to 40 days a year at the School, leading experiential

Figure 9.1 Students from Bostock House participating in a mindful meditation session led by Janet Etty-Leal.

workshops and sessions with students and staff from the ELC to Year 8. The School community greatly appreciates Janet's commitment to implementing mindfulness and meditation as part of all students' learning, and admires the experiential and vibrant nature of her work.

Janet's mindfulness lessons are a special experience. Posters, fabrics, and cushions are used to make the room a calm and colorful place. Young students take off their shoes and enter the room accompanied by peaceful music. Janet may ask students to locate their ears and give them a tug or wiggle to "prepare them for good listening," or share a simple yoga practice to "wake up their eyes, and become ready to notice everything."

By using a range of props, quotes, stories, images, sounds, and activities, the children explore what it means to be present. The different activities and exercises help the students to develop an alert, inquiring mind. Students may be invited to mindfully consider a seed, leaf, or acorn, bringing their attention to the minute details of nature that are often missed. After this introduction, Janet asks the students to consider other things in their lives that they may miss. The students volunteer insightful examples, ranging from sights and sounds to how their friends or family may be feeling at a particular moment.

Janet helps the students to develop mindfulness through increased awareness of their bodies. Through "mindful movements" the students complete mindful stretching or shaking, or assume positions based on simple yoga or qi gong poses. Janet leads children into mindful meditation practice with symbols or chimes, enabling them to progress from "outer" to "inner" listening and noticing (for a summary of one of Janet's mindfulness lessons for young children see Box 9.4, and for an *Inner Awareness Meditation* script see Box 9.5). Teachers are always invited to participate in Janet's classes, and this in turn helps them to develop ideas and strategies for implementing mindfulness in their own classrooms. As a result of the School's ongoing relationship with Janet, several teachers describe increased confidence when facilitating mindfulness exercises themselves.

Mindfulness and senior students

Mindfulness supports health and wellbeing for older students, and meditation sessions are regularly run at the Corio campus in the senior classrooms, Boarding Houses, and the Handbury Centre for Wellbeing (for a reflection on meditation sessions conducted in the Wellbeing Centre by John Hendry, Director of Student Welfare, see Box 9.6). Steve Andrew, Head of Fraser House, frequently leads students in the Boarding Houses through 30-minute relaxation or visualization exercises, accompanied by calm music, often just before bedtime (for a discussion by Steve Andrew on how he uses mindfulness in both the classroom and Boarding Houses, see Case Study 9.1).

BOX 9.4: Getting to know the body

The learning intentions of this lesson are to help children develop awareness of sensa-tions of their muscular contraction and relaxation, and for them to notice changes in alignment and balance within the body as they sit, stand, and move. The lesson resources are charts with visual displays of the muscular/skeletal systems of the body, and mirrors to be shared in a group activity.

Children are invited to share their wishes, gradually connecting them to their amazing ability to change from the inside, creating different shapes and feelings with their bodies, and ultimately creating great thoughts and ideas. The students also contemplate their amazing muscular/skeletal systems. Students are divided into groups. Each person within the group takes turns to slowly move their facial muscles, through the forehead, eyebrows, cheeks, mouth, and jaw, watching their mirror reflection and noticing the changing feel-ings and sensations through their face. This is extended to mindful movements, where chil-dren develop awareness of whole-body muscular/skeletal coordinated movement, such as swaying, rocking, stretching, and balancing. This progresses to a still "inner awareness" experience in which students notice the tiny, subtle sensations within their body.

Janet Etty-Leal, Mindful Meditation Consultant

BOX 9.5: Inner awareness script

The following script is used as a basis for quiet inner awareness practice with children. It is read slowly, with frequent pauses.

Taking up your position, settling comfortably on a chair, or lying on the floor.

Softly, gently, letting the eyelids close down. Feeling the breath moving through your nose. Listening to the sound of the breath. Easily breathing out ... letting your attention slide down ... to your chest ... tummy ... buttocks ... legs ... sliding down to the feet.

Breathing out ... feeling all the muscles in your feet softening to the number 10 ... breathing out ... loosening all the muscles through your calves and shins to the number 9 ... breathing out ... the softness spreading all through your thighs and legs to the number 8 ... the out-breath just like a beautiful waterfall of softness ...

Flowing to your buttocks ... breathing out to the number 7 ... to your tummy ... softening with the number 6 ... breathing out to the number 5 ... feeling the gentle softness spreading all through your chest and your heart ... breathing out to the number 4 ... softening the hands ... breathing out to the number 3 as the softness spreads through the arms ... letting go to the number 2 ... softening through the shoulders.

Feeling your jaw ... loosening to the number 1 ... letting softness spread through the face ... cheeks ... lips ... mouth ... tongue ... eyes ... ears ... head. ... Feeling it all through the body ... from the toes ... to the very top of your head ... feeling the whole body softly saying "Thank you."

Janet Etty-Leal, Mindful Meditation Consultant

> **BOX 9.6: Senior School meditation in the Handbury Centre for Wellbeing**
>
> For senior students, meditation is a significant means of assisting them to become more aware of their interactions with their living environment, prompting their neurophysiological responses to living and learning. The awareness they gain of what surrounds them and affects them is important for enabling students to recognize their anxiety state and act, rather than react, to ensure more positive learning circumstances.
>
> The Senior School mindfulness meditation sessions are conducted once a week for 1 hour, with many students enhancing their mindfulness by completing daily sessions of 10–20 minutes. Students selecting this Senior School mindful meditation activity come from all Houses and for a range of reasons, including anxiety, the desire to better manage day-to-day challenges, a wish to improve academic focus, the desire to develop a stronger sense of awareness in particularly demanding sporting "contest moments," and to improve their quality of sleep.
>
> The silent retreat nature of the session has been fully appreciated, and the adult example set has been significant. The mindful meditation sessions have prompted students to investigate and experience meditation more deeply. One student has now gone on silent meditation retreats elsewhere in Australia, and in India. Another student, understanding the links between meditation and performance in sport, now uses meditation when competing; this student represented Australia in the World Youth Games. Other students have simply enjoyed exploring their capacity to be more aware.
>
> Those students who engaged in mindful meditation to address spikes in their emotional responses express their belief that they are now able to better recognize "felt circumstances" when relating to others or when facing up to challenges. Over the last 3 years, more than 100 students have completed a 10-week course in mindful meditation.
>
> John Hendry, Director of Student Welfare

CASE STUDY 9.1

Mindfulness in the classroom

Steve Andrew, Head of Fraser House, Corio

In conversation with my students, I define mindfulness as being aware of what we are attending to. "Imagine that you could increase the time that you spend actively involved in learning in each class; this would increase your ability to learn, and the consequent grades you could achieve." My objective has been to increase the amount of time my students spend "attending" in class and during prep (homework). We sometimes might feel we have little to no control over our attention and how we are distracted. However, we *do* actually have control over what we do once we *realize* that we are distracted or not focused. To improve the students' focus and attention, I decided to introduce a form of meditation to be practiced at the start of each of my Mathematics classes (see Figure 9.2). This can be a body scan or

Figure 9.2 Senior students practicing mindfulness at the start of a Mathematics lesson.

breathing meditation, or take a more active form, such as a standing or walking meditation. Meditation redirects the students' focus from what they were previously doing—perhaps another class or having lunch. As their teacher, I want my students to focus on the Mathematics that I want them to learn.

In addition to mindfulness in the classroom, I have led similar meditations at the start of prep in the evening. Students have often come to me asking for a meditation because they have felt in need of it; it helps them to cope with the demands of prep and their need to focus effectively. Focused meditation works well at the start of each class and at the start of prep sessions each evening, as it sets the scene for the period of work ahead. Teaching students how to meditate before they go to sleep has also helped both male and female students. However, this type of meditation is a relaxation meditation rather than a focused exercise.

Meditation is a powerful tool—whether the aim is to increase the ability to focus or to relax. Invariably students tell me that they are better able to focus and concentrate in class, and also as they work on their own or prepare for sleep. Meditation has enhanced my students' ability to "attend," to concentrate, and therefore to learn more effectively. My students tell me they are better learners as a result of our meditations. I have now recorded my meditations, making them available on our School Intranet for individual students to listen to as they need to. Most importantly, I believe that students who complete a mindful, meditative exercise are more aware of where their attention is, and so cope better with the demands of each class, and their work. The outcome is positive learning—and positive, more mindful students.

Meditation scripts of various lengths have been recorded, and students can obtain copies to upload on to their phones, computers, or iPads. There is also a range of mindfulness phone "apps" that are recommended for older students. To create depth of understanding, students are introduced to the science that underpins mindfulness. As part of the Year 10 Pos Ed curriculum, a neuroscientist visits the School and speaks to the students about the neurological and physiological benefits of mindfulness and meditation. In Case Study 9.2 on "Small Pieces," Michelle Badior, Head of Drama, describes how students are encouraged to take a moment to reflect and be present in Senior School assemblies.

CASE STUDY 9.2

Small pieces

Michelle Badior, Head of Drama, Corio

Senior School assemblies at the Corio campus are a community event, not just a vehicle for announcements or award presentations, because so much of the culture and the spirit of the School is explored and enhanced through the formal gathering of staff and students. Student input and participation are encouraged, and students approach the Head of Campus with ideas and suggestions about topics, film clips, or great and memorable stories that could be shared. Often the School Captains will talk to the student and staff body about ideas or issues of concern, or will share reflections on aspects of school life. There really *is* a sense of community in assemblies, and not just a sense of process.

Nevertheless, it can be difficult, in the busyness of school life—in the sometimes all-consuming round of classes, co-curricular activities, meetings, sport, choir practices, rehearsals, training, and evening prep—to actually find moments of stillness and silence in which to just stop, think, and reflect. Mindfulness meditation, exploratory conversations in Pos Ed classes, the keeping of journals—all of these activities and practices, and more—are key components in the Pos Ed philosophy. However, students also need to connect with the natural world around them as much as with each other and with themselves.

This is how the idea of "Small Pieces" as a component of Senior School assemblies arose. It was felt that students, although mindful of the richness and beauty of their own worlds (their friends and peers, their families, teachers, and staff, the Geelong Grammar School community in which they live, and the many communities from which they are drawn), were sometimes so swept along by the momentum of human connections that they could forget the beauty, complexity, and wonder of the small things, of nature and the natural world. The natural world is made up of a myriad of small pieces (animals, plants, the elements, and natural phenomena) that on their own might seem insignificant, but which when enhanced through observation and stillness reinforce the wonder and magnificence of the big "earthly" sphere.

In practical terms, "Small Pieces" is a video presentation that lasts for 1 to 3 minutes. It is preceded by a short introduction that is designed *only* to explain its context. Importantly, students are not told how they should feel, or what the presentation means. They are free to feel or think whatever they like, for there is to be no commentary. Sometimes the awe is palpable;

sometimes confusion turns to irritation or wonder. Sometimes the whole community is drawn into silent contemplation of something amazing. In those small moments, something "big" and powerful occurs. Usually a "Small Piece" is shown at the end of an assembly, so that the community can be free to think a little more about what they have seen, or to share their thoughts as they leave to go to class. Once the idea of "Small Pieces" takes hold, students and staff learn to anticipate its potential strangeness or beauty. They will also search for their own "Small Piece" and ask to share it with the community.

Examples of "Small Piece" clips have included video footage of surfers riding the largest waves in the world off the coast of Nazaré, Portugal (the visual spectacle of nature's power and man's wild courage speaks for itself), a scene from the Ron Fricke film, *Baraka,* featuring the performance of the Kecak (the Balinese Monkey Chant, an extraordinarily vibrant and strange visual display that can at first alienate students, but which then draws them in), excerpts from David Attenborough's films focusing on the intricacy and beauty of plant or animal life, and a short film (without sound) showing the rhythm of balls suspended on strings in a wonderful, almost balletic parabola of motion regulated by the laws of physics.

After a very short introduction and a short clip, the community is left alone to watch, think, and feel. There have also been some restrictions. "Small Pieces" is not about issues, although of course key issues may be implicit. It is also not about human activity, although, as in the surfing clips from Portugal or scenes from *Baraka* (a very rich source of many small pieces constructing a masterful whole), "man" plays his part. "Small Pieces" cannot be a song, a speech, or an event. A "Small Piece" reflects the natural world that is all around us, stunning in its power, silent in its magnificence, an intrinsic part of our human existence.

As we sit together in assembly to watch something wonderful, strange, and weird, from part of our experience or indeed alien to our experience, our mindfulness is being redirected and enhanced. The thoughts and feelings of our community slip into engagement, curiosity, and wonder. Rejection or confusion, these thoughts and feelings are also intrinsic to who we are and how we react to change and challenge. Small and simple really *can* be beautiful.

Staff support students in implementing mindfulness by encouraging them to take a few moments to focus on their breath, draw attention to a part of the body, or even bring their awareness to an object or picture. Another technique involves selecting a yoga-inspired position and providing students with a few moments in which to pause and stretch. Students are familiar with the phrase "7–11 breathing," which involves inhaling to the count of 7 and exhaling to the count of 11. These strategies plant seeds of mindfulness in daily life, and allow the students to experience a "comma" in what can be a full and hectic day.

Feedback from students and staff has been that some students highly value and appreciate mindfulness. Many students describe finding mindfulness especially valuable in situations that make them feel nervous or anxious, such as doing a class presentation or performing in front of others. Prior to an exam period one year, students approached Justin Robinson, Head of Positive Education at the time, and asked if they could organize mindful meditation sessions for students before their exams (see Box 9.7). Students who had experienced the benefits of meditation and mindfulness themselves felt that such sessions might be useful to others.

BOX 9.7: MINDFULNESS FOR EXAMS

During 2013, the Pos Ed student committee, comprising a Year 11 student from each of the 10 Houses, suggested the possibility of offering formal mindful meditation sessions for students just prior to their mid-year and end-of-year examinations. Students took ownership of the project by seeking permission from the Director of Learning, determining which meditations they would offer, designing an advertising poster, and promoting the program in their House to their peers. A venue just beside the examination hall was open 15 minutes prior to exam start times for any students who wished to take part. A short mindfulness meditation recording, narrated by Dr Hassed, was played to guide students through simple mindfulness exercises. Every session throughout the exam period had students in attendance, with numbers ranging from 2 to 76 students. The numbers generally swelled as the examination period progressed, and it was clear that many students found the sessions valuable. Year 11 students also offered and led 30-minute mindful meditation sessions in the evening in the Hawker Library, showing admirable leadership in supporting the wellbeing of other students.

Justin Robinson, Director of the Institute of Positive Education

Other students report that they do not find mindfulness or meditation so valuable, and some describe difficulty in maintaining their practice. Individual differences in enjoyment, value, and intrinsic motivation are common features of many health and wellbeing strategies, and the objective is for each person to find ways of nurturing wellbeing that work for them. Although not all of the topics covered across the Model for Positive Education will resonate with every staff member or student, it is hoped that all members of the School community will find at least a few concepts that appeal to them (for a related discussion of "person–activity fit," see Lyubomirsky, 2007; Lyubomirsky and Layous, 2013).

Mindful learning

Students can arrive at my classes still caught up in what happened over recess or lunch. I now start the majority of my classes with 3 minutes of mindfulness—and this is coming from someone who had never done any sort of meditation before. It really helps with the productive time within each session. The skill of calming and quietening yourself literally changes the way the rest of the class runs.

Emma Grave, Drama Teacher, Corio Campus

Teachers often assume that students show up to their classrooms ready to focus on the lesson. In reality, however, students can be preoccupied by a recent conversation with a friend or distracted by an upcoming deadline for another subject. If students are experiencing strong emotions, such as anxiety, anger, or excitement, they may be especially distracted and unfocused. By taking a few moments for mindfulness at the start of the lesson or as a break between topics, staff and students become better able to maintain focus and concentration. Similarly, students may practice a short meditation prior to starting their homework, or refresh their attention when switching topics. To serve as a reminder to be mindful, sometimes a teacher will place a candle at the front of the room during a test or exam. When a student is having thoughts that the questions are too difficult or the exam is too long, they are encouraged to pause, look at the candle flame, and center themselves, before proceeding with renewed clarity.

Over time, mindfulness training helps people to become better able to direct their attention, which means that students are less susceptible to distractions and can pay attention for longer. The benefits of mindfulness for learning and academic performance are supported by research evidence (for discussions of mindful learning, see Langer, 2000; Ritchhart and Perkins, 2000). In particular, mindfulness has been found to lead to improved attention and enhanced memory (Chiesa et al., 2011). Mindfulness supports reflective and novel exploration, and helps students to make innovative connections between various concepts. A senior Psychology assignment used by Simon Haigh, Head of Barabool House, that requires students to explore the evidence for mindfulness from a personal and scientific perspective, is described in Box 9.8.

Mindfulness in Chapel

There can be a gap for kids if they don't have a sense of sacredness, a sense of calmness inside, a sense of connection. I believe we are all spiritual beings, so to be at peace with that part of your life is very nurturing. So whether it's through

BOX 9.8: Exploring stress reduction

A senior Psychology assignment requires students to explore the three stress-reduction techniques of mindfulness, relaxation strategies, and exercise. Students explore each of the techniques from both scientific and personal perspectives. First, they are asked to research the physiological and psychological benefits. Secondly, they are encouraged to implement the techniques in their lives and reflect on their unique experiences. The students make choices about how to apply the techniques. For example, in order to explore mindfulness, students may choose to attend the Handbury Wellbeing Centre for meditation sessions, or alternatively go for mindful walks around the Corio campus. The students then compare and contrast their personal experiences with the scientific evidence, and write about their experiences in a comprehensive essay. The combination of an understanding of the physiological benefits of the stress-management techniques and the personal application helps many students to make worthwhile reflections and gain insights about what is best for them.

Chapel, and/or through meditation in Positive Education, it is extraordinarily important for kids to attend to their spirit and nurture their inner selves.

Reverend Eleanor O'Donnell, Senior Chaplain

Often I would lead a guided meditation in Chapel. After these meditations, there were moments of really profound silence. Sometimes when a group of people are mindful together you can feel a sense of silence and connection that is truly deep and nourishing.

Reverend Dr Hugh Kempster, Past Senior Chaplain

A few years ago, the School had the honor of hosting a visit by four Buddhist monks. The monks spent one afternoon creating a beautiful mandala in the School Chapel (see Figure 9.3). They worked slowly and deliberately, placing the grains of sands down in an intricate design so that the vibrant colors wove together—their actions were the epitome of mindfulness. As they worked throughout the day, staff and students came to visit the Chapel to watch their work. Once the day was over, there was a blowing away ceremony. Looking on, one student commented that she felt sad that something so beautiful had been undone so soon. This led to a rich discussion between staff and students on mindfulness, the impermanence of existence, temporality, and the ability to "let go."

Figure 9.3 Visiting Buddhist monks creating a beautiful sand mandala in the School Chapel.

The role of the Chapel in the development of Positive Education at the School has been significant. The School Chaplains look for links with Positive Education, so that students' spiritual development complements their growth in wellbeing, and vice versa. Mindfulness has been a particularly strong point of connection between Positive Education and the Chapel's work in helping students to attend to their spirit and inner selves. There are many parallels between mindful meditation and the values espoused in Christianity, as well as in many other religions and spiritual traditions. Themes of mindfulness and meditation are prevalent across many religious texts, and there are commonalities between mindful meditation, contemplative prayer, and Christian meditation.

A core belief of the Chaplaincy is that it is important for students to nurture a sense of spirituality and inner calmness. One pathway to this is through prayer and the Chapel; another pathway is through meditation and mindfulness. It is understood that each individual student and staff member will find value in a different way of nurturing the self through contemplation, introspection, and meditation. One role of the Chapel is to support individuals' growth in this manner. With this end in mind, meditation and mindfulness are regularly integrated into Chapel services, and the Chaplains frequently make connections between Positive Education, faith, and spirituality. As well as supporting students' spiritual development, this helps to create the culture around the School, so that students encounter mindfulness and meditation in a range of different ways and settings.

Summary and conclusions

Mindfulness involves focusing attention and accepting the present experience without judgment. In an increasingly fast-paced society, there is great power in supporting students to quieten their mind and just "be." Mindfulness helps a child or adult to move from a state of busyness to a place of calm and balance. It emphasizes the importance of having time that is unstructured and unplanned, and encourages people to spend time being still and reflecting. This leads to renewed energy, and allows the individual to engage meaningfully and consciously with the important tasks of daily living.

At Geelong Grammar School, teachers are increasingly implementing mindfulness techniques within the classroom to help students to cultivate a state of awareness and curious attention that supports rich exploration and learning. However, mindfulness offers much more than a set of teaching tools. It helps to create a School culture where pausing for reflection and introspection are valued aspects of daily living. The benefits across the School community are profound. Mindfulness is an evidence-based pathway to reducing stress, and has valuable healing properties for physical and mental health. Mindfulness complements the other domains of the

Model for Positive Education by helping students to connect with their purpose, enter a state of flow, and consciously pursue their goals. As a result of an enhanced state of balance, children, young people, and adults are more able to remain calm when they experience strong emotions, and are more resilient when faced with difficulties and hardships.

Mindfulness has an especially powerful impact on relationships, and helps to create a culture of respectful, compassionate, and forgiving actions and interactions. A student who is mindful is more attuned to the needs and feelings of others, and is also more able to spot character strengths in action. Starting among the very youngest children, mindfulness helps members of the School community to develop a strong foundation of personal awareness and insight. It creates fertile soil for the cultivation of physical and psychological health, helping people of all ages to thrive and flourish through the ups and downs of life.

RECOMMENDED RESOURCES

Etty-Leal J (2010). *Meditation Capsules: a mindfulness program for children*. Melbourne, Australia: Meditation Capsules.

Garrison Institute. <www.garrisoninstitute.org>

Harris R (2008). *The Happiness Trap: how to stop struggling and start living*. London: Constable & Robinson Ltd.

Hassed C and Chambers R (2014). *Mindful Learning: reduce stress and improve brain performance for effective learning*. Wollombi, Australia: Exisle Publishing.

Hawn Foundation. *MindUP training program*. <http://thehawnfoundation.org/mindup>.

Kabat-Zinn J. *Guided Mindfulness Meditation Practices with Jon Kabat-Zinn*. <www.mindfulnesscds.com>

Kaiser Greenfield S (2010). *The Mindful Child*. New York: Free Press.

Mindful Schools. *Integrating Mindfulness into Education* (USA based). <www.mindfulschools.org>

Mindfulness in Education (Australia based). <www.mindfuleducation.com.au>

Mindfulness in Schools Project (UK based). <http://mindfulnessinschools.org>

Puddicombe A (2012). *All It Takes Is 10 Mindful Minutes*. *TED Talk*. <www.ted.com/talks/andy_puddicombe_all_it_takes_is_10_mindful_minutes>

Ricard M (2004). *The Habits of Happiness*. *TED Talk*. <www.ted.com/talks/matthieu_ricard_on_the_habits_of_happiness>

Siegel D and Payne Bryson T (2012). *The Whole-Brain Child: 12 revolutionary strategies to nurture your child's developing mind*. New York: Bantam Books.

Smiling Mind. <http://smilingmind.com.au> (Web- and app-based program of meditation for young people.)

Wellspring: Institute for Neuroscience and Contemplative Wisdom. <www.wisebrain.org>

REFERENCES

Baer R (2003). Mindfulness-based treatment approaches: a conceptual and empirical review. *Clinical Psychology: Science and Practice, 10*, 125–43.

Chiesa A, Calati R, and Serretti A (2011). Does mindfulness training improve cognitive abilities? A systematic review of neuropsychological findings. *Clinical Psychology Review, 31*, 449–64.

Dweck C S (2006). *Mindset: the new psychology of success*. New York: Ballantine Books.

Etty-Leal J (2010). *Meditation Capsules: a mindfulness program for children*. Melbourne, Australia: Meditation Capsules.

Fjorback L et al. (2011). Mindfulness-based stress reduction and mindfulness-based cognitive therapy: a systematic review of randomized controlled trials. *Acta Psychiatrica Scandinavica, 124*, 102–19.

Greeson J M (2009). Mindfulness research update: 2008. *Complementary Health Practice Review, 14*, 10–18.

Grossman P, Niemann L, Schmidt S, and Walach H (2004). Mindfulness-based stress reduction and health benefits: a meta-analysis. *Journal of Psychosomatic Research, 57*, 35–43.

Hassed C (2008). *The Essence of Health*. North Sydney, Australia: Ebury Press.

Hofmann S G, Sawyer A T, Witt A A, and Oh D (2010). The effect of mindfulness-based therapy on anxiety and depression: a meta-analytic review. *Journal of Consulting and Clinical Psychology, 78*, 169–83.

James W (1890). *The Principles of Psychology*. Boston, MA: Harvard University Press.

Kabat-Zinn J (1990). *Full Catastrophe Living: using the wisdom of your body and mind to face stress, pain, and illness*. New York: Delacorte.

Kabat-Zinn J (2003). Mindfulness-based interventions in context: past, present, and future. *Clinical Psychology: Science and Practice, 10*, 144–56.

Langer E J (2000). Mindful learning. *Current Directions in Psychological Science, 9*, 220–23.

Lyubomirsky S (2007). *The How of Happiness: a scientific approach to getting the life you want.* New York: Penguin Press.

Lyubomirsky S and Layous K (2013). How do simple positive activities increase well-being? *Current Directions in Psychological Science, 22,* 57–62.

Meiklejohn J et al. (2012). Integrating mindfulness training into K-12 education: fostering the resilience of teachers and students. *Mindfulness, 3,* 291–307.

Ritchhart R and Perkins D N (2000). Life in the mindful classroom: nurturing the disposition of mindfulness. *Journal of Social Issues, 56,* 27–47.

POSITIVE ENGAGEMENT

**Introduction by
Dr Sue Jackson**

Helping students to experience complete immersion in school activities may seem like a lofty goal. However, by learning the principles and practices of flow it is possible to achieve total absorption in what one is doing. Flow is an optimal psychological state, one involving total focus on the task at hand. It is comprised of several positive experiential characteristics, defined and studied over decades of research by the founder of the concept of flow, Professor Mihaly Csikszentmihalyi, and colleagues (Csikszentmihalyi, 1990).

The defining characteristics, or dimensions, of flow are skill–challenge balance, a merging of action and awareness, clear goals, unambiguous feedback, concentration on the task at hand, a sense of control, loss of self-consciousness, time transformation, and autotelic (intrinsically rewarding) experience.

Flow is the synergy created through the simultaneous experience of its defining characteristics. Flow provides a model of optimal engagement with a task. At the heart of this model is the balance between challenges and skills in a situation. For flow to occur, both challenges and skills (for the individual) need to be high and in balance. Challenging situations foster engagement, provided that the student perceives they have the skills to meet the challenge. The perception of challenge, and of skill, is more important than any objective level of challenges or skills in the flow state.

The great thing about a model defined by the relative balance of challenges and skills is that there is tremendous scope for intervention. Challenges can be progressively structured to match a student's perceived skill level. Where perceptions of skill are low, strategies to build confidence can be developed. Where students are bored, challenges can be increased according to the demonstrated skill level. In my work with Geelong Grammar School, I have witnessed the enthusiastic application of the principles of the flow model in various ways across the School. The skill–challenge balance concept has considerable practical utility for facilitating flow in educational settings.

Being in flow provides individuals with an opportunity to become completely immersed in a task, to be free from self-consciousness and self-doubts, and instead to engage fully in what they are doing. The research that I have conducted on the experience of flow has demonstrated what Csikszentmihalyi has consistently found in his research— the flow experience is a fundamentally similar, highly valued state across individuals (Csikszentmihalyi, 1990; Jackson and Csikszentmihalyi, 1999). Rich information about the qualities of being in flow, and the factors perceived to influence its occurrence, has been obtained through interview-based research with high performers across a diverse range of settings, including sports, art, and academia. The following are a few examples of how people at the top of their field have described their experience in flow: "complete task focus," "totally relaxed," "totally absorbed in what I'm doing," "endless supply of energy," and "nothing else enters awareness." Wouldn't it be great to hear our students describe their learning experiences in such ways? By helping students to understand flow, and by creating environments conducive to flow, opportunities for flow in the classroom can abound.

In my research with elite performers, flow is recognized as the blueprint for optimal performance, as well as being the benchmark for peak experience. Once flow has been experienced, people are highly motivated to find it again, as illustrated by the following elite athlete:

> Flow is what gives you the buzz to keep doing what you are doing, keep doing the sport. Because once you've got it, it just lifts you. Once you lose it, it can be a real slog until you get it back again. And once you've got it back again, and you're just grooving along, everything's going well, that's great. That's just what you want it to be.

Teachers can help students to experience flow by explaining the flow model to them, and setting the stage for students to become fully engaged in what they are doing. Learning about flow and having opportunities to experience this optimal psychological state helps students to grow and develop. Once flow is understood, the pathway to enhanced performance becomes clear, as the flow model provides a practical pathway to an optimal psychological state.

Preconditions for flow that have been identified in the flow literature include the skill–challenge balance, setting clear goals, and receiving clear feedback about progress (for a related discussion of process versus praise feedback, see Chapter 11; see also Mueller and Dweck, 1998). Teachers and students can work collaboratively on fostering these components of flow in the classroom. Learning to engage with relaxed concentration, confidence, and preparing well for upcoming challenges also facilitate flow. Additional ways in which flow can be fostered include learning the skill of being in the present moment, and identifying signature strengths.

Learning to be in the present moment is challenged by our fast-paced, technologically advanced world. Multi-tasking and multiple technologies mean that our focus is continually elsewhere. Mindfulness provides a means of reconnecting to the present moment, and is a critical skill to foster in young people. Recognizing the importance of mindfulness in school settings, Geelong Grammar School has incorporated this psychological skill into its overall program, and it has been inspiring to observe the value placed by the School on developing mindfulness in its students (for more information on mindfulness, see Chapter 9). One outcome of learning mindfulness skills is that the capacity to experience flow is enhanced. Being mindful in a challenging environment can be a pathway to flow.

Another pathway to engagement, and to flow, is developing awareness of individuals' strengths and, relatedly, helping individuals to define what is personally important to them. Character strengths allow students to recognize internal factors that are core to who they are and to what they are capable of doing.

One approach to mindfulness, known as *acceptance and commitment therapy/training (ACT)*, provides a practical model for developing mindfulness. Through ACT one identifies what is important in one's life and takes steps in the service of these identified values. The ACT approach has many useful strategies for cultivating mindfulness, as well as for understanding and reframing the role that our thoughts and feelings can play in our lives. Knowing what matters, and moving in the direction of one's identified values, is integral to ACT. The ACT model is relevant to the theme of positive engagement because greater engagement is likely to occur when students are able to find personal meaning in what they are doing, and recognize that a mindful approach to their activities is integral to their quality of experience at school.

Intrinsic motivation is likely to be fostered when students can engage in personally meaningful tasks, and in environments where they can develop and demonstrate their individual strengths. Flow, once experienced, is an optimally rewarding state.

The interconnectedness of positive psychological characteristics associated with engagement offers many possibilities for structuring classroom environments to facilitate immersion in learning. Geelong Grammar School has identified that helping all members of the School community to become engaged in meaningful, challenging, and intrinsically rewarding pursuits will lead to positive outcomes both for wellbeing and for achievement. It has been an honor to be involved in the visionary program for Positive Education developed at Geelong Grammar School. The enthusiasm for understanding flow and incorporating this Positive Psychology concept into the School's Model for Positive Education has demonstrated to me what can be achieved when visionary leadership moves education into the realm of lifelong, meaningful experiences.

Positive engagement at Geelong Grammar School

There are so many outlets for people to express their passions and individuality at this School—whether it is studying, playing netball, or performing on a stage. There are many opportunities for flow, and there is no better feeling. I encourage you to get out and make the most of your time here. Find your flow and let it flourish.

George Vickers-Willis, School Captain 2012, speaking at a School Assembly

A student explains flow in terms of his experience with surfing—he arrives at the beach early in the morning and, before he knows it, hours have passed and it is mid-afternoon. Another student describes feeling completely alive and full of joy and vitality while performing on stage. For yet another student, flow occurs when she is having meaningful conversations with her friends. During these times she is not worried about how she looks to others or concerned about upcoming assignments, but is fully present in the moment.

A goal of Positive Education is to help staff and students to live engaged, curious, and passionate lives—lives filled with flow. Whether they are learning something new, playing sport, creating music or art, or contributing to the community, it is important for all students to regularly take part in activities that provide them with meaning and fulfillment (Figures 10.1, 10.2, and 10.3 showcase highly engaged students across the School community). An equally valuable goal is for staff to be engaged in their respective roles, whether it is teaching, working in administration, or tending the School gardens. A positive consequence of this is that staff members who are engaged evoke interest, curiosity, and passion in children and young people, and vice versa.

Engagement and flourishing

Within the Model for Positive Education, positive engagement is defined as living a life high on interest, curiosity, and absorption, and pursuing goals with determination and vitality. The aim of the positive engagement domain is to promote complete immersion in activities through understanding the nature of engagement, the pathways to it, and the effect that it has on health and wellbeing.

Engagement is a key component of wellbeing and a pathway to a fulfilling life (Peterson et al., 2005; Seligman, 2011). It is associated with positive outcomes for adolescents and for adults, including enhanced optimism and self-confidence (Froh et al., 2010; Hunter and Csikszentmihalyi, 2003; Rogatko, 2009). The related concept of curiosity is also consistently linked to good mental health and high levels of wellbeing (Jovanovic and Brdaric, 2011; Kashdan et al., 2004). Engagement and curiosity can also support flourishing relationships as people embrace social situations, are open-minded to different perspectives, and make others feel valued

Figure 10.1 Students actively engaged in their learning.

Figure 10.2 Toorak student fully engaged in playing the xylophone.

Figure 10.3 Middle School student fully absorbed in a lino cut activity during Art.

through their natural inquisitiveness and interest (Kashdan and Roberts, 2004; Kashdan and Silvia, 2009).

In addition to supporting wellbeing, engagement has benefits for accomplishment and achievement (Froh et al., 2010). When in flow, people are less susceptible to distractions or thoughts about failure, and are less likely to procrastinate (Jackson et al., 2001). A person who is engaged in an activity finds it enjoyable, practices it frequently, and persists despite challenges. In turn, the investment of time, energy, and attention builds skills and capabilities. These effects have lasting consequences. For example, students' engagement at high school has been found to predict their motivation, commitment, and performance during their university studies (Shernoff and Hoogstra, 2001).

Exploring flow

Professor Mihaly Csikszentmihalyi has been instrumental in advancing our understanding of engagement through his work on flow (Csikszentmihalyi, 1990). Csikszentmihalyi's initial understanding of flow came from interviews with people who were the elite of their fields—artists, musicians, sportspeople, and chess players—who spoke of experiencing complete focus, immersion, and vitality when taking part in their activities of choice. Through this exploration, Csikszentmihalyi came to define flow as a state of intense absorption and optimal experience that occurs during inherently motivating challenges.

To introduce flow in the multi-day Positive Education training courses, Justin Robinson, Director of the Institute of Positive Education, invites people to think of a time when they have felt "in the zone" or "fully immersed" in an activity. Usually a few volunteers start by sharing their experiences of diverse activities, such as playing the piano, rowing, or spending time with their children. Their stories often lead to "ah-ha, so that is flow!" moments for others as more people identify times of high engagement and vitality. Generally most people can think of a time when they have experienced flow, although the frequency tends to vary from "seldom" to "almost every day." One of the most common examples shared in this context is teachers describing their experiences of flow in the classroom. This is perhaps unsurprising given that their role is challenging, constantly changing, and deeply rewarding. The conversation often evolves into a discussion of how wonderful it is to see children fully engaged in the moment, with staff sharing stories of witnessing their students, or even their own children, totally immersed in flow activities.

Enjoyment and absorption

On a roll ... fully immersed ... in the moment ... completely absorbed ... in the zone ... being at one with the music ... when time stands still ... total focus on the task at hand.

Students describing flow, Senior School, Corio

In her introduction to this chapter, Dr Sue Jackson thoroughly explained the features of flow. These features are often summarized as the three elements of enjoyment, absorption, and intrinsic motivation. Flow is highly enjoyable and rewarding. One student described flow as "feeling too good to put into words." As Dr Tal Ben-Shahar explains, flow occurs when people perform at their best (peak performance) while enjoying themselves the most (peak experience) (Ben-Shahar, 2007). Interestingly, people describe being so deeply immersed during flow that they are largely unaware of feeling anything, but when they reflect on the experience they recall feelings of joy and exhilaration.

Flow is also a state of complete absorption. Someone in flow is not thinking about what they would like to have for dinner or where they put their geography book, but is fully focused on the task at hand. While in flow, people are largely unconcerned about how they look to others, and are sometimes even unaware of basic needs or drives, such as feeling cold or hungry. One of the most distinguishing features of flow is a distorted sense of time—people are so immersed in the activity that often hours can seem like minutes. Less common, but still a feature of flow, is the experience of time slowing down. For example, a tennis player in flow may see the ball coming towards her in slow motion, and feel as if she has all the time in the world to prepare her return shot. There is also evidence that flow experienced with others—referred to as group or social flow—is more enjoyable than flow experienced individually (Walker, 2010). People may experience group or social flow while playing basketball, making music in an ensemble, or acting in a play with others.

Intrinsic motivation

The third summarizing feature of flow is intrinsic motivation—the activity is completed for the love of it, not because of external rewards or punishment. People do not complete flow activities out of a sense of obligation or a desire to please others, but for the joy and meaning derived from the activity itself. A student who is talented at Chemistry—but motivated by a desire to achieve high grades to please his parents—is less likely to experience flow than a student with less natural ability who finds the subject fascinating and rewarding.

Professor Richard Ryan and Professor Edward Deci have been instrumental in furthering our understanding of intrinsic motivation through their work on self-determination theory (Ryan and Deci, 2000). They propose that intrinsic motivation is most likely to occur when the three fundamental needs of competence, autonomy, and belonging are met. First, people have a need to feel competent—that is, that their actions can bring about the desired effects. People also have a need for autonomy, which is the ability and freedom to make choices that are aligned with their values. Belonging (also referred to as relatedness) is a sense of connectedness and closeness to others. Research has shown that when these needs are met, people experience high levels of wellbeing and vitality and low levels of psychological distress. In contrast, when these needs are thwarted, people can become disengaged and unmotivated (Reis et al., 2000; Van Ryzin et al., 2009).

In developing a holistic understanding of flow and engagement, it is important to consider any potential "shadow sides." It is useful to explore activities such as computer gaming or gambling that are set up deliberately to be extremely engaging, to the point that they can have a detrimental impact on a person's life. That is, although some levels of computer games may be engaging and even valuable for wellbeing, there is increasing attention within the scientific literature on the potential costs of the overuse of gaming, such as impaired academic performance and social isolation (Peters and Malesky, 2008; Thomas and Martin, 2010). Although these are complex issues, the aim is for students to understand that there is not a one-size-fits-all answer with regard to ways of enhancing engagement and wellbeing. These conversations also highlight the value of helping students to developing a nuanced understanding of all Positive Education concepts.

Skill–challenge balance

A defining prerequisite of flow is a match between skill level and the task challenge, so that skills are stretched but not overmatched, and both skill level and task challenge are perceived to be high (Nakamura and Csikszentmihalyi, 2009). Activities in which skill levels are low but the challenge is high can lead to anxiety, whereas activities in which skill levels are high but the challenge is low can lead to relaxation or boredom. Consider skiing as an example. A beginner skier on the most difficult slopes would experience fear and stress, whereas an experienced skier on the beginner slopes would most probably feel bored. With younger students, the story of Goldilocks and the Three Bears is used to describe how the challenge should not be "too hard" or "too soft," but "just right." Different levels of skill and challenge can lead to various psychological states, including anxiety, apathy, arousal, boredom, control, relaxation, worry, and flow. Boxes 10.1 and 10.2

BOX 10.1: Explaining the flow diagram

In this activity, students are presented with a flow diagram without labels, so eight blank segments are visible. They are also provided with the corresponding eight labels of flow, anxiety, apathy, arousal, boredom, control, relaxation, and worry. In groups, the students are asked to match where each segment fits on the diagram. Students often quickly identify that a high challenge–low skill activity may lead to anxiety and that a high skill–high challenge activity may lead to flow. Positioning the other segments correctly on the diagram creates opportunities for discussion, with students coming up with useful examples of times when they have experienced each state. There is often rich debate about the correct location of various terms—for example, some students disagree about the respective positions of relaxation and boredom on the diagram. From the teacher's perspective, the correct placement of a segment on the diagram is much less important than the quality of discussion and the depth of reflection.

This exploration of the flow diagram is extended by asking the students to nominate an activity that fits each segment for them. For example, a student may recall experiencing relaxation while reading a book, control while practicing the piano, anxiety during a particularly challenging English examination, and flow while taking photographs. Students are asked to brainstorm activities that they would like to move closer to flow. For example, a student may move from apathy, relaxation, or boredom while looking after his younger siblings to arousal or even flow by inventing creative games or challenges for them to do together. Reflecting on these experiences and sharing them with others helps students to explore the role that flow plays in various areas of their lives.

> **BOX 10.2: The flow test**
>
> The flow test helps students to develop an understanding of the variations in their level of engagement over the course of a week. Random or programmed reminders are set up on students' mobile phones or computers to beep five times a day. When the reminder beeps, the students ask themselves a series of questions, such as "Who are you with?", "What are you doing?", "What is your emotional state?", "What is your current level of engagement?", and "Are you in flow?" By capturing these moments, students develop insight into their unique patterns of engagement. They can explore whether flow is most likely to occur when they are alone or with others. They can also identify activities or behaviors that take them away from flow. The students are then required to write a report on their findings, thus developing their self-awareness and insight and supporting the overall theme for Positive Education of "know thyself."

provide examples of activities that help students to develop an understanding of flow and its relevance in their lives.

Nurturing curiosity and passion

> What do I look for when hiring new staff? I look for three things—passion, passion, passion.
>
> Charlie Scudamore, Vice Principal

Across the School community, students and staff are constantly provided with opportunities to participate, try new things, and get involved. Co-curricular activities such as music, drama, sports, clubs, camps, and community service are especially important in nurturing young people's well-rounded development. Through these pathways, students step outside their comfort zones and take part in new experiences that help them to learn and grow. One aim is for students to balance taking part in activities they already really enjoy with exploring new areas of skill and interest. Case Study 10.1 describes the "Make a Difference (MAD) Market," where Year 4 students from Bostock House are engaged in a diverse range of activities and projects that also help others. A Timbertop practice of helping students to cultivate new hobbies is described in Box 10.3, and the nurturing of curiosity through Year 10 Creative Workshops is outlined in Box 10.4.

Finding flow

> I often talk to students about finding something that inflames their passion, finding something that gets them out of bed in the morning.
>
> Steve Andrew, Head of Fraser House

CASE STUDY 10.1

The Make a Difference (MAD) Market

Andrew Groves, Teacher, Bostock House

How can you make a difference in the lives of others, and why should you even try to do so? The Year 4 Bostock House program is designed to help students to develop an authentic and practical understanding of leadership and service. At the start of the year, students are encouraged and supported to engage in acts of school and community leadership and service. In the second half of the year they are challenged to employ their initiative and creativity in devising and instigating their own schemes to help others.

The year begins with a leadership induction course, which is focused on building relationships between students and local community stakeholders—the local church and Rotary branch, the Red Cross, Second Bite (a community food program), Outpost (which supports homeless people in Geelong), and our primary community partner, Scope (a disabilities service provider).

MAD (the Make a Difference Market) is an empowering activity that leads students further in their community service by helping them to explore and use their initiative. MAD is a community market held at the School and run almost exclusively by the children, with teacher and parental support when necessary. The task starts with the *end* in mind—students begin by selecting the local wellbeing organizations they have encountered during the first part of the year, for which they will be trying to make a difference.

What follows is a substantial learning journey as the children work in small groups and take a product (literally!) from invention, or reinvention, to the marketplace. Business ideas range from a mindful meditation and massage service, to candy-floss making, to the traditional lemonade stand, and a sports competition group (see Figure 10.4). Students improve their literacy and numeracy skills while setting up a business team and promoting a product. However, of greater significance is each child's evolving understanding that the MAD project goes beyond aiming for good grades. Each child becomes increasingly aware of the fact that every effort they make in the project can help to make a positive difference in the lives of others.

Several teams have worked on their market business and stall in partnership with clients and staff from local community groups, such as Brett Reynolds, a talented artist, and Scope's own "Boxes n Bunches" flower-arranging business. Fleur, a Year 4 student, explains her collaboration with Taylor, a Scope client with Down syndrome and significant learning difficulties: "I learnt to see what people can do, and not just what they can't do. Taylor was amazing making the flowers with me, and I even got to shake her hand when we opened the MAD Market together." Children are ready to

Figure 10.4 Students at one of the MAD Market stalls.

see the person they know and like, and not a disability. They also realize, in the end, that the money they raise is not a sympathetic, charitable "pat on the head," but a real contribution that creates greater freedom for others.

One anecdote sheds more light on the transformational power of our students' MAD Market. In 2011, a boy named Jonah was living in Stuttgart, Germany. Like any other 9-year-old, he liked hanging out with his friends, having fun, and wished he was already a teenager. He had had a very simple dream that he longed to realize—one that most other 9-year-olds would take for granted. However, Jonah dreamed of somehow making a vital difference to his life. For as long as he could remember, he had wished that he could communicate more easily with his family and friends. Jonah had cerebral palsy, which meant that he could not speak in the conventional sense, and he badly needed some good advice to help him to overcome his growing sense of frustration.

On the other side of the world from Jonah, Brett Reynolds from Glen Park, Victoria wished that he could go to the Communication and Access World Conference in Pittsburgh, but he could not afford the flight. Extremely disappointed, he felt that he had something to give, namely his story of how finding the latest technology had enabled him to communicate more freely. He had already traveled Jonah's journey of growing up with cerebral palsy, where even the simplest task can seem like an insurmountable challenge. Then one day Brett met a Bostock House student, Drewe.

Drewe was 9 years old, too, just like Jonah. Neither boy knew the other, yet a chain reaction of kindness was about to connect them. Drewe wanted to shake Brett Reynold's hand and compliment him on the amazing painting he had created by using a paintbrush attached to his head—the only part of his body over which he had a degree of controlled muscle movement. Through the simple act of reaching out, they connected. Drewe kept in touch through the School. Soon afterwards, Brett visited the Bostock campus to present a leadership talk to the class, and he met Drewe again.

Brett had inspired another group of Bostock students, and the following year they worked with him on their hugely successful MAD Market stall. Brett—with the help of his new friends—raised the money for an international plane ticket to Pittsburgh. There at the Communication and Access World Conference he spoke to a packed hall about the latest technologies for people with cerebral palsy. Jonah was thrilled. Brett had given him hope that his dreams could come true. Back in Geelong, Drewe heard that a 9-year-old boy like him, a German boy called Jonah, had undergone a transformation in his life.

> You can start up a journey yourself and, over time, if you are on the right path, you can build on it, to make it better for the community, also for yourself.
>
> Brett Reynolds

BOX 10.3: Hobbies at Timbertop

> The Howqua River produced for me my first solo trout. I sat on the pebbles and cried. I have been tearful many times since with the beauty our country provides. But I am especially indebted to my year at Timbertop for surrounding me with good friends and so many of nature's gifts.
>
> Old Geelong Grammarian, Reflection on Timbertop's lasting impact

One of the initiatives at Timbertop is the dedication of time to exploring new hobbies. Students have the opportunity to try a wide range of activities, including skiing, snowboarding, mountain biking, fly-fishing, self-defense, golf, and rock climbing. In addition to these "active" hobbies, students are encouraged to try at least one "passive" hobby that can be used as an alternative to watching television, such as board games, baking, jewellery making, leatherwork, woodwork, international cooking, and football scarf knitting. Many students develop new skills that stay with them for years or decades to come. Often the most meaningful experiences occur when students try things that are different to their existing interests, and they are surprised by how much they enjoy their new activities. For some, these hobbies become lifelong interests. Many Timbertop students claim that their love of fly-fishing started during the activities program. For example, students have gone on to become editors of fly-fishing journals and run fly-fishing companies. Many staff members derive great enjoyment from introducing one of their favorite hobbies to students. Sharing an experience completely outside of the academic domain has the added benefit of helping to form and nurture close relationships between staff and students.

BOX 10.4: Year 10 Creative Workshops

The Year 10 Creative Workshops take place over a 3-day period after the Term 2 examinations each year. As the students have just emerged from an intense period of academic focus, the workshops are in one sense a time of "de-stressing" and using a similarly intense but very different mode of thinking. There is a quote attributed to Confucius that states "I hear and I forget. I see and I remember. I do and I understand." The workshops were established over 30 years ago to foster learning rooted in extremely practical experiences. Practitioners from a range of creative fields are invited to run sessions over the 3 days which engage students in making, performing, playing, and composing. Students often reflect on their involvement in workshop sessions such as blacksmithing, theatre improvisation, airbrushing, pizza making, or African drumming as highlights of the School year. Meeting various artisans and learning about alternative lifestyles and careers is also fundamental to the workshops. From time to time the workshops are a trigger for students to engage in an activity that becomes a lifetime passion.

Martin Beaver, Art Teacher and Head of Francis Brown House

A common observation is that two people with about the same skill level who are exposed to the same activity often experience vastly different levels of engagement. Csikszentmihalyi describes how some people are highly curious and inquisitive and constantly seek out new ideas and challenges. Such people, who are described as having an *autotelic personality,* are more likely to experience flow than other people, due to their high natural levels of concentration, focus, and persistence (Csikszentmihalyi, 1997; Nakamura and Csikszentmihalyi, 2009).

Independent of their baseline levels, all members of the School community can be supported to experience more flow. Numerous teachable skills across the Model for Positive Education are important foundations for engagement. As Dr Jackson explained in her introduction to this chapter, mindfulness provides a fertile soil for flow by helping people to attend to the present moment. Other pathways that support engagement, such as developing skills in setting clear, realistic goals and cultivating growth mindsets, are discussed in Chapter 11. Box 10.5 describes an activity aimed at changing non-flow activities into flow activities. In Case Study 10.2, Alice Macmillan, a senior student from the Corio campus, describes how she has thrived when raising awareness of epilepsy.

Supporting staff engagement

Do you love children? Don't love the kids—don't work here. I am surrounded by people who love children.

Charlie Scudamore, Vice Principal

BOX 10.5: Moving towards flow

This student activity—which is also relevant for staff, parents, and members of the School community—helps people to explore how to transform non-flow activities into flow activities. Students are asked to nominate an activity during which they would like to experience greater flow. They are then asked to identify their current level of engagement for the activity on the flow diagram. Next, the students make a plan for some realistic changes and actions that could create more flow in this activity. They identify strategies for increasing their skill level, such as increased practice, or calling upon their character strengths. They also identify strategies for decreasing the perceived level of challenge, such as removing distractions from their environment, asking for help, or breaking a large goal down into smaller steps. Discussion in pairs and small groups provides additional ideas and suggestions. The students are encouraged to implement their actions and strategies over a period of 1 week and report back on their progress, often revisiting their plans based on what worked and what did not work for them. Students have used this process to explore a range of examples, from regular school activities such as completing homework for a particular subject, increasing their engagement in different classes, or participating in the School debating team, through to more unique and personal activities such as playing chess, composing music, or rowing.

CASE STUDY 10.2

Epilepsy Awareness

Alice Macmillan, Year 12 Student, Elisabeth Murdoch House

I began my campaign for Epilepsy Awareness after a life-changing incident with the illness. My older brother Hamish, an epileptic of 4 years, had a severe seizure, resulting in his hospitalization. Before this time, Hamish's epilepsy was something I had found best not to think about or discuss. However, after watching my brother in such danger, I finally realized that not only was it my responsibility to understand this illness, but I needed others to understand the true implications, too.

After researching epilepsy, I began to develop an understanding of how common—and yet misunderstood—the illness is. Over 3.5% of Australians experience it at some point in their lives, and although it is rare to die from a seizure itself, many people can be injured, harmed, or even die because of their surroundings. Scared and incredibly anxious as to what might happen to Hamish, I decided that I would channel this negative energy into something positive by helping those I cared about.

The people from the Epilepsy Foundation of Victoria assisted me on the best way to go about raising awareness at Geelong Grammar School, starting with International Epilepsy Awareness Day—Purple Day 2013. I had so many ideas and was filled with ambition; I finally felt as if I could make a change not only for my brother but for many others out there. I wanted to stand out amongst those raising money for other charities at the School, and I wanted people to remember what I was saying.

Firstly I went around the School filming people and asking them what they knew about epilepsy and seizures and, as I had suspected, there was minimal knowledge. I compiled the video and showed it to the School community at a School assembly, explaining why I was doing what I was doing and why it needed to be done. I covered the School in posters marking March 26 as the day to dress up in purple and support the cause.

Soon another meeting was called with the Foundation and, after all my hard work, I was asked to be the Junior Ambassador for Epilepsy Victoria. My role was now not only to campaign at School, but also to work alongside the other ambassador, Joffa Corfe, and raise greater awareness of epilepsy issues. Joffa came to our Corio campus and spoke to the School community about why epilepsy knowledge is so important.

Joffa's visit stirred my ambition once again and, using some key contacts, I convinced the Australian Football League (AFL) Club, the Western Bulldogs, to get on board and help out. We took some photos for the media (as shown in Figure 10.5), and soon I was being interviewed by a radio station about my work with the Foundation. I had also convinced a long-time family friend, Mike Sheehan, that he and his guests should wear the purple ribbon for epilepsy awareness on their AFL talk show.

However, my proudest moment was on Purple Day at Geelong Grammar School, seeing so many students dressed up in purple to support everything I had done. Everyone wanted to contribute, even in the smallest ways. Putting in so many hours and so much effort was all worth it in the end because of the amazing feeling I had in helping others and being selfless, of being positively engaged—and knowing that others were positively engaged alongside me. A year later, I continue to contribute to the Foundation, with the support of all my peers behind me.

Figure 10.5 Alice Macmillan, family members, Joffa Corfe, and Western Bulldogs representatives promote Purple Day for Epilepsy.

Staff have commented that an understanding of flow and engagement has influenced their personal and professional lives. Taking part in professional development sessions on flow gives staff the time and space to identify times when they already experience high levels of engagement, and strategies that they can use to increase flow in different activities. In addition to their work at the School, many members of staff are highly engaged in service to the wider community through clubs and community organizations. Others build engagement into their lives by undertaking new training courses and even further university studies—increasingly in the fields of Positive Psychology and Positive Education. Staff engagement is supported at a broader level by providing diversity in terms of roles and projects and opportunities for staff to cultivate their interests and passions.

In a pertinent example, Keven O'Connor explains that the engagement and commitment of his team of cleaning professionals has increased noticeably since they have been involved in the Positive Education training. Involving the cleaning team in the training sends a clear message that they are an invaluable part of a thriving School, and that their ideas, experiences, and stories are valued. Perhaps most powerfully of all, the training provides an opportunity for staff to come together so that they all feel part of a wider community with a shared vision.

Understanding the need for engagement has influenced the home and family lives of many members of staff. Justin and Jeanette Robinson believe in the importance of helping their four children to experience engagement during the school holidays. They help each child to set a special project or challenge, ranging from creating a wall hanging for the family home, to passing a grade in music theory, or learning a new skill or hobby. As well as an individual project suited to the age and interests of each child, the family takes part in activities together, such as bushwalking or treasure hunts. The importance of highly engaging family time is relevant for all staff, and an activity aimed at encouraging this is discussed in Box 10.6.

Engaged classrooms

A great man once said to me that teaching is all about opening doors and not closing them—this is what I attempt to do by telling stories and posing questions. The stories often illuminate a point but then leave students with something on which to ponder. Pondering is such an undervalued pastime.

Steve Andrew, Head of Fraser House

Geelong Grammar School teachers believe strongly in the role that flow and engagement play in flourishing classrooms. Students' innate curiosity, interest, and intrinsic motivation are some of the most valuable resources that teachers can use to facilitate learning. Curious students absorb knowledge and want to learn more—they make a psychological investment in their lessons, contribute to discussions, and ask questions that help them to grow. Their enthusiasm inspires others and

BOX 10.6: Flow and family life

During the multi-day Positive Education training courses, attendees are encouraged to explore the role that flow plays in their home and family lives. After being introduced to flow theory, staff are divided into small groups and invited to consider times when they have seen each member of their family in flow, and times when the family has been in flow together. They are also asked to consider strategies and behaviors that support flow, and anything that may act as an obstacle to flow—for example, watching television over dinner may be a barrier to meaningful and engaging family conversations. Dr Kevin Rathunde's "five Cs" framework (Rathunde, 1997) is used to brainstorm strategies for moving families towards greater flow.

Dr Rathunde encourages people to nurture flow through a balance of the "five Cs": *clarity* of goals and expectations; *centering* by expressing interest in the favorite activities of each individual; allowing members of the family *choice* over behaviors and activities; providing a safe and *committed* family environment; and ensuring ongoing *challenges* that continue to evolve and develop. Through this framework, families of all shapes and sizes are able to identify strategies for achieving more flow. By sharing their insights in pairs or small groups, each person gets ideas and suggestions from others, as well as the pleasure and meaningfulness of talking about their families at their best.

creates a classroom culture in which deep questioning and exploration are valued. In contrast, disengaged students are uninterested and can distract others. There is substantial research that connects intrinsic motivation and engagement with valuable learning outcomes such as creativity, deep conceptual understanding, and overall achievement (Burton et al., 2006; Niemiec and Ryan, 2009).

David Bott, Head of Positive Education, believes that strong staff–student relationships are the most valuable pathway to engaged classrooms. Students are more likely to invest in the class if they believe that the teacher genuinely likes and values them—a notion highly consistent with the centrality of belonging and relatedness for intrinsic motivation (Ryan and Deci, 2000). David starts most of his classes by spending a few moments talking to his students as people—enquiring about important things that are happening in their lives, and asking them personally relevant questions. This reinforces David's view that the students as people are more important than the content of the lesson. He has a goal of interacting with every student at least once each lesson, using their names and providing individualized guidance and feedback. This attention to each student builds a class culture of mutual respect, and reinforces the fact that caring and positive relationships are a top priority. Across classrooms of all ages, a caring learning environment in which students feel safe to take risks without fear of criticism or judgment is essential for high-quality learning.

The teacher's passion is another important ingredient of classroom engagement. Engaged and passionate teachers go an extra step in creating learning opportunities for their students, by communicating knowledge in ways that intrigue and fuel curiosity. Finding stories, examples, and media clips that illustrate core ideas helps to create relevance for students. For example, Steve Andrew engages his students in their Mathematics lessons by telling stories, drawing from the history of how Mathematics has emerged and evolved over time, to spark students' interest and intrigue them. Perhaps most adults can recall teachers who taught them in their school years and identify those who were most passionate about their respective fields—teachers, coaches, or mentors whose love of a subject or activity ignited sparks of passion for them. The relationship between staff and student engagement is also supported by research, with evidence of a cross-over effect between students' perception of their teacher's flow and student engagement and motivation (Bakker, 2005; Radel et al., 2010).

Another pathway to engagement is to ensure that goals and expectations are clear and structured. Equally important is regular feedback, where teachers provide individual students or the overall group with guidance on what they are doing well and ways in which they can improve. A valuable strategy is to involve students in the goal-setting process. Prior to commencing a task, teachers can ask students to consider what a piece of work they would be proud of might look like—in other words, how they will know that they have done their best work. Interestingly, this strategy often highlights different students' strengths. For example, a student who greatly appreciates beauty may set goals related to creative presentation, whereas a student with a great love of learning may set goals related to understanding a challenging concept. The process of involving students in setting their own standards helps to build intrinsic motivation as students aim for goals that are personally meaningful to them in addition to the external criteria that are deemed appropriate for the whole group.

The use of character strengths has been found to be an important route to engagement—as well as to pleasure and meaning (Peterson et al., 2007). Understanding their strengths helps students and staff to focus on activities that suit their unique interests and talents. An exploration of character strengths can be the most powerful way of helping students to broaden or narrow their thinking about their subject and vocational options. By exploring character strengths, staff focus on what a student does best—what energizes and motivates them—which helps to foster self-awareness and enable students to refine their thinking about different subject or career choices.

Classroom skill–challenge balance

We don't turn the textbook over and say "All right everyone, we are starting at page 1." One student might need to start at page 60 and another at page 10. We aim to move children forward at the challenge level of their respective abilities.

Garry Pierson, Head of Toorak Campus

Essential to promoting class engagement is the creation of a match between students' skills and the level of challenge. As Garry Pierson explains in the quote that opens this section, some students may need to be stretched beyond the existing curriculum, while others require additional support. The aim is to meet students at the point where they are in terms of their abilities and competencies, so that they feel stretched but not overwhelmed—in other words, to aim for a challenge that is "just right." Just as students can become disengaged if activities are too simple, they can become stressed or anxious if activities are beyond their abilities. Many teachers can provide examples of students who procrastinate or stop trying when a task is too difficult for them.

When faced with a choice of assignment topic, or even subject, it can be tempting for students to choose something within their comfort zone, making it easier to get high grades. At Geelong Grammar School, students are continually encouraged to choose a topic or subject that will stretch them, leading to greater flow in the short term and growth over time. This is particularly important when it comes to choosing academic subjects, and great care is taken to coach and support students through this process to ensure that they are stretched without being overwhelmed.

Another important teaching tool involves providing a level of choice between activities. This encourages a sense of volition, and supports students' need for autonomy. Providing choice also helps to create a match between challenge and skill level, as students can select an activity that suits their interests and perceived abilities. Within the explicit Positive Education curriculum, students are regularly provided with options that cater for their diverse capabilities and interests. For example, students can choose from a range of workshops on character strengths, and may select a workshop on one of their signature strengths, or alternatively a workshop on a lesser strength that they would like to explore and develop.

Summary and Conclusions

Young children are very adept at being "in flow." One only has to observe a child coloring in an intricate mandala, involved in a favorite book, or simply attempting to achieve copperplate handwriting to realize that they can be totally absorbed in the moment and almost oblivious to what is going on about them.

Darryl Moorfoot, Head of Bostock House

An understanding of engagement helps to support flourishing classrooms, where students are intrinsically motivated, actively engaged in their learning, and more "alive" in the present moment. The objective is for students to invest in their learning because they find it rewarding to do so—not because of external rewards, a desire to get a certain mark, or a wish to please others. The benefits extend far beyond the classroom, with many members of the School community able to provide examples of ways in which their understanding of flow and engagement has enriched their family and personal lives. These concepts have lasting consequences as people seek out new information and take part in activities that stretch their current skills, building their knowledge and capacities over time.

Being in flow is a highly engaging and rewarding state, and potentially one of the most enjoyable human experiences. An experience that is perhaps almost as powerful as being in flow is witnessing it in others. Many members of staff find that teaching students who love their subject is one of the most rewarding aspects of their role. Parents share how important it is to them for their children to be engaged and motivated while at school, and to take part regularly in activities that they genuinely love. It is wonderful to witness students and staff showcasing their passions and talents through different subjects, assemblies, musicals, art exhibitions, sporting events, leadership activities, and service to others. In this way flow and engagement not only have a powerful impact on individuals, but also create ripple effects to enhance flourishing across the School community.

RECOMMENDED RESOURCES

Csikszentmihalyi M (2008). *Flow: the psychology of optimal experience*. New York: HarperCollins.

DeBono E (2004). *How to Have a Beautiful Mind*. London: Random House.

Hansen P (2013). *Embrace the Shake. TED talk*. <www.ted.com/talks/phil_hansen_embrace_the_shake>

Hollingsworth P and Lewis G (2006). *Active Learning: increasing flow in the classroom*. Carmarthen, UK: Crown House.

Jackson S. *Body and Mind Flow*. <www.bodyandmindflow.com.au>

Jackson S and Csikszentmihalyi M (1999). *Flow in Sport: the keys to optimal experiences and performance*. Champaign, IL: Human Kinetics.

Kahneman D (2011). *Thinking Fast and Thinking Slow*. New York: FSG Books.

Kashdan T (2009) *Curious? Discover the missing ingredient to a fulfilling life*. New York: Harper Collins.

Kaufman J (2013). *The First 20 Hours: how to learn anything … fast. TEDx talk*. <http://tedxtalks.ted.com/video/The-First-20-Hours-How-to-Learn>

Kaufman J C and Sternberg R J (2006). *The International Handbook of Creativity*. Cambridge: Cambridge University Press.

Leslie I (2014). *Curiosity—why our future depends on it. RSA Talk*. <www.thersa.org/events/video/vision-videos/ian-leslie-curiosity>

Pink D H (2011). *Drive: the surprising truth about what motivates us*. New York: Riverhead Books.

Robinson K. <http://sirkenrobinson.com>

Robinson K and Aronica L (2009). *The Element: how finding your passion changes everything*. New York: Penguin Books.

Self-Determination Theory. <www.selfdeterminationtheory.org>

REFERENCES

Bakker A B (2005). Flow among music teachers and their students: the crossover of peak experiences. *Journal of Vocational Behavior, 66,* 26–44.

Ben-Shahar T (2007). *Happier*. New York: McGraw Hill.

Burton K D, Lydon J E, D'Alessandro D U, and Koestner R (2006). The differential effects of intrinsic and identified motivation on well-being and performance: prospective, experimental, and implicit approaches to self-determination theory. *Journal of Personality and Social Psychology, 91,* 750–62.

Csikszentmihalyi M (1990). *Flow: the psychology of optimal experience*. New York: Harper & Row.

Csikszentmihalyi M (1997). *Finding Flow: the psychology of engagement with everyday life*. New York: Basic Books.

Froh J J et al. (2010). The benefits of passion and absorption in activities: engaged living in adolescents and its role in psychological well-being. *Journal of Positive Psychology, 5,* 311–32.

Hunter J P and Csikszentmihalyi M (2003). The positive psychology of interested adolescents. *Journal of Youth and Adolescence, 32,* 27–35.

Jackson S and Csikszentmihalyi M (1999). *Flow in Sport: the keys to optimal experiences and performance*. Champaign, IL: Human Kinetics.

Jackson S A, Thomas P R, Marsh H W, and Smethurst C J (2001). Relationships between flow, self-concept, psychological skills, and performance. *Journal of Applied Sport Psychology, 13,* 129–53.

Jovanovic V and Brdaric D (2011). Did curiosity kill the cat? Evidence from subjective well-being in adolescents. *Personality and Individual Differences, 52,* 380–84.

Kashdan T B and Roberts J E (2004). Trait and state curiosity in the genesis of intimacy: differentiation from related constructs. *Journal of Social and Clinical Psychology, 23,* 792–816.

Kashdan T B and Silvia P J (2009). Curiosity and interest: the benefits of thriving on novelty and challenge. In: S J Lopez and R Snyder (eds) *Handbook of Positive Psychology*, 2nd edn. New York: Oxford University Press. pp. 367–74.

Kashdan T B, Rose P, and Fincham F D (2004). Curiosity and exploration: facilitating positive subjective experiences and personal growth opportunities. *Journal of Personality Assessment, 82*, 291–305.

Mueller C M and Dweck C S (1998). Praise for intelligence can undermine children's motivation and performance. *Journal of Personality and Social Psychology, 75*, 33–52.

Nakamura J and Csikszentmihalyi M (2009). The concept of flow. In: S J Lopez and R Snyder (eds) *Handbook of Positive Psychology*, 2nd edn. New York: Oxford University Press. pp. 89–105.

Niemiec C P and Ryan R M (2009). Autonomy, competence, and relatedness in the classroom. *Theory and Research in Education, 7*, 133–44.

Peters C S and Malesky L A (2008). Problematic usage among highly-engaged players of massively multiplayer online role playing games. *CyberPsychology and Behavior, 11*, 481–4.

Peterson C, Park N, and Seligman M E P (2005). Orientations to happiness and life satisfaction: the full life versus the empty life. *Journal of Happiness Studies, 6*, 25–41.

Peterson C et al. (2007). Strengths of character, orientations to happiness, and life satisfaction. *Journal of Positive Psychology, 2*, 149–56.

Radel R, Sarrazin P, Legrain P, and Wild T C (2010). Social contagion of motivation between teacher and student: analyzing underlying processes. *Journal of Educational Psychology, 102*, 577–87.

Rathunde K (1997). Parent–adolescent interaction and optimal experience. *Journal of Youth and Adolescence, 26*, 669–89.

Reis H T et al. (2000). Daily well-being: the role of autonomy, competence, and relatedness. *Personality and Social Psychology Bulletin, 26*, 419–35.

Rogatko T P (2009). The influence of flow on positive affect in college students. *Journal of Happiness Studies, 10*, 133–48.

Ryan R M and Deci E L (2000). Self-determination theory and the facilitation of intrinsic motivation, social development, and well-being. *American Psychologist, 55*, 68–78.

Seligman M E P (2011). *Flourish*. London: Nicholas Brealey Publishing.

Shernoff D J and Hoogstra L (2001). Continuing motivation beyond the high school classroom. *New Directions for Child and Adolescent Development, 93*, 73–88.

Thomas N J and Martin F H (2010). Video-arcade game, computer game and Internet activities of Australian students: participation habits and prevalence of addiction. *Australian Journal of Psychology, 62,* 59–66.

Van Ryzin M J, Gravely A A, and Roseth C J (2009). Autonomy, belongingness, and engagement in school as contributors to adolescent psychological well-being. *Journal of Youth and Adolescence, 38,* 1–12.

Walker C J (2010). Experiencing flow: is doing it together better than doing it alone? *Journal of Positive Psychology, 5,* 3–11.

POSITIVE ACCOMPLISHMENT

Introduction by Pninit Russo-Netzer and Dr Tal Ben-Shahar

SUCCESS DOESN'T COME TO YOU, YOU GO TO IT.
Marva Collins

Today, in an age of knowledge explosion and a fast-paced, affluent society where "better, faster, and higher" are sacred values, issues such as the nature of success, its meaning, sources, and expressions, emerge more forcefully. And indeed success in and of itself, whether it is reflected in the way we praise it or experience it, is not enough. We have all heard stories of very successful people who experience themselves as failures. Furthermore, we know from the literature that accomplishments or success—whether we get promoted, or win the lottery—do not make that much of a difference in the long term because we return to our baseline level of happiness (Brickman et al., 1978; Kahneman and Krueger, 2006). In short, not all accomplishments are born equal.

Striving for and achieving any accomplishment, performance, or success, not necessarily an academic one, involves a synthesis of numerous internal as well as external components, including self-efficacy (Bandura, 1994), intrinsic motivation (Ryan and Deci, 2000), positive engagement (Akey, 2006; Heller et al., 2003), hope (Snyder, 2002), optimism (Scheier and Carver, 1985), character strengths (Park and Peterson, 2006), and praise (Dweck, 2006). The variety of models and theories reveals the complex, dynamic, and multifaceted nature of the notion of accomplishment. Positive and meaningful accomplishments or achievements may function as a potential venue for other domains of wellbeing (Seligman, 2011), as such accomplishments or achievements both facilitate and are facilitated by positive emotions, meaning, engagement, and positive relationships. The interconnection between accomplishment and flourishing (e.g. Howell, 2009) is not surprising when we consider the empowering effect that an experience of accomplishment can have on our sense of self.

According to Bandura (1994, p. 2), "the most effective way of developing a strong sense of efficacy is through mastery experiences." When we experience our own success—when we perform something effectively, or are getting noticeably better at it—our self-confidence increases. In turn, this leads to better performance and a higher likelihood of future mastery experiences. In other words, performing a task successfully reinforces our self-confidence and self-esteem, which also builds interest, motivation, and engagement. In contrast, when the experience is a poor one, where there is no mastery experience, self-confidence suffers and performance drops, which leads to lower confidence, and so on in a vicious circle of negative reinforcement. When we are using our strengths, when we are intrinsically motivated, when we believe in ourselves—that is when we can perform at our best while enjoying the process and not just the "finish line." That is also when we are most likely to enter the virtuous circle—the upward spiral.

Mastery experiences of positive accomplishment most often start with goal setting, which functions to organize and motivate behavior and efforts. In a way, goals can function as self-fulfilling prophecies, as they posit a belief that we can achieve something. Specifying what it is that we want to achieve makes it more likely to come true. Goal setting is considered a significant cognitive skill for students to master as part of a successful learning process (Saleh, 2008). To help students to set goals that will motivate meaningful achievement and accomplishment, they should be calibrated and aligned with a person's interests, personal values, and abilities. In other words, they need to be personally meaningful and freely chosen. Such self-determined or self-concordant goals, derived from intrinsic motivation, entail volitional and active engagement with activities that individuals find interesting (Ryan and Deci, 2000; Sansone and Harackiewicz, 2000), and relate to positive wellbeing and long-term success (Sheldon and Elliot, 1999).

Another important ingredient in the fostering of students' positive accomplishments has to do with agency and self-management in taking action and reaching those goals. According to Bandura (1997, 2001), human agency is essentially based on efficacy beliefs, or beliefs in personal competence. The importance of one's self-beliefs is also emphasized in Snyder's hope theory. According to Snyder (2000), agency involves motivation, willpower, and determination to initiate and implement strategies and pathways to achieve desired goals. Individuals with high levels of hope are able to focus on success rather than failure when pursuing goals, and perceive themselves as capable of problem solving (Snyder et al., 1997). The importance of cultivating optimism and hope is supported by their wide variety of positive outcomes, such as greater success and more persistence, particularly in the face of challenging tasks or obstacles (Gillham and Reivich, 2004; Peterson and Park, 1998).

Many studies also show the importance of character strengths for achievement and accomplishment. In particular, perseverance and temperance were found to predict academic achievement among school students (Peterson and Park, 2009). Furthermore, persistence in the face of challenges requires focused and long-term exertion of effort. These important qualities are reflected in the character strength of "grit," which "entails working strenuously toward challenges, maintaining effort and interest over years despite failure, adversity, and plateaus in progress. The gritty individual approaches achievement as a marathon; his or her advantage is stamina" (Duckworth et al., 2007, p. 1088). Interestingly, this character strength was found to predict success to a greater extent than intelligence (IQ) and the personality variable of conscientiousness.

Building accomplishment

When visiting Geelong Grammar School (see Figure 11.1), I (Tal Ben-Shahar) was struck by how these theories came to life. The students, although in a competitive environment, were still able to enjoy intrinsic motivation and numerous mastery experiences; they learned from their failures and humbly celebrated their successes. I remember one particular instance when I had lunch with a group of Year 12 students. We were discussing Aristotle's idea of eudaimonia and its connection to meaning when I suddenly remembered—in disbelief I must add—that these were 17-year-olds who were grappling with the deepest and most profound questions. It was not only their intellect that impressed me. The confidence with which they carried themselves—the willpower and "waypower" that they exemplified—were remarkable, quite irrespective of their age.

We can muster and nurture these important keys to empower our students to pave their own unique routes to positive accomplishments and success in different contexts and occasions throughout their daily routine in school. A few examples are provided below.

Learning from success and savoring accomplishments

Building on the appreciative inquiry perspective (Cooperrider and Whitney, 2005), it seems valuable to encourage students (as well as ourselves, as educators) to discover their own best learning experiences and positive accomplishments, and savor them. Basking, and celebrating our victories, whether small or large ones, stimulates positive emotions, such as pride of accomplishment (Bryant and Veroff, 2007). This in turn

Figure 11.1 Dr Tal Ben-Shahar addressing senior students during his stay at Geelong Grammar School.

endorses the development of a genuine and deep-rooted sense of self-esteem (see Tracy and Robins, 2004, p. 116).

Learning from the positive accomplishments of the self and others, through analyzing "why did this happen," as in What Went Well (WWW) exercises (see Seligman, 2011), focuses our attention and awareness on the processes and conditions that contribute to flourishing and optimal functioning. We can also learn a lot from failures and setbacks along the way. Much growth can stem from experiences that do not turn out as we expect or want them to, such as failures or hardships that we experience. It is what we make of the experiences that matters most. We can reinterpret a failure as an opportunity to develop and to improve.

Positive feedback

Teacher–student dialogues—providing authentic, timely, and genuine interest as well as positive and supportive feedback—validate learning experiences, promote intimacy and trust, and enable the student to focus on their strengths and possibilities. Work by Dweck (2006) illustrates the importance of effective praise to leverage students' efforts to develop a growth mindset rather than fixed mindset, and foster love of learning as well as self-esteem.

According to Dweck (2006), the messages that we receive from significant others direct the way we think about ourselves. As Dweck explains, "It can be a fixed-mindset message that says: You have permanent traits and I'm judging them. Or it can be a growth-mindset message that says: You are a developing person and I am interested in your development"

(Dweck, 2006, p. 173). Thus praising persistence and effort rather than innate intelligence, talent, or outcome can play an important role in helping students to fulfill their potential and achieve positive accomplishments. Building a student's confidence is about giving authentic and realistic positive feedback.

Rituals

As Friedrich Nietzsche noted in 1883, "He who would learn to fly one day must first learn to stand and walk and run and climb and dance; one cannot fly into flying." Success inevitably involves setbacks and failures. The key is to unpack threatening tasks into small, digestible, and manageable ingredients and turn them into rituals within daily routines. According to Loehr and Schwartz (2003), rituals can be built by planning precise, value-driven behaviors and performing them at defined times. Teachers can introduce rituals to support their students' positive accomplishments, at the beginning and/or end of a class (for example, they can ask the students to journal about how the topic learned is relevant to their own personal lives).

Positive and engaging environment

Research in the area of priming (e.g. Stadler and Hogan, 1996) demonstrates that our subconscious grasps much more than most of us think, and the subliminal messages that it receives influence where we focus our attention and ultimately how we feel about ourselves and others, as well as how we act. A positive environment can go a long way towards bringing out positive emotions and positive behavior. Teachers play an important role in nurturing student engagement that can positively influence their achievement (Akey, 2006).

Creation of a culture of achievement can be nurtured by fostering a safe and empowering environment in the classroom, developing interactive lessons and activities relevant to the students' real life, and catering for the different learning styles and multiple intelligences of students. These, together with supportive and challenging instructions, are all ways in which teachers can foster student engagement in the classroom. Encouraging mastery experiences through exploratory, collaborative, and active learning (for example, by setting self-concordant goals, initiating personal research projects, and oral presentations) is important when promoting hands-on experiences that lead to interest, autonomy, creativity, and curiosity. In a large-scale study, curious students were found to have more optimism, hope, and confidence, and a greater sense of self-determination and self-efficacy, believing that they were in control of their actions and decisions, compared with their peers who were rated as bored (Hunter and Csikszentmihalyi, 2003).

The secret to success

So what is the "best-kept secret" to success? The secret is that there is no secret. There are no short cuts to success. Looking at the most successful people in the world, we see three components to their success—optimism, passion, and hard work. It is crucial that we believe in ourselves and in our abilities. Highly successful people are optimistic—they believe that they will succeed. They also identify things that they are passionate about and set their personal goals in alignment with these passions, personal interests, and meaningful values. Finally, there is another ingredient which all successful people have, and that is available to all. It is perspiration, or hard work (Ericsson, 1996). Coupled with working at that which one is passionate about and a belief that one can do well, it comprises the "magic ingredient" of success.

Positive accomplishment at Geelong Grammar School

You don't have to be the most brilliant student in the world to achieve. What you might have to be is persistent and committed. The students who persevere are the ones accomplishing things, creating things, getting things done.

Dr John Court, Old Geelong Grammarian and Past Senior Medical Officer

One year a student on the senior rowing team made a special impression on her crew members. Initially a member of the Fourth VIII, this student did not finding rowing easy, and for weeks she struggled to get her rhythm and technique right. In addition, she was much smaller than and not as strong as many of her peers. However, instead of giving up, she approached this challenge with unbelievable determination and optimism. The student voluntarily undertook additional training, and sought out individual feedback after every training session. She worked closely with her coaches, Debbie Clingeleffer-Woodford and Robert England, and together they looked at photos and watched videos to see how she could improve. Towards the end of her season in the Fourth VIII, she had a "eureka moment" and finished the season rowing with a much smoother and more effective technique. Over the winter season she lifted weights to increase her strength, and she practiced her technique with determination and perseverance. She continued to practice using a rowing machine, while still seeking advice and feedback. Slowly this student's skills grew and she developed into a strong and confident rower. After months of consistent effort and optimism, she took her place in the First VIII, an honor reserved for the strongest rowers at the School. She continued to seek feedback and to hone aspects of her skills, and by the end of the season she had become one of the pivotal members of the crew, with excellent technique.

As this story exemplifies, it is often at the moments when things are not easy, when success does not come naturally, that the true nature of positive accomplishment emerges. The student in this story demonstrated effort, motivation, and the determination to persist despite challenges. She also had an admirable willingness to seek help, openness to feedback, and the courage to speak about her weaknesses. It is these character traits—more than external successes, prizes, or rewards—that are at the heart of the positive accomplishment domain at Geelong Grammar School.

Within the Model for Positive Education, positive accomplishment is defined as the capacity to work towards meaningful goals, the motivation and grit to persist despite challenges and setbacks, and the achievement of competence and success in important life domains. This is exemplified in a photo of students at Timbertop, hiking over snow to reach the crest of a mountain (see Figure 11.2). For some students, a sense of accomplishment may be derived from getting the grades necessary for

Figure 11.2 Year 9 students midway through a 4-day hike and collectively striving towards their goal.

them to be accepted onto their desired university course. For others, it may come from running an innovative fundraising campaign for those in need. For yet others, it may be gained by supporting a friend during a challenging time. It is understood that a dynamic blend of striving for accomplishments in a wide range of areas is necessary for a vibrant, full, and meaningful life.

"Positive" accomplishment

The foundation of the positive accomplishment domain is a rich exploration of the true meaning of success, achievement, and accomplishment. When students and staff are first asked to think about this domain, it can be tempting to think of accomplishments as awards, positions, achievements, and prizes. However, when they are encouraged to delve deeper, students can begin to see that positive accomplishment is about much more than external rewards and recognition. The positive accomplishment domain focuses on achievements that nurture the self and others academically, physically, emotionally, socially, and spiritually. In particular, there is a strong focus on accomplishment in terms of "doing good" through altruistic acts and service to the community.

An important distinction at the School is the difference between accomplishments that are pursued for *intrinsic* and *extrinsic* reasons (for a discussion of these concepts, see also Chapter 10). Extrinsic motivation occurs when a goal is pursued in order to achieve a reward or avoid a punishment. Intrinsic motivation occurs when a goal is pursued because it is valued, or because the task is enjoyable and deeply rewarding (Ryan and Deci, 2000). Research has consistently found that time spent in intrinsically motivated tasks is more nurturing to the self than time spent in extrinsically motivated tasks (Ryan and Deci, 2000; Veronneau et al., 2005). A broad aim of Positive Education is to support intrinsic motivation by helping members of the School community to develop their character strengths and apply them to activities that are personally engaging and meaningful.

Academic accomplishment

Academic achievement represents a large component of the positive accomplishment domain. One of the fundamental objectives of schools is to support young people in developing skills and knowledge across a diverse range of subjects, creating promising pathways for their future career prospects. A vision shared by Professor Martin Seligman is for schools to teach the skills needed for academic success and the skills and mindsets needed for flourishing, without compromising either of these (Seligman, 2008). It is also important to note that accomplishment in academics involves more than high performance—the aim is for students to take ownership of their learning, to question, to take risks, to collaborate, to discover, and to continually refine their skills. Academic goals that are pursued solely for extrinsic or external reasons detract from students' love of learning, and contribute to a short-term focus. True academic accomplishment comes from intrinsic self-motivation supported by excellent teaching.

Although Geelong Grammar School did not embark on its journey with Positive Education out of the desire to enhance academic outcomes, but with the intention of supporting students' mental and physical health and wellbeing, a common observation is that student flourishing and academic performance are closely linked. Students with healthy sleep habits, nurturing diets, and active lifestyles are more physically capable of maintaining concentration and focus in the classroom than students who do not take good care of their health. The interconnected relationship between learning and wellbeing is supported by substantial research evidence (Durlak et al., 2011; Suldo et al., 2011). Adolescents who are flourishing have been found to report higher grades, more self-control in relation to their studies, and lower levels of procrastination than students who are moderately mentally healthy or languishing (Howell, 2009). Performing well academically helps students to feel a sense of competence and confidence that in turn supports their physical and mental health. However, it is important to note that students who feel overwhelmed by their studies can experience *academic stress*, which contributes to decreased wellbeing and psychological distress (Suldo et al., 2008).

Although academic achievement is an important component of the positive accomplishment domain, it is not the only element. An overarching objective of Positive Education is to broaden the definitions of success and achievement within schools, so that there is equal focus on a range of positive accomplishments that nurture flourishing for self and others across the lifespan. In Box 11.1, Charlie Scudamore, Vice Principal, summarizes how he encourages students to expand their understanding of the concepts of success, resilience, and intelligence during their Year 10 Values and Ethics classes.

Mindset theory

The most valuable concept we've learnt this year is the idea of having a growth mindset over a fixed mindset. This has been particularly helpful during the exam period. Rather than thinking our results would be disappointing, we encouraged ourselves by acknowledging the growth mindset perspective that doing well is possible, with hard work and persistence. Our mindset allowed for us to be less stressed and have more self-confidence.

Imogen and Hannah, Year 10, Senior School, Corio Campus

BOX 11.1: Success, resilience, and intelligence

I teach all Year 10 students Values and Ethics. In Term 1 each class focuses on one key word. The first three words to be considered are "success," "resilience," and "intelligence." Success is looked at in terms of positive relationships and wellbeing. I stress that a successful person, for me, is one who is respected by peers, who exhibits a strong moral compass, and who is supportive of others. The concept of post-traumatic growth is the focus of the resiliency class. What allows some people to grow from traumatic experiences? What enables a person to bounce back? Reference is made to the "Resiliency Model" taught at Timbertop. It highlights the need for people to learn how to cope with failure in order for there to be growth and a real sense of achievement. Howard Gardner's work on multiple intelligences (Gardner, 1999) is at the core of our exploration of the word "intelligence." I also make use of Sir Ken Robinson's rewording of an age-old question, from "How intelligent are you?" to "How are you intelligent?" An emphasis is placed on exploring a person's emotional and social intelligences as well as highlighting numerical, linguistic, musical, kinesthetic, and other types of intelligences. By conducting these classes I hope that it will be possible to enable all Year 10s to broaden their understanding of success, resilience, and intelligence. I want them all to have knowledge of their innate talents and to recognize and appreciate the talents of others. I also want each student to apply their character strengths in all that they do.

Charlie Scudamore, Vice Principal

Mindset theory is a foundation of positive accomplishment at the School. According to Professor Carol Dweck, people embody one of two mindsets (Dweck, 2006). A fixed mindset corresponds with the belief that intelligence and talents are set in stone—that people are born with a limited amount of intelligence or strength and there is little they can do to change this. In contrast, a growth mindset corresponds with the belief that talent and intelligence can be developed, and that effort and determination are essential components of success (see Figure 11.3).

People with a growth mindset believe that hard work and persistence are essential to achieving their goals. They are willing to step outside their comfort zones and try activities that stretch their abilities. People with a growth mindset persevere when things get challenging, and they actively seek out feedback that may improve their performance. When they experience setbacks or disappointing results, they try to learn from their experiences. The features of fixed and growth mindsets are summarized in Table 11.1 (developed from Dweck, 2006).

Fixed mindsets influence student learning in powerful ways. Students may label themselves in a fixed way, such as "no good at Science," "terrible at writing," or "unable to sing." This attitude greatly influences how they feel about the subject and how they engage with the learning content. Equally, staff can create labels such as "a difficult student," "a challenging class," or even "a clever year group." The labels that teachers have for their students can have a lasting impact, as there is

Figure 11.3 Year 10 student exploring fixed and growth mindsets.

Table 11.1 Characteristics of fixed and growth mindsets

Fixed mindset	Growth mindset
Intelligence is stable and fixed	Intelligence can be developed
Avoid challenges	Pursue and embrace challenges
Give up when faced with obstacles and setbacks	Persist when faced with obstacles and setbacks
See effort as futile	See effort as necessary for accomplishment and growth
Avoid negative feedback	Seek out feedback and view criticism as an opportunity for learning
Feel threatened by the success of others	Find inspiration in the success of others

well-established evidence that teachers' expectations positively and/or negatively affect their students' academic growth and achievement (Rosenthal and Jacobson, 1968). A teacher who is informed that a class is "below average" may set relatively easy tasks and not stretch the students or foster a growth mindset, resulting in limited learning and development.

In an example of the power of overcoming fixed mindsets and undoing labels, a parent explained that his son had ongoing reading difficulties. Some teachers seemed to have the idea that the boy would always struggle in this way, and gave him reading tasks within his limits in an attempt to boost his confidence. However, one teacher noticed that the young man recited every single one of his lines in the Middle School play perfectly. The teacher prompted the student to apply the strategies that he used to learn his lines for the play to his reading across his subjects. She also continually challenged other teachers' perceptions of the young man's capabilities. Over the following years the student became a competent reader, and his improved reading skills deepened his love of performing.

Fostering growth mindsets

> Sometimes you hear the attitude "I am not a fast runner so I am not going to go in running events anymore." Together, we consider the question—if you wanted to do better, what could you do? Students are great at coming up with ideas such as doing more training, learning from a friend, or choosing athletics as their sport, so they might do better next time.
>
> Marshall Radcliff, Head of Physical Education, Toorak Campus

Dweck (2006) recommends four steps for developing a growth mindset—learning to identify growth and fixed mindset voices, recognizing the choice between interpreting challenges with a fixed or growth mindset, cultivating a growth mindset voice, and taking action and embracing new challenges. A foundational step is the creation of a common language and understanding of growth and fixed mindsets around the School. Even the youngest children in the School community are encouraged to reflect on their mindsets and whether their thinking is helping or harming a situation. With young students, metaphors such as "red light thinking" and "green light thinking" are used to highlight the difference between fixed mindset thoughts that stop them and growth mindset thoughts that help them to move forward (for an example of how this metaphor is used with Prep students at Bostock House, see Box 11.2). Case Study 11.1, written by David Bott, Head of Positive Education, describes how growth mindsets are taught in the explicit Positive Education program with senior students, including how research in psychology and neuroscience is used to create depth of understanding for students.

Once the staff and students have a foundational understanding of growth mindsets, the next step is to create personal relevance and meaningful understanding. Knowledge of mindsets is particularly helpful when individuals in the School community experience setbacks such as a poor mark, a disappointing sporting

---

BOX 11.2: Red and green light thinking

In Prep we have been learning about mindsets and how they can affect our progress. We use the analogy of a traffic light to differentiate between fixed and growth mindsets. When we are faced with a challenge we have a choice of whether to use red light thinking (fixed mindset) or green light thinking (growth mindset). When we use green light thinking and give things a try, we are able to make new connections in our brain and learn more. Green light thinking has helped us to learn so much this year because a lot of what we do in Prep is a new challenge for us but we can use it in other places as well. We thought of some times we have used green light thinking to help us try new things and challenge ourselves:

- "I was scared to ride my two-wheel bike in case I fell off, but I used green light thinking and now I can do it." Hamish
- "I couldn't read when I got to Prep, but every night I use green light thinking, even on the hard words, and now I can read." Aryan
- "I used green light thinking the other day to go down the purple waterslide, because I had never done that before." Violet
- "When I started in Prep I couldn't hold scissors and cut things, and I used to tell Ms Marney it was too hard for me, but then I used green light thinking and she taught me how to hold them, so now I can cut things on my own. I'm a good cutter now." Adam

Jane Marney, Teacher, Bostock House

CASE STUDY 11.1

Year 10 Neuroplasticity Project

David Bott, Head of Positive Education

Increasingly, the psychological research that has underpinned the growth of Positive Psychology is being supplemented by exciting advances in neurobiological research. This "hard" science has always captivated me, but it is the concept of neuroplasticity in particular that seems to intersect most neatly with my passions for psychology and education. The ability of the brain to constantly rewire itself in response to experience not only explains learning itself, at a biological level, but also explains why beliefs, mindset, and practice are so powerful in learning.

While reading Norman Doidge's book, *The Brain That Changes Itself* (Doidge, 2007), I began to visualize ways in which we could bring the abstract concept of neuroplasticity alive for students. We wanted to design a single lesson that could clearly illustrate the brain's ability to change rapidly. It was fortuitous that Todd Sampson's documentary series, *Redesign Your Brain*, happened to be on television at the time. In one episode, Sampson learns to juggle three balls by means of a clear strategy and sustained practice. This was obviously an ideal, demonstrable, and enjoyable way for students to experience neuroplasticity in action. And so the Geelong Grammar School "Neuroplasticity Project" was born.

As part of the Year 10 Pos Ed curriculum, students (most of whom cannot juggle three balls) are given a single juggling ball. Through a series of carefully choreographed practice strategies over a 30-minute period, the students progress through increasingly difficult training goals before finally being given three balls to juggle (see Figure 11.4). By this stage, the students can throw a reliable arc with two balls; for most students, it is a matter of a few minutes of practice before they complete their first "juggulation." Even students who fail to complete this final goal in the session see a significant improvement in their juggling ability. The fun and excitement throughout the session are palpable. It is always hard to get the students to stop juggling at the end of the session.

As a teacher, however, the most rewarding part of the lesson is the subsequent debrief discussion. When asked the question "What has happened in the last half hour?," the students inevitably reach the conclusion that their brain has changed. Further discussion explores questions such as why the learning was so fast, why mistakes were so important in the process and, ultimately, how learning to juggle might be analogous to tackling academic and co-curricular challenges.

This task is certainly a very effective way of teaching students about the brain's remarkable plasticity. The empirical nature of the lesson is also consistent with our desire to balance student theoretical understanding with experiential learning.

Figure 11.4 David Bott teaching Year 10 students how to juggle as part of their neuroplasticity project.

result, or a conflict with a friend or colleague. These moments of difficulty provide invaluable opportunities for helping individuals to start to understand their mindset voices and identify areas for growth and improvement. Although it is easy to think of growth mindsets in terms of specific topics or subjects, mindset theory actually has much richer and broader implications. Staff and students share examples of trying to become more patient, more accepting of others, and more mindful. There are also important links between growth mindsets and character strengths, and members of the School community are continually reminded that they can grow and develop all 24 strengths, not just the ones identified as their top signature strengths.

Feedback and growth mindsets

Often it is the natural instinct of parents and teachers to praise children for their intelligence and talents. Comments such as "Wow—you are so clever!" or "You have a natural talent for this subject" are well-intentioned efforts to increase children's and students' self-confidence and motivation. However, research suggests that feedback which is focused on abilities, referred to as "person praise," can foster a fixed mindset as students start to believe that success should come easily to them (Dweck, 2007; Mueller and Dweck, 1998). The student may label him- or herself as naturally talented and look for easy challenges that enable high scores and more person praise. In contrast, "process praise" that is directed towards effort and persistence supports a growth mindset, as students realize that their performance is influenced by factors that are within their control.

In order to foster a growth mindset, when a student performs well on a task, teachers focus on the effort that the student has put in (e.g. "I like the way you tried all kinds of strategies on that challenging problem until you finally got it" or "You really studied for your test, and your improvement shows it"). When a student does not perform well, discussion focuses on how effort can be improved in the future (e.g. "This assignment does not reflect your best effort—can we please discuss some areas and strategies for improvement?"). This approach is strengthened by introducing parents and family members to mindset theory, and encouraging them to use process praise with their children. Mindset theory also informs the staff performance appraisal process, and the aim is to provide staff with both positive and constructive feedback in ways that support a growth mindset.

Striving for meaningful goals

> At the "Make a Difference" Market my group was Jack, Ethan, and Sebastian. I think we worked well together because we had goals. We didn't argue and we all worked towards the same goal. That was a valuable lesson for me about teamwork.
>
> Oscar, Year 4, Bostock House

Striving for meaningful goals plays a central role in the positive accomplishment domain. Goals can be short term, such as going for a run, or long term, such as achieving success in a chosen career. The benefits of goals are abundant (Covington, 2000), and goal setting has been found to be an effective strategy for use with students of all ages, from young children (Szente, 2007) to adolescents (Scarborough et al., 2011). When levels of motivation and confidence are high, goals provide a focal point for effort and action. When motivation is low, looking back at progress towards the goal renews confidence and serves as a reminder of successes to date. Goal commitment is highest when the goals are specific, highly valued, and challenging but attainable (Locke and Latham, 2002). Features of highly motivating goals are often represented by the SMART mnemonic—specific, measurable, attractive, realistic, and timely. There is also substantial research evidence that goals completed for intrinsic reasons do more to enrich wellbeing and foster motivation than goals which are completed for extrinsic reasons (Sheldon and Elliot, 1999).

BOX 11.3: Hot air balloon goals

At the start of each school term, Pam Barton, who teaches Year 5 at Middle School, Corio Campus, and her class explore SMART goals. In collaboration with their parents, students set three goals for the term. The students come up with a range of goals, such as improving their spelling scores, getting along better with their siblings, or eating healthier food. Pam encourages the students to explore concrete strategies for how they are going to achieve their goal—that is, what they need to do to make it possible. After the goals and strategies have been formalized, the class create colorful visual representations of the goals. Each term the theme is different, with themes including athletes running towards the finish line, hikers climbing a big hill, and miners digging towards gemstones.

One favorite theme is hot air balloons. Each student has their own hot air balloon (representing the goal) and a basket (representing their progress). Each week the class revisits their goals, moving the basket closer to the balloon if they have made good goal progress and leaving it where it is if they have not. If students have not progressed towards their goals, Pam helps them to explore what they could do differently over the coming week. Pam observes that the students demonstrate remarkable honesty during this process and appear to understand that it is not a competition, but rather it is about how they are developing and can improve in the future.

Across the Geelong Grammar School campuses, students are regularly encouraged to set SMART goals. An activity for Year 5 students that uses classroom visuals to represent goal progress is described in Box 11.3. Goal setting is also greatly enhanced by collaborative work between peers, referred to as "goal coaching." This process draws on the literature on evidence-based coaching to help students to support each other in setting and striving for valued goals (for details, see Box 11.4; see also Green et al., 2007).

BOX 11.4: Peer goal-coaching

To set a context for goal-coaching, senior students first spend some time individually exploring examples of times when they have achieved, and failed to achieve, goals. The students often come up with useful insights, such as "Goal achievement is most likely if motivation is intrinsic, not extrinsic," "Sometimes to achieve goals you need to ask for help," and "Having a growth mindset helps you to persist when things get tough." In the next step, the students brainstorm SMART goals for each of the domains of the Model for Positive Education. After the students have set their goals, they are divided into pairs and each member of the pair takes turns to share one of their valued goals. The partners' instructions are to listen attentively and provide feedback on any ways in which the goals could be made more "SMART." The goals are revisited over the following weeks, with students regrouping in their pairs to discuss their goal progress, and revising their goals as needed.

Grit and persistence

Trying new things and having a turn.

When you keep going and going.

Trying things you don't know until you can do them.

Definitions of persistence, Early Learning Centre Students, Toorak Campus

Dr Angela Duckworth and her colleagues define grit as "perseverance and passion for long-term goals" (Duckworth et al., 2007, p. 1087). Grit involves self-regulation, discipline, and sacrificing short-term rewards for long-term gain. Seligman (2011) proposes the following formula: grit = skill × effort, where skill is natural ability, and effort is the amount of time devoted to practice and obtaining experience.

In numerous research studies, grit has been found to be important for goal attainment and academic performance, and often plays a more powerful role than concepts traditionally viewed as important to achievement, such as intelligence, personality, and natural talent (Duckworth et al., 2007). Although applicable to many domains of their lives, grit has particular relevance to students' studies, especially during demanding exam periods when students need to maintain energy and focus. One interesting research finding is that teachers who score high on grit have been found to have students who display the greatest improvements in learning over a school year (Duckworth et al., 2009). Duckworth suggests that "grittier" teachers work longer and harder with students who are experiencing difficulties, and do not give up when situations become challenging.

Throughout their time at the School, students are exposed to challenges that develop their capacity for grit and persistence. In the Bostock Year 4 Adventure Challenge, students work together to travel the 12 kilometres from Bostock House to the Corio campus by using a combination of walking, public transport, and even boating across Corio Bay. The Lorne 160, in which students undertake a relay of 160 kilometres as a fundraiser for charity, is another activity that fosters grit. Throughout the months leading up to the relay, students demonstrate great commitment to raising money for their selected cause, and dedicate time to training to ensure that they are physically prepared for the ambitious physical challenge. Timbertop is the epitome of grit and persistence for many students. In addition to their academic learning, students at Timbertop perform a variety of tasks and chores that ensure the campus community runs smoothly, and they also take part in a rigorous outdoor education program. (For a story about grit at Timbertop written by Clare Bennetts, Agriculture and Land Management Coordinator, see Box 11.5.)

Hope theory

During a School assembly in 2012, Xara Kaye, School Captain at the time, made a speech that prompted the audience to think about the phrase "You've made your

---

BOX 11.5: Top of the mountain

Recently we did the "Over the Top" run, which takes us up to the Saddle and then over the top of Mount Timbertop. Over the other side of Mount Timbertop the students had the choice of turning down the fire trail to school or keeping going up and over Mount Buller to complete the "King of the Mountain." I had the opportunity to be the tail runner over Mount Buller, but only if I made the cut-off time at the intersection. While we were running up Timbertop, the mist followed us up the mountain and the atmosphere was quite magical. I was struggling to keep running, and every time I started to walk a student who was running behind me kept saying "Come on Miss Bennetts, you can do it, don't stop now." All I could do was turn around and smile at her because I was so out of breath.

We made it to the summit of Mount Timbertop together feeling that we must be on top of the world. Both of us ran through the rising mist, the red leaves that spring had brought to the snow gums between the cliff edges falling off to the side of the narrow path. We reached the intersection in time and kept running up onto Mount Buller, and I thought "I have made it here because of the student helping me, and not the other way round."

Most of the 55 students who made it up Mount Buller ran every step of the way—20 km across and 1200 m in elevation—and truly inspired the teachers with their persistence and enthusiasm. There was great emotion at the end of the run, and a deep sense of accomplishment. Flourishing and pride filled the campus for the rest of the day as we, in our contented and exhausted states, all reflected on what we had achieved.

Clare Bennetts, Agriculture and Land Management Coordinator, Timbertop

---

bed, now you must lie on it." Xara encouraged the students to consider that this is an unhelpful point of view, as it implies that it is often too late to change. She urged the students to consider that hope is always possible, and she asked them to consider the relevance of change in their own lives, as well as in terms of community and environmental issues. Xara concluded her speech by urging the students to "always remember you are never past the point of being able to remake the bed and start again with some awesome new sheets."

Often when people think of hope, they think of a general intention to cross their fingers and hope for the best. Developments in the field of Positive Psychology have clarified that hope is more than wishful thinking, and is actually a cognitive process that enhances motivation and inspires action. Professor Rick Snyder's model of hope (Snyder, 2002) is a useful framework that encompasses the value of setting goals with the grit and determination to achieve them. The model is based on the three interconnected elements of goals, pathways, and agency. Goals are the anchors of hope theory; they provide the targets that guide action. Pathways are strategies for achieving the goals. Agency is the motivation to achieve the pathways. Language that makes sense to many students is that hope is having the will (agency) and the ways (pathways) to work towards goals (Lopez et al., 2009).

> **BOX 11.6: Hope for the "Journey"**
>
> Each year, the Year 8 students take part in a "Journey," which is either a 9-day cycling expedition or a 5-day hiking and paddling expedition. Both options are physically and emotionally demanding and require many months of training and preparation. Just prior to the expedition, the students take part in a Positive Education Focus Day based on teamwork and hope. The students spend time exploring how the "will" and the "ways" can help them in the upcoming Journey, and guest speakers share personal stories of resilience and grit. The Focus Day often culminates in the creation of a team dance or song which is re-performed or re-sung by smaller groups of students on various occasions throughout the Journey as a reminder not to give up. This combination of the Focus Day and camp is a good example of the value of explicit teaching which, when connected with real-life experiences, gives students the opportunity to put their skills into action.

There is substantial evidence that hope is related to good mental and physical health (Snyder, 2002; Valle et al., 2006). A school-based hope program has been found to lead to increased feelings of self-worth and improved satisfaction with life (Marques et al., 2011). High levels of hope have also been found to be associated with strong performance academically and in sports (Curry et al., 1997; Snyder et al., 1997).

Schools provide an invaluable opportunity for inculcating hope (Lopez et al., 2009). Hope can be enhanced by supporting students to learn skills for setting goals, and by developing pathways and agency (motivation) thinking. Strategies for building hope include working in teams, using goals that are progressively more challenging, brainstorming multiple pathways to achieve the goal, and breaking large goals down into small steps. Box 11.6 describes a "Hope for the Journey" Positive Education Focus Day, where Year 8 students learn about the character strengths of hope and teamwork prior to putting their learning into action in an outdoor adventure camp.

Summary and conclusions

> May we stand up for what is right, even if it may cause us harm; may we be able to find opportunity in the midst of difficulty, and may we not be afraid to make mistakes, but use them instead as a means for learning.
>
> Rogan Kennedy, School Prefect 2012, Extract from a prayer at a School assembly

Teachers and parents want what is best for their students and children, and one of their deepest wishes is to equip young people with the skills and knowledge that will

CASE STUDY 11.2

Running at Timbertop

Kate Hood, Head of Unit, Timbertop

John Landy worked at Timbertop in 1955 and used the Timbertop terrain as a training ground for his 1956 Olympic appearance. It was during this time that boys became involved in his passion for running, and a more formalized running program developed from there. With the introduction of teacher/student ratios and workplace health and safety laws, the running program became a whole community event, with all teachers, assistants, and students participating.

At the beginning of a Timbertop year, students from Bangkok, Deniliquin in New South Wales, the North Shore in Sydney, Hong Kong, and many places in between set foot on the gravel, all with a common nervousness. The more athletic students wonder whether Scrubby Hill—a short steep hill that is part of Term 1 "crossies"—is really that tough, and whether they can keep up with the staff, and the less fit students hope that they will not come last. After the first 2 weeks at Timbertop, the students and new staff realize that this physical adventure has nothing to do with comparison of self against others. It is a personal journey—a year-long journey. Most likely it will be littered with small strains and pains, good days and bad days, disappointments and achievements. Figures 11.5, 11.6, and 11.7 showcase the Timbertop running program.

The accomplishment is one of personal growth and satisfaction. When I began at Timbertop 5 years ago, I had always considered myself fit, but I was not a runner. In fact I strongly disliked running. I was fit because I played sport that gave me social connections. Just like the students, I grew to love running throughout my first year. I clearly remember the first time I ran all the way up Scrubby Hill, and I remember the "woo hoo" I let out when I did. I remember the feeling of being lost on a path somewhere—lost physically because I had not yet explored the Timbertop surrounds so I had no idea where I was, and lost mentally because my mind had wandered from the pain and exhaustion to a pleasant daydream. Now I can clearly remember each of the Timbertop marathons that I have run, the students whom I spent time with out there on the 29-km track through the bush and mountains, and the peaks and troughs that my body endured.

A wonderful part of the year is that everyone gets through the Timbertop marathon. A year of training, preparation, and progressive overload ensures that 228 15-year-olds get to enjoy the achievement of completing up to a possible 500 km on the track in a year. Some have a sad tale of injury or illness that prevents them from taking part in the final run. However, it is the journey that matters for those unlucky few, and they can easily see the bigger picture of what they have achieved, rather than what they missed, because of the mental growth they have enjoyed over the

Figure 11.5 The nerve-racking roll check before each run commences at Timbertop.

Figure 11.6 Students part of the way through a weekly long run at Timbertop.

Figure 11.7 Beautiful terrain is covered throughout the year, providing accomplishment within every run at Timbertop.

year. The learning that occurs on the running track is greater than any physical change. The beauty of running is that everyone can do it, but the way that they do it differs greatly. Psychological strength pushes them up and down hills and through strains and pains; ultimately it is what provides self-awareness, personal growth, and resilience, and that is a priceless life lesson to hold on to.

allow them to create a secure and fulfilling place for themselves in the world. In the increasingly complex, competitive, and global environment in which we live, the skills and mindsets for accomplishment are becoming more important than ever. Through the positive accomplishment domain, students learn skills and mindsets that will set them up for flourishing futures. The domain is not about short-term successes, but about developing an optimistic outlook that embodies hope in progressing towards goals, and the persistence, grit, and determination to manage the ups and downs of the journey.

Through learning about growth mindsets, staff and students are supported in understanding that it is all right to fail sometimes, and that difficulties and challenges are powerful pathways to growth and leaning. Through their learning in Positive Education—as well their learning throughout the broader curriculum—students are prompted to reflect on the wider consequences of their actions. It is hoped that through meaningful discussion and reflection the students grow to understand positive accomplishment in its true depth—to resist the temptation to think of success only as it relates to themselves, and to be continually mindful of the ways that their actions can enrich the lives of others. In this way, in addition to reaping the rewards personally, staff and students can use the skills and mindsets for accomplishment to pursue goals that benefit others and the greater community.

RECOMMENDED RESOURCES

Baumeister R F and Tierney J (2011). *Willpower: rediscovering the greatest human strength.* New York: Penguin Press.

Briceno E (2012). *The Power of Belief: mindset and success.* TEDx Talk. <http://tedxtalks.ted.com/video/Social-Media-Changing-Learning>

Chains.cc <www.apple.com> (App for creating good habits.)

Dean J (2013). *Making Habits, Breaking Habits: why we do things, why we don't, and how we make changes stick.* Boston, MA: Da Capo Press.

Doidge N (2008). *The Brain That Changes Itself.* New York: Scribe Publications.

Duckworth A (2013). *The Key to Success? Grit. TED Talk.* <www.ted.com/talks/angela_lee_duckworth_the_key_to_success_grit>

Duhigg C (2012). *The Power of Habit: why we do what we do in business and life.* New York: Random House.

Dweck C (2006). *Mindset: the new psychology of success.* New York: Random House.

Dweck C. Mindset website. <http://mindsetonline.com>

Lopez S J (2013). *Making Hope Happen: create the future you want for yourself and others.* New York: Atria Books.

McGonigal K (2010). *The Willpower Instinct: how self-control works, why it matters, and what you can do to get more of it.* New York: Avery.

Mindset Works. <www.mindsetworks.com> (Brainology programme.)

Raschka C (2013). *Everyone Can Learn to Ride a Bicycle.* New York: Random House. (Children's picture storybook.)

Syed M (2010). *Bounce: the myth of talent and the power of practice.* New York: HarperCollins.

Tough P (2012). *How Children Succeed: grit, curiosity and the hidden power of character.* New York: Houghton Mifflin Harcourt.

REFERENCES

Akey T M (2006). *School Context, Student Attitudes and Behavior, and Academic Achievement: an exploratory analysis.* New York: MDRC.

Bandura A (1994). *Self-Efficacy.* Hoboken, NJ: John Wiley & Sons.

Bandura A (1997). *Self-Efficacy: the exercise of control.* New York: W. H. Freeman.

Bandura A (2001). Social cognitive theory: an agentic perspective. *Annual Review of Psychology, 52*, 1–26.

Brickman P, Coates D, and Janoff-Bulman R (1978). Lottery winners and accident victims: is happiness relative? *Journal of Personality and Social Psychology, 36*, 917–27.

Bryant F B and Veroff J (2007). *Savoring: a new model of positive experience.* Mahwah, NJ: Lawrence Erlbaum Associates.

Cooperrider D and Whitney D D (2005). *Appreciative Inquiry: a positive revolution in change.* San Francisco, CA: Berrett-Koehler Publishers.

Covington M V (2000). Goal theory, motivation, and school achievement: an integrative review. *Annual Review of Psychology, 51*, 171–200.

Curry L A et al. (1997). Role of hope in academic and sport achievement. *Journal of Personality and Social Psychology, 73*, 1257–67.

Doidge N (2007). *The Brain That Changes Itself: stories of personal triumph from the frontiers of brain science.* New York: Penguin Books.

Duckworth A L, Peterson C, Matthews M D, and Kelly D R (2007). Grit: perseverance and passion for long-term goals. *Journal of Personality and Social Psychology, 92*, 1087–101.

Duckworth A L, Quinn P D, and Seligman M E P (2009). Positive predictors of teacher effectiveness. *Journal of Positive Psychology, 4*, 540–47.

Durlak J A et al. (2011). The impact of enhancing students' social and emotional learning: a meta-analysis of school-based universal interventions. *Child Development, 82*, 405–32.

Dweck C S (2006). *Mindset: the new psychology of success.* New York: Ballantine Books.

Dweck C S (2007). The perils and promises of praise. *Educational Leadership, 65*, 34–9.

Ericsson K A (1996). *The Road to Excellence: the acquisition of expert performance in the arts and sciences, sports, and games.* Mahwah, NJ: Lawrence Erlbaum.

Gardner H (1999). *Intelligence Reframed: multiple intelligences for the 21st century.* New York: Basic Books.

Gillham J and Reivich K (2004). Cultivating optimism in childhood and adolescence. *Annals of the American Academy of Political and Social Science, 591*, 146–63.

Green L S, Grant A M, and Rynsaardt J (2007). Evidence-based life coaching for senior high school students: building hardiness and hope. *International Coaching Psychology Review, 2*, 24–32.

Heller R, Calderon S, and Medrich E (2003). *Academic Achievement in the Middle Grades: What does research tell us? A review of the literature.* Atlanta, GA: Southern Regional Education Board.

Howell A J (2009). Flourishing: achievement-related correlates of students' well-being. *Journal of Positive Psychology, 4*, 1–13.

Hunter J P and Csikszentmihalyi M (2003). The positive psychology of interested adolescents. *Journal of Youth and Adolescence, 32*, 27–35.

Kahneman D and Krueger A B (2006). Developments in the measurement of subjective well-being. *Journal of Economic Perspectives, 20*, 3–24.

Locke E A and Latham G P (2002). Building a practically useful theory of goal setting and task motivation: a 35-year odyssey. *American Psychologist, 57*, 705–17.

Loehr J and Schwartz T (2003). *The Power of Full Engagement: managing energy, not time, is the key to high performance and personal renewal.* New York: Free Press.

Lopez S J et al. (2009). Measuring and promoting hope in school children. In: G Rich, E S Huebner and M J Furlong (eds) *Handbook of Positive Psychology in Schools.* New York: Routledge. pp. 37–50.

Marques S C, Lopez S J, and Pais-Ribeiro J L (2011). "Building hope for the future": a program to foster strengths in middle-school students. *Journal of Happiness Studies, 12*, 139–52.

Mueller C M and Dweck C S (1998). Praise for intelligence can undermine children's motivation and performance. *Journal of Personality and Social Psychology, 75*, 33–52.

Nietzsche F W (1883) *Thus Spoke Zarathustra: a book for everyone and nobody* (trans. by P Graham). New York: Oxford University Press (2005 edition).

Park N and Peterson C (2006). Moral competence and character strengths among adolescents: the development and validation of the Values in Action Inventory of Strengths for Youth. *Journal of Adolescence, 29*, 891–909.

Peterson C and Park C (1998). Learned helplessness and explanatory style. In: V B Van Hasselt and M Hersen (eds) *Advanced Personality.* New York: Plenum. pp. 287–310.

Peterson C and Park N (2009). Classifying and measuring strengths of character. In: S J Lopez and C R Snyder (eds) *Oxford Handbook of Positive Psychology*, 2nd edn. New York: Oxford University Press. pp. 25–33.

Rosenthal R and Jacobson L (1968). *Pygmalion in the Classroom: teacher expectancies and pupils' intellectual development*. New York: Holt, Rinehart & Winston.

Ryan R M and Deci E L (2000). Self-determination theory and the facilitation of intrinsic motivation, social development, and well-being. *American Psychologist, 55*, 68–78.

Saleh A (2008). Debunking myths in brain research. *Principal's Research Review, 3*, 1–8.

Sansone C and Harackiewicz J M (2000). *Intrinsic and Extrinsic Motivation: the search for optimal motivation and performance*. Waltham, MA: Academic Press.

Scarborough M K, Lewis C M, and Kulkarni S (2011). Enhancing adolescent brain development through goal-setting activities. *Social Work, 55*, 276–8.

Scheier M F and Carver C S (1985). Optimism, coping, and health: assessment and implications of generalized outcome expectancies. *Health Psychology, 4*, 219–47.

Seligman M E P (2008). Positive education and the new prosperity: Australia's edge. *Education Today, 12*, 20–21.

Seligman M E P (2011). *Flourish*. London: Nicholas Brealey Publishing.

Sheldon K M and Elliot A J (1999). Goal striving, need satisfaction, and longitudinal well-being: the self-concordance model. *Journal of Personality and Social Psychology, 76*, 482–97.

Snyder C R (2000). *Handbook of Hope: theory, measures, and applications*. San Diego, CA: Academic Press.

Snyder C R (2002). Hope theory: rainbows in the mind. *Psychological Inquiry, 13*, 249–75.

Snyder C R et al. (1997). The development and validation of the Children's Hope Scale. *Journal of Pediatric Psychology, 22*, 399–421.

Stadler M A and Hogan M E (1996). Varieties of positive and negative priming. *Psychonomic Bulletin & Review, 3*, 87–90.

Suldo S M, Shaunessy E, and Hardesty R (2008). Relationships among stress, coping, and mental health in high-achieving high school students. *Psychology in the Schools, 45*, 273–90.

Suldo S M, Thalji A, and Ferron J (2011). Longitudinal academic outcomes predicted by early adolescents' subjective well-being, psychopathology, and mental health status yielded from a dual factor model. *Journal of Positive Psychology, 6*, 17–30.

Szente J (2007). Empowering young children for success in school and in life. *Early Childhood Education Journal, 34,* 449–53.

Tracy J L and Robins R W (2004). Putting the self into self-conscious emotions: a theoretical model. *Psychological Inquiry, 15,* 103–25.

Valle M F, Huebner E S, and Suldo S M (2006). An analysis of hope as a psychological strength. *Journal of School Psychology, 44,* 393–406.

Veronneau M H, Koestner R F, and Abela J R (2005). Intrinsic need satisfaction and well-being in children and adolescents: an application of the self-determination theory. *Journal of Social & Clinical Psychology, 24,* 280–92.

POSITIVE PURPOSE

**Introduction by
Professor George Vaillant**

Purpose is captured by the concept of intentionality. Wellbeing is promoted through many actions that are sponsored by conscious thought, and conscious thought finds a way to establish purpose through the processes that the body has established through evolution. Purpose gives direction to decision making and the consequential action initiated by the decision made. We are beings that have evolved over time to need purpose to guide action, and the evolution of the brain has developed both the facility and the capacity for making decisions consciously (i.e. with thought but also with heart). The establishment of the conscious brain, the frontal cortex, following the evolution of the midbrain (the "emotional brain"), has enabled the process of establishing considered and heartfelt purpose. Such loving purpose is critical to the management of wellbeing, although for wellbeing to be advanced in a psychosomatic sense it must have an "intention of care" (i.e. be moral in an ethical sense and loving in an emotional sense).

Geelong Grammar School has addressed wellbeing in a truly holistic sense, and it has been a wonderful privilege to be a member of the original and ongoing body of people involved in this commendable and significant project. My life work, as a psychiatrist and as an academic, has been to explore the components of wellbeing and to try to establish ways of educating all to the better management of their lives in reference to their own wellbeing and the wellbeing of those near and dear to them, and also of the community in which they live. The Grant Study, which I supervised and have written about, indicated that wellbeing is complex and multifaceted (Vaillant, 2012). However, many of the pillars of wellbeing are now known and can be identified and enhanced in the individual. These known contributors to wellbeing can be taught, and Geelong Grammar School has embarked on an important and significant educative project to teach children about these fundamentals and how they can live better and healthier lives by employing them actively, from moment to moment, in life. Purpose is defined by actions, and actions are sponsored by decisions made. The positive nature of purpose for wellbeing is clearly tied to living a meaningful and productive life within a relational world. Other people matter.

I had the pleasure of working closely with Geelong Grammar School staff specifically to add further to the already established, morally important, behavioral actions of kindness (compassion) and forgiveness. Kindness and forgiveness, together with gratitude, love, hope, faith (trust), and joy, are the defining elements of what it means to be human and are fundamental to wellbeing. I presented a lecture on forgiveness, which has been established as a transcendent strength in the Values in Action character strengths model, as have kindness and gratitude. My lecture clearly tied the capacity to forgive to physical and relational health as well as individual psychological states that promote physical and emotional wellbeing. Forgiveness is the lubricant that enables individuals to truly accept that an event has occurred. In this acceptance the nervous system reconciles all the angry sympathetic nervous system physical responses and moves them to the trusting parasympathetic nervous system responses that rebalance the physical determinants of health within the body. Forgiveness is essential to life, as everyone makes mistakes and everyone makes judgments that can damage others. The act of forgiving permits a healthy way forward both for the individual being forgiven and, perhaps more critically, for the person who is forgiving. This is positive purpose in action. Desmond Tutu states:

> Forgiveness gives us the capacity to make a new start ... and forgiveness is the grace by which you enable the other person to get up, and get up with dignity, to begin anew. ... In the act of forgiveness we are declaring our faith in the future of a relationship and in the capacity of the wrongdoer to change.

The purpose of Geelong Grammar School is to educate the young, holistically, to become empathic, trusting contributors to society. The School has established, and lives, a clear understanding that unselfish character and positive purpose are truly complementary. The understanding that to err is to be human, and that the management of errors requires a positive purpose approach to ensure the wellbeing of individuals and communities, is the basis for living and learning together at Geelong Grammar School. The empathic (not-about-me) character/positive purpose is the basis of all behavioral policies at the School. Kindness and forgiveness are the foundations of all policies. All policies guide behavior, and behavior is relational in every respect. The Hippocratic Oath, "first do no harm" and "The Golden Rule"—along with the precepts of the Anglican Christian faith—direct and guide the way that relationships are established and sustained.

Wellbeing is substantiated personally and in a relational and communal sense through positive purpose and care (i.e. *caritas* or love). St Paul, in his Letter to the Corinthians (1 Corinthians 13), tells us that:

love is patient, love is kind. It does not envy, it does not boast, it is not proud. It is not rude, it is not self-seeking, it is not easily angered, and it keeps no record of wrongs. Care does not delight in evil but rejoices with the truth. Like love, care never fails, but even where there is knowledge, it will pass away. And now these three remain: forgiveness, kindness and love. But the greatest of these is love.

It is the caring "common good" found in "caritas/love" that enables the body and mind to promote wellbeing. Being centered on "care" establishes an about-the-other endeavor in all action. This care is doing what is good for others and the community and, as such, cultures are created which promote wellbeing. These principles are illustrated in this chapter. Meaning is registered through caring for others and by making actioned contributions to others to add value to their lives. Contributions that are freely given add value to the caregiver in a wellbeing sense. This is service to others, and in this chapter many examples are given of students and staff giving service. Again the fundamentals of wellbeing that exist in all situations of kindness, forgiveness, love, and gratitude are found implicitly in service.

The culture established at Geelong Grammar School is one of service, which expresses care holistically in all living circumstances. This establishes a sense of connection and a sense of worth. Both are lived in the life of the School. Care also ensures that individuals will be "upstanders" and not "bystanders" when mistakes are made or challenges present. Communities that exhibit service and care encourage individuals and groups to "step up to the plate" when things go wrong or have the potential to go wrong. This covenant of caring behavior is promoted and the transcendent nature of such action reinforces the underpinnings of the culture. Love, gratitude, hope, and spirituality unite to promote kindness and forgiveness, and such expressions are found in action.

It has been a pleasure to be involved with the staff at Geelong Grammar School and to contribute to this important project. I thank Mr John Hendry in particular, for his ongoing and significant leadership and for the wonderful steps he has taken to lead the School to a culture that promotes care and therefore wellbeing. My ongoing support is registered by my continued interest and involvement. I encourage you to read this chapter with care.

Positive purpose

Positive Education has not only encouraged us to be emotionally healthy in ourselves, but also to help and support others. We explore meaning and purpose in life and are encouraged to contribute to something larger than ourselves.

George Vickers-Willis, School Captain (2012)

In Japanese culture, the origami crane is a symbol of hope and peace. Giving 1000 origami cranes is a traditional way of communicating goodwill to people who are unwell or undergoing hardships. After the Japanese earthquake and tsunami in 2011, two senior Geelong Grammar School students, Ellie Carless and Camille Nock, wanted to send a message of support, empathy, and hope to communities in Japan. Camille and Ellie came up with the idea of creating strings of origami cranes and sending them to schools in earthquake- and tsunami-devastated regions of Japan—but they could not do it alone. They enlisted the help of the School community, which responded with enthusiasm, and the "Cranes for Japan" project was formed.

Over the course of "Cranes for Japan" week, more than 600 students and 60 staff members at the Corio campus made more than 3000 origami cranes out of colored paper. As they worked, the students and staff were encouraged to reflect mindfully on the ongoing difficulties facing the children and families living in earthquake-devastated regions (for guidelines written by Ellie and Camille outlining the purpose of the activity, see Box 12.1). Once completed, the cranes were strung together and hung in the Chapel of All Saints in a beautiful display of vibrant color (see Figure 12.1). The cranes prompted visitors to the Chapel to pause and send a wish or prayer to people across the globe. After 1 month the cranes were taken down, carefully packed into boxes, and sent to three different primary schools in Japan, where they were received with gratitude.

BOX 12.1: Paper cranes instructions

As students at this School we are very fortunate. We regularly, however, hear and see human tragedies unfold around us, which have the capacity to significantly move us. Unfortunately, often society moves too fast to allow us to mindfully reflect and remember those who are suffering. This is why we are donating our time and prayers. It is so rare that we get to take a moment to write a message and prayer for those who have suffered—emotionally and physically. Please take the time to fold some cranes and send a message of hope across to Japan. These cranes will grace the Chapel and serve as a gentle reminder of the world around us.

Many thanks in anticipation of your support,
Ellie and Camille

Figure 12.1 More than 3000 cranes, made by students, adorning the Chapel prior to being sent to three different schools in Japan.

This story represents much of the essence of the positive purpose domain at Geelong Grammar School. Positive Education is about more than helping students to "feel good," and involves encouraging staff and students to think beyond themselves to how their actions can benefit others. Throughout the "Cranes for Japan" project, members of the School community worked together and, in doing so, achieved much more than any one individual could have done alone. It is symbolic that the completed cranes were displayed in the Chapel of All Saints, which is often thought of as the physical and spiritual "heart" of the Corio campus, a place that represents great purpose and meaning for many.

Positive purpose at Geelong Grammar School

Within the Model for Positive Education, positive purpose is defined as believing in and serving something greater than the self, and deliberately engaging in activities for the greater good. Positive purpose has a rich history at Geelong Grammar School. Michael Collins Persse, former Head of History and current Archives Curator, has been a valued member of the School community for more than 50 years. Michael explains that throughout its history, Geelong Grammar School has strongly espoused the importance of service to others. He credits the School's founding Headmasters, including John Bracebridge Wilson and James Darling, with embedding the values of contribution and civic responsibility deeply into the underpinning ethos and philosophy of the School.

In addition to the strong focus on community service, the School has a rich and proud Anglican tradition and, in regular Chapel services and Religious Education classes, students are encouraged to cultivate purpose and meaning through a sense of faith and spirituality. Recent scientific advances that have emphasized the importance of altruism, belonging, and spirituality for wellbeing have affirmed what the School has long known—that a consideration of purpose and meaning in life is essential to the development of the whole student.

Purpose and meaning

In her first Chapel address as Senior Chaplain in 2012, Reverend Eleanor O'Donnell explained that a life of purpose must *feel* worthwhile. A life of purpose is one that is personally and meaningfully rewarding; the most noble of aspirations may seem meaningless if it does not ignite a sense of passion or involve the use of signature strengths. Eleanor explained that a life of purpose must also *be* worthwhile—it must be of benefit to the community and the larger world. This understanding of purpose has many parallels with definitions from within the academic literature, where purpose is defined as "a stable and generalized intention to accomplish something that is at once meaningful to the self and of consequence to the world beyond the self" (Damon et al., 2003, p. 121). Both of these understandings exemplify the fact that a sense of purpose is achieved by making a difference and contributing to others.

A sense of purpose provides people with a central mission or vision for life (Bronk et al., 2009). A metaphor that resonates with many members of the School community is that purpose is like a compass which provides a sense of direction, informing choices and decisions throughout life. Substantial empirical research has found that a strong sense of purpose in life is linked with wellbeing and physical health (Bronk et al., 2009; McKnight and Kashdan, 2009; Sone et al., 2008). There is an especially important connection between purpose and resilience, and when people have a sense that life is worthwhile they cope more successfully with stressful life events, and have the strength to persist through hardships and difficulties (McKnight and Kashdan, 2009; Wang et al., 2007).

Closely related to positive purpose is the concept of meaning in life. Meaning concerns the way in which people understand themselves and the world around them (Steger et al., 2008b). Meaning is a subjective and personal experience—some students may derive meaning from being a member of a close sporting team, whereas others derive meaning from their religious faith. In his seminal book, *Man's Search for Meaning* (Frankl, 1948), Dr Victor Frankl proposed that humans have a "will to meaning" or an innate drive to experience their lives as purposeful and significant. Frankl proposed that failure to achieve this sense of meaning can lead to distress, emptiness, boredom, and apathy. Having a sense of meaning in life has been associated with wellbeing and reduced mental distress for different age groups (Steger et al., 2009).

Exploring meaning and purpose at school

Rita Jenkins, senior Music teacher, explains that within the media there are many messages about what it means to live a good life—young people are bombarded with pictures of constantly changing fashions, airbrushed models, and bigger, faster, shinier material possessions. One of the benefits of Positive Education, in Rita's eyes, is that it helps students (and staff) to develop a strong personal foundation that protects them from being blown around by the pull of materialistic and superficial pursuits. The aim is to help students to connect with deeper sources of meaning and fulfillment in their lives, thereby supporting them to develop sustainable sources of self-worth and fulfillment. In doing so, it is hoped that students will become more resistant to messages in society about things that may have adverse consequences for the wellbeing of the self and others.

The schooling years are the opportune time to help young people to explore the role of meaning and purpose in their lives. Developmentally, adolescence is a period of exploration and curiosity; it is when young people form an idea of who they are, who they want to be, and what they want to accomplish in life (Damon et al., 2003; Yeager and Bundick, 2009). A commitment to purpose also has consequences for accomplishment, as students who feel a sense of meaning and purpose at school are more committed to their learning and more inspired by their future career aspirations (Yeager and Bundick, 2009).

Although it is well established that having a sense of purpose is valuable for young people's wellbeing, it is also understood that it is inherently difficult to "teach" someone how to have purpose or meaning in life. However, it is possible for schools to create safe and supportive environments for questioning and exploration. Geelong Grammar School aims to support students to cultivate purpose in life by providing a forum through which different ideas, experiences, and philosophies can be considered and explored. The objective is to help students to get to know themselves and their world. Epitomizing this concept, the Honorable Frank Callaway runs a philosophy club, where students meet together and discuss how timeless wisdom integrated into ancient and modern texts can inform their present life choices (see Box 12.2).

Making a difference through altruism and service

> The reality is that giving is firmly embedded in the life and culture of Geelong Grammar School.
>
> Charlie Scudamore, Vice Principal

Professor Martin Seligman explains that people experience meaning when they develop their signature strengths and use these strengths in the service of others

> **BOX 12.2: Philosophy Club**
>
> The Philosophy Club began spontaneously when Mr Callaway first visited the School in May 2010 as a Richard and Janet Southby Visiting Fellow. In addition to speaking to the Legal Studies students, he gave two lectures on the nineteenth-century German philosophers Arthur Schopenhauer and Friedrich Nietzsche. Some Year 11 students expressed an interest in exploring philosophy further, which eventually led to an entirely off-the-syllabus series of activities, now in its fifth year (2014–2015).
>
> They begin with two seminars at the end of Year 11, one being an introduction to a wide range of ideas and thinkers, including Aristotle, Thucydides, Machiavelli, Burke, Tocqueville, Wittgenstein, Lao Tzu, and Bankei. The ideas explored in the seminar include the Delphic injunctions "Know yourself" and "Nothing to excess." The second Year 11 seminar is an introduction to Plato's *Republic*, which the students, usually about 15 in number, read during the summer vacation.
>
> Year 12 begins with a third seminar, this time on the *Republic*, followed by a fourth, more wide-ranging discussion of reasons for reading philosophy—for example, to ask questions about how we know things, or what might be the elements of the good life, or to open our eyes to new ideas or help us to clarify existing ideas, such as the way the writer of St John's Gospel used the idea of the Logos ("word" or "reason") to explain Christianity to readers familiar with Greek thought.
>
> There are three concluding activities. In the first activity the students are divided into teams and each given a topic arising from their reading of Plato, followed by a team presentation on that topic a few weeks later. The second activity is a reading session in which some of the books mentioned in the first seminar in Year 11 are handed out for the students to read for themselves. The third activity is a 2- to 3-hour fireside chat in the third term on almost any subjects that the students wish to explore, such as freedom and equality, the meaning of life, art, and literature.
>
> The Philosophy Club has been aptly described as "an intellectual Timbertop."

(Seligman, 2002). Cultivating a sense of purpose often involves a pro-social or altruistic intent, such as a commitment and passion for helping others or improving the world (Hill et al., 2010). As Professor Vaillant described in his introduction to this chapter, throughout the Geelong Grammar School community there is a deepseated commitment to altruism and to community service. This commitment has powerful implications, as one of the most consistent findings of wellbeing research is that giving to others is related to good physical and mental health (Post, 2005; Post and Neimark, 2008; Steger et al., 2008a).

Throughout the campuses there are many pathways through which students can contribute to the School, local, national, and global communities. Although service and civic responsibility have been part of the School's foundation for a long time, many staff members reflect that this focus has blossomed since the implementation of Positive Education. In particular, students are constantly thinking of new ideas and projects aimed at helping others. Staff members also share stories of being inspired to give more, and several even describe being motivated by their learning in Positive Education to join community service groups that provide regular opportunities to give meaningfully to others.

Across the campuses, opportunities to make a positive contribution to others are numerous. One of the most memorable experiences at Bostock House is the Make a Difference Market, where Year 4 students explore themes of leadership and service (for a case study on this project, see Chapter 11). Students at the Toorak campus take part in a meaningful "Build-a-Bear" campaign, raising money for the Good Friday Appeal (see Box 12.3). A culture of service pervades Timbertop, in particular during Term 2, when students spend their weekends working at local farms, schools, wineries, and national parks, giving back to the wider community.

Making a difference is also central to the Corio campus. After dedicated Pos Ed classes in the Year 10 curriculum on exploring meaning and purpose, students put their learning into action through community service projects. With the support of their teachers, students select a way that they would like to give back to their local community. In the past, groups of students have assisted at a local primary school, made food and visited Middle School boarding houses, cleaned up the Corio Bay foreshore, and participated in the Salvation Army Wishing Tree Appeal (see Figure 12.2).

BOX 12.3: Build-a-Bear

For the past 2 years the Toorak campus has volunteered to be actively involved in an initiative to help to raise money for the Royal Children's Hospital as part of the Good Friday Appeal. Students across different year levels have come together to organize a fundraiser. Collaboratively they make posters, promote the cause in assembly, gather donations through tin collections, and make an assortment of food to be sold at bake sales on campus (see Figure 12.3). The students organize their own roster, are responsible for the setting up and dismantling of the stall, and are in charge of account keeping and counting the donations.

In conjunction with the fundraiser, the students have gone to the Build-a-Bear shop at Chadstone Shopping Centre and made two bears each (see Figure 12.4). One of these bears has been donated to the Adopt-a-Teddy Centre on Good Friday, and the other bear has been given to a child who has had to remain in hospital over the Easter period. As the students make the bears, they are encouraged to think of the young children who are receiving them—a process that assists the development of empathy. Each student makes a wish for the recipient and attaches a letter of hope or gratitude.

This has proved to be a fantastic opportunity for the young students of our School to become involved in a philanthropic event. It is an opportunity for them to learn lessons in the value of giving, as well as to develop their personal strengths in citizenship, leadership, and kindness.

Jacqui Moses, Teacher, Toorak Campus

Figure 12.2 Senior students purchasing and decorating presents for the Salvation Army Wishing Tree Appeal.

Figure 12.3 Junior students enjoying the experience of selling their baked goods.

Figure 12.4 Toorak students on completion of their Build-A-Bear workshop.

The Karen community

One pertinent example of making a difference has been an ongoing relationship with the Karen refugee community. The Karen people are an ethnic-minority group from South East Asia. The majority of the refugees have come to Australia after living for numerous years in refugee camps on the Thai–Myanmar border. In 2009 a request was made to the School for spare blankets to be donated to the local Karen refugee community. This request could not have been made at a better time. The School was preparing for the annual "Lorne 160," in which a team of Year 11 students undertake a running relay to Lorne and back—a distance of 160 km—and raise money for a worthy cause. That particular year it was decided that the worthy cause was the Karen refugee community.

The School communicated with the Karen community and explained that although they did not have any spare blankets, they would like to provide $40,000 for the Karen people. Leaders from within the Karen community expressed their two primary needs—land for a community garden, and support for education. A plot of land at the Corio campus was therefore made available to the Karen community for them to grow food and vegetables (see Figure 12.5). The School also helped to set up the Karen refugee homework club to support the learning of Karen students (this is described in Case Study 12.1). An ongoing and mutually caring

Figure 12.5 Senior students from Geelong Grammar School working together to prepare the Karen refugee garden plot.

CASE STUDY 12.1

The Karen Refugee Homework Club

Eleanor O'Donnell, Senior Chaplain, Geelong Grammar School

The Karen Refugee Homework Club is run in Terms 2, 3, and 4 at St Andrew's Anglican Church, Corio. Facilitated by a staff member of the parish along with two Geelong Grammar School teachers, the club is actually run by Geelong Grammar School students for local refugee students from a range of local schools (both primary and high schools). The club was established to help to address the needs of recently arrived Karen refugee children from Myanmar (Burma), who struggle with assimilation into a new culture of schooling and a new language, but it welcomes students from other cultural backgrounds as well.

Geelong Grammar School students from Years 10, 11, and 12 are bussed to the Church hall after their classes end for the day. A simple afternoon tea is shared, and then our students find someone to work with. There are usually 40 students working together on any afternoon. The purpose of the Homework Club is to give one-on-one assistance with homework tasks to students who are new to Australia, and who may have very limited English skills. Giving refugee students a space in which they have time and support to complete their schoolwork has been beneficial educationally and socially—both for the Karen community and for the Geelong Grammar School community. The students who come to the club complete more of their homework and also have an opportunity to practice their English.

The friendly relationships that are built nurture communication. Geelong Grammar School students are often humbled by the life stories that the Karen students share with them and their desire to make the most of the possibilities of life in Australia. They feel a sense of privilege that the time they spend with the refugee students, the efforts they make to support them with homework tasks, and their gestures of friendship through conversation and mutual storytelling are received so warmly. There is recognition that the giving of oneself to another—in terms of time, energy, and empathy—often rewards the giver as much as those whom the giver seeks to assist.

As Minnie (a Senior Student) reflected after a Homework Club session:

> It is often really hard to do things that are out of our comfort zones, but this Karen girl was able to do so. I helped her with Maths and I really enjoyed working with her as she was willing to learn, she asked me a lot of questions, and if she did not understand anything I said she would ask me to repeat. We worked productively and she was able to complete her Maths homework by the end of that session. I felt really good about myself because I felt like she actually learnt something from me. I respected and valued her work ethic highly, which was what I learnt from her.

The Karen Homework Club is an ongoing community service activity that is much sought after by Geelong Grammar School students. Each term we have more students volunteering for this activity than we can productively use. I am sure this is because our students have learned that their own wellbeing increases when they do something real in the service of others.

relationship has emerged between the two communities, who have come together through music performances, Chapel services, and soccer games. Many members of the School community attest that Geelong Grammar School has received as many gifts from the Karen people as they have given to them, and that the warmth and generosity of spirit of the Karen community has certainly "made a difference" at Geelong Grammar School.

Core values

> Deep down inside, what do you really want? What do you want to stand for in life? What sort of personal qualities do you wish to cultivate? How do you want to be towards others?
>
> Exploring Values Questions, Year 10 Positive Education curriculum

As part of the Year 10 Positive Education curriculum, students spend time exploring their own personal life philosophy. As a foundation for this exploration, staff members share a wide range of poems, stories, and media clips that provide a range of insights and perspectives on what it means to live a good life. The students are then encouraged to explore their own life philosophy by drafting five "I believe" statements that reflect how they see the world. After they have decided on their statements, the students share them with each other and also journal about their experience in their Pos Ed folios. Some examples of "I believe" statements that students have created include the following:

- I believe that no matter how good a friend is, they are going to hurt you, every once in a while, and you must forgive them for that.
- I believe that you can keep going long after you think you cannot.
- I believe that sometimes when I'm angry I have the right to be angry, but that does not give me the right to be cruel.
- I believe two people can look at the exact same thing and see something totally different.

This is a valuable activity that helps students to explore a particularly powerful route towards meaning and purpose—exploration of their personal values. One way to think about values is to consider people who epitomize certain beliefs and philosophies. Dame Elisabeth Murdoch, a past student of Clyde School and the namesake of one of the School's Boarding Houses, devoted much of her life to making a difference to the world, inspiring others to do the same. She is a role model of the values of service and community to many within the School community.

Values are enduring beliefs that guide and motivate people as they move through life. Whereas actioned character strengths often represent what a person does, lived core values can be thought of as who they are, what they believe, and what defines them as a person. Another important distinction is between values and goals. Goals are desired outcomes that can be achieved, whereas values are enduring and unending.

Taking part in activities that are consistent with personal values is an important source of meaning and fulfillment in life (Waterman, 1993). Knowing and acting in accordance with values is central to psychological health and growth (Rogers, 1964). As part of their learning in Positive Education, students are given the time and space to explore their values. They are asked to explore the consequences of living in (and out of) accordance with their values. They are invited to explore the ways in which values can and do change throughout life, and to understand that particular core values may soften or strengthen over time. An activity that is aimed at helping students to identify their core values is described in Box 12.4.

> **BOX: 12.4: Identifying core values**
>
> This activity, which is used with senior students, focuses on helping each student to identify their core values. The students are provided with a list of 100 words that represent different values, such as achievement, adventure, compassion, family, freedom, honesty, independence, friendship, responsibility, respect, truth, and wisdom. They are encouraged to add to the list any other values that are important to them. The students then select from the list 20 to 25 values that resonate strongly with them. Next, they are encouraged to group like values together, and to select one word that represents each group. For example, the values of family and friends may be grouped together with an overarching theme of connectedness or loyalty. Although the students often find much meaning in thinking about their values, an important step is for them to explore the extent to which they are living in alignment with their values, and what they could do to enact these values more fully. The activity concludes with a prompt for the students to think about what they might start to do differently in order to live with more meaning and purpose on a daily basis.

Belonging and community

> The Geelong Grammar School community embraces many people and many ideas on a daily basis. It supports the notion that everyone is valued, that everyone is worth listening to, and that everyone can make a difference.
>
> Garry Pierson, Head of Toorak Campus

> Bostock isn't just like friends. It is like a really big and nice family which treats everyone how they want to be treated. Every morning I can't wait to go to school and see all my friends. This School is like my second family and Bostock is like my second home.
>
> Hugo, Year 4, Bostock House

In a professional development training session that was conducted on all campuses, teaching and non-teaching staff members came together to explore what makes a community. Different staff members shared stories of "fondly remembered community experiences" and described in three words what made these experiences special. Staff shared their favorite memories of being part of a range of close-knit groups, such as sports teams, surf life saving clubs, cultural communities, and groups of people who traveled together. The different words that represented these experiences were put together, resulting in a list of over 100 words, such as "sharing," "team," "excitement," "belonging," "humor," "compassion," "family," "mateship," and "fun." Although communities come in all shapes and sizes, a common feature is that a strong community exists when members feel valued, loyal, and connected to each other.

One of the greatest gifts that schools can give children, young people, and adults is a sense of belonging and connection to others. Feeling part of a community is one of the most powerful protective factors in mental and physical health (Osterman, 2000; Stewart et al., 2004). The Geelong Grammar School community is one of diversity, and students come from over 15 different countries, from all states of Australia, and from metropolitan and rural areas, to study at the School. Although people may travel from far and wide, once they arrive at the School they often quickly feel like part of a close community. The sense of belonging and connectedness is influenced by the four physical campuses which, although vastly different in terms of size and structure, are alike in the sense that they are all designed to foster a sense of closeness and community among students and staff. The story of how students from Garnett House, a senior girls' Boarding House, showed gratitude for the School community is included in Box 12.5.

A respectful, caring, supportive community, in which difference and diversity are valued, is pivotal to Geelong Grammar School and the sustainable implementation of Positive Education. John Hendry, Director of Student Welfare, explains that the School's culture of kindness, forgiveness, and collaborative relationships creates a firm foundation for nurturing a sense of belonging and community. The legacy of belonging persists through the Old Geelong Grammarians (OGGs), where past students often maintain their connections with the School and form a wide community with a shared history.

BOX 12.5: Garnett House Gratitude People

During a discussion of gratitude in Garnett House, the girls started thinking about all of the "hidden" people who support their life at the School. First they thought of obvious people who work behind the scenes to make the community run smoothly, such as the staff in the kitchen and offices. They then started to delve more deeply and ask questions about what happened behind the scenes to keep the School functioning. Through this exploration the students identified many less obvious but very important people, such as security staff, maintenance staff, and staff in the sewing room. The students cut out and decorated "gratitude people" from stickers, and wrote messages of appreciation on them for each of the different groups of staff members. Together the Garnett girls scurried around at night under cover of darkness and placed the gratitude stickers around the School community, so that they would be a surprise in the morning. The next evening the students thought about even more important people within the community, so more messages of gratitude were created and displayed. The feedback to the girls was really wonderful. One security man said that he had cried because he was so happy that we had noticed what he and his colleagues did for the community.

Margaret Bennetts, Head of Garnett House

Faith and spirituality

More than a set of beliefs, Christianity is a framework for living a meaningful life—a life that serves a higher power. That service overflows into ways of being with other people that are generous and good.

Reverend Eleanor O'Donnell, Senior Chaplain

Be open to God. Be open to God's mysterious Spirit. And if this is not your culture, then I encourage you to be open to the great spiritual traditions from your own background. Because through these traditions you will find profound truth; you will tap into a reality that nurtures goodness and wellbeing in your own life and in the lives of those around you.

Reverend Dr Hugh Kempster, Past Senior Chaplain

Geelong Grammar School has a strong Anglican tradition, and staff and students are encouraged to cultivate a sense of spirituality and to engage in meaningful reflection and introspection. Students regularly attend Chapel services, and many influential members of the School community model a genuine love of God. Since the implementation of Positive Education, a few concerns have been raised—both by parents and by the wider community—that the focus on Positive Education may detract from the School's religious and spiritual foundation. Rather than seeing Positive Education as a challenge to the place of religion at the School, the quest has been to celebrate both, so that the science of wellbeing complements the integrity of the Anglican tradition. The connection between the School's Christian faith and Positive Education was eloquently expressed in a recent article by Reverend Eleanor, extracts of which are included in Box 12.6.

There are many important links between spirituality and Positive Education. The Christian spirit of "Love thy neighbor as thyself" and "the Golden Rule" have natural synergies with the focus on altruism and giving to others within Positive Education. In turn, through Positive Education, language that has long had a home within the Chapel—the discussion of virtues such as love, gratitude, forgiveness, hope, and spirituality—has blossomed in other contexts, such as classrooms and Boarding Houses. In particular, the Values in Action character strengths, based on virtues present in the religions and cultures that have helped to shape humanity, can be seen as a place where ancient wisdom meets modern science and psychology (Dahlsgaard et al., 2005; Peterson and Seligman, 2004).

The Chaplains have also taken leadership in promoting this conversation beyond the School grounds, sharing their learning with the Christian community. In 2010, the School organized a "Faith and Positive Psychology Conference," which was attended by almost 100 clergy, chaplains, priests, and bishops, and provided a forum for exploring the meeting point between faith, spirituality, and Positive

BOX 12.6: Faith and Positive Psychology in an educational setting

Part of the story of Geelong Grammar School's embracing and shaping of "Positive Education" is explained on the School website. It points out that "there is substantial evidence from empirical studies that skills to increase resilience, positive emotion, engagement and meaning can be successfully taught to school children and achieve meaningful outcomes." The Geelong Grammar School project is also presented in overview in Chapter 5 of *Flourish* (Seligman, 2011). In it, Seligman rightly notes that "Positive Education at Geelong Grammar School is a work in progress and is not a controlled experiment;" it is a work in progress that has not escaped criticism, especially by some Chaplains and religious educators who insist that it has the potential to dilute the principles and narratives of the Christian Gospel in schools like Geelong Grammar which have faith links with the Anglican Church.

It is an interesting, if somewhat slippery, critique. Positive Education/Psychology has been suggested by some to be merely a marketing device, and one which takes over "Anglican" (in the case of Geelong Grammar) as a descriptor of the ethos that shapes the School. The implication is that the Christian identity of the School is subsumed by the secular human sciences in a slick but eminently marketable public relations coup. Further, critics have maintained that Chaplains in schools such as Geelong Grammar are forced to become social workers rather than Christian ministers, and that Positive Education/Psychology has become a substitute for religious and values education in the classroom and the Gospel of Christ in the Chapel. Whether or not this criticism has any foundation in some schools, it has no basis in the day-to-day reality of life at Geelong Grammar School, which continues to celebrate its shared life through the Anglican Christian tradition, while, at the same time, using the insights of Positive Psychology to develop our wellbeing and education programs within and beyond the School.

Critics of Positive Education, whether their starting point is the fear of losing the unique wisdom of the Christian faith tradition to an emerging human science, or concern about the ethics of a genuinely good and generous life being subsumed by the short-sighted pursuit of success and happiness, need to look closely to see if their concerns have any real foundation in the lived experience of specific schools. Geelong Grammar School is a front runner in the development of Positive Education; it is also an active Anglican School with a clear Christian identity, and one which seeks to engender a life of commitment and service to others as a way of living the good life individually and collectively. These things are not mutually exclusive. Positive Psychology, the Christian faith, altruism and The Golden Rule are all taught explicitly and implicitly in each of our campuses—we are an educational institution before all things.

Extracts reproduced from Reverend Eleanor O'Donnell (2014)
Learning optimism – faith and positive psychology in an
educational setting. *Dialogue Australasia Journal, Issue 31*,
23–5. © 2014, Dialogue Australasia Network.

Education. The central place of both Positive Education and the Anglican faith in the School's Purpose Document (see Figure 3.5 on p. 46 in Chapter 3) is a testament to how highly both aspects of the School's ethos and philosophy are regarded. The School also respects the wisdom of other spiritual faiths. Special visitors to the School have included Indigenous elders, Buddhist monks, and Jewish rabbis. When staff members from schools of other religious dominations are welcomed into the School during Positive Education training courses, the recommendation is that they too find meaningful points of connection between their own guiding religion and the growing science of wellbeing and flourishing. A powerful project that was completed at the Toorak campus, which celebrated Indigenous culture by creating a possum-skin cloak, is described in Case Study 12.2.

CASE STUDY 12.2

The Possum-Skin Cloak

Sarah Bell, Toorak Campus Art Coordinator, Indigenous Curriculum Coordinator

During Term 3 in 2011, Geelong Grammar School (Toorak Campus) and the Kirrae Whurrong/Gunditjmara artist, Vicki Couzens, began a conversation about respect. The result of this encounter was called "kareeta—mayapa kani kooramooyan" (growing-up possum cloak).

I had come across Vicki's work in the field of possum-skin cloak revival, and was fascinated and impressed by her persistence in researching and reviving this lost cultural practice. Initially I had hoped that she would come and speak at our School about her experiences, and I never dreamed that such a meaningful and important community project could develop. During our initial discussions, Vicki emphasized the importance of Indigenous students from the Corio campus being part of the project.

Before beginning such a project we did not consider the question "How?" but rather the question "Why?" We sat in a circle with the Toorak campus Year 4 students and their teachers, and a number of Year 7 and 8 Corio Indigenous scholars. We spent much time discussing questions relating to our common values, such as "What is respect?" and "What are important shared values and beliefs?" The students found that they shared the common values of family, kinship, place, and connection. Vicki generously shared her cultural knowledge with the students.

The purpose of making a possum-skin cloak is usually for an individual or elder to wear it for ceremony and healing. As we sat together, we needed a new purpose for this unusual undertaking. After much discussion it was decided that the cloak would come to be a symbol of our commitment to respect, and the students put forward many ideas about how this could be represented on the cloak. Jodene, in Year 7, suggested that our hands might represent our individual identities. We could include a symbol representing Australia, as we all come from places far and wide, and it is this land that connects us all. Andrew, in Year 4, felt that a tree could symbolize our commitment. He quoted Aunty Di Kerr, a Wurundjeri elder in her Welcome to Country ceremony at the Toorak campus: "From the tops of the trees to the roots in the ground I welcome you."

Working together on the possum-skin cloak, the students deepened their understanding of perseverance when developing their designs in a team with the goals of inclusiveness and meaning: "We were learning about the values and beliefs of different cultures. This project was important because it made us more aware and appreciative of Indigenous culture. Making a possum-skin cloak was really special because there are very few old cloaks in Australia" (Yasmin, Year 4).

Shanni (an Indigenous scholar in Year 7) explained part of the process: "On the fourth day, Vicki and Mrs Bell came up with the design that was going to cover the cloak that had a big circle representing Australia, a tree representing our connection with nature, and the Yarra River which is the veins of the earth that connects us all together. It was such a great experience that we had as young artists working on the cloak. This cloak will be used for the Indigenous scholars at graduations, ceremonies, National Aboriginal and Islander Day Observance Committee (NAIDOC) week, Welcome to Country, and many more Aboriginal cultural celebrations."

Hannah (in Year 4) reflects on the shared pride felt by the members of the group: "We all feel great about how the cloak has turned out. It is an amazing feeling because we all participated in the project. It feels great to be able to contribute something to the School."

The significance of the experiences shared by the Indigenous artist, the students, and the teachers is clear in the summary by Andrew (Year 4): "We learnt that you need to have lots of patience because the project was a long process: from the first discussions through to the final burnings. We also had to be open-minded when we were adding all our ideas together about our personal values. We had to show respect for other people's values when we were discussing our ideas."

As new relationships were formed, deep understandings and connections were made. This very special cloak (see Figures 12.6 and 12.7) is a gift that has added an enriched sense of both healing and ceremony for our Indigenous and non-Indigenous students since its completion, and is a symbol of our collective hope and humanity: "We have learnt countless things about our ancestors, ourselves and our culture, the significance of the cloaks, and their role in Victorian Aboriginal culture" (Jodene, Indigenous scholar, Year 7, 2011).

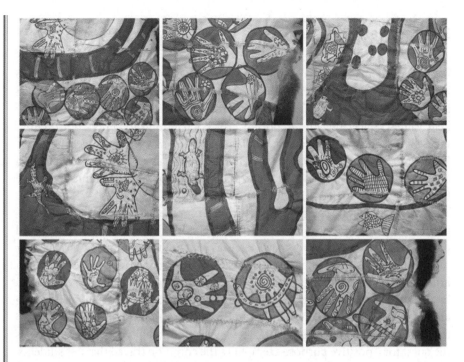

Figure 12.6 Detailed images of the possum-skin cloak.

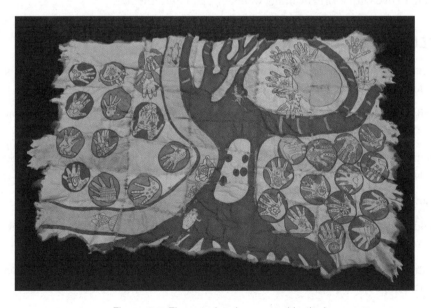

Figure 12.7 The completed possum-skin cloak.

Summary and conclusions

Instilling students with a sense of responsibility to the world and a commitment to helping others has been an integral part of Geelong Grammar School throughout its history. The implementation of Positive Education has seen a renewal of deeply held values concerning the importance of contributing to others both within the School community and beyond. Through the growing language of Positive Education, conversations across the School about what it is to live with meaning and purpose, to cultivate a sense of spirituality, and to belong to a community have been embraced by staff and students alike.

At first glance, developing a sense of purpose may seem like a grandiose or daunting task. At Geelong Grammar School it is understood that living with meaning and purpose is as much about everyday choices as it is about finding a long-term goal or mission for life. A sense of purpose is evident in the decision to forgive rather than hold a grudge, to be kind rather than critical, and to have courage rather than stand by and watch someone being treated unfairly. In the short term, a sense of meaning and purpose helps a person to make choices that are aligned with their values. In the long term, it provides a sense of cohesiveness and stability to life. In many ways the quest for a positive purpose exemplifies the common thread that ties students' learning in Positive Education together—the belief that strengthening the wellbeing of the individual enriches their capacity to give to others, and in doing so helps them to live with more meaning, wellbeing, and fulfillment.

RECOMMENDED RESOURCES

Center for Compassion and Altruism Research and Education, Stanford School of Medicine. <http://ccare.stanford.edu/tag/compassion>

ChildSpirit Institute: understanding and nurturing the spiritual life of the young. <http://childspirit.org>

Damon W (2009). *The Path to Purpose: how young people find their calling in life.* New York: Free Press.

Frankl V (1946/2006). *Man's Search for Meaning.* Boston, MA: Beacon Press.

Haidt J (2012). *The Righteous Mind: why good people are divided by politics and religion.* New York: Pantheon.

Keltner D (2009). *Born To Be Good: the science of a meaningful life.* New York: W. W. Norton & Company.

Kennedy M (2013). *Reaching Out: messages of hope.* Sydney, Australia: ABC Books/ HarperCollins Publishers.

Muth J J (2002). *The Three Questions: based on a story by Leo Tolstoy.* New York: Scholastic Press. (Children's picture storybook.)

Post S G (2011). *The Hidden Gifts of Helping.* San Francisco, CA: Jossey-Bass.

Reynolds P H (2009). *The North Star.* Boston, MA: FableVision Press. (Children's picture storybook.)

Ricard M. <www.matthieuricard.org>

University of California, Berkeley. *Greater Good: the science of a meaningful life.* <http://greatergood.berkeley.edu>

Vaillant G (2008). *Spiritual Evolution: a scientific defense of faith.* New York: Three Rivers Press.

Wong P (2012). *The Human Quest for Meaning: theories, research, and applications.* New York: Routledge.

Zimbardo P (2007). *The Lucifer Effect.* New York: Random House, Inc.

REFERENCES

Bronk K C et al. (2009). Purpose, hope, and life satisfaction in three age groups. *Journal of Positive Psychology, 4,* 500–10.

Dahlsgaard K, Peterson C, and Seligman M E P (2005). Shared virtue: the convergence of valued human strengths across culture and history. *Review of General Psychology, 9,* 203–13.

Damon W, Menon J, and Bronk K C (2003). The development of purpose during adolescence. *Applied Developmental Science, 7,* 119–28.

Frankl V (1948). *Man's Search for Meaning.* New York: Washington Square Press.

Hill P L, Burrow A L, O'Dell A C, and Thornton M A (2010). Classifying adolescents' conceptions of purpose in life. *Journal of Positive Psychology, 5,* 466–73.

McKnight P E and Kashdan T B (2009). Purpose in life as a system that creates and sustains health and well-being: an integrative, testable theory. *Review of General Psychology, 13,* 242–51.

Osterman K F (2000). Students' need for belonging in the school community. *Review of Educational Research, 70,* 323–67.

Peterson C and Seligman M E P (2004). *Character Strengths and Virtues: a handbook and classification.* New York: Oxford University Press; Washington, DC: American Psychological Association.

Post S G (2005). Altruism, happiness, and health: it's good to be good. *International Journal of Behavioral Medicine, 12,* 66–77.

Post S G and Neimark J (2008). *Why Good Things Happen to Good People: how to live a longer, healthier, happier life by the simple act of giving*. New York: Broadway Books.

Rogers C R (1964). Toward a modern approach to values: the valuing process in the mature person. *Journal of Abnormal and Social Psychology, 68,* 160–67.

Seligman M E P (2002). *Authentic Happiness: using the new positive psychology to realize your potential for lasting fulfillment*. New York: Free Press.

Seligman M E P (2011). *Flourish*. London: Nicholas Brealey Publishing.

Sone T et al. (2008). Sense of life worth living (ikigai) and mortality in Japan: Ohsaki Study. *Psychosomatic Medicine, 70,* 709–15.

Steger M F, Kashdan T B, and Oishi S (2008a). Being good by doing good: daily eudaimonic activity and well-being. *Journal of Research in Personality, 42,* 22–42.

Steger M F, Kashdan T B, Sullivan B A, and Lorentz D (2008b). Understanding the search for meaning in life: personality, cognitive style, and the dynamic between seeking and experiencing meaning. *Journal of Personality, 76,* 199–228.

Steger M F, Oishi S, and Kashdan T B (2009). Meaning in life across the life span: levels and correlates of meaning in life from emerging adulthood to older adulthood. *Journal of Positive Psychology, 4,* 43–52.

Stewart D et al. (2004). Promoting and building resilience in primary school communities: evidence from a comprehensive "health promoting school" approach. *International Journal of Mental Health Promotion, 6,* 26–33.

Vaillant G E (2012). *Triumphs of Experience: the men of the Harvard Grant Study*. Cambridge, MA: Harvard University Press.

Wang M C et al. (2007). Purpose in life and reasons for living as mediators of the relationship between stress, coping, and suicidal behavior. *Journal of Positive Psychology, 2,* 195–204.

Waterman A S (1993). Two conceptions of happiness: contrasts of personal expressiveness (eudaimonia) and hedonic enjoyment. *Journal of Personality and Social Psychology, 64,* 678–91.

Yeager D S and Bundick M J (2009). The role of purposeful work goals in promoting meaning in life and in schoolwork during adolescence. *Journal of Adolescent Research, 24,* 423–52.

RESEARCH AND EVALUATION

With Dr Meredith O'Connor

Research Fellow, Institute of Positive Education, Geelong Grammar School; Honorary Fellow, Department of Paediatrics, University of Melbourne

Do I have any regrets about deciding to embrace Positive Psychology? Not at all. I have no doubt that we are a richer and more fulfilled School than we were before and, I think, a happier, more purposeful, more connected place. If you can create that for your staff and students, what more could you ask for?

Stephen Meek, Principal

I think Positive Education has taught me many things, such as how to get on with my friends, how to make new friends quickly, and how to be an honest and encouraging person. I think that Positive Education will help me in later life by making me a more patient person, a better sportsman, a good senior school classmate, and a kind father.

Year 4 Student, Bostock House

Positive Education has changed my outlook as both a student and a citizen of the world. As I travel through life, I know that when the inevitable issues and adversities come along, I will be ready because of the tools that Positive Psychology has helped me possess. I have learnt to keep things in perspective and understand that my own beliefs have consequences on my actions and emotions, and that by changing those beliefs I can act accordingly in times of trial; I can learn and grow from these times.

Year 10 Student, Senior School, Corio Campus

Figure 13.1 Year 10 students reflecting on their learning in Positive Education.

In the early days of the School's journey, a clear and deliberate decision was made to progress with Positive Education as a whole-school commitment, not as a research trial. Key concepts were consistent with the School's values, and staff felt excited about taking Positive Education to a new level by applying it across the entire School community. Nevertheless, processes were put in place to try to understand the impact of Positive Education on staff and students, including gathering anecdotal evidence and stories, asking for feedback from students and staff, and comparing wellbeing data with averages from the general population. Figure 13.1 shows Year 10 students reflecting on their Positive Education learning. From these efforts, a collective understanding has grown that Positive Education has brought many gifts to Geelong Grammar School. Complementing this anecdotal evidence, a formal, independent evaluation of the Geelong Grammar School Positive Education program is now under way, led by the University of Melbourne. Together, the evidence and evaluation are starting to provide a rich and encouraging picture of the potential of Positive Education to have a real-world impact on students' health and wellbeing.

Students' social and emotional wellbeing

Timbertop students have outstanding levels of wellbeing, which is in stark contrast to the general population.

ACER Social and Emotional Wellbeing Survey, 2011,
Summary for Geelong Grammar School

In order to make Positive Education as relevant to student needs as possible, it was important to first understand the wellbeing profile among students at the School—that is, in what areas students were flourishing and in what areas they could benefit from additional support. The Australian Council for Educational Research (ACER) Social and Emotional Wellbeing Survey is designed to provide Australian schools with empirically validated tools for assessing the wellbeing of their students (Bernard et al. 2007). Professor Michael Bernard led the survey that measure seven aspects of wellbeing—school life, home life, community life, social skills, learning skills, emotional skills, and a composite of social and emotional wellbeing indicators. Comparative averages have been calculated from the responses of over 32,000 students nationwide.

Students across Years 7, 9, and 11 from Geelong Grammar School completed the survey in 2011, three years after the initial implementation of Positive Education (Bernard et al., 2011). The results revealed that Geelong Grammar School students had social and emotional wellbeing scores that were significantly above national averages: 37% of students reported wellbeing levels at the very high or highest levels, compared with 21% of the national sample. Geelong Grammar School students scored above national averages for all seven indicators of wellbeing, and rated their school life, home life, and community life particularly favorably. In addition, Geelong Grammar School students had highly developed social skills and pro-social strengths, such as volunteering and caring about the community. Overall, this indicates that the majority of the students felt connected to their friends, teachers, and families, and valued the caring and supportive relationships that they experienced across the School.

Year 9 students were even further above the national averages for wellbeing, with 45% of students scoring at the very high or highest levels of social and emotional wellbeing. These students reported especially strong feelings of belonging, connectedness, and safety. This is a striking finding, as it contrasts the national trend for social and emotional wellbeing to dip in Year 9, and is a testament to the Timbertop program and its strength in helping students to thrive. It may be that Positive Education and Timbertop are an especially powerful combination in supporting students to be physically and mentally well.

The survey also revealed that, although the rates were low compared with national averages, some Geelong Grammar School students were experiencing mental health difficulties, such as symptoms of depression, feelings of loneliness, and concerning levels of stress. Nurturing wellbeing across the community is important, but there will always be some students who require additional help and support, and providing counseling services for these students is viewed as a priority. Support by psychologists and counselors, as well as pastoral care by teaching staff, to address mental health difficulties continues be an essential complement to the Positive Education approach of promoting student flourishing.

Staff experiences of Positive Education

> The cleaning staff have benefited a lot. They are more confident. They know that people respect what they have to say and what they do. They also understand each other better and work as a team. They are always going out of their way to help each other out.
>
> Keven O'Connor, Alliance Cleaning Manager

Positive Education has had an observable impact on the School staff. There are stories of closer relationships between staff members and between staff and students. Staff have shared examples of how Positive Education has brought them closer to their families and equipped them with useful parenting ideas and tips to use with their own children. There are moving stories of staff members using their learning in Positive Education to help them through life challenges. Several staff have commented that it has enriched their capacity to support their friends and family through ups and downs. Staff have also enjoyed learning from the diverse range of Positive Psychology books and literature (see Figure 13.2).

Staff feedback on the multi-day training courses is especially promising. In feedback after a 3-day staff training course (in 2012), 95% of staff members believed that the training had given them valuable skills and knowledge. Over 90% felt equipped

Figure 13.2 Positive Education is underpinned by the science of Positive Psychology.

to apply Positive Education principles in their work and personal lives. Almost all of the staff said that they would recommend the training to others. Of the concepts that were covered, active constructive responding, detecting thinking traps, and character strengths were rated by staff as the most interesting and helpful. One valuable piece of feedback taken on board by the School is the necessity to balance a continual focus on Positive Education professional development with training in other imperative areas, such as curriculum advancement.

Positive Education has been a unifying factor between staff from different campuses. The training program allows staff from all four campuses to come together and get to know each other at both personal and professional levels. The commitment to Positive Education provides a shared vision for staff, and it is apparent that many feel pride in the initiative and leadership that the School has shown in bringing wellbeing to the forefront of education. Most notably, Positive Education has helped to close the gap that can exist between teaching and non-teaching staff. The dedication to including non-teaching staff has enriched their connection with the School community and strengthened their sense of purpose and belonging at the School. Staff and student feedback has been supplemented with quantitative questionnaires at various time points, in particular data from the *Individual Flourishing Questionnaire* (Huppert and So, 2013), as described in Box 13.1.

BOX 13.1 Flourishing data

The central aim of the School's Model for Positive Education is "flourishing." During a visit to the School in 2010, Professor Felicia Huppert—who has completed pioneering work in measuring flourishing in large populations—kindly invited the School to use her 15-item *Individual Flourishing Questionnaire (IFQ)* (Huppert and So, 2013). This has enabled the School to measure levels of student flourishing (in Years 7 to 12) in September of each year. Beginning in 2011, all staff—including teaching and non-teaching staff on all campuses—were also invited to complete the IFQ.

Although the IFQ has not yet been validated for use in smaller school populations (see Huppert and So, 2013), the results allow general longer-term trends in student and staff wellbeing to be monitored. Over the 4-year period, student flourishing levels have fluctuated between 19% (in 2012) and 26% (in 2011), with the average for the 4 years being 23%. Average flourishing rates across the 4 years for each of the six year levels are as follows: Year 7, 28%; Year 8, 26%; Year 9, 31%; Year 10, 22%; Year 11, 21%; Year 12, 21%. It is interesting to note the higher overall average in Year 9 as students experience the Timbertop program. With the exception of the peak in Year 9, there is a small general decline in levels of flourishing from Years 7 to 12. There was no striking gender difference in flourishing rates among the student population (females, 22%; males, 24%).

> **BOX 13.1** *(Continued)*
>
> Over the 3 years (2011–2013), staff flourishing levels have fluctuated between 44% (in 2011) and 49% (in 2012), with the average for the 3 years being 46%. Average flourishing rates over the 3 years (2011–2013) are almost identical in teaching (47%) and non-teaching (45%) staff populations, which is both interesting and encouraging. Higher levels of male staff (52%) were flourishing compared with female staff (41%).
>
> Work is continuing on the establishment of several measures of flourishing (Diener et al., 2010; Keyes, 2006), and it is exciting to recognize the continual growth in this area. In the future, the hope is that robust student and adult scales will be devised that will comprehensively measure each of the six elements of the Model for Positive Education. This will support the School in monitoring flourishing levels in their staff and students— and potentially even in parents and other members of the School community—well into the future.

The Positive Institution Project

As the School's experience evolved, the team began to reflect more comprehensively and strategically on how best to measure and evaluate the approach taken with implementing Positive Education. The first step in this process was the Positive Institution Project (PIP), initiated and led by Paige Williams, Positive Psychology Project Manager from 2009 to 2013, and a significant element of this was Paige's PhD research project undertaken at the University of Melbourne. Launched in 2010, the PIP explored ways in which Positive Psychology could be applied at the organizational level to create a positive culture and work environment for all staff. A number of initiatives were implemented within the broader scope of the PIP, including the introduction of *appreciative inquiry (AI)* as a method for exploring the creation of change. AI was successfully used with the School's senior leadership group to explore what Geelong Grammar School as a flourishing organization looks like (for further details, see Williams, 2011), with the Diversity Committee to develop a new 5-year strategy, and in a review of the Middle School co-curricular program.

The research project embedded within the PIP focused on staff training as a pathway for schools to create positive cultural change that will support efforts to apply Positive Education to the curriculum. The first phase of the research analyzed the pattern of relationships between positive psychological capital (Luthans et al., 2004), perception of a virtuous organization culture (Cameron et al., 2004), and levels of happiness at work (Fisher, 2010). This involved staff completing a series of surveys at three time-points over an 18-month period. Building on the knowledge from Phase 1, the second phase of the study investigated the impact of a

Positive Psychology intervention in developing one variable of interest (psychological capital) on the other variables under study, and examined more closely the underlying mechanisms that explain these relationships, specifically the influence of attitude change. The "intervention" for this study was the 3-day *Introduction to Positive Psychology* training course undertaken by staff at the School. This phase of the research involved staff completing surveys immediately before and after the training course, and again 6 weeks after its completion. The results of the study are currently being analyzed, and will be published in 2015.

The PIP research study makes a valuable contribution to the field of Positive Psychology by extending current understanding of how Positive Psychology interventions influence wellbeing (Lyubomirsky and Layous, 2013). In an applied context, the research will help schools and other organizations to understand the impact of developing the psychological resources of their staff through training, and explain why the starting point for positive culture change may be with the individual.

Building research capacity at Geelong Grammar School

Given the capacity of Geelong Grammar School to both contribute to and benefit from developments in scientific understanding of Positive Education, in 2012 the School decided to make the substantial investment of employing a Research Fellow to coordinate research efforts at the School. This role was taken up by Dr Meredith O'Connor, an Educational and Developmental Psychologist with a background in researching healthy developmental pathways over the life course. Few schools make such a strong commitment to research and evaluation by creating such a role, but doing so has opened up a range of possibilities.

Having a researcher embedded within the School setting has been valuable in allowing unusually strong bridges to be built between academic research and the "on-the-ground" implementation of Positive Education. A Positive Education research advisory group was formed in 2013, with academics from multiple institutions across Australia generously providing their time and expertise to advise on the strategic direction of the Geelong Grammar School research program. Promoting two-way conversations between the academic world and school practice, a paper on the Geelong Grammar School Model for Positive Education was published in the peer-reviewed *International Journal of Wellbeing* (Norrish et al., 2013).

Helping to develop this research program, a number of postgraduate research students have completed their thesis projects at the school. For example, Emily Toner explored character strengths, and how these related to wellbeing levels, in students from Geelong Grammar School (Toner et al., 2012). Two questions currently being explored by Master of Psychology students from Deakin University and the University of Melbourne are how schools can promote teacher "buy-in" during the process of implementing Positive Education, and the impact of Positive Psychology training for parents on their own and their children's wellbeing.

In addition, having a researcher based at the School has provided opportunities for staff to engage with the scientific research relating to Positive Education, and upskill themselves as discerning consumers of science. The establishment of a Positive Education journal club at the School is just one example of this. Each term an appropriate journal article is selected, and a group of staff members come together to discuss the research methods, strengths, limitations, and implications for the School. This promotes not only staff members' skills, but also their interest and engagement with empirical knowledge, thereby promoting evidence-based practice.

As well as scientifically based research, the School is beginning to put in place processes that will allow "local evaluations" to become a routine part of Positive Education practice. Local evaluations provide insight into how Positive Education strategies are working in the specific Geelong Grammar School setting. The outcomes can then be used to inform decisions about what strategies should be prioritized, and how they can be made even more effective. This contributes to a cycle of continuous improvement in Positive Education at Geelong Grammar School, allowing the program to continually move forward and develop.

Independent evaluation

Our challenge is to demonstrate that Positive Education enhances student wellbeing, and to lead in establishing wellbeing as an essential component of a thriving educational system.

Geelong Grammar School, Purpose Document, 2012

Although the difference that Positive Education has made is apparent in reports from staff and students, the School is now invested in taking evaluation to the next level by collecting extensive quantitative and qualitative data. The School is inundated with enquiries and visitors from other Australian and international schools and organizations interested in learning about the School's journey. Unsurprisingly, as schools consider embarking on their own journeys, questions about whether the program is working and how it is evaluated are often at the forefront of their minds. Geelong Grammar School is uniquely placed to answer these questions, as well as to provide additional insight into how Positive Education can be further developed and enhanced, what aspects of the program are most critical, and who benefits most from the program. To this end, the School has taken substantial steps in the direction of rigorous evaluation.

A major milestone for the School has been to embark on a 3-year longitudinal research program under the direction of two Chief Investigators, namely Associate Professor Dianne Vella-Brodrick from the University of Melbourne, and Associate Professor Nikki Rickard from Monash University (other investigators include Professor Donna Cross from the University of Western Australia, and Professor John Hattie from the University of Melbourne). The collaboration between the School and the research experts commenced in 2011 with an application for an Australian Research Council (ARC) Linkage Grant to explore the efficacy and effectiveness of Positive Education at Geelong Grammar School. When this application was unsuccessful, Geelong Grammar School made the commitment to fund the project from the commencement of 2013. The Chief Investigators and the School then reapplied to the ARC in 2012, submitting a project of enhanced size and scope. This time, the ARC Linkage Grant was successful, enabling an additional element of a randomized controlled trial of the Positive Education curriculum at two neighboring government schools. The project will thus provide insight into the efficacy and effectiveness of the Positive Education program in different contexts.

The project, titled "Enhancing Adolescent Mental Health through Positive Education," involves two stages—one at Geelong Grammar School, and one at the two local government schools. At Geelong Grammar School the study is following Year 9 students over a period of 3 years, from 2013 to 2015, in order to determine the effects of Positive Education on students' daily functioning and wellbeing. Students will complete online measures of wellbeing and mental health at key time points over the 3 years. Focus groups will be used to explore young people's thoughts and feelings about what they have learned. This will be supported by students' attendance and academic records, which will provide insight into their school engagement and performance. An external control group of adolescents of the same age who have not completed Positive Education has been recruited from the general population to function as a comparison. The results obtained from the first year of this study (i.e. 2013) are briefly described in Box 13.2 (see also Vella-Brodrick et al., 2014).

BOX 13.2: Preliminary research findings: a snapshot of 2013

In February and December 2013, a total of 383 students from across Years 9, 10, and 11 from Geelong Grammar School completed a range of mental health and wellbeing indicators as part of the independent evaluation led by the University of Melbourne. To provide a point of comparison, 138 students from socio-demographically matched schools completed the same measures of mental health and wellbeing. Year 9 Geelong Grammar School students, who were living at Timbertop at the time, reported significant improvements in wellbeing across the school year, as well as decreased symptoms of depression and anxiety. In comparison, Year 9 students from the control group reported a decline in wellbeing over the course of the year. Interestingly, Year 9 students who arrived at Timbertop from

BOX 13.2: *(Continued)*

the Corio campus reported significantly higher wellbeing at the beginning of the year than students who arrived at Timbertop from other schools. Furthermore, the largest gains in wellbeing during Year 9 were experienced by students who were new to Geelong Grammar School at the start of 2013. A subset of Year 9 Geelong Grammar School students who took part in focus group interviews described a range of benefits and positive attributes concerning both Positive Education and the Timbertop program more generally.

The data from the Year 10 students yielded a more complex picture. Year 10 students from Geelong Grammar School experienced higher levels of wellbeing than students in the control group at both the beginning and end of the year, although the differences between the groups were not statistically significant. The wellbeing of students from Geelong Grammar School remained stable over the course of 2013, which is in contrast to expectations that wellbeing would increase as a result of students participating in the comprehensive Year 10 Positive Education Program. The opportunity for Year 10 students to provide feedback via the focus groups revealed several points of constructive critique. Themes in students' evaluations of Positive Education, in terms of suggestions for improvement, included reducing the didactic nature of some of the lessons, placing less emphasis on writing and completing worksheets, and integrating more experiential activities. The students highlighted the fact that they valued peer-to-peer learning and felt they could learn from each other's experiences. They commented on the multi-faceted, individualized, and dynamic nature of personal wellbeing, and a key take-away message for the Positive Education teachers was to ensure that they were "describing" and not "prescribing" wellbeing concepts and related activities. These suggestions provide useful insights into areas for improvement for the Year 10 Positive Education Program, and substantial revisions to the content and delivery were made prior to the commencement of the 2014 program.

Year 11 students from Geelong Grammar School reported higher levels of wellbeing than students from other socio-demographically matched schools. Year 11 students from Geelong Grammar School and students from the comparison group reported decreased levels of wellbeing and increased levels of anxiety and depression over the course of the year. One reason for this decrease in wellbeing may be the increasing academic stress that young people experience as they work towards their final exams. In is important to note that Year 11 students at Geelong Grammar School do not take part in an explicit Positive Education curriculum. It may be that refresher sessions delivered over the course of Year 11 help students to continue to apply, and benefit from, their Positive Education learning.

Overall, these initial research findings provide support for the Geelong Grammar School Positive Education Program, especially in relation to the Year 9 program as students live in the Timbertop community. The results also indicate that the positive effects diminish over the course of Years 10 and 11, with focus group data suggesting some areas for improvement in terms of program content and delivery. Although these results are preliminary, they are consistent with other sources of information which indicate that students' level of wellbeing at Timbertop is particularly high. It may be that students benefit most from Positive Education programs that are highly experiential, and when they have opportunities to apply their learning to real-life situations.

In order to obtain deeper and more nuanced information about how students are benefiting from Positive Education as they go about their daily lives, a sample group of 50 students has been randomly selected to take part in experience sampling and biological sampling components of the study. The experience sampling method (ESM) is a research strategy that uses a device such as an iPod Touch to prompt students to answer questions about their current experience (Larson and Csikszentmihalyi, 1983). Asking students about what they are feeling and doing "in the moment" minimizes bias and inaccuracies that result from trying to recall past experiences.

Four times a year the 50 students carry an iPod Touch around with them for 1 week. The iPods are programmed to beep four times per day, prompting the students to complete a short assessment of what they are doing and how they are feeling at that time. Students respond to questions about whether or not anything of significance (either good or bad) has happened since they were last beeped, and if so, what strategies they employed to respond to the situation. This research will provide invaluable insight into how various activities and strategies influence students' thoughts, feelings, and behaviors as they go about their daily lives. Biological samples, including levels of the hormone cortisol (which give an indication of students' physiological levels of stress), will provide an important complement to these subjective reports of their wellbeing. A final measure, which involves testing students' heart rate variability, is taken at four different time points over the duration of the project. Heart rate variability analysis is a new objective measure that has been found to be an indicator of emotional regulation (Appelhans and Luecken, 2006). Based on the study results and students' feedback, the Positive Education program will be amended to better suit students' needs and interests.

In the second stage of the study, a component of the Positive Education explicit curriculum will be evaluated at a neighboring school. The first step in this stage will be training a small number of teachers who will be directly involved in delivering the Positive Education curriculum. Following the teacher training, and after the collection and analysis of student baseline wellbeing data, staff from the three schools (Geelong Grammar School and the two local schools) will work together to tailor a 15-session Positive Education program to be delivered over one semester. Initially half of the Year 10 students at the local schools will experience the program, with the other half receiving the schools' existing curricula. In this study, classes of students will be randomly allocated to the two study conditions, and a broad range of wellbeing assessments will be conducted at pre-intervention, post-intervention, and 6-month follow-up time points. Taken together, the findings of this research study will provide a rich picture of the impact of Positive Education on students' wellbeing and positive mental health, both within the Geelong Grammar School community and beyond.

The research journey continues

Geelong Grammar School has become an international leader in demonstrating how an educational institution can apply Positive Education in a meaningful, integrated, evidence-based, and sustainable way. The impact on the School is tangible—many staff and students are flourishing, students have shown a renewed commitment to helping others, and the School is a more connected and cohesive place. Across the community there is a consistent message that good mental health is as important as good physical health, and that it can be promoted through valuable skills for wellbeing.

The power of Positive Education is that it combines the knowledge gained through scientific research with the expertise and wisdom of the teaching profession. Through its move towards scientific evaluation and establishing an ongoing research program, Geelong Grammar School has the chance to give back to the scientific community and contribute even more to shaping conversations about the role of wellbeing in education. This research will no doubt yield invaluable information on how schools can support their students, staff, parents, and communities so that they can flourish. The hope is that this will empower other schools looking to increase their focus on helping students to live resilient, connected, and purposeful lives.

REFERENCES

Appelhans B M and Luecken L J (2006). Heart rate variability as an index of regulated emotional responding. *Review of General Psychology, 10,* 229–40.

Bernard M E, Stephanou A, and Urbach D (2007). *ASG Student Social and Emotional Health Report.* Melbourne, Australia: Australian Council for Educational Research and Australian Scholarships Group.

Bernard M E, Stephanou A, and Urbach D (2011). *Social-Emotional Wellbeing Survey: full summary of ACER data for Geelong Grammar School.* Melbourne, Australia: Australian Council for Educational Research and Australian Scholarships Group.

Cameron K S, Bright D, and Caza A (2004). Exploring the relationships between organizational virtuousness and performance. *American Behavioral Scientist, 47,* 766–90.

Diener E et al. (2010). New well-being measures: short scales to assess flourishing and positive and negative feelings. *Social Indicators Research, 97,* 143–56.

Fisher C D (2010). Happiness at work. *International Journal of Management Reviews, 12,* 384–412.

Huppert F and So T (2013). Flourishing across Europe: application of a new conceptual framework for defining well-being. *Social Indicators Research, 110,* 837–61.

Keyes C L M (2006). Mental health in adolescence: is America's youth flourishing? *American Journal of Orthopsychiatry, 76,* 395–402.

Larson R and Csikszentmihalyi M (1983). The experience sampling method. *New Directions for Methodology of Social and Behavioral Science, 15,* 41–56.

Luthans F, Luthans K W, and Luthans B C (2004). Positive psychological capital: beyond human and social capital. *Business Horizons, 47,* 45–50.

Lyubomirsky S and Layous K (2013). How do simple positive activities increase well-being? *Current Directions in Psychological Science, 22,* 57–62.

Norrish J M, Williams P, O'Connor M, and Robinson J (2013). An applied framework for Positive Education. *International Journal of Wellbeing, 3,* 147–61.

Toner E, Haslam N, Robinson J, and Williams P (2012). Character strengths and well-being in adolescence: structure and correlates of the Values in Action Inventory of Strengths for Children. *Personality and Individual Differences, 52,* 637–42.

Vella-Brodrick D, Rickard N, and Chin R C (2014). *An Evalution of Positive Education at Geelong Grammar School: a snapshot of 2013.* Melbourne, Australia: The University of Melbourne.

Williams P (2011). Pathways to positive education at Geelong Grammar School: integrating positive psychology and appreciative inquiry. *AI Practitioner, 13,* 8–13.

LOOKING TO THE FUTURE

Wellbeing is at the heart of what we want for our children. We want them to flourish and we want them to be happy. If we can get that right, then they will make so much more of the opportunities which their education will provide.

Stephen Meek, Principal

Geelong Grammar School made its commitment to wellbeing in 2005, to Positive Psychology in 2007, and to Positive Education in 2008. The School has come a long way since the early days of discussing the plans for the Wellbeing Centre, meeting Professor Seligman through Dr Trent Barry, and having Dr Karen Reivich and the team from the University of Pennsylvania arrive in Australia for the first multi-day training course. The growth has been remarkable—from the early days when most of the staff and students had never heard of concepts such as growth mindsets, active constructive responding, or thinking traps—to the current state where such language is built into the culture of the School across the four campuses.

Although there has been tremendous progress in Positive Education, both within Geelong Grammar School and beyond, there remains much more to be done (as symbolized in Figure 14.1). There are research, curriculum, and staff training directions to pursue. Longitudinal research in different cultural settings must be conducted in order to determine effective wellbeing activities and to measure the impact of Positive Education programs. Additional research must be undertaken to determine how best to promote flourishing among students, staff, parents, and wider school communities. There is a need for further curriculum materials to be developed. And, of course, there is a need to enable staff in all schools to receive training in Positive Education so that they can not only benefit personally from the science of wellbeing, but also embed the principles and practices authentically within their own school environments.

Figure 14.1 Positive Education is an ongoing journey at Geelong Grammar School.

As pioneers of Positive Education, and from the considerable experience gained over the past 6 years from both the achievements and the setbacks, the team at Geelong Grammar School has confidence in its role in driving the growth of Positive Education on a broader scale. The School has been fortunate to learn from many of the national and international experts in the fields of Positive Psychology and Positive Education. Over 25 scholars have resided at Geelong Grammar School and enriched the community and the Positive Education program. With this privilege comes a sense of responsibility to share this knowledge and to assist other school communities in making efficient and effective progress. With these considerations and hopes in mind, in 2014 the School took the next significant and exciting step of the journey—the launching of the Institute of Positive Education (see Box 14.1 for an extract of an article describing the Institute by Stephen Meek, Principal, from *Light Blue,* 2013).

BOX 14.1: Institute of Positive Education

I am delighted to announce that we are establishing the Institute of Positive Education in 2014. The Institute will enable us to develop and strengthen Positive Education within the School, but it will also give us the capacity to share our knowledge with other schools, to undertake more research in connection with leading universities, and to train more teachers from other schools, as well as our parents and Old Geelong Grammarians.

We have come a long way with Positive Education in the last 6 years. We have gradually increased the size of the Positive Education Department as we have increased the scale of our operations. We are now in a position to take a bigger step forward, through the creation of the Institute of Positive Education.

The Institute will be led by the Director of the Institute of Positive Education, assisted by a team of (initially) six staff. The Institute will be overseen by the Vice Principal, Charlie Scudamore, who will play a key role in setting up and working with the Institute. This is a very exciting initiative, and I am confident that it will help us to scale ever greater heights in the development of Positive Education.

Stephen Meek, Principal, *Light Blue*, September 2013

The Institute of Positive Education

My colleagues and I feel a tremendous sense of meaning and purpose in the work we are doing at Geelong Grammar School. To see the impact we are having on our own School community, and to hear many examples of the influence we are having on schools throughout Australia, and indeed internationally, is extremely exciting.

Justin Robinson, Director of the Institute of Positive Education

The Institute of Positive Education operates under the banner of Geelong Grammar School, and is dedicated to promoting the science of wellbeing in educational contexts—at the School and more widely, both in Australia and beyond. Led by Justin Robinson, and with the collaboration of Charlie Scudamore, a team of teachers, psychologists, and other professionals work to promote excellence in Positive Education (see Figure 14.2). The Institute's objective is to have a meaningful impact on the wellbeing of people, and in particular young people, so that they can flourish and contribute to the world in positive ways. The School deliberately chose the tagline *Learning to Flourish* for the Institute of Positive Education. It is taken from the focus statement of the Geelong Grammar School Purpose document, and indicates that Positive Education is not a finished product. It illustrates that the School has begun an ongoing journey of learning how to describe, measure, and promote flourishing within all members of the community. The vision and mission of the Institute are described in Box 14.2.

The Institute has six departments or "arms." "Positive Teaching and Learning" is responsible for the explicit and implicit teaching of Positive Education. "Positive Organization" focuses on how Geelong Grammar School can embed the philosophy of Positive Education even further into everyday life at the School. "Positive Research" focuses on advancing scientific understanding of Positive Education. "Positive Training" involves the planning and delivery of training courses within

Figure 14.2 The Institute of Positive Education staff team on its first day of operation in 2014.

BOX 14.2: Vision and mission of the Institute of Positive Education

Our **Vision** is "to lead by example and innovate in the field of Positive Education", and we do this through our **Mission**, which is "to provide transformational educational programs to our stakeholders in a sustainable delivery model. This results in our **Purpose**, which is "to make a positive difference in the world through inspiring students, individuals and communities to flourish."

the School community and beyond. "Positive Resources" aims to create books, materials, and resources to support schools in Positive Education. Finally, "Positive Development" focuses on keeping abreast of advancements in the science of well-being and flourishing, and using this knowledge to create content, curriculum, and training materials.

"Getting it right in our own backyard"

I support this program because I believe that our children need as much preparation for the job of "living life" as they do for "earning a living." This is about helping students become rounded individuals who can contribute to their world in ways we have not even imagined yet.

Paddy Handbury, Chair, Geelong Grammar Foundation

The School has grown with Positive Education, and that is why so many people from different places want to come and have a look. We still have a long way to go and we are still learning and developing, but we are actually living it and actually doing it.

Ildi Anderson, Academic Office Manager

It is frequently said at the School that the first priority for Positive Education is "getting it right in our own backyard" and "ensuring Pos Ed is humming at home. (See Figure 14.3)" An area for ongoing growth in this regard is the development and expansion of the teaching and learning of Positive Education. Over the past few years, the explicit teaching of Positive Education at Geelong Grammar School has grown from Years 7 and 9 (in 2009) to Year ELC through to Year 10 (in 2014). The plan is to continue to expand this so that Positive Education is taught in a systematic way across all years—from ELC to Year 12. The goal is to identify specific social and learning needs of children at different ages, and to create a scope and sequence for Positive Education so that students' understanding of concepts builds sequentially and logically over the course of their time at the School. Complementing the high-quality explicit curriculum is well-developed implicit teaching, and a long-term objective is to create curriculum materials and other resources to assist with the implicit teaching of Positive Education, both within Geelong Grammar School and more widely.

Figure 14.3 Members of the Year 11 Focus Day committee with Steve Andrew, Head of Fraser House, at the end of a meaningful day.

Another core growth area is for Geelong Grammar School to become, and remain, a flourishing institution. In many ways it already is a thriving community, but an overarching objective is for the science of wellbeing and flourishing to be reflected in everything that happens at the School. Thus the School is committed to exploring how the diverse aspects of School life—from the way that staff are hired and appraised, to how students are awarded colors and commendations, to what is included in the School newsletters—can be informed by the science of wellbeing and flourishing. The ongoing and comprehensive training of teaching and non-teaching staff has been an important step in embedding wellbeing into the School community. The more recent implementation of parent training programs is helping to spread Positive Education even further, and a vision for the future is for all members of the wider community—including Old Geelong Grammarians and staff families—to benefit from the science of wellbeing and flourishing.

Sharing with the other schools

Geelong Grammar School has a long history of working with the community on a broader basis. The Positive Education program and sharing it with other schools is an extension of the School philosophy from way back in the early days.

Dr John Court, Senior Medical Officer (1995–2010)

I feel unbelievably privileged to have done the training and to now be standing on the cusp of a new state of education. I love that people come here all the time wanting to know more, and we tell them. We are helping it grow.

Annabel Meek, Head of Highton House

Geelong Grammar School has a deep commitment to sharing its learning and experience with regard to Positive Education with other schools and educational institutions. The interest in the School's journey has been remarkable, with regular enquiries coming from all over Australia and the world. Each year, school staff groups ranging from as far away as the UK and Finland through to the closer neighbors of Singapore and New Zealand travel to Australia to visit the School and learn about the implementation of Positive Education. The significant interest from wider educational communities suggests that Positive Education is capable of fulfilling a need, and that it is something for which many school communities are searching. This need and this search are for a comprehensive, scientific, and whole-school approach to acquiring the concepts and skills for promoting wellbeing.

The School's commitment to sharing its learning and resources has led to the development and implementation of training courses for staff from other schools

Figure 14.4 Janis Coffey, Associate Director of the Institute, leading a training session.

and organizations, and as of 2013 a range of multi-day courses are delivered each year (see Figure 14.4). Teams from the Institute frequently travel to different states of Australia to train entire groups of staff from other schools in Positive Education. Staff members have delivered keynote presentations and workshops at education and psychology events and conferences in different countries around the world. Charlie Scudamore and Justin Robinson were both key presenters in the first ever university course on Positive Education at the University of Melbourne, namely the Professional Certificate in Education (Positive Education), in 2014. The School also takes great pride in the role that students have played in sharing Positive Education with others. A major achievement for the School was when three students travelled from the Corio campus to Shanghai, China, to run a workshop on Positive Education and mindfulness at the World Leading Schools Association Student Conference.

Of the many opportunities that the School has had to share Positive Education with others, a few stand out as especially meaningful accomplishments. In 2013, an invitation was extended to Principal Stephen Meek to attend and present at the Positive Education Summit at 10 Downing Street, London. The Summit brought together approximately 35 leading thinkers and educators from across the world to the British Prime Minister's official residence to explore and brainstorm how to grow Positive Education globally. In another highlight, Charlie Scudamore, Vice Principal, was invited to travel to Finland to present a keynote speech to civil servants from the Ministry of Education, as well as staff from Vassa University who were interested in how they too could take proactive and preventative steps towards supporting the mental health and wellbeing of their young people.

A peak moment of the School journey occurred in October 2013. Charlie Scudamore was invited to deliver a keynote presentation to Masters of Positive Psychology students at the University of Pennsylvania. After Charlie had finished speaking about Positive Education at Geelong Grammar School, he received a standing ovation. Unbeknown to Charlie at the time, Professor Seligman was waiting to come up on to the stage to present him with the Pioneer Award in Positive Psychology, for "bringing Positive Psychology to Geelong Grammar School and thereby igniting the Positive Education movement." It is safe to say that, once ignited, this movement has spread like wildfire, with schools across the world taking steps to place student and staff wellbeing at the core of their day-to-day business.

Leading the shift in education

> It is hard for schools—and the education system more broadly—to change direction. It is much easier for schools to keep doing what they have always done. As a community, we have to step back, ask the hard questions, and look at the bigger picture. It is time to say: "this is the new direction that we feel our children and young people need in the education that we offer them."
>
> Jeremy Kirkwood, Chair of the Geelong Grammar School Council

For too long, academic models have dominated the educational landscape, and success has been defined in terms of academic excellence. The objective of Positive Education is to broaden the focus so that the term "a good education" refers to more than academic learning, and instead supports the growth of the whole student. Geelong Grammar School has been instrumental in sharing Positive Education with the Australian community and the world, and in doing so has helped to shape the conversation about what is important in education. The vision for the future is that all schools will have elements of Positive Education embedded within their cultures and their curriculums. A shared hope among members of the Geelong Grammar School community is that all schools will prioritize the training of staff in the principles of Positive Education, and that key wellbeing concepts will be addressed in pre-service teacher training courses.

This discourse is gaining momentum—not just through the thriving field of Positive Education, but from related and complementary fields such as social and emotional learning (Collaborative for Academic, Social, and Emotional Learning, 2003) and positive youth development (Lerner et al., 2003). Progress in this regard is garnered from wider-scale Australian government initiatives such as Kidsmatter (<www.kidsmatter.edu.au>), Mindmatters (<www.mindmatters.edu.au>), and the National Safe Schools Framework (<www.safeschoolshub.edu.au>). For a School

BOX 14.3: PESA vision and Founding Board Members

Vision: To foster the implementation and development of Positive Psychology and its applications in education settings.

Chairman:
Simon Murray (Headmaster, St Peters College, South Australia)

Founding Board Members:
Roger Bayly (Deputy Principal, Christ Church Grammar School, Western Australia)
Steven Bowers (Principal, Burgmann Anglican School, Australian Capital Territory)
Alan Campbell (Headmaster, Anglican Church Grammar School, Queensland)
Stuart Johnston (Principal, The Peninsula School, Victoria)
Anne Johnstone (Principal, Seymour College, South Australia)
Stephen Meek (Principal, Geelong Grammar School, Victoria)
Julie Townsend (Headmistress, St Catherine's School, New South Wales)
Scott Watson (Principal, Euroa Secondary College, Victoria)
Steve Zolezzi (Director of Positive Education, Knox Grammar School, New South Wales)

like Geelong Grammar School—one of the largest and most well-known schools in Australia—to be so deeply committed to supporting wellbeing across the whole school, and taking leadership in this way, augurs well for this larger picture.

The number of schools that are embracing Positive Education, both in Australia and internationally, is growing. The launch in 2014 of the Positive Education Schools Association (PESA) (<www.pesa.edu.au>) is testament to the expanding interest in wellbeing in schools. PESA aims to provide a forum for collaboration between teachers, schools, researchers, and academics, and to continue to refine and expand the understanding of how wellbeing can be embedded into education. PESA's vision and Founding Board Members are outlined in Box 14.3. It is believed that by building awareness of wellbeing, and deliberately focusing on enhancing and nurturing it, all schools can assist students in experiencing positive emotions, fostering positive relationships, recognizing the value of positive health, increasing positive engagement, striving for positive accomplishments, and further developing a sense of positive purpose.

A flourishing future

Education is about hope. One hopes that students will be successful. One hopes that they will lead a meaningful life. One hopes that they will make long and lasting relationships. One hopes that they will accomplish something worthwhile.

Charlie Scudamore, Vice Principal

Everyday researchers and scientists are expanding and refining our understanding of what it means to flourish, and how this can be achieved. In a comprehensive review of progress in the field, Rusk and Waters (2013) identified 18,401 articles on Positive Psychology concepts that have been published in peer-reviewed journals. The vast majority (86%) of these articles were published after 1998, and the field had increased in size, breadth, and scope each year since this time point. This progress is notable, and indicates that scholars and researchers in a diverse range of fields have responded to the call to further our understanding of positive aspects of human functioning, as made by Professor Seligman in 1998 (Seligman and Csikszentmihalyi, 2000). However, unless there is communication of this knowledge more broadly, scientific progress will have little practical impact. In this regard, schools are uniquely placed to communicate the skills, knowledge, and mindsets of flourishing to wide audiences and, in doing so, to contribute to increasing the percentage of people who experience good mental health and wellbeing across the lifespan.

Central to the School's approach is the understanding that Positive Education is about much more than individual flourishing. Fundamental aspects include building character strengths, exploring ethics and morals, and cultivating values such as compassion, kindness, and forgiveness. Central to Positive Education are *eudaimonic* behaviors and values—where the welfare of others, the community, and society are considered just as important as the wellbeing of the self (for a discussion of the importance of eudaimonic behaviors for young people, see Hallam et al., 2013). If such considerations become a fundamental part of the way that all children and young people are educated, the result will no doubt be a kinder, more compassionate, and ultimately more peaceful world.

In the end, it is the students themselves who will make the biggest difference to the future of wellbeing in the wider population. Students who have come through the program at Geelong Grammar School have gone on to set up or contribute to Positive Education initiatives beyond the School. For example, past students have played key roles in founding wellbeing programs at tertiary colleges such as St Paul's College at the University of Sydney and Ormond College at the University of Melbourne. In other cases the difference made by Positive Education is less obvious, as students use the skills they have learned to be mindful in their interactions, to respond to challenges with hope and persistence, or to maintain their commitment to making a difference. Thus investing in the wellbeing of students in this way is a gift to them, which ultimately extends to others and the wider world.

REFERENCES

Collaborative for Academic, Social, and Emotional Learning (CASEL) (2003). *Safe and Sound: an educational leader's guide to evidence-based social and emotional learning (SEL) programs.* Chicago, IL: CASEL.

Hallam W et al. (2013). Association between adolescent eudaimonic behaviours and emotional competence in young adulthood. *Journal of Happiness Studies*, 15, 1165–1177.

Lerner R M, Dowling E M, and Anderson P M (2003). Positive youth development: thriving as the basis of personhood and civil society. *Applied Developmental Science*, 7, 172–80.

Rusk R D and Waters L E (2013). Tracing the size, reach, impact, and breadth of positive psychology. *Journal of Positive Psychology*, 8, 207–21.

Seligman M E P and Csikszentmihalyi M (2000). Positive psychology: an introduction. *American Psychologist*, 55, 5–14.

BIOGRAPHIES OF
EXPERT CONTRIBUTORS

Professor Roy Baumeister

Roy Baumeister is one of the world's most prolific and influential psychologists. He has published well over 500 scientific articles and over 30 books. In 2013 he received the highest award given by the Association for Psychological Science, namely the William James Fellow award, in recognition of his lifetime achievements. He is currently Eppes Eminent Scholar and Professor of Psychology at Florida State University, as well as holding distinguished visiting professorships at King Abdulaziz University, Saudi Arabia, and at the VU Free University of Amsterdam, the Netherlands. Although Roy made his name with laboratory research, his recognition extends beyond the narrow confines of academia. His 2011 book, *Willpower: rediscovering the greatest human strength* (co-authored with John Tierney) was a *New York Times* best-seller. He has appeared on television shows such as NBC Dateline and ABC 20/20, Discover, PBS, National Public Radio, and countless local news shows. His work has been covered or quoted in the *New York Times, Washington Post, Wall Street Journal, Los Angeles Times,* the *Economist, Newsweek, Time, Psychology Today, Self, Men's Health, Business Week,* and many other outlets.

Dr Tal Ben-Shahar

Tal Ben-Shahar is an author and lecturer. He taught two of the largest classes in Harvard University's history, "Positive Psychology" and "The Psychology of Leadership." Tal consults and lectures around the world to executives in multinational corporations, the general public, and at-risk populations. The topics he lectures on include leadership, education, ethics, happiness, self-esteem, resilience, goal setting, and mindfulness. His books in the area of Positive Psychology have been translated into more than 25 languages. He is the co-founder and chief learning officer of the Wholebeing Institute and Potentialife. Tal is also the founder and chairman of Maytiv, a center committed to the spread of Positive Psychology in education. An avid sportsman, Tal won the US Intercollegiate and Israeli National squash championships. He obtained his PhD in Organizational Behavior and BA in Philosophy and Psychology from Harvard.

Professor Barbara Fredrickson

Barbara Fredrickson has been advancing the science of positive emotions for more than 20 years. She is currently Kenan Distinguished Professor of Psychology at the University of North Carolina at Chapel Hill, where she directs the PEP Lab (<www.PositiveEmotions.org>). Her books, *Positivity* and *Love 2.0*, have been translated into more than 20 languages. Barb's research, funded by the US National Institutes of Health, reveals how our positive emotions were sculpted by the discerning chisel of Darwinian natural selection to serve as life-giving nutrients for growth. Her innovative contributions have been recognized with numerous honors, including the inaugural Templeton Prize in Positive Psychology from the American Psychological Association, the Career Trajectory Award from the Society of Experimental Social Psychology, and the inaugural Christopher Peterson Gold Medal from the International Positive Psychology Association. Barb's scientific work has influenced scholars and practitioners worldwide, in disciplines ranging from education and business to healthcare, the military, and beyond. Her work has been featured in the *New York Times*, CNN, NPR, PBS, *The Atlantic*, *The Economist*, *Oprah Magazine*, and elsewhere. She has been invited to present her research findings at the White House and for the Dalai Lama.

Dr Craig Hassed

Craig Hassed is a general practitioner and a senior lecturer and mindfulness consultant at Monash University. His teaching, research, and clinical interests include mindfulness-based stress management, mind–body medicine, meditation, health promotion, integrative medicine, and medical ethics. Craig is regularly invited to speak and run courses in Australia and overseas in health, professional, and educational contexts. He was the founding president of the Australian Teachers of Meditation Association, and is a regular media commentator. He writes regularly for medical journals, and has published eight books: *New Frontiers in Medicine* (Volumes 1 and 2), *Know Thyself* (on mindfulness-based stress management), *The Essence of Health* (on the lifestyle approach to health and chronic illness), *General Practice: the integrative approach* (a textbook co-authored with Kerryn Phelps), *Mindfulness for Life* (a book written with Stephen McKenzie), and, most recently, *Mindful Learning* (a book co-authored with Richard Chambers, on the role of mindfulness in education), and *Playing the Genetic Hand Life Dealt You: epigenetics and how to keep ourselves healthy*.

Professor Felicia Huppert

Felicia Huppert is internationally renowned for her work on the science of wellbeing and the promotion of human flourishing. Her research examines the causes and consequences of wellbeing, using data from large population samples, longitudinal studies, and intervention programs such as the Mindfulness in Schools Project. Felicia is a Professor of Psychology, and spends part of the year in the UK, where she is Director of the Well-being Institute at the University of Cambridge, and part of the year in Sydney, Australia, at the Institute for Positive Psychology and Education. She advises the UK Government and international bodies on the measurement of wellbeing and policies to enhance wellbeing. In addition to numerous published papers, her edited books include the seminal publication *The Science of Well-Being*, a four-volume set entitled *Major Works in Happiness and Well-Being*, and a new book, *Interventions and Policies to Enhance Well-Being*.

Dr Sue Jackson

Sue Jackson has been involved in positive psychology and the psychology of performance enhancement since completing a PhD on the flow state in the early 1990s. She has been working in academic and professional capacities since 1993, bringing a wealth of experience to her work and clients. She has completed degrees in Education, followed by graduate degrees in Sport and Exercise Psychology, an MSc and a PhD. Sue is a registered psychologist and member of the College of Sport and Exercise Psychologists of the Australian Psychological Society (APS). She is also a member of the APS Psychology and Yoga Interest Group. Her work on flow has helped to make this optimal psychological state understandable and more accessible to all levels of performers, from weekend warriors to Olympic champions. She has extensively researched flow, using a combination of qualitative and quantitative approaches. The latter work has included the development of a suite of Flow Scales—self-report instruments that have applicability across a diverse range of settings. With her mentor and the founder of flow, Professor Mihaly Csikszentmihalyi, Sue has written a popular book on flow for athletes and coaches, *Flow in Sports: the keys to optimal experiences and performances*.

Dr Jacolyn Norrish

Jacolyn Norrish is passionate about mental health promotion, and views schools as one of the most powerful avenues for building flourishing communities. Her PhD involved developing and testing a Positive Education program for Australian adolescents, which explored concepts such as hope, kindness, meaning, character strengths, and gratitude. Jacolyn has worked with a range of schools and organizations during their application of evidence-based wellbeing initiatives, including Berry Street School and the AFL Players Association. Her interests include mindfulness, acceptance commitment therapy, compassion, and altruism. She has taught wellbeing and Positive Psychology across the Psychology, Medicine, and Business faculties of Monash University, and she is the co-founder of Share Well, which is a movement that fosters collaboration and innovation in the practical application of the science of wellbeing.

Professor Nansook Park

Nansook Park is Professor of Psychology, Director of Michigan Positive Psychology Center at the University of Michigan, and a nationally certified school psychologist in the USA. She completed her graduate work both in Korea and in the USA, and has a research and practice background in clinical and school psychology. Her work on developing ways to measure character strengths and virtues, and studying consequences and ways to cultivate good character, is considered to be the most ambitious undertaking within the field of Positive Psychology. She has also been working on soldier resilience and a psychological fitness project with US Army and Positive Education projects in Australia. Her main research interest is the promotion of positive development and wellbeing across the lifespan in different cultural settings. Her expertise includes character strengths, happiness, positive relationships, meaning and purpose, and positive experiences and their applications to resiliency, strength-based practice, education, family, work, health, and wellbeing. She has over 100 scholarly publications to her name, and has received several national and international honors, including the Fellow Awards (Association of Psychological Science, International Positive Psychology Association) and the Academic Excellence Award (China). She is a member of the International Positive Psychology Association steering committee, the Annenberg/Sunnylands Commission on Positive Youth Development, and a Consulting Editor for *The Journal of Positive Psychology*.

Dr Karen Reivich

Karen Reivich is Co-Director of the Penn Resiliency Project at the Positive Psychology Center, and a Research Associate in the Department of Psychology at the University of Pennsylvania. She is also an Instructor in the Master of Applied Positive Psychology program at the University of Pennsylvania. She is a leader in the fields of resilience, optimism, depression prevention, and Positive Psychology interventions. Her work focuses on helping leaders, parents, and educators to promote resilience and wellbeing in adolescents and adults. During the past 20 years she has been a Co-Principal Investigator of studies of the Penn Resiliency Program funded by the National Institute of Mental Health and the US Department of Education. In addition, Karen works with the US Army, as part of Comprehensive Soldier and Family Fitness, an initiative designed to teach resilience skills to soldiers and their families. She conducts workshops and training for leaders, parents, educators, clinicians, and corporations throughout the USA and internationally, and she lectures extensively on the topics of resilience, optimism, and Positive Psychology. In addition, she has a coaching practice and provides consultation to organizations on the themes of resilience and strength development. Karen has published extensively and is a co-author of the books *The Optimistic Child* and *The Resilience Factor*.

Pninit Russo-Netzer

Pninit Russo-Netzer is a researcher at the Department of Counselling and Human Development at the University of Haifa in Israel. Her main research and practice interests focus on Positive Psychology, meaning in life and Logotherapy, change and development, spirituality and education. Pninit has published several articles, developed programs and curricula for various organizations on these topics, and is the co-editor of *Meaning in Positive and Existential Psychology*. She lectures on Positive Psychology and related topics in a number of academic institutions, and conducts workshops and training for various organizations. Pninit has acquired much experience in working with children and adolescents, especially at-risk young people, both individually and within the framework of group interventions. She serves as academic advisor and consultant to both academic and non-academic institutions.

Professor Martin Seligman

Martin Seligman is the Zellerbach Family Professor of Psychology and the Director of the Positive Psychology Center at the University of Pennsylvania. His main research interests are learned helplessness, depression, optimism, Positive Psychology, and comprehensive soldier fitness. He is a best-selling author, having written 25 books which have been translated into more than 40 languages. His best-sellers include *Learned Optimism*, *The Optimistic Child*, and *Authentic Happiness*. His latest book, *Flourish*, was published in 2011. Martin was President of the American Psychological Association in 1998, during which one of his presidential initiatives was the promotion of Positive Psychology as a field of scientific study. He is the recipient of several Distinguished Scientific Contribution Awards from the American Psychological Association. Martin and his family resided at Geelong Grammar School for 6 months in 2008, and were instrumental in the embedding of Positive Education within the School community.

Professor George Vaillant

George Vaillant is a Professor of Psychiatry at Harvard Medical School and the Department of Psychiatry, Massachusetts General Hospital. He is a graduate of Harvard College and Harvard Medical School, and did his psychiatric residency at the Massachusetts Mental Health Center. He has spent his research career charting adult development, the importance of involuntary coping mechanisms, and the recovery process in heroin addiction and alcoholism. From 1970 to 2005 he was Director of the Study of Adult Development at the Harvard University Health Service, which prospectively charted the lives of 724 men for over 75 years. A major focus of his work in the past has been individual adult development; more recently he has been interested in positive emotions and their relationship to Positive Psychology. In 2000 he became a founding member of Positive Psychology. He has been a Fellow at the Center for Advanced Study in the Behavioral Sciences, a past Class A (non-alcoholic) trustee of Alcoholics Anonymous, and is a Fellow of the International Positive Psychology Association. His published works include *Adaptation to Life, The Natural History of Alcoholism Revisited, Aging Well, Spiritual Evolution,* and *Triumphs of Experience.*

GLOSSARY

ABC/ATC model A model of how people interpret events, devised by Professor Albert Ellis and Professor Aaron Beck. The model refers to how an *activating* event (or *antecedent* event) influences *beliefs/thoughts*, which in turn leads to emotional and behavioral *consequences*. The ABC model is foundational to cognitive–behavioral therapy. The ATC model is another version of the ABC model, commonly used at Geelong Grammar School.

Actioning strengths Putting a character strength into action—for example, engaging in an activity such as painting, which uses the character strength of creativity.

Active constructive responding (ACR) Enthusiastic and interested responding by one person to another's good news.

Agency A person's awareness of the influence and control that they have on their environment (see **hope theory** for information on how agency is conceptualized within the hope model).

Appraisal patterns The ways in which people interpret and make decisions about situations. Within psychology, theories of appraisal propose that emotions and behavioral reactions arise from different appraisals of situations. Typical or frequent ways of interpreting situations contribute to appraisal patterns.

Appreciative inquiry (AI) A strengths-based approach to analysis and decision making that is used primarily within organizations, and comprises four stages—discover, dream, design, and destiny.

Authentic happiness What it means to lead a good and happy life. *Authentic Happiness* is the title of Professor Martin Seligman's early and influential Positive Psychology book (published in 2002), and of the University of Pennsylvania website developed by the Penn Positive Psychology Center.

Autotelic personality The type of personality that occurs in people who are internally driven and display a sense of their own purpose and curiosity. People with an autotelic personality regularly experience flow.

Broaden-and-build theory A theory postulated by the researcher, Professor Barbara Fredrickson, according to which positive emotions such as happiness, enjoyment, and love broaden one's awareness and boost creative thinking and actions. As people broaden their ways of behaving through positive emotion, their skills and knowledge build, leading them to become better equipped to function well and flourish across different situations and challenges.

Cardiac vagal tone The continuous activity of the vagus nerve, which is thought to be a reliable physiological measure of a person's stress levels and their vulnerability to stress. Vagal tone has a strong effect on the parasympathic nervous system, which in turn influences and regulates heart rate.

Character strengths Ways of thinking, feeling, and behaving that come naturally and easily to a person, enabling high levels of functioning and performance. Character strengths constitute a recognized subset of personality traits that are morally valued.

Cognition The mental processes of thinking, knowing, and remembering.

Domains Important, interrelated, and necessary focus areas of wellbeing. The Geelong Grammar School Model of Positive Education comprises six domains—positive relationships, positive emotion, positive health, positive engagement, positive accomplishment, and positive purpose.

Engagement A state of mind that is characterized by participation, focused attention, and immersion in an activity.

Environmental mastery The sense of mastery or control that a person feels over their environment.

Eudaimonic wellbeing A conceptualization of wellbeing that prioritizes having a sense of meaning and purpose and living a virtuous and value-based life.

European Social Survey (ESS) A survey that has been conducted across European countries every 2 years since 2001, and which measures the attitudes, beliefs, and behaviors of different populations.

Explicit learning Learning by students of the tenets of wellbeing and flourishing in classes specifically dedicated within the academic timetable to Positive Education.

Extrinsic motivation A desire to perform an action or complete a task that is driven by the promise of external rewards or threats of punishment.

Fixed mindset The mindset from which those looking at tasks or challenges see intelligence and talents as naturally determined and unchangeable (see also **mindset**). Having a fixed mindset limits growth and learning over time.

Flourishing Optimal wellbeing on a spectrum of wellbeing. It is at the opposite end of the spectrum to mentally languishing. At Geelong Grammar School, flourishing is understood as "feeling good and doing good."

Flow A state of intense absorption and optimal experience that results from taking part in intrinsically motivating challenges. Flow occurs when there is a match between a person's skill and the level of challenge.

Forgiveness The letting go of negative emotions such as resentment held by one person against another person who has harmed or wronged them.

Gratitude Thankfulness or the feelings of appreciation that result from perceived fortune or the kindness of others.

Grit The mixture of perseverance and passion that a person has for their long-term goals. Components of grit include self-regulation, discipline, and sacrificing short-term rewards for long-term gain.

Growth mindset The mindset from which those looking at tasks and challenges see intelligence and talents as malleable (see also **mindset**). Having a growth mindset enhances learning and development over time.

Hedonic wellbeing Good psychological health characterized by high levels of satisfaction with life, and the predominance of positive emotions such as happiness over painful or negative emotions such as sadness.

Hope Positive expectations and feelings about the likelihood of desired events and outcomes occurring in the future.

Hope theory A cognitive–motivational theory based on three interrelated elements—goals, *pathways* or strategies for achieving the goals, and *agency* or motivation for achieving the pathways.

Implicit learning The integration of the skills for wellbeing and flourishing throughout the broad curriculum, so that wellbeing is explored and supported in ways that also align with academic goals and competencies (e.g. students learning about character strengths by considering books and stories in English lessons or historical figures in History lessons).

Intrinsic motivation A desire to perform an action or complete a task that is driven by interest, enjoyment, or valuing the task itself, rather than by external rewards or punishments.

Kindness A state and a character strength that is characterized by helpfulness towards another when there is no advantage to the helper or expectation of receiving anything in return.

Learned helplessness The situation that occurs when an animal or human being has learned to become helpless or out of control of the situation as a result of experiencing a series of aversive events and not being able to escape or change the situation.

Loving-kindness meditation A Buddhist meditation practice that aims to cultivate goodwill and love towards oneself, others, and all sentient beings. Scientific studies sometimes describe this practice as compassion meditation.

Mastery experience The experiencing of a sense of accomplishment and/or control—in other words, the mastering of a task that the person has set out to achieve.

Meditation A broad family of practices, the common feature of which is the deliberate direction of attention and awareness.

Meta-analysis A statistical term used to describe the process of combining the results and effect sizes of different studies on one area of focus, in order to analyze whether clear patterns of similarity or difference emerge across the findings.

Mindfulness A meditation practice that involves moment-to-moment awareness of one's present experiences. Mindfulness is a state of acceptance, openness, and non-judgment.

Mindset The way in which a person views their ability to learn and change (see also **fixed mindset** and **growth mindset**).

Model for Positive Education A model that provides an evidence-based guideline for promoting flourishing across the whole school community. This model includes six domains—positive engagement, positive accomplishment, positive health, positive emotions, positive relationships, and positive purpose, with character strengths interwoven throughout.

Negativity bias The tendency of human beings to experience and recall negative emotions as stronger and more influential than positive emotions when making decisions and evaluations.

Neural pathways The bundles of connected neurons that have a fundamental role in communication between the different parts of the brain and the nervous system.

Neurons Nerve cells that link together to create neural pathways, which constitute the nervous system operating throughout the body. Neurons consist of axons, cell bodies, and dendrites.

Neurophysiology The study of the functioning of the nervous system.

Neuroplasticity The malleability of brain structures, functions, and the brain itself in response to experiences. Changes to the brain's structure and organization can occur as a result of changes to behavior, brain damage, and the environment.

Pedagogy The method and practice of teaching. It includes the theories, techniques, and approaches of teaching, learning, and leading.

Penn Resiliency Program (PRP) A group intervention program for students from late childhood to mid-adolescence, designed by the Positive Psychology Center at the University of Pennsylvania. The lessons teach cognitive–behavioral and social problem-solving skills, and aim to build resilience, wellbeing, and social and emotional learning skills.

PERMA An acronym, created by Professor Martin Seligman, which stands for positive emotions, engagement, relationships, meaning and purpose, and accomplishments. The acronym describes Seligman's broad theory of the essential components of living a good life as set out in his book *Flourish* (published in 2011).

Person praise Positive feedback or statements about a person's performance, characterized by a global evaluation of their traits—for example, "Good job, you are such a creative person."

Positive organizational behavior (POB) The study and application of psychological capacities and behaviors that build relationships and productivity within organizations.

Positive organizational scholarship (POS) The study of the positive outcomes, processes, and attributes of organizations that support high levels of performance and functioning.

Positive psychological capital A positive psychological state of development that is characterized by four constructs—self-efficacy, optimism, hope, and resiliency.

Positivity toolkit A toolkit designed to broaden one's understanding and awareness of positive emotions, as well as to build upon specific positive emotions through conscious intention and practice. This toolkit is presented in Professor Barbara Fredrickson's book, *Positivity* (published in 2009).

Post-traumatic growth A term used to describe the experience of positive change resulting from how a person responds to and rebuilds their life after a significant event such as trauma.

Process praise Positive feedback or statements about a person's performance, characterized by a focus on their effort or strategy—for example, "Good job, I can see you tried really hard."

Psychological wellbeing A term that is used to discuss both the theory and measurement aspects of positive functioning. Most commonly this term refers to a theory developed by Professor Carol Ryff, where psychological wellbeing has six components—self-acceptance, personal growth, purpose in life, environmental mastery, autonomy, and positive relationships with others.

Relationship reparation The process of repairing and restoring a relationship bond after there has been some sort of damage caused by conflict, grief, loss, or separation.

Resilience A person's ability to adapt and flourish in the face of challenges, stress, and adversity.

Savoring Behaviors or thought patterns that aim to prolong, maximize, or build positive emotions. Savoring can be directed to the past, the present, or the future.

Self-compassion A combination of kindness towards oneself, mindfulness, and connecting to a sense of common humanity.

Self-efficacy The strength of a person's belief in their ability to achieve their goals or perform a task—in other words, how effective they believe they are at achieving or mastering goals.

Self-forgiveness In a person's relationship with him- or herself, a decrease in directing resentment and blame towards the self, and an increase in directing empathy and compassion towards the self.

Signature strengths The character strengths that a person identifies as their top strengths. The person values such strengths and finds drawing upon them easy and natural.

Skill–challenge match The balance between a person's perceived ability and the challenge at hand. Skill and challenge are thought to match when a person is confident in their ability to take on a challenging task. Skill–challenge match is a prerequisite for flow.

SMART goals Goals that are Specific, Measurable, Attainable, Realistic, and Timely. SMART is an acronym that originated in management literature, with the aim of helping people to be specific and clear about goals.

Strath Haven Positive Psychology Course A curriculum designed for adolescents by the Positive Psychology Center at the University of Pennsylvania. The program aims to build character strengths, supportive relationships, and meaning, as well as to increase positive emotion and reduce negative emotion.

Strengths paragons People who can be viewed as models of excellence for a particular strength—for example, Picasso is a strength paragon for creativity.

Strengths spotting The process of identifying and communicating the strengths that one notices in another person, of which they may not be aware.

Subjective wellbeing The way that a person perceives and thinks about their wellbeing. Subjective wellbeing consists of a cognitive component that is associated with satisfaction with life, and an affective component that relates to the balance between positive and negative feelings and emotions.

Synapse The small gap between the axon end of one neuron and the dendrite end of an adjacent neuron.

Vagus nerve A nerve that is located in the medulla oblongata within the brainstem, and which plays a key role in regulating the body's internal systems through the parasympathetic nervous system.

Values in Action (VIA) Classification of Character Strengths The name used by researchers Chris Peterson and Martin Seligman to describe their character strengths framework, which is based on character strengths that have been valued across time and cultures. The VIA consists of 24 character strengths that come under six broad virtues.

Virtuous organization An organization in which employees are collectively supported to behave in ways that display moral excellence and lead to benefits both for the organization and for the wider community and environment.

Wellbeing A state of being healthy, happy, and comfortable. Wellbeing can refer to an individual or to groups of people, and can be divided into different subtypes, such as physical, social, subjective, and psychological wellbeing.

Whole-child approach An approach to the support and teaching of children that is holistic in its outlook, taking into account the child, their family, and the community. It emphasizes the long-term development and success of children, as opposed to short-term academic outcomes.

NAME INDEX

SUBJECT INDEX

Note 1: Entries in bold refer to glossary entries.

Note 2: As many entries are prefaced with 'positive' this has been generally been inverted.